POLITICS OF LANGUAGE IN THE
EX-SOVIET MUSLIM STATES

'The fate of the language
is the fate of the people'

Kyrgyz saying

JACOB M. LANDAU
BARBARA KELLNER-HEINKELE

Politics of Language in the ex-Soviet Muslim States

Azerbayjan, Uzbekistan, Kazakhstan, Kyrgyzstan, Turkmenistan and Tajikistan

ANN ARBOR

THE UNIVERSITY OF MICHIGAN PRESS

Copyright © Jacob M. Landau and Barbara Kellner-Heinkele, 2001
All rights reserved
Published in the United States of America by
the University of Michigan Press
Manufactured in Malaysia

2004   2003   2002   2001   5 4 3 2 1

A CIP catalog record for this book is available from the Library of Congress.

ISBN 0-472-11226-0

The map on page xii was produced by the
Institut für Geographische Wissenschaften, Freie Universität Berlin.
The photographs were taken by Barbara Kellner-Heinkele.

PREFACE AND ACKNOWLEDGEMENTS

This work seeks to contribute to the study of politicolinguistics in the six newly independent ex-Soviet Muslim republics. While there are many facets of the interaction between language and politics, we are concerned with one main domain. Our intention is to observe, analyze and compare the mutual impact of language issues and ethnopolitics in these states. For this purpose in March-April 1997 and September 1998 we visited the five Turkic states: Azerbayjan, Uzbekistan, Kazakhstan, Kyrgyzstan and Turkmenistan. On both occasions, however, we were unable to visit Tajikistan due to security problems. In each of these states, we collected and analyzed printed materials; interviewed public officials and scholars involved in language policymaking; and also engaged a research assistant in the capital city to send us required information and check the needed data. For Tajikistan we had to rely mainly on published sources, which unfortunately did not always offer complete information. We sifted through a large amount of material, including texts of laws, decrees and constitutions, statistical data, school information, numerous books, reports and newspapers in several languages as well as surveys carried out by others (mentioned below), which we could not undertake ourselves. The time-span, though focused on the period of independence since 1991, had to include the last few years of the Soviet Union – without the discussion of which the processes we examined would be less intelligible; thus the period of our study stretches approximately over the decade 1988-98. The result is a comparative description and analysis of the central topics in the politics of language in the area, taking into account the fact that some subjects have received more attention in certain communities than in others. Our presentation, while not final due to the non-availability of certain data (e.g. statistics at times incomplete and at others inaccurate), may assist those interested in the subject and in the region to understand it somewhat better.

We wish to express our heartfelt thanks to the German-Israeli Foundation for Scientific Research and Development, which gave us a generous grant, particularly to the Director of the Foundation's Israel Office, Dr Amnon Barak; to the Rockefeller Foundation in New York City, for enabling us to prepare our first draft at its Bellagio Study and Conference

Center, and to the staff of the Center for cordially providing the conditions to achieve this; to our assistants in Berlin and Jerusalem, respectively, Brigitte Heuer and Leonid Kogan; to our research assistants in Azerbayjan and Central Asia: Haläddin Ibrahimli (Baku), Leyla Zhubanova (Almaty), Vladimir Salaridze (Ashgabat), Dr Tynchtykbek Chorotegin (Choroev) (Bishkek), Nodira Bakhramova and Aziz Nazirov (Tashkent), and, finally, Dr Hairullo Saifulloev (Dushanbe), who unstintedly gave us of their time; and to all those who offered us advice both at home and in the Muslim states. We are grateful to Dr Isabelle Kreindler, who read the entire work and offered valuable comments; to Mira Reich, style editor; Richard Wittmann, who compiled the index; and Esther Porat, who uncomplainingly typed the text several times. Finally the publishers in London, C. Hurst and Co., who saw our work through the press. It was a pleasure to work and consult with them all. We alone, however, are responsible for the study itself.

BARBARA KELLNER-HEINKELE
Institut für Turkologie
Freie Universität Berlin

JACOB M. LANDAU
Department of Political Science
Hebrew University of Jerusalem

June 2000

CONTENTS

ILLUSTRATIONS

TABLES

ABBREVIATIONS

BBC	British Broadcasting Corporation
BR	*Bakinskii Rabochii*
CAM	*Central Asia Monitor*
CAS	*Central Asian Survey*
CIS	Commonwealth of Independent States
Extracts	*Extracts from BBC Monitoring Service, Interfax and RFERL Daily Reports for [country] by [date]*
FBIS	Foreign Broadcasts Information Service
KP	*Kazakhstanskaya Pravda*
KT	*Kommunist Tadzhikistana*
NaG	*Narodnaya Gazeta*
NG	*Nezavisimaya Gazeta*
NS	*Narodnoe Slovo*
NT	*Neitral'nyi Turkmenistan*
PV	*Pravda Vostoka*
RG	*Rossiiskaya Gazeta*
RL	Radio Liberty
RFE/RL	Radio Free Europe/Radio Liberty
RSFSR	Russian Soviet Federated Socialist Republic
SI	*Sotsiologicheskie Issledovaniya*
SK	*Slovo Kyrgyzstana*
SoK	*Sovetskaya Kirgiziya*
TASS	Telegraph Agency of the Soviet Union
TI	*Turkmenskaya Iskra*
ŬTA	*Ŭzbek Tili va Adabiëti*

TRANSLITERATION

We have attempted to transliterate foreign words as accurately as possible, but have preferred to apply standard usage to place names, such as Baku, or commonly accepted personal names, such as Gorki, Elchibey or Yeltsin. We have also respected certain persons' preferences in transliterating their own names into Latin characters. Otherwise, for transliteration from Russian, we have followed Bruhn's (1968) 'English transcription', using however 'y' for 'yeri'. Modern Turkish presented no problem, as it is written in Latin script. For the Turkic languages and

Tajik, we refer to the transliteration tables on these pages. Uzbek, Turkmen and Azeri personal names and titles of books and newspapers written in the new Latin-based alphabets are given in their original form except for Azeri 'a', which is rendered as 'ä' (cf. illustrations).

TRANSLITERATION OF RUSSIAN
(CYRILLIC) ALPHABET

А a	a	Р p	r
Б б	b	С c	s
В в	v	Т т	t
Г г	g	У у	u
Д д	d	Ф ф	f
Е e	e	Х x	kh
Ж ж	zh	Ц ц	ts
З з	z	Ч ч	ch
И и	i	Ш ш	sh
Й й	i	Щ щ	shch
К к	k	ъ	''
Л л	l	ы	y
М м	m	ь	'
Н н	n	Э э	ė
О о	o	Ю ю	yu
П п	p	Я я	ya

Source: Adapted from Bruhn 1968 (English transcription)

TRANSLITERATION OF SPECIAL SIGNS FOR
CYRILLIC-BASED ALPHABETS OF TURKIC
LANGUAGES AND OF TAJIK

Г[1]	q	j[3]	ĭ	Ү	ü
Ғ	gh	Қ	g	Ұ	ū̄
ё	ё	Қ	q	h	h
ә	ä	Ң	ng	Ҳ	h
Җ	j	ө	ö	Ч	j
Ӣ	ī	ȳ	ū	Ҷ	j
i[1]	i	ў	ŭ	apostrophe[3]	'
й	ĭ	ў[2]	w		

Source: Adapted from Bregel 1995.

1. In Kazakh
2. In Karakalpak
3. In Azerbayjanian

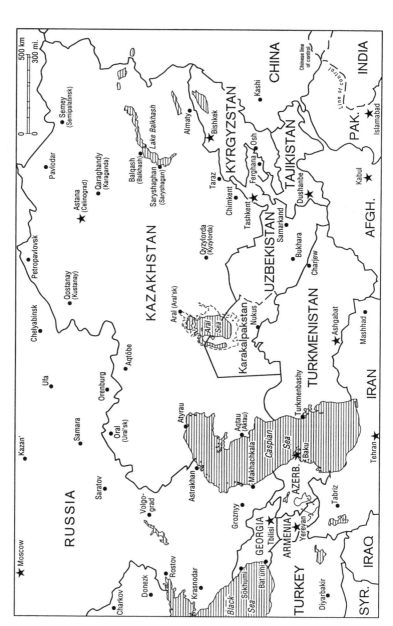

Central Asia

1

LANGUAGE AND THE SEARCH FOR IDENTITY

A central issue for many social scientists, politicians, educators and others is what is known as 'the modern ethnic problem'. This in itself may be rather surprising, for until the early 1980s one could read and hear frequent pronouncements by both Marxist and liberal thinkers, as well as by integrationists and proponents of 'the melting pot' theories, predicting the imminent demise of ethnicity. However, since then ethnicity has raised its head assertively not only in African polities like Somalia and Rwanda, but also in Europe as in the Soviet Union and former Yugoslavia. If anything, ethnic problems show signs of becoming more inescapable and more visible almost everywhere in the world.

Ethnicity is linked, indeed, to many focal issues of our times, such as globalization, increasing migration, multi-culturalism, economic development, social relationships, contemporary nationalism (in support or in opposition), inter-communal and inter-state conflicts, terrorist activities, and the creation and promotion of diasporas. We are witnessing in the 1990s the growing importance of ethnopolitics – a mobilization of ethnic groups for political ends. Sometimes this is a relatively moderate continuation, political and cultural, of developments in earlier years, as in the cases of the Welsh and Scottish in the British Isles, Corsican and Breton in France or Catalan in Spain. More violent ethnopolitics – those which Zvi Gitelman (1992:7) has labeled 'ethnic rage' – presented a serious challenge to Soviet leaders. Soon afterwards followed the disintegration of the Soviet Union in a process leading to further fissiparous activities in the Russian Federation, Yugoslavia and elsewhere. Ethnopolitics or the political demands and activities of discontented ethnic groups seeking more power and cultural rights, as well as better access to education, jobs, and resources, have been increasingly complicating the general situation in numerous states, pitting nationalisms against one another. There are many similarities of substance between ethnicity and nationalism, the main difference being one of scale (Fishman 1972:3; Hoffmann 1991:196-7). It is probably inevitable that assertion by one ethnic group results in counter-claims by one or more competing ones. Ethnicity is the province of minority groups which feel, rightly or wrongly, that they suffer discrimination. Majority groups, which seldom perceive themselves as 'ethnic', but rather as nation-builders in their states and societies, are obliged to respond to such conflicts when challenged by minority *ethnies*. The nationalism of such a majority group, to paraphrase Ernest Gellner, is expressed in the desire to make its political unit and national borders congruent. Naturally, variations in the essence of inter-ethnic conflicts occur frequently, depending on the history and specific situation of each land. What is common to all these conflicts, however, most particularly in developing countries, is the almost ubiquitous search of ethnic groups for a collective identity for themselves.

Both personal and national identity are difficult to define precisely and the debate about an accepted definition still goes on, as indicated, for instance, by Laitin (1998:10-28). In their search for identity, ethnic groups, when they seek national characteristics, tend to emphasize one or more of the following commonalities: origin, territoriality, religion, history, culture, and language. They may base themselves on scientific facts, or invented myths, or a mixture of the two, promoting both legitimacy and loyalty. In various contexts, identity characteristics have been subject to strategies of maintenance, display, or avoidance. In certain instances, the common origin, or even the origin itself, is unknown or unclear or not sufficiently ancient, and therefore has to be invented. Thus, some ideo-logues of Palestinian nationalism have been searching for Canaanite antecedents. Territoriality is not always an effective criterion of nation or group identity for diaspora peoples, nor for areas inhabited by more than one group. Religion sometimes offers only a doubtful frame of refer-ence, as its impact has been eroded by secularism, and is less decisive in countries where the nation or *ethnie* is divided between two or more religions, as is quite common nowadays. Besides, religion is sometimes perceived as combined with nation: many Italians see themselves as both Catholics and Italians, while numerous Persians consider themselves both Shiites and Iranians – without consciously distinguishing between the two identities. Indeed, many Persians and Arabs seem to opt for a na-tional Islamic identity. History may be manipulated by selectivity and emphasis in order to serve the cause of national identity, as has happened in some colonialist empires as well as recently decolonized societies (Seckinger 1988).

A process of change is taking place in the perception of national iden-tity at the end of the twentieth century, as in the states and societies emerging from the breaking up of certain federal units like the former Soviet Union, Yugoslavia, and Czechoslovakia. In the six newly independent ex-So-viet Muslim states, identity is still largely conceived as loyalty, real or imagined, to an *ethnie*, clan, or locality, with Islam, generally in a mod-erate expression, providing a source for supra-loyalty. In the centralized Soviet Union, all six had been akin to protostates, lacking control of many of their material and spiritual attributes but already possessing names, boundaries, legislatures, administrative staffs, political and cultural elites. After independence, these elites had to concentrate on the identity aspect of nation-building, that is, to have all the *ethnies* – not merely the titular *ethnie*, i.e. the one after which the republic is named – transfer their political loyalties to the new state (Kolstø 1998:51ff.). In all six, the political leaders have been attempting, to various degrees, to foster sentiments of nationalism overriding parochial, regional, clannish or tribal loyalties in an effort to have all citizens identify with a conception of nationalism that is not primarily directed against outsiders but rather fosters a feeling of cohesion among the members of the nation. The element of territoriality has now added another common factor of patriotism in each of the newly independent states, frequently absent in pre-independence years. In their struggle for nation-building, the leading elites of the titular *ethnie* are compelled to take into account the institutionalized multinationality inherited from the Soviet Union (Brubaker 1994:49). This implies finding a *modus vivendi* with the counter-elites of other ethnic groups, with their particularist aspirations, some of them living close to their own homelands (below, ch. 2).

In this context, the centrality of ethnocultural perceptions is obvious. Culture in its manifold aspects has been and frequently still is a focal and probably essential component of national or group identification – and in the past this has sometimes been used selectively. A well-known example of the uses and misuses of culture is the Soviet Union, whose regime determined not only the politics and economy of the Union's citizens, but also most aspects of life and society, including religion, education, history, and many facets of culture. Soviet rulers (particularly Lenin) repeatedly stressed their desire to preserve and foster the culture of the numerous nationalities making up the Union: 194 in the 1926 count and 101 in the 1979 one (Brutents 1998:545). This they did by fostering literacy – up to and including university level – in the Central Asian republics and the Caucasus, and by preparing much-needed studies, textbooks and dictionaries in many languages. Sometimes, however, they promoted the less significant identity characteristics, such as time-hallowed headgear and clothes (in a folkloric vein) or traditional foods and dietary customs (Sansone 1983:53-7). The literary and linguistic heritage was variously fostered or rejected – frequently the latter – during sovietization and russification (Carley 1995:300-1). In several of the successor states of the Soviet Union, such as the Baltic republics, the Russian minorities are nowadays being repaid for real or perceived injustice, chiefly insofar as language preferences are concerned. In any event, the general perspective shows that cultural assimilation, also, did not invariably succeed in the Soviet Union. Looking at the six new Muslim states, one is tempted to agree with Shenfield (1994:10), 'However linguistically and culturally russified many Kazakhs may in reality be and however uncertain Kazakhs may be about what it "means" to be Kazakh, everyone seems to feel that Russians and Kazakhs do belong to different cultures and civilizations, in contrast to the shared Slavic and Orthodox tradition of Russians'. This characterization, although very broad, seems to apply generally to the other five ex-Soviet Muslim states as well, compounding the problem of shaping a new comprehensive national identity in each of these multiethnic societies (for which Zhilina and Cheshko 1992). Their common denominator, in addition to the Soviet legacy, is the Muslim majority in their populations (Shami 1999:189-91).

Very understandably, peoples and groups in the ex-Soviet states, including the six new Muslim ones, are looking into their own past for the cultural elements suppressed under the Soviets. This they do in an attempt to authenticate their distinguishing characteristics, consciously or unconsciously seeking to shape the national identities. Special emphasis is laid on their respective languages – in an energizing, mobilizing, and unifying effort which aims at strengthening their ethnic identity. In each of the six, the state leaders have been attempting to use the new sense of independence in a defined national territory for nation building – not merely consolidating their own group in a top-down drive, but also striving to include together with their own *ethnie* all (or most) of the others (*CAM* 1994, no. 1:10). An example is the declaration of Heidar Aliev, Azerbayjan's President, on 12 November 1995, that 'Azerbayjan is the homeland of all those living in Azerbayjan regardless of their nationality, religion, language, and origin; including the Armenians' (Black 1995: II, 385). Despite the emphatic tone of such declarations, popular views have often tended to exclude the Russians and others, often because of their ignorance of the local languages.

It was only natural that the native language of the largest *ethnie* would serve as an important means of determining titular identity and building a nation. In other words, language is seen not only as a medium, but as the message; not merely as the means for communication, but as a symbol as well. It has frequently been perceived as one of the chief dimensions of national or ethnic identity, probably as the main single component defining its uniqueness, shaping and maintaining its sentiments of solidarity. In many societies, language has been used as the authentic device for claiming one's legacy; it is often considered not just a component of culture, but an issue of politics, economics and religion. In some countries, indeed, it was the main criterion investigated in official statistics to determine nationality, as in the Soviet Union or, in a different context, in the republic of Turkey (until language use recently ceased to be recorded systematically in the latter by the census takers). Of course, the information collected was sometimes misleading, for there are people who frequently speak more than one language and are more fluent in a foreign language than in that of their *ethnie*, as are numerous Africans (such as many Senegalese) in French. At other times, people are fluent in two languages, such as certain inhabitants of Uzbekistan, equally competent in Uzbek and Tajik and unable to define their identification automatically with either nationality. Difficulties in evaluation are compounded by 'fluency' not being precisely defined in statistics concerning the republics discussed, while 'nationality' is not always clear to respondents, as for instance in the case of descendants of ethnically mixed marriages.

All things considered, the commonality of language was and has remained an important factor, often the decisive element in both identity self-perception and ethno-cultural conflict. The cases of Canada and Belgium are very well-known, but there are numerous other instances in recent history. Even the United States is now struggling with multiculturalism, at least as expressed in the English-Spanish debate in the schools of a number of states. One may even predict that the language issue, already alive in the English-French competition in the European Union, may well increase in scope and diversity in the twenty-first century. But to return to the past: since 1938, everyone in the Soviet Union was encouraged to study Russian because the Soviet Union, albeit a federation, was largely a unitary state shaped by Stalin in which one could not advance, or even lead a normal life, without knowing Russian, the language of the majority. The law of 13 March 1938 required everybody to learn Russian at school, on the premise that bilingualism was a common sense solution to both communication and language inequality. This assumption can be seen as an example of ideology based on power (Tollefson 1991:10-11), more so than in many other societies, and it provoked certain minorities in the Soviet Union. As will be explained below (ch. 4), from September 1938 onwards Russian was introduced everywhere as a compulsory subject at school and in extracurricular activities. Although reactions varied in the republics, criticism of these moves served as a contributory factor in fashioning the mood leading to the Soviet Union's collapse.

In newly independent states, when societies are bilingual or multilingual, the struggle over language is largely a conflict over ethnic dominance. Without necessarily serving as a direct cause for conflict, it is frequently an aggravating factor. Nigeria, India, Sri Lanka and others are cases in point. By the 1970s and 1980s, many of the non-Russian peoples in the Soviet Union felt that they were losing control over their language situation (Kagedan 1991). Russian societal hegemony was being actively promoted and large sections of the local populations had mastered Russian, a central subject at school. At the same time, very few Russians who had moved into the various Soviet republics knew the native languages, which they did not really need and considered, anyway, less developed than Russian. This was the inverse of what has been happening in almost all societies, where the minority has learned and used the language of the majority, not the other way around (Motyl 1987:95-105). In many cases, the greater the number of other minority languages in the area, the greater the need for a Russian (rather than a titular) *lingua franca*; there never was any other choice. The situation resembles, to some extent, that in countries colonized by France, Great Britain, the Netherlands or Portugal, although the Soviet republics were never designated as colonies of Russia. However, language laws and decrees in the various republics, since 1989 and even more so after independence in 1991 (below, ch. 6), have indicated growing popular language nationalism, overturning the earlier linguistic situation by making the titular language of each republic the one to be employed in education and public services – foreshadowing 'the demise of the Soviet language' (Motyl 1990). Non-Russian nations were becoming increasingly hegemonic in their own republics in both linguistic and other domains, with language frequently emerging as the most powerful symbolic vehicle of nationalism, a catalyst for political ideologies and movements, in which a bond between nation and language has increasingly been taken for granted (below, ch. 5). As for the titular nations in Central Asia, the results of a 1996 study in Kazakhstan are quite characteristic. Among 1761 respondents throughout the state, the highest number among the Kazakhs (20.7%) as well as among the Slavs – that is, the Russians and kindred *ethnies* (e.g., Ukrainians and Poles) – (18.6%) placed language above other criteria as the marker of their national identity (Arenov and Kalmykov 1998:53).

Segments of the frustrated non-titular minorities, chiefly the Europeans, preferred to emigrate (below, ch. 3), for economic and other reasons; in part, this was a reaction to the fact that important sectors within the titular *ethnie* (and others) in each republic had advocated limiting the impact of Russian in education and public life. Nonetheless, the widespread knowledge of Russian and its frequent use could not change markedly within a very few years and the current language situation still substantially reflects the main features of the 1980s, even in the field of education, where change is more palpable. As the research of Laitin (1996), Hough (1996) and others has shown, Russian will not be easily displaced in the near future. Although varying in essence, language issues have remained an important bone of contention and source of competition in many of the Soviet Union's successor states. Language contact frequently breeds language conflict which, in turn, expresses and sometimes exacerbates political, social or economic friction (Nelde 1989). This situation is particularly relevant to the multiethnic and multicultural societies of the six independent states, where language conflict both reflects political conflict and has an impact on it.

If language can be (and it often is) idealized by a dominant group as a symbol of national unity, dominated groups obviously can – and do – employ the same reasoning to make political counter-claims based on their own linguistic identity. For many of these, language is not merely a means of communication but, no less importantly, the genius of their nationhood and a focal factor in nation-building, perceived as pivotal for their respective ethno-cultural identities (Fishman 1972:3). Language both provides for uniqueness of the group or the *ethnie* (frequently nourished by sentiments of primordial attachment) and differentiates it from others. It can provide both elites and masses with an extrapolation to political independence. Thus, language may be a cohesive as well as a disruptive political force in the bilingual or multilingual states which form the pattern most commonly found in modern and contemporary times. Linguistic nationalism in the six newly independent ex-Soviet Muslim states has, indeed, been much less researched than that in states with Germanic (Wood 1981) or Romance languages (Rogers 1981). This is so, while other markers of ethnonationalism (Smith 1979:24-6) in the area discussed are either blurred or non-existent: religion, common to other Islamic peoples, also is as yet a less potent factor than in other Islamic communities, due to seventy years of official atheistic indoctrination; colour is highly irrelevant in this area. For most or perhaps all communities in Central Asia and Azerbayjan, then, language issues are crucial for their future no less than for their present. Some of their leading thinkers perceive language as the means for authentication and self-identification or, rather, for re-identification. Hence the steps taken for alphabet change (below, ch. 7), language intervention (below, ch. 8) and improving education (below, ch. 9).

Remembering that the six independent states resemble one another in some respects and differ in others, a basic issue applies to them all – how they rise to the occasion of nation-building in the first years of statehood. The problem is a difficult one for them, due to the multiethnic and multilingual character of each (Heuer 1999). The language factor is especially complex, due to the predominance of Russian in all areas of life, to the uneven development of several local languages, and to cultural demands by some other *ethnies*. With varying emphasis, the decision in each state is to opt for nation-building on the basis of the culture and language of the titular *ethnie*.

In order to understand the issue better, we pose such questions as the following. First, *why* should the governments of the six newly independent states opt for titular languages, often less familiar to city elites than Russian; moreover, why opt for languages often lower in status (that is, in prestige) and poorer in corpus (i.e., in the subtlety of grammar or breadth and depth of vocabulary), at a disadvantage in technological and other terms needed for modernity and development? Secondly, *how* would the governments reverse or reduce language shift by legal means, public use, alphabet change, orthographic and lexical intervention, school instruction and similar strategies for asserting the primacy of the titular language – in the teeth of the lack of financial resources and the need to cope urgently with other pressing matters? Thirdly, *how* did this work out, in view of only partial support amongst the titular population and very strong opposition – even some resistance – by other *ethnies*, chiefly the Russians? Fourthly, *what* differences were there among the six republics and how did they affect the various results, as of now? Bearing in mind that we are discussing ongoing processes, we shall attempt to offer some tentative answers to these questions.

2

THE ADVENT OF THE INDEPENDENT MUSLIM STATES

The story of the disintegration of the Soviet Union in the late 1980s and its demise in late 1991 – the only instance of a superpower collapsing in peacetime – has often been retold and analyzed (e.g., Zaslavsky 1997; Zdravomyslov 1997: ch. 2). In order to understand better the background of the creation of the six newly independent Muslim states in the Caucasus and Central Asia, we shall briefly recapitulate some of the main lines of development, basic data and figures (keeping in mind that some of the available statistics are uncertain or incomplete).

The political, economic, ideological, ethnic, social, and cultural pressures (with their numerous interconnections) besetting the Soviet Union brought about its end, with Gorbachev's repeated calls for *glasnost'* and *perestroika* being interpreted as appeals for democratization and resulting in increasingly insistent demands for the decentralization of central power in favour of each nation in its homeland. The long process of devolution of political and economic decision-making authority to national elites in their homelands, sometimes named 'indigenization', had brought about a shift in the balance of power from centre to periphery since the late 1970s (Beissinger 1993; Kaiser 1994:325-77). In the late 1980s, serious riots – several with nationalist ingredients – occurred in some of the republics (Carrère d'Encausse 1993:31-3). It took a failed coup against Gorbachev in August 1991 to achieve the breakup of the Soviet Union along the territorial lines defining the fifteen nations whose homelands were union republics, including the six Muslim ones. These lines had been drawn in the 1920s and 1930s with the apparent intention, among others, of creating situations facilitating manipulation and intervention. In 1991 they became the borders of independent states.

The pervasive role of the state in multiethnic societies is well exemplified in the use the rulers of the Soviet Union made of their coercive force to foster or alter ethnic identities. The artificial boundaries imposed by a totalitarian state ruled from Moscow, with numerous *ethnies* in each republic, were in a way a 'recognition of distinct national territories... critical in transforming the fluid relationships between language and ethnicity into a cohesive sense of nationality' (Dave 1996b:76-7). This was true, to an extent, only for the titular *ethnie* in each territory. Otherwise, these dividing lines were, no less, a prescription for cultural rivalries, preferential economic policies, ethnonationalist conflicts and separatist or irredentist dreams within most of the newly independent states (examples in Hunter 1996:9-10; Kaiser 1997:22-7). The decentralization issue found its final expression to date in the Commonwealth of Independent States (CIS), created by Russia, Belarus and Ukraine on 8 December 1991, joined on 21 December 1991 by the other ex-Soviet republics, Georgia and the Baltics excepted. In 1992 Azerbayjan left the CIS, but rejoined it in 1993; Georgia, also, joined in 1993. This is a rather weak structure, performing an economic coordinating function and providing an instrument for military cooperation. The Russian Federation, although formally only one of the CIS members, casts a long shadow everywhere; it is the only natural candidate for regional hegemony (Kubicek 1997:638-53). Briefly stated, the CIS has not yet worked out very well, as some leaders of its component states have wished to strengthen its super-national structures, while others preferred to focus on their respective nation-states. In various states, despite pronouncements about 'equal rights', the titular group tried hard to become 'the first among equals' in order 'to take responsibility for the fate of the nation'. Leaders of the titular community have sensed that the call of nationalism was strong in several of the independent states and have responded to it, even when not fully inclined to do so (examples in Fuller 1992:13-16). Some have used newly acquired statehood to 'restore' the primacy of the titular *ethnie*, including its culture, with an emphasis on language. At least several of these leaders must have hoped that, by promoting the titular language in the name of nationalism, they would also strengthen the bases of the nation.

The reduced effectiveness of the Soviet Union's form of government and its reduced legitimization, among other factors leading to its disintegration, caused profound disarray in its economy and presented serious problems and dangers, usually interconnected, in the inheritance of the fifteen successor states. To obtain creative order instead of destructive disorder, the newly independent states had to strive for de-sovietization so as to assert their own identity, construct their political and administrative institutions, reform their economy, and resolve their ethnic and cultural rivalries in the way most suitable for each community. Among large segments of the population in several of the ex-Soviet independent Muslim states there was a pervasive feeling of economic and psychological dislocation and an instinctive desire to prevent a descent into a chaotic Absurdistan by maintaining some of the conservative structures. Thus, many aimed at consensual modernization, sometimes expressed, paradoxically, by authoritarian methods (Biryukov 1997 for Uzbekistan), ensuring stability under the unaccustomed conditions of national independence, when the ruling elites in each republic had to make their own decisions in key issues instead of following Moscow's instructions as before. Since elite circulation was limited, some leading politicians and bureaucrats lacked the experience and training needed for independent decision making. In this new situation, competing elites in 'the new states and ancient societies' (to use a term of Gleason 1997:1) found themselves antagonistically positioned in pressing for competing economic advantages and diverging security interests.

All of the fifteen independent republics also had to face serious domestic challenges: for examples, turning themselves into states for which they had to create nations, forming new political and social orders while struggling to liberate themselves from the Soviet legacy and resolving formidable economic and other problems. These issues were common, in varying degrees, to the six Muslim republics: Azerbayjan in the Caucasus, and Uzbekistan, Kazakhstan, Kyrgyzstan, Turkmenistan, and Tajikistan in Central Asia (Götz and Halbach 1996; Uzel 1993). The leaders of the titular *ethnies* had to make a choice between polyethnic diversity and monoethnic supremacy. In their preference for the latter, they had to minimize ethnic, clannish and local attachments and instill instead a public sense of patriotism, loyalty to nation and devotion to the republic (in certain cases, barely concealing their nostalgia for the defunct Soviet Union), while simultaneously contending with the difficult process of transition to a market economy and democratization. The rulers of the ex-Soviet Muslim states, when faced with the choice, succinctly phrased by Hélène Carrère d'Encausse (1993:231), of nation *versus* democracy, or nation *and* democracy, selected the former option and did not favour democracy.

Throughout Soviet rule, probably the most visible continuity in Moscow's attitude towards the six republics was a rejection of their cultural otherness and a persevering attempt to effect change. This worked out only in part. While all six states have developed in different ways since independence due to their differing size, ethnic makeup, cultural characteristics, resources and location, some common patterns are discernible in their response to challenges. A prominent feature of the response was a certain rise in self-assertiveness of identity and culture – a process which had started as early as the 1960s in varying degrees in each republic and became more prominent later, displaying signs of emerging national awareness in the 1980s. This process was essentially a backlash stimulated by economic, political and cultural grievances (Hyman 1996:13); it was also the effect of modernization in education and life styles that had created new elites. While still part of the Soviet Union, all six had been characterized by economic underdevelopment (although most are rich in mineral resources) and conservative political culture (expressed by docility to Moscow's instructions). The exception was Azerbayjan where, like some other areas in the Caucasus (chiefly Georgia and Armenia, with their longer cultural continuity), nationalism had fomented certain aspirations for independence somewhat earlier; the Azeri language had already been promoted to a special status in 1936 (for language politics in Georgia, see Enokh 1998). In the Soviet Muslim republics of Central Asia and Azerbayjan, the top Communist-bred bureaucracy, despite growing anti-Russian grassroots' sentiment, was generally supportive of Gorbachev's intention to preserve the Soviet Union, in whose parameters they found it easier to contain or suppress opposition groups. In the 17 March 1991 referendum on the Soviet Union's future, Azerbayjan's and all Central Asia's leaders had their populations vote in favour of preserving the Union: Azerbayjan by 93.3% (although only 75.1% participated in the voting), Uzbekistan 93.7%, Kazakhstan 94.1%, Kyrgyzstan 94.6%, Turkmenistan 97.9% and Tajikistan 96.2% (Karasik 1992:400; Khazanov 1995:140-1).

When the swift disintegration of the Soviet Union practically compelled the republics – which had not taken any steps to break away – to declare their independence in 1991, most ruling elites were hardly prepared for the new situation and the consequent challenges of balancing different, often contradictory interests and pressures. They had not expected this change and, in many instances, probably did not welcome it. All had been Soviet-trained; the changes that they introduced into the *apparat* consisted mainly of replacing Russian high-level and sometimes middle-level managers with native ones, similarly Soviet-trained. Most decision-makers continued to prefer stability to openness; they relied on authoritarian strong-handed governments based on cadres of former Communist parties, the military and the police, while variously banning reform-minded opposition parties and groups (which are often split on ideological or ethnic lines, anyway) or severely limiting and marginalizing their activities. This has often been the case even following official declarations promising responsiveness to change. Opposition parties, insofar as they still exist, have been further weakened by internal rifts and by the state leaders' successful appropriation of nationalist programmes and slogans and recruitment of certain opposition leaders with offers of lucrative jobs within the bureaucracy. In general, Tajikistan (until 1992) and Kyrgyzstan have been somewhat less restrictive than the other states in their years of independence. All in all, however, the political styles favoured by the leaders of the six newly independent states have more or less followed the Soviet model.

The six states have many features in common, at least partly due to a shared history in the Russian Empire and then in the Soviet Union (Saray 1996: xiii-xiv). During those years, no political frontiers separated them; even today, despite state-centred attitudes, the borderlands continue in part to be scenes of intense interaction in face-to-face relations and frequent moving, authorized or not, across the frontiers. The scarecrow of Islamic fundamentalism which most of the six new states have been raising is only partly real, at least in the short term, since Islam, although on the rise, is often politically moderate in this area – except perhaps in Tajikistan and Uzbekistan, both threatened by the situation in Afghanistan. Relations with Russia, China, Turkey and Iran are crucial, while those with Pakistan, Saudi Arabia and the industrial states of the West are important especially in the areas of economics and development. Turkey, in particular, has invested serious efforts towards economic cooperation, but with only limited success, as it has not had sufficient economic clout and several of the six states have preferred to establish links directly with the West rather than via Turkey (Robins 1993:593).

Despite a high degree of commonality, there are, however, visible differences in territory and population among the six. Kazakhstan is the largest in area, while the others range from about 86,600 to 491,200 sq. km. (table 2.1 below). Population (table 2.1 below) is not commensurate with size, Uzbekistan having the highest number. Moreover, overall population growth during the last decade of Soviet rule was considerable but varied for each community throughout the region, according to official figures for 1979 and 1989 (*Vestnik statistiki* 1980, 1990, summarized in Hyman 1996:21). It rose in that decade by 23.6% for the Azeris, 34.1% for the Uzbeks, 24.1% for the Kazakhs, 32.7% for the Kyrgyz, 34.6% for the Turkmens, and 45.5% for the Tajiks. Average annual population growth continues to be rather high: in 1992, it was about 1.3% in Azerbayjan, 2.4% in Uzbekistan, 1.0% in Kazakhstan, 1.9% in Kyrgyzstan, 2.4% in Turkmenistan, and 1.3% in Tajikistan (Haghayeghi 1995:173-4). It is no accident that the lowest birthrate was registered in Kazakhstan, where approximately half the population was not Muslim (chiefly Slavic); it was the only one of the six in which the overall population decreased after independence due to out-migration (tables 2.1 and 3.6). In the other republics, non-Muslims formed a small minority only, in relative numbers, with the exception of Kyrgyzstan where the non-Muslims still represented a quarter of the entire population. Further, it is not surprising that population growth, percentagewise, was highest amongst the Tajiks, where Islam is an important factor within a population with the lowest per capita income and very modest living standards (Turkmenistan seems however to overtake it recently in proportionate population growth). Looking at more recent data, one notes that during 1994 the population of the six Muslim states changed as follows.

Table 2.1. AREA AND POPULATION OF AZERBAYJAN AND THE
CENTRAL ASIAN STATES, 1994-95
(*rounded figures*)

	Area (sq. km.)	Jan. 1994	Jan. 1995	Increase	Relative growth (%)
Azerbayjan	86,600	7,364,000	7,420,000	56,000	0.8
Uzbekistan	447,000	22,192,000	22,633,000	441,000	2.0
Kazakhstan	2,717,300	16,942,000	16,683,000	-269,000	-1.5
Kyrgyzstan	199,500	4,463,000	4,476,000	13,000	0.3
Turkmenistan	491,200	4,361,000	4,455,000	94,000	2.2
Tajikistan	143,000	5,704,000	5,777,000	73,000	1.3

Sources: Statistical Yearbook of Azerbayjan 1997, Baku 1998: 3,8,13; State Committee for Forecasting and Statistics of the Republic of Uzbekistan, *Economy of the State of Uzbekistan 1991-5*, Tashkent, n.d.; *Ekspress Kazakhstana* 15 June 1995; State Committee on Statistics of Turkmenistan 1997, Ashgabat 1997: *Brief* 3; official data of the Government of Tajikistan, reported by Sokolova 1998:14; Pomfret 1995:4; Kulchik a.o. 1996:61-96. For some 1997 data, Smith a.o. 1998:153.

Table 2.2. MAIN ETHNIC GROUPS IN AZERBAYJAN
AND CENTRAL ASIA, 1989

	Azerbayjan	Uzbekistan	Kazakhstan	Kyrgyzstan	Turkmenistan	Tajikistan
Azeris	5,804,980	44,410	90,083	15,775	33,365	3,556
Uzbeks	1,379	14,142,475	332,017	550,096	317,333	1,197,841
Kazakhs	1,639	808,227	6,534,616	37,318	87,802	11,376
Kyrgyz	224	174,907	14,112	2,229,663	634	63,832
Turkmens	340	121,578	3,846	899	2,536,606	20,487
Tajiks	702	933,560*	25,514	33,518	3,149	3,172,420
Russians	392,304	1,653,478	6,227,549	916,558	333,892	388,481
Ukrainians	32,345	153,197	896,240	108,027	35,578	41,375
Belorussians	7,833	29,427	182,601	9,187	9,200	7,247
Germans	748	39,809	957,518	101,309	4,434	32,671
Tatars	39,118	656,601	331,151	72,282	39,257	72,264
Karakalpaks	102	411,878	1,387	142	3,062	163
Koreans	94	183,140	103,315	18,355	2,848	13,431
Uyghurs	9	35,762	185,301	36,779	1,308	566

Source: 1989 Soviet Population Census.

*The number of Tajiks in Uzbekistan seems to be higher than officially reported, since some Uzbek-speaking Tajiks were registered as Uzbeks (US Department of State 1999).

Table 2.2 lists only the more important nationalities in the six multiethnic republics. Many of these groups are native; others, like the Slavs, have immigrated; others found refuge there during the years 1941-5; yet others were resettled there before the war or deported there during the war as 'security risks' – including Germans, Crimean Tatars and Koreans (Um 1996:218-9). Between 1979 and 1989, according to census returns (rounded to thousands, cf. table 3.1), overall figures of Russians had grown in Kazakhstan (by 236,000) and Kyrgyzstan (by 5,000), while they dropped moderately in Uzbekistan (by 14,000), Turkmenistan (by 16,000) and Tajikistan (by 7,000). In the 1990s, the decrease in population in Kazakhstan – the only case among the six states – was due not only to generally falling birthrates, but to the exodus of non-Kazakhs. In 1993 alone, about 50,000 Russians left Kyrgyzstan (Hyman 1996:53; also below, table 2.7) and 40,900 left civil war-torn Tajikistan (Smith a.o. 1998:206). A few emigrants later returned, saying that they had not been welcomed in Russia, the Ukraine and elsewhere. Some titulars, too, have been returning to their own republic, e.g. to Uzbekistan and Kazakhstan, in varying numbers (Robertson 1996:124).

All six states are landlocked with far-reaching implications for their economy. Kazakhstan is not only the largest in territory but probably in mining resources, as well as the only one bordering the Russian Federation; thus it is an important transit area. So is Uzbekistan, the state with the largest population and the biggest capital city, Tashkent; it is the only state bordering on all the new Muslim states in Central Asia as well as on Afghanistan.

Azerbayjan

Since the 1828 Peace of Turkmanchay, Azerbayjan has been divided between Russia and Persia. Russian Azerbayjan, in the eastern Caucasus, was briefly independent between 1918 and 1920; it was then conquered by the Red Army. According to official Soviet propaganda, progressive Azeris joined Soviet efforts to build socialism and to promote world revolution; Azeri nationalists have claimed that their pre-Soviet republic was a perfect democracy, marking the resurrection of Azeri national identity (Entessar 1993:122-3), and that those Azeris who cooperated with the Soviets did so under the misconception that they were thus assisting their country's national cause (Altstadt 1992:109-10). Azerbayjan's sovietization had two main objectives, encountered elsewhere as well: to harness its economic resources, chiefly Caspian Sea oil, to serve Soviet interests; and to shape a population loyal to the regime. The former endeavour was more successful than the latter.

On 23 September 1989, Azerbayjan was the first Muslim republic in the Soviet Union to declare its sovereignty; on 5 October 1991, it proclaimed its independence, adopting a new constitution in November 1995. Azerbayjan joined the CIS on 21 December 1991, but withdrew in

1992, following Ebulfeyz Elchibey's election to the presidency in June. It rejoined the CIS on 19 September 1993 by order of its new president, Heidar Aliev (Willerton 1992:191-222), a veteran Communist official, who came to power by a coup in June 1993, replacing the pro-Turkish Elchibey (Elçi Bey 1993; Goldenberg 1994:119ff). Azerbayjan's leaders opted for a presidential system, in which the state President appoints a Prime Minister and a Council of Ministers. The 125-member unicameral parliament is composed as follows: 100 are elected by single-member constituencies and 25 seats are distributed proportionately among representatives of political party slates which have won at least 8% of the vote. Several parties attempt to compete for power. The largest is President Heidar Aliev's New Azerbayjan Party. Former President Elchibey and the veteran *Müsavat* (Equality) Party chairman, the former Speaker of parliament, Isa Gambar, lead jointly the opposition Democratic Congress, which unites several opposition parties (Robertson 1998:206-7). A smaller Talysh People's Party promotes the interests of this minority. Some parties have been closed down during the 1990s and new ones set up (Robertson 1997:206; Gaebel and Jürgensen 1996; Helly 1998 for these and other political groupings). In the parliamentary elections of 1995, only eight out of forty-eight parties were allowed to run; the Azerbayjan Islamic Party and the Communist Party were among those not admitted (Auch 1995:164ff; Fuller 1996:121-30; Batalden and Batalden 1997:114-15). Azerbayjan's principal exports are crude and residual fuel oils.

In 1989, about 78% of the republic's population of 7,019,739 (the 1998 estimate is 7,631,600) were Azeris, of whom about 54% were urban; 75% were Shiites, about 11% were Christians and the rest Sunnis. Baku, the capital, had 1,725,900 inhabitants in 1998. Although Islam is more visible nowadays, the 1992 Law on Religion, guaranteeing freedom of religious worship, is generally observed in what amounts to a mild form of secularism. The most important minorities in 1989 were made up of Russians (5.6%) and Armenians (7.9%); others were the Lezghins and Avars (less than 3% each) and smaller groups like the Talysh and Tats; there is also a small Ukrainian community, mostly visible in Baku (*Vyshka* 10 Apr. 1998). For years, the Armenians and Lezghins have been raising nationalist claims of their own (Grigoryan 1992: 4ff., 25ff.). The Armenians were living mainly in the province of Nagorno-Karabagh, then an Armenian populated enclave within Azerbayjan. Powerful tensions had grown since 1988, accompanied by physical violence in 1989-90, erupting into a bloody war between Azerbayjan and Armenia in 1992-4 (Altstadt 1992:195ff; Borovali 1992:114ff; Zdravomyslov 1997:14-27), which severely harmed the nation's economy and left the Azeris traumatized. Armenian forces occupied Nagorno-Karabagh as well as a corridor of land connecting it with Armenia. Because of this loss of territory, the ratio of Azeris in Azerbayjan has increased to more than 90% in 1998 (according to Yunusov 1998:101), while that of Russians has decreased and that of Armenians drastically, now that Nagorno-Karabagh has been occupied by Armenia and is no longer governed by Azerbayjan. According to various sources, there has occurred an unscheduled population exchange: during the years 1988 and 1992, about 270,000 Armenians fled Azerbayjan and some 217,000 Azeris fled from Armenia to Azerbayjan (Anderson and Silver 1996:503-4). To the south lies the Azerbayjan province of Iran, with an Azeri population larger than that of ex-Soviet Azerbayjan, of whose existence the Azeris in the new state of Azerbayjan are very much aware.

An unintended result of Gorbachev's politics was an upsurge of cultural particularism in Azerbayjan, as in some other republics. The ensuing search for identity and nationalist self-assertion (Gadzhi-Zade 1998:62-4), both in the last years of the Soviet Union and in those immediately following, show signs of pro-Turkish and pro-Iranian sentiments, as well as Pan-Azeri tendencies, Shiite sympathies and the seeking of Azeri origins, particularly as 99.1% of Azeris in Azerbayjan considered Azeri as their primary language, while only 31.7% claimed fluency in Russian (1989 Soviet Population Census, reported in Henze 1991:167). A revival of old ethnic and cultural rivalries (Hunter 1993:225ff) has occurred, tending to foster ethnocentric culture and slow down the process of nation-building (Hunter 1994:58-96). It was no secret that just about 14.4% of Russians in Azerbayjan knew Azeri, that the prestigious Oil and Gas Institute in Baku conducted classes exclusively in Russian, and that all its experts were Russian (Altstadt 1992:185-91), as was the case in faculties of science.

Azeri patriots focused on the efforts by their intellectual elites to highlight the importance of the Azeri literary heritage (strongly influenced by Iranian culture) and to give special attention to the enrichment and promotion of their language (which belongs to the Turkic group), as will be explained below. In a parallel way, there was a resurgence of Islam, expressed in a wave of mosque and religious school construction (Kappert 1994:128-30). Perhaps this can be explained by the fact that almost 50% of the population is rural, in whose villages Russian culture remained somewhat remote; moreover, the survival of the pre-Soviet quasi-feudal clan system has affected Azeri townspeople, too, through kinship (Huttenbach 1995:338).

Uzbekistan

The country as it is today was never a political unit. Russia dominated parts of what is now modern Uzbekistan since conquering Tashkent in 1865. Soviet rule was established in Tashkent (now the capital) in November 1918. The old Emirate of Bukhara and the Khanate of Khiva, which had become Russian Protectorates in 1868 and 1873, respectively, became the People's Soviet Republics of Bukhara and Khorezm in 1920, both dissolved in 1924. In the Soviet 'national delimitation' of 1924-5, the Uzbek Soviet Socialist Republic included the Tajik Autonomous Soviet Socialist Republic, which was separated from it later, in 1929; in 1936, the Karakalpak Autonomous Soviet Socialist Republic was added to Uzbekistan from Kazakhstan. The main role of Uzbekistan in the Soviet Union was to provide it with cotton; heavy demand affected the environment, with serious consequences. The economy continues to be largely dependent on cotton, with industrialization progressing at a slow pace.

Uzbekistan proclaimed its sovereignty on 20 June 1990 and independence on 31 August 1991, issuing its new post-Soviet constitution on 8 December 1992. It joined the CIS on 21 December 1991. It has adopted a presidential system of government by order of President Islam Karimov who is also head of the ruling People's Democratic Party. Several other parties were and are sporadically active, such as *Birlik* (Unity), *Ėrk* (Freedom), *Adolat* (Justice), *Dehqon* Freedom Party (of Peasants), National Revival Party, the Greens, Progress of the Fatherland Party, Independence Party, and several other groups (details in Ginzburg 1994-5: I, 193-298; Robertson 1998:494). Although not all have been permitted to register (*Birlik* and *Ėrk*, among others, have not), they continue to exist. A new law on political parties was adopted in 1996, stipulating a minimum membership of 5,000 per party and prohibiting the establishment of parties on a religious or ethnic basis. The banned *Ėrk* Democratic Party, led by Muhammed Salih, who has been forced to live abroad since 1993, issued a plea to the world community, on 10 September 1998, calling for the legalization of all opposition parties and the creation of a political environment conducive to the opposition parties' joining in the approaching parliamentary elections (text in *CAM* 1998, no. 5:38). Inasmuch as there is opposition to the government, most of it is carried out abroad (Fierman 1997a:367-88). The unicameral parliament now comprises 150 members (formerly it had 250), elected by universal suffrage for five years. Real power, however, is concentrated in the President's office. In April 1997, two laws were adopted in parliament, 'On Guarantees of and Freedom of Access to Information' and 'On the Protection of the Professional Work of Journalists'. However, the government severely limits the freedom of speech and the press, and an atmosphere of repression stifles public criticism. A new law of January 1999 increases government supervision of the media: press censorship continues and the government restricts citizens' access to foreign media (US Department of State, 1998; 1999).

Table 2.3. ETHNIC GROUPS IN UZBEKISTAN, JANUARY 1995

	%		%
Uzbeks	75.8	Ukrainians	0.6
Russians	6.0	Azeris	0.2
Tajiks	4.8	Armenians	0.2
Kazakhs	4.1	Belorussians	0.1
Tatars	1.6	Jews	0.1
Kyrgyz	0.9	Germans	0.1
Turkmens	0.6	Others	4.9

Source: State Committee for Forecasting and Statistics of the Republic of Uzbekistan, *Economy of the State of Uzbekistan 1991-1995,* Tashkent n.d., 31; Kulchik a.o. 1996:91.

Uzbekistan borders on Kazakhstan, Tajikistan, Kyrgyzstan, Turkmenistan, and Afghanistan. It has the largest population of the six newly independent Muslim states, 23,867,400 in January 1998, of whom more than 2.1 million live in the capital, Tashkent. About 1.6 million Uzbeks live in other CIS lands and some 1.65 million in Afghanistan (Haase 1994:131; Şahnazarov 1996-7:105). One of the problems facing the Uzbek majority and their government is that the Persian-speaking population, since early Soviet times known as Tajiks, has a long history of both cohabitation and rivalry with the Uzbeks (Fragner 1998; Shorish 1994:53-73). Nowadays the Tajiks in Uzbekistan, chiefly in and around Bukhara and Samarkand, claim that their overall number is larger than that given in the official data and raise cultural and other demands (Foltz 1996), while some of their brethren in Tajikistan would dearly love to see Samarkand and Bukhara incorporated into Tajikistan. Uzbeks' forming almost a quarter of Tajikistan's population and their involvement in the civil war there constitute an added complication to Uzbek-Tajik relations in Uzbekistan. The Uzbek majority in Uzbekistan, fearing separatist campaigns, often proclaims the slogan 'Every inch of the motherland is like gold!' A common national language of elevated status is perceived as a means for preventing breakaways; another slogan emphasizes this attitude, viz., 'All independence starts with language and depends on it!'

A further issue has to do with religion: *ca.* 88% of Uzbekistan's population are Muslims (mostly Sunnis), *ca.* 9% Russian Orthodox, and 3% adhere to other religions. While Islam was generally kept low-key during the Soviet era, due to central control and containment, it has become vocal and visible since independence (Bazarov 1997:122-9). Sufi brotherhoods, which had existed during the Soviet period underground, increased their activity in Uzbekistan after independence (Babazhanov 1999). An indication of the interest in cultural-religious heritage among the intellectuals can be seen in the prestigious literary monthly *Sharq Yulduzi* (Star of the East) publishing the Koran in instalments between March 1990 and February 1992; responding to the success of this feature, a complete edition of the Koran was published as number 8-9 (1992) of this journal.

In May 1998, Uzbekistan, Kyrgyzstan and Tajikistan decided to co-operate in order to limit the advance of Islamic fundamentalism, which they perceive as a political danger (*CAM* 1998, no. 3: 38). In the case of Uzbekistan, according to government reports, the determined efforts by President Karimov and the Uzbekistan authorities to stop penetration by politically radical Islamist groups have been moderately successful. While Tashkent is still mostly a secularized city and Samarkand and Bukhara are generally characterized by moderate Islam, the densely populated Ferghana Valley is alleged to house militant Islamic tendencies (Khal-mukhamedov 1998:55). In June 1999 a Tashkent court found a number of 'Islamic radicals' guilty of allegedly carrying out an assassination attempt against President Karimov on 16 February 1999 (*CAM*, 1999, no. 2:20-1; Abbas 1999; *Moskovskie Novosti* 22-28 June 1999). Aware of the potent appeal of Islam, Karimov issued a decree, on 7 April 1999, establishing an Islamic university in Tashkent (*Ma"rifat* 10 Apr. 1999; *Uchitel' Uzbekistana* 21 Apr. 1999). His basic approach was to have the projected university teach and analyze the ideas of Islam 'in a contemporary spirit' – under government control.

Sovietization, which aimed at remoulding Uzbek society by administrative measures, propaganda against 'bourgeois nationalism' and the supposedly retrograde character of religion, had some success in urban centres but much less in rural areas. However, Uzbek intellectuals who had started their search for identity in the late nineteenth and early twentieth centuries continued their quest in later years – until many of them were purged in the 1930s – and again, more actively so during the Gorbachev era (Fierman 1989:5ff.). Uzbek intellectuals started discussing a 'national awakening' based on cultural revival, with emphasis on language.

The ingrained Soviet model of centralism has apparently contributed to preventing Uzbekistan's political leadership from granting fully equal cultural and other rights to the non-titular *ethnies,* some of which have been voicing their apprehension lest Soviet domination be replaced by Uzbek (Akiner 1996:345). As in the neighbouring states, political, economic and cultural public rivalries are fed by competing groups – ethnic, familial, regional, religious, or attached to special interests (professional and otherwise). Such competition and cooperation among the groups, which intended to advance their own agendas and control the new institutions, constitute complex and changing processes of solidarity in which, for instance, certain inter-group coalitions cut across national loyalties, thus questioning the nature of national identity (Gleason 1993:331ff). President Karimov has responded by selecting the medieval tribal leader and conqueror Timur (Tamerlane) – a non-Uzbek – as the main political icon of Uzbekistan, trying to enhance national identity with a new historical myth.

Kazakhstan

Around the end of the fifteenth century, the Kazakhs emerged as a distinct people. Their lands, however, came under strong colonization pressures from Russia, China and Mongol tribal federations. Desperate, Kazakh khans turned to Russia for protection, but in the course of the eighteenth and nineteenth centuries, Russia extended its rule in the northwest of the territory claimed by Kazakh pastoral nomadic federations. In the east, China's Manchu dynasty increased its control. Thus, large areas of today's Kazakhstan have been under Russian domination longer than Turkic lands in Central Asia proper. Since the mid-nineteenth century, intensive colonization by Russian peasants continued unabated in what was considered unoccupied fertile land. The number of Russian and Ukrainian settlers in the Kazakh steppes increased from 533,915 (12.8% of the entire population) in 1897 to about 1.5 million (30% of the entire population) in 1917. By 1918, about 150,000 hectares (approximately 370,000 acres) of the most fertile lands had been appropriated by the settlers (Khazanov 1995a:245).

The number of Kazakhs and their ratio in the population had changed by then and continued to do so under Soviet rule, first diminishing because of Soviet economic and other pressures (such as forced collectivization in which many Kazakhs perished or fled to China), later improving due to a higher birthrate.

Table 2.4. KAZAKH POPULATION IN KAZAKHSTAN, 1830-1992
(rounded figures)

		% of entire population
1830	1,300,000	96.4
1850	1,502,000	91.1
1897	3,000,000	79.8
1926	3,713,000	57.1
1939	2,640,000	38.2
1959	2,755,000	30.0
1970	4,234,000	32.6
1979	5,289,000	36.0
1989	6,531,000	39.7
1992	7,297,000	43.2

Sources: Official censuses, summed up in Khazanov 1995:266. The 1830 and 1850 censuses are approximate; the 1992 estimates, not based on a census, may be too high.

Kazakh nationalism emerged in the late nineteenth century and was apparently reinforced by contact with foreign nationalists exiled to Kazakhstan. Between 1917 and 1920, a Kazakh national movement demanded autonomy, but ultimately the country was incorporated into the RSFSR (Russian Soviet Federated Socialist Republic) as the Kirghiz Autonomous Soviet Socialist Republic (until 1925, the Kazakhs were known as Kirghiz, while the Kirghiz were called Kara Kirghiz). In 1925, it was renamed the Kazakh Autonomous Socialist Republic, which became a Union republic in 1936. Under Russian and Soviet rule, the Kazakhs became more and more marginalized and, except in the south, confined to relatively unproductive areas. From 1926 to 1970, the number of Russians and other Slavs in Kazakhstan increased from 2 to 6.5 million. Many of these were skilled workers, technicians and engineers, coming to jobs in new enterprises and settling in the towns, whose population increased visibly, with European elements dominant (Melvin 1995:100-5). In Kazakhstan the main religions are Sunni Islam and Russian Orthodox Christianity (Twining 1993:145).

Kazakhstan has a huge territory of 2,717,300 sq. km. (larger than Saudi Arabia) as one of its most salient features (it was the second largest republic in the Soviet Union – following the RSFSR – and it remains so in the CIS). It borders on Russia, China, Kyrgyzstan and Uzbekistan. Undeniably, 'Kazakhstan is an accidental country, a nation that was carved out of a Soviet republic whose boundaries were never intended to be those of an independent state' (Olcott 1997:201). Although it has a huge potential (Giroux 1997), at present the economy seems to be only recovering slowly from the deep recession which followed the dismemberment of the Soviet Union. In 1999, the authorities of Kazakhstan appealed to the population to donate their jewels to the state. Unemployment remains high, particularly in the cities and towns. Much depends on the state's ability to exploit its large oil and gas reserves and market them as well as other raw materials. Only about sixteen million people were living in this vast country at the start of 1997. The total population number has constantly declined through the emigration of Russians, Germans and others (below, table 2.5); it was only 15,048,500 according to the first results of the population census in April 1999. The same census reported 1,120,700 inhabitants in the former capital, Almaty (called Alma-Ata in Soviet times) and 319,300 in the new capital, Astana. Another four-and-a-half million form the Kazakh diaspora: in 1997, there were some 2,477,000 Kazakhs in the republics of the former Soviet Union and about 2,023,000 in twenty-five other states (Mendikulova 1998:73). Over time, waves of immigration have composed Kazakhstan's population. In 1989 the main ethnic groups were Kazakhs (39.7%), Russians (37.8%), Ukrainians and Belorussians (6.5%) and Germans (5.8%). Annual population increase was then 1.2% to 1.3%. By 1993, due to emigration, the percentages were closer to 44%

Kazakhs, 36% Russians, 5% other Slavs, and 4% Germans (Esenova 1996:697). For the following years, we have the more detailed official Kazakh figures, which however do not always give data for the smaller *ethnies*.

Table 2.5. ETHNIC GROUPS IN KAZAKHSTAN, 1995-8

	Number (1000) 1995	Share in population 1995 (%)	Number (1000) Jan. 1997	Share in population Jan. 1997 (%)	Number (1000) Jan. 1998	Share in population Jan. 1998 (%)
Kazakhs	7,636	46.0	8,033.4	50.6	8,129.7	52.0
Russians	5,770	34.7	5,104.6	32.2	4,905.0	31.4
Ukrainians	821	4.9	720.3	4.5	684.3	4.4
Germans	507	3.1	303.6	1.9	247.8	1.6
Uzbeks	379	2.3	358.7	2.3	n.d.	n.d.
Tatars	319	1.9	277.6	1.7	268.2	1.7
Uyghurs	205	1.2	n.d.	n.d.	n.d.	n.d.
Belorussians	172	1.0	n.d.	n.d.	n.d.	n.d.
Koreans	105	0.6	n.d.	n.d.	n.d.	n.d.
Azeris	103	0.6	n.d.	n.d.	n.d.	n.d.
Others	592	3.6	1,062.5	6.7	1,406.9	9.0
Total	16,609	99.9	15,860.7	99.9	15,641.9	100.1

n.d. = no data
Source: Official Kazakh statistics, reported in *Mysl'* 9: Sep. 1996, 65; slightly different data for 1995 in Benner 1996:146; *Statisticheskoe Obozrenie Kazakhstana* 1:1997, 3; data given by Dr. Y. K. Shokamanov, Kazakhstan's Institute of Statistics (interviewed on 11 Sep. 1998). According to the April 1999 population census, the Kazakhs numbered 53.4% of the inhabitants (*Extracts*: 14 May 1999. Available: http://www.soros.org/kazakhstan/omri/0177.html.28 Mar. 2000).

The table indicates that, by January 1997, the six largest *ethnies* together formed 93.2% of the entire population. Further, it shows the increase in Kazakh numbers since 1992 (above, table 2.4), in both absolute and proportionate figures, at the expense of other ethnic groups, along with a decline in the state's overall population. Europeans were emigrating. The Germans, for instance, were leaving for Germany and those who remained reduced their cultural activities in education and publishing.

Russian colonization rested on the concept of bringing civilization, progress and Christianity to a backward population; Soviet ideology added 'socialism' to 'progress' and substituted 'Christianity' with 'atheism'. Under the Soviets, with their sustained drive for education, the Kazakh intelligentsia expanded and, with it, a Kazakh particularist awareness emerged. It expressed itself, for instance, in student demonstrations, in December 1986, against the dismissal of Dinmuhammad Kunaev, a Kazakh who had long served as the First Secretary of the Kazakhstan Central Committee of the Communist Party, and his replacement by a non-Kazakh, Gennadii Kolbin. With the bloody response of the Soviet

forces in Alma-Ata (Zdravomyslov 1997:13-14), identity awareness assumed a nationalist character, whose most evident expression was perforce
cultural, chiefly in the domain of language. In August 1989, taking advantage of *perestroika*, the Supreme Soviet of Kazakhstan adopted a law
instituting Kazakh as the official state language (with Russian as the language of inter-ethnic communication). Local Russians started lobbying
for an amendment, and conflict on this and other issues has constantly
accompanied Kazakh-Russian relations ever since. The Kazakhs passed
a moderate bill to proclaim their sovereignty, on 25 October 1990, post-
poning their declaration of independence to 16 December 1991, only
after the Soviet Union had finally collapsed (Kazakhstan, not coinciden-
tally, being the last of the Soviet republics to announce its independence).
Five days later, the new state joined the CIS. In December 1997, the
Government moved the capital of the republic from Almaty, in the
southeast, to Akmola, further north, in a symbolic gesture to assert its
hold on that area, populated by a heavy Russian majority (Kulchik a.o.
1996:37; Huttenbach 1998 lists additional reasons for the move to Akmola,
renamed in 1998 Astana).

Both the January 1993 and the August 1995 constitutions as well as
daily practice have been laying the groundwork for the primacy of the
Kazakhs in their republic. The last Supreme Soviet of 1990 had already
been dominated by Kazakhs, because in 1990 the delegates had been
elected not only by districts, but also by many public organizations,
whose leadership had traditionally been Kazakh (Khazanov 1995:169;
Ponomarev 1991:6ff.). In independent Kazakhstan, this parliament functioned until 1993. The President, Nursultan Nazarbaev, formerly First
Secretary of the Central Committee of the Kazakhstan Communist Party
(for whose career, Olcott 1992:371-6), persuaded parliament to dissolve
itself in December 1993 and ruled for a while via the government he had
appointed and the Assembly of the Nationalities of Kazakhstan, which
he set up in 1995. This was a 260-member institution representing the
102 recognized ethnic communities (some official publications mention
130 nationalities, Nysanbaev a.o. 1996:97) – but in practice state-ap-
pointed. The Assembly established cultural centres for some of the *ethnies*
represented and encouraged their language maintenance (details below,
ch. 5; *KP* 13 June 1997; 6 Oct. 1998). A separate body, a unicameral
178-seat parliament, was elected in March 1994, but never met and was
dissolved by the Constitutional Court a year later. In December 1995, a
new bicameral parliament was made up of a 47-member Senate and a 67-
member *Majlis* or Lower House. In the Senate, 40 members had been
elected, while 7 others were appointed by the state President. In all three
parliaments, Kazakh representation was higher, and Russian lower, than
their respective share in the population. The bicameral parliament elected
in 1995 comprised in all 68 Kazakhs, 31 Russians and the rest from other

ethnies: Ukrainian, Uyghur, German, and Korean (Dave 1996b:200-1; Smith a.o. 1998:152); the Korean community included many descendants of those deported there by Stalin. Several political parties and groups are registered, although the regularity of their activities has varied: the People's Congress, a communist, a socialist, and a social-democrat party, as well as *Azat* (Liberty), *Alash* (named after a legendary Kazakh hero), and others (Robertson 1997:282-3; Karsakov 1998:76-81; Petrov and Gafarly 1998:42-5). A new party, *Otan* (Fatherland), founded on 1 March 1999, enjoys the President's support (*KP* 2 Mar. 1999).

While careful to preserve relations with the Russian Federation and to appear as the defendant of equal rights for all *ethnies*, the authorities have sought to enhance Kazakh identity (Akiner 1995:52-9). They have not merely visibly encouraged the search for roots in Kazakh culture and language (Söylemez 1996), but have also altered access to land, favouring the Kazakhs (in Kazakhstan, alone among the new Muslim republics, many Russians are agricultural workers – Roy 1993:146-8), while also promoting them in most spheres of public administration, the financial sector and the judiciary – with some emphasis on kinship and clannishness (Naumova 1991:300-5; Eschment 1997:75). Also, the Kazakh diaspora has been encouraged to return home. Between 1991 and 1998, about 40,000 families returned to Kazakhstan, mainly from other CIS countries and Mongolia, many of them speaking Kazakh, but the latter little or no Russian (*The Economist* 3 Apr. 1999; Smith a.o. 1998:157). Since the Kazakhstan Government wished to regulate the 'return' (or 'repatriation') of Kazakhs, so as to have the state and local authorities take proper care of them, a Presidential decree on 3 April 1998 limited it to 3,000 families for that year and 500 families for 1999, and assigned quotas and assistance for those arriving from the CIS states, Mongolia, China, Iran, Turkey, Pakistan, and Saudi Arabia (*KP* 4 Apr. 1998). There are some signs that Almaty, still largely a Russophone city, is becoming increasingly Kazakhized, demographically (Kirchner and Zöller 1996).

Nonetheless, society still maintains its largely dual or, rather, bi-ethnic character, the indigenous Kazakhs holding on to political power, while the Europeans still manage much of the industrial and a sizable part of the educational sector (Svanberg 1996:324). A fragile ethnic peace is maintained among the numerous *ethnies*, with the Kazakhs striving to bolster their own national identity by officially insisting on theories about their descent from earlier peoples who inhabited the area, emphasizing the primordial and perennial bond between the Kazakhs and the territory of the present state (Smith a.o. 1998:146).

Kyrgyzstan

The Kyrgyz nomads adopted Islam by the mid-seventeenth century and came under Russian control between 1863 and 1876, when the Khanate of Kokand – on the territory of which most Kyrgyz then lived – was annexed to the Russian Empire. This territory was incorporated into the Turkestan Autonomous Soviet Socialist Republic in 1918, and became an Autonomous Region in 1924, an Autonomous Soviet Socialist Republic in 1926, and a Socialist Union Republic of the Soviet Union in 1936. The republic declared its sovereignty on 5 December 1990 and independence on 31 August 1991, joining the CIS on 21 December 1991. On 5 May 1993, it changed its name from the Republic of Kyrgyzstan to the Kyrgyz Republic – apparently to emphasize its ethnicity. A mountainous country, Kyrgyzstan (formerly spelt 'Kirgiziya' in Russian) comprises 199,500 sq. km. and borders on China, Kazakhstan, Uzbekistan and Tajikistan. Its economy is largely based on its gold production, its hydro-electric stations and its animal husbandry. Almost two thirds of its population have been rural in recent times: 66% in 1959, 61% in 1979, and 62% in 1989 (Huskey 1997:249). As in the other states discussed, Kyrgyzstan has suffered from the breakdown of the Soviet Union, with indicators for national income, industrial output and the production of consumer goods plummeting. Still, alone of all CIS states, it is a member of the World Trade Organization. It had 4,634,900 inhabitants in January 1998, 34.2% of them urban and 65.8% rural, about 606,000 of them in the capital, Bishkek, with a countrywide annual population increase rate of about 1.3% in 1997 (down from 1.9% in 1989) (the official *Kyrgyzstan v tsifrakh 1997*, Bishkek:1998, 16). Kyrgyzstan comprises more than eighty ethnic groups.

Table 2.6. KYRGYZSTAN'S ETHNIC COMPOSITION, 1926-98 (%)

	1926	1939	1959	1970	1979	1989	1996	1997	1998
Kyrgyz	66.8	51.7	40.5	42.6	47.9	52.4	60.3	60.8	61.2
Russians	11.7	20.8	30.2	29.2	25.9	21.5	15.7	15.3	14.9
Uzbeks	10.6	10.4	10.6	11.4	12.1	12.9	14.2	14.3	14.4
Ukrainians	6.4	9.4	6.6	4.1	3.1	2.5	1.6	1.6	1.5
Germans	0.4	0.8	1.9	3.1	2.8	2.4	0.5	0.4	0.3
Tatars	0.5	1.4	2.7	2.0	2.0	1.6	1.2	1.2	1.1
Others	3.6	5.5	7.5	7.6	6.2	6.7	6.5	6.4	6.6

Sources: Official census, summed up by Achylova 1995:16; Pomfret 1995:107; *SoK* 22 May 1990; Smith a.o. 1998:153; TÜRKSAM 1999:89; *Kyrgyzstan v tsifrakh 1997:* 20, refers to January 1998.

From the 1920s through the 1950s, numerous Europeans came to Kyrgyzstan as administrators, technicians, teachers, workers and peasants. In 1941-5, Germans living in the European parts of the Soviet Union were deported there (as well as to Kazakhstan). Most Russians and Ukrainians and some Germans live in the towns (only 38% of the entire population were town dwellers in 1989). Since independence, a number of Slavs, Germans, Jews and other Europeans have left, as follows:

Table 2.7. MIGRATION FROM KYRGYZSTAN BY MAIN ETHNIC
GROUPS (NET LOSS), 1990-4
(*rounded figures*)

	1990	*1991*	*1992*	*1993*	*1994*
Russians	16,300	17,400	48,500	50,900	31,600
Ukrainians	2,400	2,300	6,700	10,600	4,000
Germans	15,200	12,800	12,000	10,600	7,800
Jews	1,000	600	500	600	400

Source: Kyrgyzstan v tsifrakh 1997:25; Huskey 1997:256; Hyman 1996:53.

One notes that the emigration of non-titulars has recently decreased. But the small German minority in Kyrgyzstan has already lost half its numbers during the first years of independence; these emigrated to Germany or to the Russian Federation (*Wostok*, Frankfurt am Main, Oct.-Nov. 1993: 36-9; July-Aug. 1994: 55-60). The main religions are Sunni Islam and Russian/Ukrainian Orthodox Christianity (*SK* 2 Oct. 1998). Almost all issues – political, cultural, or economic – are debated and decided by ethnic criteria. President Askar Akaev was formerly president of the Academy of Sciences of Soviet Kyrgyzstan and, although he was a member of the Central Committee of the Kyrgyzstan Communist Party, is not a typical *apparatchik*. Akaev is attempting strenuously to balance ethnic interests and safeguard minority rights, granting however some advantage to the Kyrgyz majority. Nevertheless, he is blamed by some Kyrgyz for not being patriotic enough, while the Europeans display little interest in learning the Kyrgyz language, although he is continually prodding them to do so.

A new constitution was proclaimed on 5 May 1993. Parliament was at first a unicameral body of 350 members, but was replaced in February 1995 by a bicameral one, popularly elected: a 35-seat Legislative Assembly, constantly in session; and a 70-seat Assembly of Representatives of the People, which convenes twice a year. Of the total 105 seats, 85 went to Kyrgyz, 8 to Uzbeks, 6 to Slavs, and the remainder to others (Smith a.o. 1998:152) – an over-representation of the Kyrgyz. Kyrgyzstan has formally adopted a presidential system in which, despite squabbles with parliament, Akaev remains the main decision-maker. He is expected to be above party himself, while about twenty political parties and groups are active, in various degrees, none of them officially identified with the President. Most consider themselves oppositionist and their brisk activity and open attacks in the press on the president and government are an indication that Kyrgyzstan's domestic politics are rather more liberal and pluralistic than those in the other four new Muslim republics in Central Asia. Among the parties are the Republican People's Party of Kyrgyzstan (unofficially supported by Akaev), the Democratic Movement of Kyrgyzstan, *Ėrkin Kyrgyzstan* (Free Kyrgyzstan), the Democratic Party of Kyrgyzstan, *Ata Meken* (Fatherland Party), the Party of Communists of Kyrgyzstan, the Agrarian Party, *Asaba* (Banner) – the National Revival Party (ultra-nationalist), the Uzbek Justice Party (staffed by Uzbeks), the Civic Accord (comprising ethnic Russians and other minorities), and others (*Bitiğ: Journal of the Turkish World* 7(12):Jan. 1997, 10-11). A new opposition party, *Ar-Namys* (Dignity), was founded in July 1999. (*RFE/RL Newsline*, 3(133), part I:12 July 1999. Online Posting). Apart from a broad spectrum of parties, there were registered in 1998 in the entire state, according to the data of the Ministry of Justice, 18 sociopolitical movements and 150 religious associations. Much political power rests with various councils and committees attached to the state President's office (as can also be understood from the new constitution, approved after months of wrangling in May 1993). In the early 1990s, Akaev appeared inclined to pluralism and a civil society characterized by interethnic tolerance (Koichuev 1998:106-7; Galieva 1998). But from the midnineties, faced with an economic crisis and deep political division, the regime has moved somewhat more slowly towards democratization.

Soviet pressures towards uniformity notwithstanding, Kyrgyz national aspirations before independence were fed by a literary revival based on the national epic *Manas*. There was renewed interest in the country's historical and cultural heritage, along with demands for greater linguistic autonomy, emphasizing the need to improve the teaching of Kyrgyz, its orthography and status. Since independence, the Kyrgyz are striving to form a national identity by combining rediscovered history with newly shaped traditions. Their nationalism is at least partly a reaction to linguistic russification, represented by those 'Russified Kyrgyz' elites who were educated in Russian literature and language and now feel culturally rather alien in both the Kyrgyz and the Russian camps (Bohr and Crisp 1996:386-95). This situation is similar to Kazakhstan's, in many respects. There are tensions, also, between the Kyrgyz and the third largest *ethnie*, the Uzbeks, in the southern part of the country, Osh and Jalalabad, where in 1990 bloody clashes occurred. This reminds us of the ethnic rivalry between Uzbeks and Tajiks in Uzbekistan.

Turkmenistan

Until the final Russian conquest, the main political forces in the area were the Khanate of Khiva and the Emirate of Bukhara, the Turkmen tribes preserving a high degree of independence. Russia gained definite ascendancy in the years 1868-73, after having overcome strong Turkmen resistance. In the Soviet 'national delimitation' of 1924, the greater part of the Transcaspian district of the Turkestan Autonomous Soviet Socialist Republic, most of the People's Soviet Republic of Khorezm (Khiva) and a small part of the People's Soviet Republic of Bukhara were joined together to form the Turkmen Soviet Socialist Republic. Some other regions which Turkmen tribes had traditionally inhabited became part of Kazakhstan and Uzbekistan. Turkmenistan proclaimed its sovereignty on 22 August 1990 and independence on 27 October 1991, joining the CIS on 21 December 1991. In Soviet times, tribe, clan and ethnicity preserved their force under the surface. Since independence, they have re-emerged.

In 1995, 4,483,300 people lived in an area of 491,200 sq. km., much of it desert, bordering on Iran, Afghanistan, Kazakhstan and Uzbekistan. 54.9% of the population then resided in towns, the rest were rural, preserving many tribal traditions. Ashgabat, the capital, now has *ca.* 500,000 inhabitants. Annual population growth is close to 2.4%. About 100 *ethnies* live in Turkmenistan today, but the Turkmen, Russian and Uzbek ones are prominent numerically. The main religions are Sunni Islam and Russian Orthodox Christianity. While opinions differ about Islam's power in Turkmenistan today (some observers say that it has grown stronger, due to the impact from Afghanistan), Islamic cultural practice seems to pervade many aspects of daily life. Islam, driven underground under Soviet rule, has now become socially acceptable, as in all the six republics discussed.

Table 2.8. MAIN ETHNIC GROUPS IN TURKMENISTAN, 1989-95

	1989		1995	
	Absolute figures	*%*	*Absolute figures*	*%*
Turkmens	2,536,606	72.0	3,401,900	77.0
Russians	333,892	9.5	298,800	6.7
Uzbeks	317,333	9.0	407,100	9.2
Kazakhs	87,802	2.5	87,000	2.0
Tatars	39,257	1.1	36,400	0.8
Ukrainians	35,578	1.0	23,100	0.5
Azeris	33,365	0.9	36,600	0.8
Armenians	31,800	0.9	33,600	0.8
Beluch	26,300	0.7	36,400	0.8

Sources: 1989 Soviet Population Census; State Committee on Statistics of Turkmenistan, Ashgabat 1997:12; Nissman 1993:386-7; Ochs 1997:333.

The search for a national identity, in which new nationalist overtones replace the subnational and regional ones of tribe and clan which remain strong, was initiated by some Turkmen intellectuals chiefly as an expression of resistance to the overbearing Soviet domination. Although their number was small, they articulated demands focused on allocating more power to local spokesmen as well as for greater industrialization. In a society poised between tradition and modernization, mounting calls were heard during *perestroika*, from 1987 on, for an improvement in the status of the Turkmen language and an uncensored re-examination of Turkmen history (Bohr 1996:353). Soon, demands focused on a 'strong' national language. On 24 May 1990, Turkmenistan passed a language law which raised Turkmen to the status of official state language. After obtaining independence, numerous national holidays were initiated as unifying symbols, reinventing tradition and paying homage to customs or objects associated with Turkmen culture (Smith a.o. 1998:145). There are nineteen non-religious holidays nowadays – more than in any of the other five states – of which ten are days of rest. Another aspect of ethnonationalism is the effort invested since 1990 in establishing closer contacts with the Turkmen diaspora, chiefly in Iran and Afghanistan, but also in Turkey and Western Europe. A society named *Vatan* (Fatherland) has been active in this as well as in encouraging research in Turkmen history and language (Nissman 1993:394-6).

The new state's constitution, adopted on 18 May 1992, concentrated political power in the President, Saparmurat Niyazov, called *Turkmenbashy*, or 'head of the Turkmens'. In this authoritarian presidential system, with an extreme form of personality cult, Niyazov controls all organs of the state completely. A 50-member permanent parliament is formally the legislative organ. The first elections were held in December 1994, when 50 candidates ran unopposed: 45 were Turkmens, 3 Uzbeks and 2 Russians (Smith a.o. 1998:152) – an over-representation for the Turkmen. Another body, the People's Council, which meets at least once a year, comprises the President, members of parliament, ministers, the Chief Justice, the Solicitor General as well as members elected by sub-districts and other dignitaries. Its main roles are to determine broad policies and propose constitutional changes (Anderson 1995:511-2); the ministers are subordinate to its decisions. The only registered party, formerly the Communist, has been renamed the Democratic Party of Turkmenistan, chaired by Niyazov himself, and has accepted many new members. A government-sanctioned opposition party, named the Peasant Justice Party, was also allowed to exist. In mid-1992, a six year moratorium was proclaimed on multi-partyism and no new parties were permitted to register. Others have been either banned or kept peripheral in size and activity. Among these are *Agzybirlik* (Consensus), a popular front organized in September 1989, the Democratic Party, the Movement for Political

Reforms and the Islamic Renaissance Party (*Bitiğ: Journal of the Turkish World* 7(12):Jan. 1997, 9). Opposition is not permitted (Götz and Halbach 1996:348). In December 1999 parliament approved an amendment to the constitution allowing the incumbent President Niyazov to remain in office for life (*Extracts* 30 Dec. 1999. Available: http://www.soros.org/turkstan/omri/0239.html. 29 Jan. 2000).

Niyazov insists on his declared policy of neutrality in foreign affairs, striving not to commit his state whenever feasible. A decision of the United Nations General Assembly, in December 1995, proclaimed Turkmenistan's neutrality. Turkmenistan has hesitated regarding the CIS collective security pact, preferring a direct security guarantee from Russia. This was not renewed and, in May 1999, Niyazov decided to terminate in November of that year Turkmenistan's agreement with the Russian Federation which had permitted it to station 300 border guards on the frontier with Afghanistan and navy vessels in the Turkmenistan sector of the Caspian Sea. Also, Turkmenistan is manoeuvering among Iran, Turkey and others, avoiding regional pacts while trying to join larger neutral bodies such as the Non-Aligned Movement. The strategy adopted by Turkmenistan's leader is domestic risk avoidance and maintenance of tight societal control, targeted at stability, combined with a campaign for international recognition (Ochs 1997:314; Halbach 1997:308). Turkmenistan's foreign policy is largely mandated by its need for economic development coupled with its modest level of industrialization under the Soviets. With considerable reserves of oil and gas and an important production of cotton and manufacture of carpets, it needs highways, railroads and pipelines to carry its exports.

Tajikistan

The Tajiks belong to the oldest ethnic components of Central Asia's population mosaic, linguistically representing the Iranian element in the Persian-Turkic cultural symbiosis (Fragner 1998; Perry 1996a: 280). They form a complicated ethnogram differentiated according to geography (Götz and Halbach 1996:303). The term Tajik, which has acquired a number of meanings over time in Islamized Central Asia, became with Russian colonial rule at the end of the nineteenth century an ethnolinguistic designation for the inhabitants of Turkestan speaking Iranian languages (Fragner 1998).

By the late nineteenth century, the area of present-day Tajikistan was controlled in the north by Russia and in the west and south by the Emir of Bukhara. By 1920, most of the area was governed by the Soviets, who in 1924 created the Tajik Autonomous Soviet Socialist Republic as a part of the Uzbek Soviet Socialist Republic; in 1929 this became a separate union republic, the Tajik Soviet Socialist Republic. Official efforts at russification were carried out since the 1930s, chiefly in imposing the

Russian language and culture, while downgrading Tajik traditions (Conermann 1994:161-5). However, socialization in the Marxist-Leninist spirit had little impact. Opposition to Soviet cultural policies continued; since the 1980s, Islamic activity was increasing, partly as a result of the war in Afghanistan.

The republic announced its sovereignty on 24 August 1990 and independence on 9 September 1991, joining the CIS on 21 December 1991. Opposition of the democratic-Islamic alliance to the Communist hardliners of the government, which had started in 1990, turned into a civil war which went on from spring 1992 well into 1993; it traumatized and impoverished the new state. For several years an unsettled situation prevailed on and off, with Islamist groups, nationalists and democrats pitted at first against the Communists, both sides supported by regional interest groups. Back in power, the Communists were assisted since November 1992 by a CIS peace-keeping force, largely made up of Russian units, invited in to prevent infiltration from Afghanistan and possible 'Afghanization' of the new state (Zdravomyslov 1997:61-2). The coalitions shifted in composition according to clan, regional and ideological rivalries (Niyazi 1993; Akhmedov 1997; Brown 1998; Dudoignon 1998). Civil wars have a momentum of their own; peace negotiations and cease-fires in the following years had only a limited influence on the warring parties (Dadmehr 1998; Nourzhanov 1998:18). A 'General Agreement on the Establishment of Peace and National Accord in Tajikistan' was reached on 27 June 1997 (Kuz'min 1998:215-21; Nourzhanov 1998a:163).

Imomali Rakhmonov, a former hard-line Communist and a local leader, was elected President on 6 November 1994 and re-elected five years later. On the day of Rakhmonov's first election, a new constitution was approved by a popular referendum. Still, patron-client networks continue to wield considerable influence (Dani 1993:119-22; Atkin 1997:283-91), probably more than elsewhere in the republics discussed. Both the former and the current president attempted to manoeuver between various political, tribal and regional forces (Abazov 1999:87) while drawing closer to Russia, whose economic and military assistance they badly needed. A 20,000-strong Russian military contingent was present for several years to defend Tajikistan from the incursion of militant Muslims from Afghanistan; it was cut down to 14,000 – still a sizable number after the June 1997 agreement had formally ended the civil war in Tajikistan (*CAM* 1998, no. 3:35). In 1999, the peace-keeping force dwindled to one Russian division of about 6,000 men (*Izvestiya* 2 Mar. 1999), which would constitute a Russian military base (according to an agreement reached in Moscow, in April 1999, between Russia and Tajikistan), along with a small number of Uzbek and Kazakh troops.

The system is mostly presidential and autocratic, with a Council of Ministers and a 181-member unicameral parliament, the Supreme

Assembly, elected in February and March 1995 by universal suffrage. It includes, besides the Tajiks, 18 Uzbeks, 2 Russians and 1 Kyrgyz. In accordance with the 27 June 1997 peace agreement, in 1998 representatives of some parties in the United Tajik Opposition (UTO), led by Said Abdullah Nuri, joined the government. Nuri is at the same time the leader of the Tajikistan Islamic Movement, also called the Islamic Renaissance Party (interview with him in *CAM* 1997, no. 6:18-19). Recent information about the parties is not easily obtainable (some details in Robertson 1997:384). Apart from the above mentioned, the most active ones are the following: the Communist Party of Tajikistan, the Democratic People's Party of Tajikistan, the Party of People's Unity, and the National Revival Movement. In a nationwide referendum held on 26 September 1999 voters endorsed a package of constitutional amendments – including the creation of a bicameral parliament and the extension of the presidential term of office from five to seven years, but limiting it to one term. The formation of religious-based parties was also allowed (*Extracts* 28 September 1999. Available: http://www.soros.org/tajik/omri/0321.html. 24 Jan. 2000.)

Tajikistan is a poor country and the civil war has affected its economy adversely; even agriculture was harmed (Djalili a.o. 1998:179). Cultural life has suffered as well (Nizamov 1995). Other problems adding to Tajikistan's political and economic troubles are the migration of many thousands of its citizens to other lands, fleeing from civil war and financial hardship; and, compounding it, the inflow (largely illegal) of tens of thousands of Tajiks as political and economic refugees from Afghanistan, some of whom are only transiting, while others are staying and getting involved in politics (*NG* 9 Sep. 1994; Olimova 1998).

Tajikistan, a mountainous country bordered by Uzbekistan, Kyrgyzstan, Afghanistan and China, covers 143,000 sq. km. and has almost 6 million inhabitants, with a recent annual population growth of about 1.85%. In the capital, Dushanbe, live *ca.* 602,000 people. The population is about 32.3% urban. According to the 1989 census, the Tajiks (including the Pamiri peoples) constituted *ca.* 62.3%, the Uzbeks 23.5%, the Russians *ca.* 7.6%, and the Tatars *ca.* 1.4% (these are also the figures for 1992, cited by Hunter 1996:17, although some changes must have occurred). According to preliminary figures for early 1996 supplied by the Government Agency for Statistics, Tajikistan's population of 5,860,600 was divided ethnically as follows: Tajiks 68.4%, Uzbeks 24.8%, Russians 3.2%, Kyrgyz 1.3%, Tatars 0.7%, Ukrainians 0.4%, Turkmens 0.3%, others in insignificant numbers (*NaG* 11-18 Apr. 1997). In early 1997, the population reached 5,969,700 people (official statistics, quoted in Sokolova 1998:35). Most non-Russians are Sunni Muslims; the Pamiri peoples are Shiites.

Ethnic tensions exist, chiefly between Tajiks and Uzbeks, and over the decades have prevented the formation of a unified national identity

(Eisener 1991). While some Uzbeks in Uzbekistan suspect Tajikistan's alleged intention to take over Samarkand and Bukhara, some Tajiks in Tajikistan suspect the loyalties of the Uzbeks, the largest minority there, of being oriented towards their compatriots in Uzbekistan, thus potentially being a destabilizing factor in Tajikistan (Tadjbakhsh 1996:337-9; *Zerkalo* 23 Aug. 1997; Olimova 1999). Many Tajiks identify themselves as Muslims rather than ethnically, although the ethnic element as well as the local-regional (north versus south) and the cultural are present and influential in their antagonisms (Chvyr 1993:250-8; Clement 1994:97-105; Halbach 1995:206-7). Iran's involvement lends this situation an international dimension (Mesbahi 1997). Nevertheless, Tajiks, Uzbeks and others in Tajikistan, as well as most political groups, including the communists, are prone to use nationalist concepts and slogans in their efforts to enlist public support, including popular interest in the Tajiks abroad and advocacy for the Tajik language (Payne 1996:375-8).

3

LANGUAGE ISSUES: THE
RUSSIAN DIASPORA

'The presence of large Russian minorities in the newly independent Central Asian states', as Teresa Rakowska-Harmstone (1994:28) has put it, 'has been the most important and the most troublesome demographic legacy of Russian/Soviet rule'. We have noted that under the late Russian Empire and the Soviet Union the Slavs in Azerbayjan and Central Asia lived in what they considered their own territories (Brubaker 1994:68). Only with the disintegration of the Soviet Union did the old Russian diasporas become 'new minorities' (Yamskov 1994) in the independent ex-Soviet republics, constituting a newly dimensioned type, not quite belonging to the category of Safran's (1991:83) definition of a diaspora as 'an expatriate minority community'. Although their homeland exists, it is no longer a welcoming place (Safran 1991:91). A sizable number of Slavs still live in all six republics discussed, occupying an important role in the economy, the administration and cultural life. An understanding of their situation is essential to the understanding of language politics and language policies in all six – our main concern in this work. Since in the earlier chapters we have mentioned these diasporas only very briefly, a somewhat more detailed evaluation of their role in the current language conflict seems necessary in order to examine the implications of this phenomenon for public policy in the domain of language.

As mentioned earlier, during the second half of the nineteenth century, Tsarist Russia succeeded in seizing control of most territories now forming the six Muslim states. Russian colonization followed soon after the conquests. Fertile lands (e.g., in parts of the Kazakh steppes) were handed to Cossacks, driving the nomads out. In many towns, Russian settlers worked as administrators, railroad builders and merchants, constructing new residential quarters; in the territories inhabited by Kazakhs and Kyrgyz, a majority of the settlers were farmers. Few efforts were made to 'russify' the new possessions (Rywkin 1993:35). However, Russian language and culture followed immigration; by the turn of the century, these increasingly penetrated native communities without a sufficiently strong cultural base of their own (Lewis 1980:45ff).

Under Soviet domination, russification, in various phases, became part of general state policy from the 1930s onward. Along with efforts at forced collectivization and settlement of nomads, reducing the influence of Islam and confiscating religious property, Russians were encouraged to migrate within the Soviet Union (data in Kabuzan 1996:238-42) and take up many leading positions in the civil administration, the Communist Party, the courts of law, mining and industry, the military establishment, and public education – although in numerous instances local people were put in charge of middle and lower positions. After 1945, most Russians came of their own volition and apparently felt comfortable in their new homes, during the 1950s and 1960s at least (Olcott 1996:540-1). The newcomers included much needed experts, for there were few natives skilled in modern professions required for development; eventually, the newcomers trained local personnel, resulting in the formation of modern elites who later presented nationalist demands. Under the prevailing Communist ideology, the values of the incoming Europeans soon influenced the power structure; their advantages were increased by sharing a common language – Russian. Literary works and periodicals in Russian were published regularly (Graffy 1993). Although policies varied, knowledge of Russian remained a *sine qua non* condition for obtaining most positions and approaching the centres of power – political, military, economic, scientific, or educational. Since 1938, the whole system was so geared that education in Russian became imperative and was so programmed as to enable aspiring local persons to acquire the language in order to promote their careers. The conditions for russification and the necessary structures, also, were set up. The situation created for the locals by the official and unofficial support given by Moscow and its agents to the Russian settlers and their economic and cultural interests was one of the factors that brought about nationalist reactions in the late Soviet era and a set of problems in the newly independent Muslim states.

The difficulties were compounded by the large number of Russians in both absolute and relative figures in the six Soviet republics (for absolute figures, tables 3.1 and 3.2, below; see also Khazanov 1995: table 4.5; for relative ones, see table 12 in Rywkin 1993), even though their percentage somewhat diminished during the 1980s. In the 1989 Soviet Census, Russians formed 37.6% of Kazakhstan's population, versus 40.8% in 1979, 21.4% of Kyrgyzstan's versus 25.8% in 1979, and between 5.6% and 9.5% in each of the four others, also down from 1979 (Rywkin 1992:99). Russians, according to the 1989 Soviet population census, were largely towndwellers: 70% of them in Kyrgyzstan, 77% in Kazakhstan, 95% in Azerbayjan, and between 94% and 97% in Uzbekistan, Turkmenistan and Tajikistan. They were and remain very visible in the population of the capitals (Khazanov 1995:258-9), where the centres of decision making are naturally located. In 1989, only in Baku did Russians represent merely 16.5% of the population, while in Almaty (then, Alma-Ata) they reached 59.1% and in Bishkek (then, Frunze) 55.7%, in Tashkent 34%, Dushanbe 32.4% and Ashgabat (then Ashkhabad) 32.3% (Harris 1993:

table 2). Substantial rural communities of Russians existed only in Kazakhstan and Kyrgyzstan. Most Slavs in Azerbayjan and Central Asia were working in specialized jobs, chiefly technical, industrial, medical and educational, as well as political and administrative (Ginzburg 1992). Many were teachers and active in cultural work, others were employed in commerce and services.

Table 3.1. RUSSIANS IN THE SIX SOVIET REPUBLICS, 1979-89
(rounded figures)

	1979	*1989*	*Total population 1989*
Azerbayjan	475,000	392,000	7,020,000
Uzbekistan	1,666,000	1,653,000	19,808,000
Kazakhstan	5,991,000	6,227,000	16,436,000
Kyrgyzstan	912,000	917,000	4,258,000
Turkmenistan	349,000	333,000	3,512,000
Tajikistan	395,000	388,000	5,090,000

Source: 1979 and 1989 Soviet Population Censuses, as given in Pollard 1991: 498-502.

Table 3.2. RUSSIANS IN THE SIX INDEPENDENT STATES, 1996
(rounded figures)

	Total population	*Titular Nationality (%)*	*Russians (%)*
Azerbayjan	7,511,000	82.7	2.0
Uzbekistan	22,700,000	72.0	6.0
Kazakhstan	16,600,000	44.3	34.8
Kyrgyzstan	4,400,000	60.0	15.7
Turkmenistan	5,400,000	77.0	6.7
Tajikistan	5,500,000	60.0	3.2

Source: Obozrevatel' (Moscow) 1998, no. 3:169. Other sources – such as Kuleshov a.o. 1997:487ff – give different data.

Russians formed 34% of the population of Tashkent in 1989, but 43% of the inhabitants were Russophones. Contrariwise, few Russians saw any need to learn the titular language; in 1989, 14% in Azerbayjan, but in the five republics in Central Asia from 1% to 5% only: 1% in Kyrgyzstan and Kazakhstan, 3% in Turkmenistan and Tajikistan, 5% in Uzbekistan (table 3 of Harris 1993:22). Throughout the period since the 1930s the focus on studying and using Russian rather than other languages was no more than a logical conclusion of living in what was essentially a unitary state. Active language competition increased only in the late 1980s and even more in the early 1990s in the capitals, where political and scientific institutions are located, most books, newspapers and magazines published, radio and television studios centred, films produced and frequently viewed, and inter-ethnic rivalry is influential. Some polls carried out since independence among the Russians in the newly independent states (e.g., Marchenko 1994:150) indicate a possible change of mind, i.e., that many presumably intended then to study the titular languages; if so, they have done little to implement this design during the 1990s (see ch. 9).

When the six Muslim republics obtained independence in late 1991, more than 10 million Russians and others (table 3.1, above) found themselves suddenly living abroad, without Moscow's protection, as a minority group (even in Kazakhstan, where in 1989 the Slavs had approximately equalled the Kazakhs), with their social and economic future unclear. The British traveller Colin Thubron (1994), who visited the new Muslim republics in 1991-2, noticed how uncertain and worried the Slavs were about their future, even in the capital cities. In Kazakhstan's rural communities, mainly in the northern and northeastern regions, Kazakh villagers attacked their Slav neighbours physically several times in 1990-3, which sparked retaliation (Babak 1996:5). Since then many Slavs have been experiencing a feeling of deprivation, indeed of a beleaguered minority, as their status switched to that of undesirable aliens (Lewis 1992:35). Whether oldtimers or newcomers, many were not interested in and ignorant of the local culture, language and customs. Since they had always considered themselves protected by Moscow, they were hardly accustomed to organizing for the promotion, or even the safeguarding, of their particular interests in the new circumstances (Brusina 1992:48). While international law has devised means for protecting immigrants and diasporas (Kloss 1971; Capotorti 1991; Gurr a.o. 1993), few Russians seemed interested in legal niceties. They may have derived some comfort from the fact that elsewhere, in the Republic of Moldavia, parliament suspended a language law stipulating that all non-native speakers (i.e., 1.5 million non-Moldavians) in responsible positions should take a compulsory language test in Moldavian, the state language (*International Herald Tribune* 2-3 Apr. 1994:2). Latvia and Estonia were much more insistent on this issue. The Russians responded to perceived discrimination mostly by articles in the press. In Kazakhstan, however, local Russians have organized to defend their positions (Bremmer 1994) more than elsewhere in Central Asia.

Michael Rywkin (1993:90) divides the Russian diaspora, professionally, into four main categories: a. bureaucratic cadres; b. engineers and technicians; c. industrial workers; d. low-grade blue- and white-collar workers. He could have listed a fifth group – agricultural workers (important chiefly in Kazakhstan and Kyrgyzstan). Of the four, he argues, the first and fourth groups were bound to lose their jobs soon, the third later, while the second served a basic need and had a good chance to continue for some time. One might add that the situation was unequal in the six states, with different levels of native elites and different needs for the skills of resident Europeans. The prognosis applies in part only, for the Russians in the six states have serious identity problems also (Kolstoe 1996).

Some out-migration of a limited number of Russians from Soviet Azerbayjan and Central Asia into other parts of the Soviet Union had already taken place during the decade 1979-89 and earlier (data in Tishkov 1995:291; Shnirelman and Komarova 1997:212; Brubaker 1997:170-1; table 3.3 below). This seems, however, to have been mostly voluntary.

Table 3.3. TOTAL BALANCE OF MIGRATION TO
AND FROM CENTRAL ASIA, 1961-88
(rounded figures)

	1961-70	*1979-88*
Kazakhstan	+431,000	-789,000
Uzbekistan	+257,000	-507,000
Kyrgyzstan	+126,000	-157,000
Turkmenistan	+4,000	-84,000
Tajikistan	+70,000	-102,000

Source: Khazanov 1995:264; Tishkov 1997:118.

Since 1992, it has not been easy for those who were not needed or who could not adapt to the new situation in the six independent states either to remain or to emigrate. The latter was particularly difficult for those who had been born and bred there (sometimes in families going back for generations). But anxiety about loss of social status and the future of their jobs and financial resources, their children's education, eventual conflict, and life in countries where they did not speak the state language were among the reasons for large-scale emigration (*KP* 16 Nov. 1994; Buškov and Sitnjanskij 1997; Heuer 1998). A contributing cause was the Slavs' reluctance to acquire the citizenship of the new republic they were living in, although it would have been desirable for them to do so in order to obtain or keep certain jobs. The new Muslim states refused dual citizenship (Paniko 1994), except for Turkmenistan and Tajikistan, which concluded such agreements with the Russian Federation in 1993 and 1995, respectively (Harris 1994:197; Hunter 1996:44-7; Moiseev 1997:206, 218; Smith a.o. 1998:161). It is understandable that the Government of Kazakhstan rejected Russian demands in this matter (Eschment 1997:45ff).

Different Russian communities estimated variously the primacy of the above causes as reasons for emigrating; in some, as in Azerbayjan (during the Nagorno-Karabagh War) and Tajikistan (during the civil war), fears of violence induced many to leave. In many cases, emigrants were from areas inhabited by small numbers of Europeans, where economic conditions had deteriorated, from environmentally hazardous areas, or from those in which violence was on the increase (Clem 1993:231); perceived loss of dignity and language difficulties were other causes (Dunlop 1994). One systematic poll, carried out in 1995 in Uzbekistan, Kyrgyzstan and Kazakhstan, found that in Uzbekistan language difficulties were the main reason, in Kyrgyzstan these ranked second to third, while only in Kazakhstan did they come out sixth (Vitkovskaya 1996:101). This, for Kazakhstan, seems to agree with a poll carried out there a year earlier, which found that 28.2% of those leaving had said that they were emigrating because 'not knowing Kazakh caused work-related difficulties' (Olcott 1996:546-7). Davis and Sabol (1998), also, have argued that, at least in Kazakhstan, economic considerations have been crucial in prompting the Slavs to emigrate. This is undoubtedly so, but dissatisfaction with language policies also has been a sufficient motive there and elsewhere in the six states (Nikolaev 1994:117-18).

Emigration from the ex-Soviet states, in a process Brubaker (1997:155ff) called 'the unmixing of peoples' or 'ethnic unmixing', became an all-pervasive phenomenon. In the Caucasus and Central Asia it generally occurred from south to north, mostly towards the Russian Federation (Halbach 1997a). Russia itself was in serious economic plight after the Soviet Union's dismemberment and could hardly be counted upon to welcome immigrants and assist them in finding jobs and housing. A statewide plan set up in the Russian Federation to assist migrants arriving from the post-Soviet space (*Izvestiya* 11 Aug. 1992) had only limited success. According to a 1998 article by Kim Tsagolov, then Deputy Minister in the Russian Ministry of Nationality Affairs and Federal Relations, the main problems in accommodating the Russian immigrants remained the cumbersome existing mechanisms and the immense sums required (Tsagolov 1998:2-4). So the authorities of the Russian Federation, up to the highest levels, including President Yeltsin, proclaimed their wish to help the cause of the diaspora Russians, declaring repeatedly that the Russian Federation was interested in the members of the Russian diaspora everywhere, watching over their equality in civil rights and expecting their full integration into the countries in which they were living and their contribution to the development of those countries (*KP* 10 Oct. 1998). Much of this was mere rhetoric. Russian bureaucrats had to be careful that their intervention did not further antagonize the majority *ethnies* in the ex-Soviet states and raise the spectre of double loyalty; consequently, they generally had to resort to quiet negotiation (Zviagelskaya 1995:12-15). Official moves to assist the ethnic Russians in what was then officially termed the 'Near Abroad' (*The Economist* 22 Apr. 1995:35) were rather exceptional. Some non-governmental political circles reacted differently, however. Ultra-nationalist spokesmen in Russia, such as Vladimir Zhirinovskii, had no such compunctions and loudly expressed their support in threatening style, with a part of the press chiming in (*Novoe Pokolenie* 26 May 1995; Savoskul 1995). Some scholarly studies discussed the 're-integration', but not 'incorporation', of Kazakhstan and Kyrgyzstan into Russia (Sitnyanskii 1996), which is the official policy of the Russian Federation, e.g., in the economic sphere.

On 11 August 1994, Yeltsin issued a presidential decree, 'On Basic Points of State Policy of the Russian Federation Concerning Compatriots Living Abroad'. This was followed, twenty days later, by a resolution of Russia's Government, entitled 'On Measures to Support Compatriots Abroad'. Both offered assistance in several domains, including the cultural one (Moiseev 1997:42-6). It is noteworthy that, in both documents, the Russian Federation perceived itself as the protector of all its compatriots, which meant not exclusively Russians but also members of other *ethnies* that had national centres in the Russian Federation (such as Lezghins, Tatars, and others). In May 1996, the authorities of the Russian Federation issued a detailed programme for helping such communities abroad (*RG* 30 May 1996). Later, parliamentarians in the Russian State *Duma* expressed support for the Russian language in the successor-states of the Soviet Union (*Zerkalo* 28 Mar. 1998).

Russia's assertive options, however, have been limited (Konarovsky 1994:235-46; Shashenkov 1994:170-5); Russians in the six states have come to expect only politicians like Zhirinovskii and writers like Alexander Solzhenitsyn (1998:36-75) to proclaim their support openly. Top-level Russian statesmen have only rarely tried to intervene. Thus, then Foreign Minister Andrei Kozyrev, speaking at the Foreign Policy Council of the Russian Federation's Ministry for Foreign Affairs, on 18 April 1995, contented himself with merely expressing dissatisfaction with the linguistic situation in the ex-Soviet republics (*Diplomaticheskii Vestnik* May 1995). The Russians in the six states, well-aware of the nationalist rhetoric directed against them, increasingly feel abandoned by the Russian Federation (Kolstoe 1995: ch. 10; Laitin 1998:102-4). Figures supplied by the United Nations High Commissioner for Refugees (summed up by Wehrschütz 1997:33) indicate that Slav emigration from the new Muslim states, Kazakhstan excepted, peaked in 1991-5, becoming more moderate since 1996 (below, tables 3.4 and 3.5). However, a few repatriates came back from the Russian Federation; this is also true, on a smaller scale, for the Germans who emigrated to Federal Germany and were faced with unemployment and cultural isolation there (Baum 1999:27ff). The returnees were hoping for better economic opportunities and for a chance to continue their cultural life (Chebotareva 1994:67). On the other hand, there was an almost constant trickle of immigration into the new Muslim states by members of the titular *ethnies*, who were being encouraged 'to return home'. This process, which had started already in the 1980s, further tipped the demographic balance in favour of the titular groups.

Table 3.4. EMIGRATION OF MAIN SLAVIC GROUPS FROM
THE SIX REPUBLICS, 1989-95
(*rounded figures*)

	Russians	Ukrainians	Belorussians	Total
Azerbayjan	169,000	15,000	3,000	187,000
Uzbekistan	400,000	n.d.	n.d.	n.d.
Kazakhstan	614,000	82,000	16,000	712,000
Kyrgyzstan	296,000	39,000	3,000	338,000
Turkmenistan	100,000	n.d.	n.d.	n.d.
Tajikistan	300,000	30,000	10,000	340,000
Total	1,879,000			

n.d. = no data
Source: U.N. estimates, summed up by Wehrschütz 1997:33; more detailed figures for 1991-2, Robertson 1996:119-23; acc. to other sources, Russian emigration from Kazakhstan in those years amounted to 467,800 only – Eremin 1996:37.

Table 3.5. OVERALL EMIGRATION TO THE RUSSIAN
FEDERATION, 1990-7
(*rounded figures*)

	Emigrants to the Russian Federation							
	1990	*1991*	*1992*	*1993*	*1994*	*1995*	*1996*	*1997*
Azerbayjan	91,400	48,000	69,900	54,700	49,500	43,400	40,310	29,800
Uzbekistan	104,000	69,100	112,400	91,200	146,700	112,300	49,970	39,300
Kazakhstan	157,400	128,900	183,900	195,700	346,400	241,400	172,860	233,400
Kyrgyzstan	39,000	33,700	62,900	96,800	66,400	27,800	14,020	13.800
Turkmenistan	15,000	13,100	19,000	13,000	20,200	19,200	22,840	16,700
Tajikistan	50,800	27,800	72,600	68,800	45,600	41,800	32,508	23,200
Total	457,600	320,600	520,700	520,200	674,800	485,900	332,508	356,200

Source: Argumenty i Fakty 40: October 1997; *NaG* 18 Apr. 1997; *Demograficheskii ezhegodnik Kyrgyzskoi Respubliki 1996 g.* (Bishkek 1997):235; Tishkov 1997:133; official statistics of the Russian Federation, repr. in Kosmarskaya 1998; Vechkanov 1998:107.

The emigration figures are high, proportionately, when compared with the data on the Russian diaspora in the six states versus the titular nationality (above, table 3.2). They are high also in another perspective: during 1992-5, emigration from the six states made up half of the entire immigration from the 'Near Abroad' into the Russian Federation (calculated by Makarova a.o. 1998:49; Iontsev 1998).

In the six states, the Slavs who elect to stay have three political choices:

a. to wait and see; b. to learn the titular language and attempt to integrate into local society (not everyone is ready and willing to do this as there are few incentives although the pressures are there; besides, in some European circles, an antagonistic attitude prevails to what they consider languages of lower status); c. to strive for a bilingual situation in which Russian is an official language or, at least, close to this in education and public use (Alimov 1994:228-30). For the third option, they require the support of the Russian Federation, as diaspora Russians have shown little efficacy in organizing themselves politically to preserve their interests (except perhaps in Kazakhstan and Kyrgyzstan – and even there only moderately so). Anyway, many Russians seem genuinely alarmed concerning language in the six new states: education is shifting to the state language; preference in admission to higher education is given to the titular nationalities; Russian managers are being replaced and hardly any new ones are being hired; conferences, meetings and official memoranda (and even road signs) increasingly employ the state language (Pilkington 1998:135-40).

Some Russians chose the first option and did little or nothing on the language issue. A few chose the second. Those who chose the third obtained a mixed response from the government of the Russian Federation. The problems caused by migrants and refugees prompted the Russian Government, two years later, in May 1996, to initiate an international conference, held in Geneva. The participants adopted a comprehensive programme of action regarding migration problems (Halbach 1997a: 5-7). The actions taken seem however rather modest (Helton 1998).

The government of the Russian Federation intervened a few times on behalf of the diaspora, cautiously rather than otherwise, so as not to antagonize public opinion in the ex-Soviet states. One instance was the Russian-Kazakh treaty of 25 May 1992, in which both sides agreed to protect the ethnic, cultural, linguistic and religious identity of national minorities; another, a joint declaration on 20 January 1995 to prevent discrimination in the above domains (Moiseev 1997:160-1). However, there does not seem to have existed a definitely formulated policy on the issue, nor a mechanism to respond to challenges concerning the Russian communities in the diaspora (Blank 1994:47-9). The policy was, in general, a reaction to events there (Kuleshov a.o. 1997:442-4; Vasil'ev 1998:21). It was rather non-governmental militant groups in the Russian Federation that demanded help for their compatriots in a spirit of 're-integrating' the Soviet Union. Thus the International Congress of Russian Communities – which belongs to the ultranationalistic spectrum – convened in Moscow in early 1994. Its leaders also voiced economic and cultural demands – preserving Russian in schools and higher education, setting up cultural centres, and publishing books and newspapers (*Obozrevatel'* 1994, no. 18: suppl. 164).

A few specific instances concerning the Russians and the language issue in the six states follow, taking into account that some statistical data are incomplete and conflicting.

Azerbayjan

The leaders of the Russian community in Azerbayjan have repeatedly declared that they were not the heirs of imperial politics and that they considered themselves well-integrated (e.g., *Zerkalo* 11 Feb. 1995). Russians did not complain so much about the enforcement of Azeri as the state language in the new state, evidently unavoidable, but rather about the speed of language transition, which some considered a means of pressure (Kolstoe 1995:205-6). Russian emigration from Azerbayjan to Russia was influenced first by the climate of conflict and Azeri anti-Armenian physical violence in 1990 in Baku, where about 75% of all Azerbayjan Russians lived in the late 1980s, and then by the turmoil of the war with Armenia and the resulting instability. Russians emigrated to the Russian Federation in sizable numbers since 1990 (above, table 3.5; Chinn and Kaiser 1996:259-64; Vechkanov 1998:107ff). Russian emigration has continued since, albeit at a slower pace recently. Reliable figures are not always available, but estimates put the total Russian emigration in the years 1990-6 at more than 200,000. Azeri sources cite lower figures and Russian ones higher (Yunusov 1997:71). Those remaining have set up cultural centres in Baku, apparently to promote the cause of their language, such as the *Tsentr Kultury Slavyan* (Centre for the Culture of the Slavs) and *Bakinets Kulturnyi Tsentr* (Bakuan Culture Centre) (Mikhailovskaya 1994:47; Kuleshov a.o. 1997:490). They also established and maintained contacts with Russian communities abroad (*Zerkalo* 29 Apr. 1995).

Uzbekistan

In Uzbekistan, the government has been trying to persuade the Russians (many in vital industrial and technical professions) to remain, but many claimed that they were leaving due to language difficulties (Olcott 1996: 547; Halbach 1997a:18-19) – one of the symptoms of 'ethnic discomfort' (Vitkovskaya 1996:99ff.; Heuer 1998). Russian and other citizens of non-Uzbek background find the practical consequences of language policies discriminatory. One Russian regarded as 'language exercises' the process by which the underground stations in Tashkent were renamed and the signs rendered in Latin script. Another Russian, a physician, reported how he had been forced to note down patients' descriptions in the state language and invented the terms himself for that purpose with the help of a nurse. Bank transfer forms, work sheets in factories, and applications for employment are often available only in Uzbek and therefore not easy to handle, even for Uzbeks, since it is still true that many Uzbeks prefer

Russian as a means of communication (*Literaturnaya Gazeta* 5 Mar. 1997, 5). Some of the Russians are apprehensive that the language law of 1989, even though it left an eight-year term of grace for the acquisition of the titular language, would eventually discriminate against them (Kolstoe 1995:221-3); meanwhile, the period has been extended. It appears that their economic situation, too, has worsened since independence and the emigration figures of Russian speakers seem to support this impression in sizable figures when compared with the relatively small number of Russians there (table 3.5, above; Buškov and Sitnjanskij 1997:18). The number of emigrants declined from the mid-1990s, but the trend continued: almost 40,000 left Uzbekistan for the Russian Federation in 1997 (data of the Uzbekistan Ministry of the Interior, in *NG* 27 Mar. 1998; also table 3.5, above).

Kazakhstan

In Kazakhstan there are more Russians, absolutely and proportionately, than in any of the other five new Muslim states. They are grouped, in addition to the towns, in the north, in areas contiguous to the Russian Federation. They are connected to Russia not merely by sentiment, but also by family ties as well as by education and military service. They have been complaining continually of discrimination in employment, schooling, publishing and of cuts in Russian broadcasts (e.g., FBIS-SOV-94-038-S: 25 Feb. 1994). The Russian community insisted on making Russian, too, a state language, again deploring their discrimination. One of the Slavic movements in Kazakhstan demanded the status of a state language for Russian in areas predominantly inhabited by Russian populations as well as suitable administrative appointments for them there, hoping to put a halt to Russian emigration. A Slavic Movement was set up in Kokchetav in February 1992 to protect the Slavs from perceived discrimination in matters of language and citizenship (*RG* 28 Feb. 1992). A more comprehensive organization of the Russians in Kazakhstan, *Lad* (Concord), protests the situation, but does not seem to be very effective beyond presenting petitions and organizing street demonstrations. Among its activities are letters to the press. Alexandra Dokuchaeva (1995), an ex-parliamentarian and one of the leaders of the Democratic Party of Kazakhstan, an organization with limited political clout, claims that in a poll among the Russians of Almaty in September 1994, 97.5% of the respondents asserted that they would leave the country if two state languages were not introduced.

The issue of language serves as the main battleground (Svoik 1998; Ayagan 1998), with the Russians gaining a new language law in 1997 declaring their language the means for inter-ethnic communication, and in many domains on a par with Kazakh, but the latter is the state language. Russian remains dominant in numerous technological, academic and some administrative jobs, mostly in those areas inhabited by a sizable Slav population. According to the 1994 research of the State Committee for Languages, conducted in 55,008 governmental offices, only 16.6% of clerical work was carried out in Kazakh, versus 70.3 % in Russian (*Novoe Pokolenie* 7:26 May 1995, 7). Kazakh newspapers have been pointing out that, even in late 1998, Russian is used in parliament, on the radio and television, in the press and other publications, and in most (or, at least many) schools (e.g. *Egemen Qazaqstan* 13 Oct. 1998). Contrariwise, the Russians complain that Kazakh is favoured, as ethnic Kazakhs increasingly acquire public positions of power (e.g., *RG* 5 June 1993; Melvin 1995:106-10). They maintain that 85% of the state President's staff, 72% of the government and the civil service, and 77% of the employees in the local authorities are Kazakhs (*Obshchaya Gazeta* 15 Oct. 1998).

There was a sizable non-titular emigration – more than a million Slavs and Jews as well as *ca.* 300,000 Germans – from Kazakhstan between 1989 and 1995 (according to various statistics, Dave 1996b:194; Vechkanov 1998:107; lower figures in Breuer 1995:A 341). A sizable Russian repatriation has occurred in recent years (table 3.5, above). The Slav emigration was motivated by a complex of reasons: falling living standards, linguistic and ethnic discrimination, and others. For the Germans, the same reasons were true, but it was mainly their desire for – and the possibility of – a return to their historical homeland that caused them to leave. There are also Russians who have been returning to Kazakhstan: 102,800 in 1990; 99,400 in 1991; 87,300 in 1992; 68,700 in 1993 (Esenova 1996:696-8; Vechkanov 1998:124). Some of these figures seem inflated. In 1996, only the Kazakhs gained in number from migration (table 3.6 below), probably drawing on the sizable Kazakh diaspora (on which Mendikulova 1998).

Table 3.6. MIGRATION TO AND FROM KAZAKHSTAN, 1996-7

	Immigration		Emigration		Population balance	
	1996	1997	1996	1997	1996	1997
Kazakhs	16,446	11,582	9,543	11,759	6,903	-177
Russians	24,043	17,154	120,427	174,616	-96,384	-157,462
Ukrainians	3,038	2,349	16,459	29,080	-13,421	-26,731
Germans	2,023	1,410	58,956	49,505	-56,933	-48,095
Tatars	1,530	981	5,754	8,239	-4,224	-7,258
Belorussians	501	386	3,195	5,900	-2,694	-5,514
Uzbeks	588	522	2,478	3,992	-1,890	-3,740
Azeris	748	489	813	890	- 65	-401

Source: Statisticheskoe Obozrenie Kazakhstana 1:1997, 3; *Karavan* 8 May 1998, based on official statistics.

Kyrgyzstan

In Kyrgyzstan, in 1989, there were 916,558 Russians or 21.5% of the entire population, more than 55.7% of them in Bishkek (Kustov 1997). By 1994 the percentage of Russians had declined to 18% of the state's population and by 1995 to 16% (Kuznetsova 1999:23-4). Russian emigration had serious effects on the state's economy. In 1993, a conference on 'Kyrgyzstan and Russia' was convened by leaders of the Russian community and another was held in 1994 on 'Kyrgyzstan: Our Common Home'. Both debated the impact of the emigration of Russian experts on the state's economy (Kuznetsova 1999:25).

In Kyrgyzstan, too, well-established Russians are undecided whether to stay, as expressed in an eloquent paper by a Moscow-based scholar (Kosmarskaya 1998a). Many have been leaving, complaining about discrimination in the work-place on an ethnic basis – despite the President's repeated intervention in their favour. Akaev's attitude was praised by V. Uleev, the chairman of an association named The Slav Diaspora, who, in an article entitled 'Are Russians Needed in Kyrgyzstan?' (*Yuzhnyi Kur'er* 18 Mar. 1994) declared that granting Russian the status of a state language would curtail the emigration of ethnic Russians considerably. In 1995, B.I. Silaev, a Russian, was elected mayor of Bishkek; soon afterwards, Akaev invited him to be Deputy Prime Minister (in 1999 he was still First Deputy Prime Minister), one of the few Russians in a prominent government position. Kyrgyz nationalists, for their part, insist on a special standing for their language. In May 1999, the Kyrgyzstan parliament adopted a Civil Service Law, which laid down the rule that all civil servants ought to know Kyrgyz (*Argumenty i Fakty* 9 June 1999).

While parliament has condemned discrimination on the basis of language, Russians have complained again and again, in the early 1990s, that there were not sufficient places in the universities for all the students who applied. But in 1999, the Kyrgyz-Russian Slavic University in Bishkek had a majority of Russian students (information by T. Choroev, 3 Sep. 1999). The Slavic Foundation (*Slavyanskii Fond*) had been largely responsible for initiating the establishment of the university. This organization was established in 1990 as a literary-cultural one, but soon became politicized. The Foundation not only collected books from emigrating Russians to increase the Slavic collection at the city library in Bishkek, but organized (since 1994) lectures, exhibitions, theatrical shows, and competitions (*Yuzhnyi Kur'er* 1 Apr. 1994); it also served as a pressure group. Several tiny Russian organizations were also set up, but they had little influence on public affairs. The only important group was the Kyrgyz-Russian Friendship Association, organized in 1993 in the north (Kustov 1997). Russians unwilling to adapt to the new situation in Kyrgyzstan have been leaving (Kolstoe 1995:236-44). The same is true for other non-Kyrgyz, too, as for many ethnic Germans (they had been deported to Kyrgyzstan during World War II) (Timirbajew 1998).

Table 3.7. RUSSIAN EMIGRATION FROM KYRGYZSTAN, 1990-6

	1990	*1991*	*1992*	*1993*	*1994*	*1995*	*1996*
% of Russians in total number of emigrants	39.7	44.9	57.2	62.7	58.2	50.2	50.8

Source: Tarasova 1997:85; for more figures, Vechkanov 1998:107.

According to official Russian sources, about a third of the emigrating Russians moved to the Russian Federation (*CAM* 1995, no. 4:8). Their main arguments, like those of the Russians in the other five states, against what they perceived as language discrimination at school and office, were that in a democratic society, Russian should be fostered as a world language; and that, in the 1989 Soviet Census, more than two million out of four million respondents in Kyrgyzstan had considered Russian their native language.

Turkmenistan

In Turkmenistan, President Niyazov has been reminding everyone that he has a Russian wife. He has tried hard to placate the Russians by granting them dual citizenship, signing, in December 1993, treaties of cooperation with Russia which guaranteed the status quo of Russians in Turkmenistan. Still, in March 1999, the government announced that, as from 9 June of that year, CIS citizens (Uzbekistan and Kazakhstan excepted) would need entry visas to Turkmenistan (*Izvestiya* 20 Mar. 1999). Turkmenistan is the only CIS state in which the Russian Community has not been permitted to register in the Ministry of Justice as an organization and, for all purpose, is therefore acting illegally. The official reason for this is that ethnic organizations are forbidden (Kuleshov a.o. 1997:506).

Local Russians have also complained about perceived second-class status, preferential working conditions for Turkmens, and their own inability to learn Turkmen. Niyazov stated in December 1994 that about 3,000 people were emigrating each month (Ochs 1997:336-8). The trend continued, although in lesser numbers, subsequently, perhaps about 1,000 per month in 1995 on the average (Buškov and Sitnjanskij 1997:5, 20). Movements across the borders are not always recorded; but it appears that in 1997 about 20,870 people emigrated from Turkmenistan and 4,079 immigrated into it (interview with Dr. Juma Durdy Bairamov, President of the Union of Economists of Turkmenistan, Ashgabat, 22 Sep. 1998). This seems to fit with the above estimate of about 1,000 persons' loss monthly, but does not inform us of the exact figures of Russian migration. According to Turkmen sources, the ratio of ethnic Russians diminished in Turkmenistan between 1989 and 1995 from 9.5% to 6.7% (*CAM* 1996, no.2:11), while the number of Turkmens in the republic rose in the same period from 72% to 77% of the entire population, according to the same sources – a rather steep increase in such a short timespan.

Tajikistan

In Tajikistan, many Russians were concerned mostly about the civil war, but also about the 1989 language law making Tajik the state language, even if implementation was minimal under the circumstances. They also voiced fears both about their children's education and about the rise of Islamic militancy. In 1992, various Russian groups organized themselves in an umbrella association, the Coordinating Council of National Unions, of which the Russian Community was one (Kuleshov a.o. 1997:510). Its chairperson, Valerii Yushin, explained its goals and activities in a Tajik-language newspaper in Dushanbe as follows (*Minbari Khalq* 6 Dec. 1996): To unite common national-culture elements, especially Russians and Russophones, in order to defend their cultural, socioeconomic and political freedoms, on the one hand, and to contribute to harmonizing inter-ethnic relations in Tajikistan, on the other. A rapprochement to the Russian Federation by bilateral treaties and an improvement in the community's cultural activities, chiefly in education, were other objectives. Building amical bridges between Tajikistan and the Russian Federation would be of major significance to both. Yushin's article ends with detailed demands in the domain of schooling. Whatever the activities of the Russian Community, they failed to stop emigration (Marchenko 1994:152-3; Tadjbakhsh 1996:339; Atkin 1997:298). Another association of Slavs in Tajikistan, named *Migratsiya*, was established in February 1993 to assist Slav emigrants relocating in the Russian Federation (*NG* 2 June 1993). There are thus Russian organizations working both ways – to stop

Table 3.8. MIGRATION TO AND FROM TAJIKISTAN, 1989-1996

	Immigration	*Emigration*	*Population loss*
1989	25,100	44,200	19,100
1990	22,200	81,200	59,000
1991	20,000	48,600	28,000
1992	11,300	104,700	93,400
1993	12,000	86,300	74,300
1994	6,600	55,100	48,500
1995	5,500	45,300	39,800
1996	26,300	53,000	26,700

Source: Official data, reproduced in Sokolova 1998:43; Kuleshov a.o. 1997:510; somewhat different figures in Vechkanov 1998:107, 124.

Russian emigration and to support it. By 1996, only about 60,000–80,000 Russians remained in Tajikistan (Kuz'min 1998:220).

Recent figures for 1996 and 1997 demonstrate the proportions of the overall emigration from the six states to the Russian Federation (above, table 3.5), which are only insignificantly balanced by those of emigrants from the Russian Federation (some of them returnees). Russians and other Slavs had the lion's share in emigration from the six states in recent years. Overall movement from and into the six republics since independence, difficult to calculate in precise figures due to somewhat irregular registration of migration, still prevents ethnolinguistic geographers from predicting future trends conclusively (Breton 1991:25ff; Halbach 1997a:7-8).

The leaders of all six states still have to decide whether they want the Russians, many of them skilled in their professions, to stay or leave. In Azerbayjan, Uzbekistan, Turkmenistan and Tajikistan, the small numbers of Russians and other Europeans, comparatively, do not seriously affect the nation-building plans of the titular *ethnies*. Kyrgyzstan and Kazakhstan, both bifurcated societies, have demonstrated different tendencies in coping with the existence of the Russian communities – the former by urging them to stay, the latter by encouraging them (albeit not openly) to leave.

The Russians remaining in the area are still numerous enough to cause some worry to the more extreme native nationalists by their very presence. This has also placed constraints on the basically integrationist tendencies of the titular elites. They have reacted in various ways to the steps taken by the Russian diasporas to organize themselves: their associations have not always been permitted to register and have sometimes been harassed in Uzbekistan, Kazakhstan and Turkmenistan, but given more leeway to act in Azerbayjan and Kyrgyzstan (Smith a.o. 1998:158-9). In the six independent states the position of the Russians, however, is not as strong as the native nationalists consider them to be, nor as weak as some wish them to become.

PERCENTAGE OF RUSSIAN POPULATION IN THE SOVIET/POST-SOVIET
REPUBLICS WHO HAVE OUT-MIGRATED, 1990-4
(compared to total Russian population in 1989)

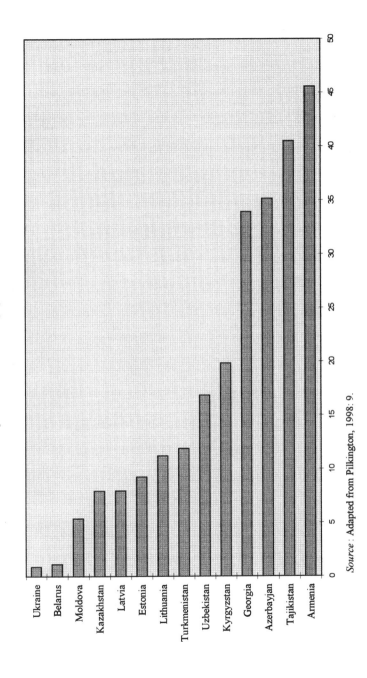

Source : Adapted from Pilkington, 1998: 9.

4

LANGUAGE POLITICS: THE SOVIET ERA

Language, an important element in developing a community's political awareness, has often been manipulated in the interests of the state, not least in the Soviet Union. To understand language politics in the six newly independent Muslim states, a brief presentation and analysis of former Soviet language policies is necessary. By 'language policies' we understand decisions taken by official circles regarding language in a certain state. We shall discuss these from the early Soviet period up to and including the *perestroika* years, emphasizing the issues relevant to the post-Soviet period, to be treated in subsequent chapters. Language politics in the Soviet era have been quite exhaustively dealt with (e.g., Lewis 1972; Isayev 1977; Isaev 1978; Desheriev a.o. 1980; Kreindler 1982; Kreindler 1985; Bruchis 1987; Bruchis 1988; Berezin a.o. 1992; Alpatov 1996; Alpatov 1997), so that we can focus on the main aspects only.

One cannot understand Soviet language politics unless they are perceived as an integral part of the regime's general purposes and a component of the very sensitive issue of its nationality policies (Halbach 1997a:18) whose objectives were to form a new *homo sovieticus,* shaped by Communist ideology and ethnic engineering (Tishkov 1997:24ff), as well as to ensure the future of the Soviet Union. In the 1920s, the more flexible nationalities policy of the Soviet central power coopted loyal non-Russian elites into the new Communist leadership in the spirit of equality of all nations within the Union. Support for and development of non-Russian languages and cultures were expected to make the national antagonisms disappear and create stability in the multi-national state. Contrary to the expectations of the central power, this policy led to the consolidation of the nationalities and the spread of nationalist ideologies. In the late 1920s, Stalin switched to a centralistic line and pursued a repressive nationalities programme. By the early thirties, all republics had been placed under the full control of the central leadership. Cultural diversity was replaced by integrationist sovietization (Kappeler 1993: 302-7).

In a major effort during the 1920s and 1930s, the Soviets advanced towards wiping out illiteracy in a country in which some 130 languages were spoken, out of which only about 20 possessed written alphabets in Tsarist times (Isaev 1979; Perks 1984:89ff; Kozlov 1988:159-63) – a remarkable achievement. Minority languages were raised to the status of literary ones and, in fact, some of them were saved from extinction (Coulmas 1984:12-14). Language construction went hand-in-hand with a tremendous expansion of education. In the multiethnic, multilingual Soviet society, ethnic relations remained closely congruent with language attitudes as well as the extent of mutual language knowledge and the consequences of language policies for cultural, political and socioeconomic considerations (Karklins 1986:55-6). Over time, as we have already pointed out, native intellectual elites grew up, who prized their own languages and would use them later for nationalist expression, reminding one of Caliban's reply to Prospero, in Shakespeare's *The Tempest*: 'You taught me language and now I can use it against you'. While the constitutions, laws, proclamations, and texts were not entirely irrelevant, the Communist Party was not reluctant to alter them in order to suit new policies (Hazard 1990). Essentially, deeds are more meaningful to our analysis.

Soviet language policies fluctuated regarding both language status and language corpus (Garkavets 1990:61-76; Dave 1996b:87-97; for the Turkic languages, Pool 1976). Briefly, three basic successive modernizing steps are noticeable in the case of Azerbayjan and the Central Asian Muslim republics: a. enrichment of local languages through codification and standardization – introduction and development of normative grammar, phonetics and morphology, and the compilation of dictionaries, including the encouragement of a new literature in each language; b. manipulation of the vocabulary by removing foreign accretions, chiefly Persian and Arabic, and subsequently introducing Russian or other loanwords needed to create a new technological vocabulary; c. introduction of Russian as a language of inter-ethnic communication, a dominant *lingua franca* for the entire area, encouraged in education and obligatory for advancement in officialdom and public careers (Ornstein 1968:121; Rakowska-Harmstone 1970:242; Wheeler 1977:210-6; Shorish 1984).

At the expense of local languages, Russian was, in time, employed in government, industrial and commercial enterprises, medicine, transport and communications, as well as in specialized secondary schools and colleges, particularly in technological, engineering and medical studies and in the training of many specialists. The other side of the same coin was the unavoidable downgrading of the native languages and their cultures (Gitlin 1998:405-6). This situation was not new. The Spanish sociolinguist Tortosa (1982:74-6) remarked that practically every empire promoted 'the language of the empire'. This is true also of many unitary states, of which the Soviet Union was one for all practical purposes.

The question remains: what were the consequences? In our case, the resulting policy of bilingualism was a lop-sided one, in which the native populations studied Russian, but the incoming Russians did not acquire the local languages. Among the elites, widespread language shift to Russian was observed, especially in Kazakhstan and Kyrgyzstan, while in the other Muslim republics the phenomenon was more one of the spread of Russian than of language shift to Russian, as remarked by J.A. Fishman (in his introduction to Kreindler 1985:vii). At all events, certain dimensions of language policy remained unsolved, such as one probably unintended result of literacy – a greater ethnolinguistic awareness among many of the region's nationalities (Hiro 1994:310).

Resolving the language problem in a multilingual situation was consistently for the Soviet leaders an ideological-political and social issue (Khanazarov 1982a: 13-16), dictating linguistic manipulation, and they returned to it again and again. The key issue was – and has remained until today – how to manoeuvre between two approaches: identification through language, favouring native languages carrying an emotional load, with possible nationalist overtones, for each *ethnie*; and language (in our case, Russian) as a common tool between various *ethnies* in an era of industrialization, common economic space, urbanization, a joint army, mass communication, and synchronized education (Alpatov 1997:10-26). The language policies of Lenin and Stalin, respectively, more or less expressed the two possibilities. Basically, Lenin gave the various peoples considerable cultural freedom, in preparation for a world revolution; Stalin was resolved to shape a unitary state with a definite language policy. While largely arising from differences in their personalities and views, such approaches were also visibly influenced by the change in the overall situation in the Soviet Union. The first years after the Bolshevik revolution were a time of emancipation from the former regime for one and all. It was only natural for groups in various administrative units to campaign for a leading role for their own languages, exploiting also the chaotic situation in the lands which were to become the Soviet Union. Institutionalized multilingualism was emerging.

Subsequently, however, as the better organized regime moved from 'the emancipation phase' to 'the coordination phase', the centre dictated policies to the periphery that were intended to achieve its own ideological and economic goals. For these, a communication language, a *lingua franca*, which the Russian sociolinguist M.I. Isayev (1977:334) called 'an interlanguage' for all components of the Soviet Union, was mandatory – and the selection of Russian was a foregone conclusion (Jachnow 1982:91-3; Bruchis 1988:216).

In the 1930s, some Soviet republics still provided education for many of their *ethnies* in their own respective languages, as the continuing struggle against illiteracy could best be carried out in the native tongues. Thus, in the 1937-8 school year, more than seventy languages were serving as a medium of instruction, with Uzbekistan alone using twenty-two

(Kreindler 1982:10). However, native language and culture were already suffering in that decade from the Stalinist purges of the indigenous intelligentsia and the destruction of historical treasures. Soon centrist policies prevailed, which held that the Latin alphabets interfered with the literacy campaign and the learning of Russian, and with the ultimate aim of russifying, languagewise, all *ethnies* in the Soviet Union (Bruchis 1984: 135-6). The Latin script, adopted in 1929 for many of the Union's languages, was changed accordingly to Cyrillic by 1940. During a relatively short time, different versions of the Cyrillic alphabet were introduced for writing the various languages, not only to fit the peculiarities of each but also probably to isolate related linguistic groups from one another (Shahrani 1992:337). By a decree on 13 February 1935 (Gitlin 1998:407), reinforced on 13 March 1938 by a Resolution 'On the Obligatory Study of the Russian Language in Schools of National Republics and Regions' (Isaev 1978:11-31; Alpatov 1997:69-80; Brutents 1998:543), the study of Russian as a second language soon became compulsory in all Soviet schools. The teaching of very 'small' languages, although continued, was discouraged selectively and often ignored – particularly when only small groups of pupils were to be taught. Hence centrifugal tendencies changed into markedly centripetal ones.

The subsequent phases of this process were no less influenced by *raison d'état* than those described above. Following the attack by Nazi Germany in 1941, the leadership of the Soviet Union decided to freeze the compulsory introduction of Russian and let other languages alone, partly because it did not then have the means to enforce Russian, but mainly because it did not wish to awaken opposition in the republics. After victory in the Second World War, the Union, greatly strengthened both domestically and internationally, and with the awareness of a Great Power, returned to highly centralized policies in all spheres. In language issues, as the Soviet leaders perceived them, an industrial state aiming at advanced technology needed a language of communication, in which case they could hardly bestow equality on the some hundred and thirty languages in use. Further, they concluded that a Great Power cannot allow itself to be weakened by internal trends towards autonomy, including language autonomy; particularly so since several *ethnies* had relatives using kindred languages beyond the frontiers. While repeatedly proclaiming the *de jure* equality of all languages in the Soviet Union, Soviet leaders preferred *de facto* to promote Russian in both education and administration – achieving a bilingual situation in the towns (Haarmann 1985:324-6), in which the primacy of Russian was felt everywhere in all important matters and even in everyday life. Publications in Russian exceeded those in other languages and their circulation in the Soviet Union buttressed the favoured position of this language (Haarmann 1992:120). There was a reciprocity in this process: the more bilingualism progressed, the less the need for publications in the native languages; the fewer publications in the native languages, the greater the need for bilingualism – and the use of Russian (Rogers 1987:101). Without Russian being officially declared the language of inter-ethnic communication in the Union, it became the *koine* between Russians and non-Russians as well as among the various *ethnies* in this multinational state (on this bilingualism, Silver 1976; Khanazarov 1990; Guboglo 1990).

While the official promotion of Russian in the Soviet Union was not always consistent (Adler 1980:195-6), it hardly wavered in practice in education, the key to enforcing Soviet policies, including language ones, from the 1920s to the end of the Union. In Nikita Khrushchev's years as First Secretary of the Central Committee of the Soviet Communist Party (1953-64), the radical shift to Russian was not least expressed in education reforms. The 1958-9 laws, while vague in some respects, encouraged the study of Russian at school, in addition to the native languages or, more correctly, at their expense: the titular language became *de facto* an elective in schools with Russian instruction (Rywkin 1993:132), thus further diminishing the probability that Russian and non-titular children would know the titular language. Whatever the formulation, Russian – although not proclaimed a state language – was cast into a primary role as a basic component consolidating the community of peoples within the Soviet Union: it was no longer merely one foreign language in the curriculum but definitely the prime objective of schooling. In other words, it was to be not only the *lingua franca*, but a 'second mother tongue of the Soviet peoples'. Under Leonid Brezhnev as party leader (1964-82), Russian was considered a national treasure and endowed with the role of facilitating the convergence of nationalities and their eventual fusion, thus forging the 'new historical community' – the Soviet People (Lapierre 1988:214-16). Russian, glorified, should henceforth cease to be merely a *lingua franca*; it should also rise above ethnolinguistic loyalties, forging a supra-national identity for the common Soviet nationality, 'the language of socialism' and a 'cement of the Union' (Kreindler 1993:262). Russification, formerly cloaked under the guise of sovietization, was thus blatantly promoted not only on the linguistic and educational levels, but in a concentrated Soviet effort to obliterate the collective national memory of all peoples in the Union. 'The rapprochement of nations' and 'the friendship of peoples', important elements in Marxism-Leninism, served also as slogans masking these objectives (Urjewicz 1991:118). The extreme ideological push for Russian in its magnified role was expressed in numerous writings, such as one published in Alma-Ata in Russian and entitled *Russian: the Mightiest Means for International Contact*; the heading of the first chapter was 'The Victory of the Russian Language: An Objective Inevitability' (Tursunov 1984:3). The long process of linguistic russification had been a covert one in a policy of language spread, as Harald Haarmann (1992:109ff) phrased it. It seems to have been successful to some degree (Khazanov 1991:40-4), even though its long-term objective of creating a new person, the *homo sovieticus*, ultimately failed (Simon 1986:369ff).

During the 1960s, 1970s and 1980s, knowledge of Russian spread as a second language (Henze 1984) among the major Turkic peoples, if one accepts the official results of the Soviet censuses. These should be treated with caution because the census takers asked about 'language knowledge' immediately after 'nationality', so many respondents may have given the same reply to both (Tishkov 1997:87).

Table 4.1. KNOWLEDGE OF LANGUAGES IN THE SOVIET
MUSLIM REPUBLICS BY TITULAR GROUP, 1970-89

| | *% claiming good command of their native language* | | | *% claiming good command of a second language of the Soviet Union* | | | | | |
| | | | | *Russian* | | | *Others* | | |
	1970	*1979*	*1989*	*1970*	*1979*	*1989*	*1970*	*1979*	*1989*
Azeri	98.2	97.9	97.7	16.6	29.5	34.4	2.5	2.0	2.2
Uzbek	98.6	98.5	98.3	14.5	49.3	23.8	3.3	2.8	3.8
Kazakh	98.0	97.5	97.0	41.8	52.3	60.4	1.8	2.1	2.8
Kyrgyz	98.8	97.9	97.8	19.1	29.4	35.2	3.3	4.1	4.6
Turkmen	98.9	98.7	98.5	15.4	25.4	27.7	1.3	4.1	2.0
Tajik	95.0	93.2	97.7	15.4	29.6	27.7	12.0	10.6	12.2

Source: 1970 and 1979 Soviet Population Censuses, reported in Crisp 1991:86; *Soviet Population Census 1989* (slightly different figures in Olson 1994:App. F; Rashid 1994:59). We have added 'claiming' to the headings of the table to indicate some doubt as to the reliability of the response. It seems strange that Kazakhs considered Kazakh as native tongue when so many hardly knew it (as will be explained later); and that the knowledge of Russian rose threefold in nine years among Uzbeks.

On paper, there was full equality among all nationalities in the Soviet Union, as guaranteed in the constitution and other documents (Weiner 1987). In practice, however, Russian, the language of inter-ethnic communication, expanded throughout the fifteen Union Republics and the thirty-eight Autonomous Republics and Districts as the medium of instruction in Russian schools, or as a second language in non-Russian ones (details in Kreindler 1982:21-4; Anweiler 1982). While many rural schools used local languages, in urban localities the professional technical schools and institutions of higher education offered instruction in Russian, with titular languages predominating in the arts, humanities and social sciences (Rakowska-Harmstone 1994:31). A landmark was the crucial Decree no. 835, adopted by the Council of Ministers of the Soviet Union on 13 October 1978, entitled 'On Measures for Further Improving the Study and Teaching of the Russian Language in the Union Republics' (Solchanyk 1982:113-5; Simon 1986:384-5). The decree called for: a. a new syllabus for the Russian language, along with suitable textbooks and teaching aids for all schools where Russian was not the medium of instruction; intensive study in smaller groups was proposed as well; b. Russian should get a larger share in such schools as the language of instruction, instead of the native languages, in various disciplines; c. learning Russian was prescribed for pre-school establishments. d. re-training and raising the level of all teachers of Russian language and literature was strongly recommended; e. providing all schools with Russian language and literature centres, equipped with language-apparatus, was enjoined.

All this, combined with the material advantages of knowing Russian, led to certain results in the different republics. For the six Muslim titular nationalities of the Soviet Union, which retained in some degree their mother tongues as the language of instruction, the official census recorded a very high loyalty to the national language, usually more than 90% (tables 4.1, 4.2); but Russian was making serious inroads due to an increase in the study hours assigned to it. By 1982, some 70% of pupils in Kazakhstan were studying in Russian-language schools (a large ratio, even when the children of the large Russian community are accounted for). In the 1989 Soviet Population Census, although 97% of Kazakhs considered Kazakh to be their first language, 60.4% regarded themselves as bilingual (Svanberg 1996:326) and many preferred to use Russian, chiefly in Alma-Ata. In 1990, the Kazakh writer Anuar Alimjanov remarked that almost 40% of Kazakh children did not speak Kazakh; if correct, this contradicts the above data of the Soviet censuses. Uzbeks were more successful in preserving their own language, despite the prodding from above, chiefly since the early 1950s, to encourage substantially the teaching of Russian (Gitlin 1998:408-9). In the late 1980s, *ca.* 17% of class hours in Uzbek schools were allocated to the study of Russian.

Almost everywhere among the Muslim populations, publishing in the native languages was in retreat, although important works did come out in these languages. Allworth (1989:544-5) has calculated that during 1958-86 the annual number of book titles in Central Asian languages remained stable, despite the sizable population increase. The Russian language share in all publications in Kyrgyzstan rose from 36% in 1970 to 50% in 1975 (Friedgut 1982:84) and, in the decade 1967-77, between 93% and 95% of all scientific publications were in Russian (Kreindler 1995:197). At the end of the 1980s, only 4% of the books in the National Library were in Kyrgyz (Kuznetsova 1999:24). William Fierman (1995:577) has calculated, however, that in Uzbekistan, even if more titles were published in Russian than in Uzbek (1,160 versus 974) in 1986, the number of copies was lower in Russian – but, one may observe, still not reflecting the fact that Russians then formed only about a tenth of the population; of course, an increasing number of non-Russians, too, could and did read Russian. Further, numerous newspapers and periodicals were published in Russian and widely read in the six republics during the 1970s, 1980s and early 1990s by Russians and non-Russians alike (Rogers 1987; Graffy 1993; different figures in Fierman 1995:577). Local elites began to know Russian better than their own language, and their best writers increasingly published in Russian or had their works translated into Russian.

This situation, already current both before and after the issuing of the 1978 decree, gave rise to numerous objections and some opposition in various republics of the Soviet Union, bracing to meet the challenge of Russian. Following the riots in Georgia in the same year – protesting at the downgrading of the state language in the draft of the new constitution in that republic – Moscow took a conciliatory stand. Azerbayjan (as well as Armenia and Georgia) retained in their new constitutions, in the same year, the paragraphs bestowing the status of 'state language' on the titular language. At the same time the introduction of the pre-school study of Russian and the projected increase in the number of hours assigned to it in all schools were criticized, at first mainly in the Baltics and Georgia. While administrative difficulties considerably slowed down the carrying out of these plans, opposition to them continued and complaints were voiced that a situation was developing in which pupils would not master any language sufficiently (Kirkwood 1991:124-5). Criticism of what was perceived as the marginalization of the non-Russian languages in school and everyday life became more articulate in the republics in the late 1980s. Some critics pointed out the marked preference given to Russian over other languages on television (Norr 1985:95-105). Others protested that in cities like Dushanbe one could not send a telegramme in Tajik, or in Tashkent one could not send a telegramme or call an ambulance in Uzbek and that applications for employment had to be filled out in Russian (Khazanov 1991:42). Yet others in Kyrgyzstan complained that one could not get any employment at all without knowing Russian (*Sovettik Kyrgyzstan* 5 Aug. 1988). The Tajik press in Tajikistan, since 1987, protested against the low standing of the language and demanded its elevation to a state language; similar demands for language status were voiced in other republics (*Central Asia and Caucasus Chronicle* 8(3): July 1989, 11-13). Such remarks were directed against both the privileged status of Russian and the low level of knowledge of the native languages among Russians living in Azerbayjan and Central Asia: again, numerous indigenous people were bilingual or multilingual, but most Russians were monolingual; moreover, many among the minority *ethnies* were learning Russian rather than the titular language, as data from the 1989 census indicate (tables 4.1-4.4). Not only was there a high ratio of people claiming fluency in Russian in the six republics, but also more books and magazines in Russian than in the titular language were stocked in their public libraries (Azerbayjan excepted) and borrowed (Azerbayjan and Uzbekistan excepted) (cf. table 4.4). Regrettably, such detailed data are as yet unavailable for the 1990s.

Table 4.2. KNOWLEDGE OF NATIONAL AND RUSSIAN LANGUAGES
IN THE UNION REPUBLICS, EXCEPT RSFSR, 1989

	People who know national language (1000)	% of total population	People who know Russian (1000)	% of total population
Ukraine	40,140	78.0	40,340	78.4
Belorussia	7,885	77.7	8,400	82.7
Moldavia	2,904	67.0	2,968	68.5
Latvia	1,662	62.3	2,176	81.6
Lithuania	3,136	85.3	1,737	47.3
Estonia	1,055	67.4	921	58.8
Georgia	4,169	77.2	2,223	41.2
Armenia	3,214	97.2	1,466	44.4
Azerbayjan	6,072	86.4	2,694	38.4
Kazakhstan	6,612	40.2	13,686	83.1
Uzbekistan	14,939	75.4	6,617	33.4
Kyrgyzstan	2,283	53.6	2,416	56.7
Tajikistan	3,392	66.6	1,851	36.3
Turkmenistan	2,631	74.7	1,025	29.1

Source: Marchenko 1994:144, calculated on the basis of: *1989 All-Union Population Census Data. National Structure of the Population*, vol.7, part 2 (Moscow:1992).

Table 4.3. KNOWLEDGE OF THE TITULAR LANGUAGE AMONG
VARIOUS NATIONAL GROUPS IN THE UNION REPUBLICS,
EXCEPT RSFSR, 1989 (%)

	Russians	Ukrainians	Jews	Others
Ukraine	34.4	–	48.6	29.4
Belorussia	26.7	16.1	29.5	48.2
Moldavia	16.5	14.3	15.2	12.7
Latvia	22.2	8.7	26.3	24.6
Lithuania	37.5	20.0	42.5	37.0
Estonia	15.0	6.3	28.0	19.5
Georgia	23.8	15.4	60.0	24.0
Armenia	34.0	27.5	–	33.7
Azerbayjan	14.4	6.3	23.6	38.4
Kazakhstan	0.9	–	–	2.8
Uzbekistan	4.5	3.3	6.2	21.5
Kyrgyzstan	1.2	1.9	–	4.7
Tajikistan	3.6	2.4	30.0	14.6
Turkmenistan	2.4	1.7	–	15.8

Source: Marchenko 1994:145, calculated on the basis of: *1989 All-Union Population Census Data. National Structure of the Population*, vol.7, part 2 (Moscow:1992); slight variations in Rudensky 1994:61 and Buckley 1996:16. The data refer to those *claiming* full mastery of the language.

Table 4.4. BOOK STOCKS AND BOOKS BORROWED IN THE LIBRARIES
OF THE UNION REPUBLICS, EXCEPT RSFSR, 1988 (%)

	Stocked books and magazines		Borrowed books and magazines	
	In Russian	*In titular language*	*In Russian*	*In titular language*
Ukraine	61	38	62	37
Belorussia	82	16	88	12
Moldavia	69	30	68	31
Latvia	47	46	55	41
Lithuania	31	64	27	68
Estonia	35	58	39	55
Georgia	42	55	24	71
Armenia	43	52	28	66
Azerbayjan	31	68	20	80
Kazakhstan	79	20	78	21
Uzbekistan	52	44	40	57
Kyrgyzstan	77	20	69	29
Tajikistan	63	29	45	41
Turkmenistan	65	33	45	54

Source: *Narodnoe obrazovanie i kul'tura v SSSR* (Moscow, 1989:274), cited in Marchenko 1994:148.

Language intervention was increasingly met by language nationalism,
also in Central Asia (Sultan 1968:261-3; Kreindler 1991:227). Language
grievances were first expressed in half-veiled terms, when Moscow still
held tight control; then, during *perestroika,* in more openly nationalist
ones, with the local elites increasingly involved. At times protests erupted
into street demonstrations, as in Alma-Ata in December 1986. The central authorities decided to release some steam and permitted certain
moves to appease the periphery on language issues. Thus, in March 1987,
the Central Committee of the Kazakhstan Communist Party and the Council
of Ministers adopted parallel resolutions for amelioration of the study of
both Kazakh and Russian in the republic (texts in *KP* 5 March 1987).
These measures did not appease the nationalists. In Tajikistan, a group
of writers, journalists and historians set up an informal organization in
1988 entitled *Ëvaroni Bozsozi* (Helpers of *perestroika*) demanding,
along with democratization and environmental preservation, the introduction of Tajik as state language (Stölting 1991:184). In Kazakhstan,
Russian was dominant, due to the massive non-Kazakh presence and to
special efforts to assist the penetration of Russian into large social strata
(Kopylenko and Saina 1982:10ff.). As a result, the number of Kazakh-
language schools declined as did that of books published in Kazakh,

and the periodical *Kazakhskii Yazyk i Literatura* (Kazakh Language and Literature) was discontinued (*KP* 26 May 1988). On 15 October 1988, the Central Committee of the Kyrgyzstan Communist Party issued a resolution 'On the Further Development of National-Russian Bilingualism, the Improvement of Learning and Teaching Kyrgyz, Russian and other Languages in the Republic' (text in *SoK* 20 Oct. 1988). In this, a more balanced approach than in earlier resolutions was evident. In the street demonstrations, there was almost always an articulate element of protest about language, considered a valued national component. Complaints centred on the quality of the teaching of the titular language and its relegation to a minor role in the conduct of official business.

In March 1989, demonstrators in Tashkent demanded the elevation of Uzbek to state language status; Kazakhs and Kyrgyz participated, but no Tajiks (Stölting 1991:183), a sign of Uzbek-Tajik rivalry and the reluctance of the Tajiks to accept Uzbek as the state language. Soon afterwards, in October 1989, large opposition demonstrations in Tashkent, organized by a new popular movement, *Birlik*, attacked a first draft of the language law, claiming that the law's support for bilingualism was merely a cover for the continued preference of Russian over Uzbek (Batalden and Batalden 1997:191). This attitude was consonant with *Birlik's* platform of 28 May 1989, whose art. 3 insistently demanded a special status for Uzbek as state language (text in Ginzburg 1994-95: I, 194).

The awareness of protests regarding language matters in several of the Union republics influenced the centre in Moscow to initiate in the late 1980s and very early 1990s a new language policy rather than one merely reacting to events and demands in the periphery. At an All-Union Conference of the Soviet Union Communist Party, in June-July 1988, the resolutions also touched on language policies (published, e.g., in *TI* 6 July 1988) and practically instructed the republics to deal with their own national language policies. These resolutions, while calling on educators to emphasize 'respect for the traditions, language and history of the peoples of [our] land and of the peoples of other lands' (para. 5), insisted on 'the free development and equal use by all the Soviet Union's citizens of their own languages and the mastery of the Russian language' (para. 4). In answer to the 1988-9 language laws in the Baltic republics and Moldavia, instituting their respective titular languages as state ones (details below, ch. 6), the Supreme Soviet started debating a language law. The decisions reached indicate that the centre in Moscow was no longer in full control. On 20 September 1989, the Plenum of the Central Committee of the Communist Party (convened to discuss national affairs) adopted an important resolution on 'The Nationality Policy of the Party in the Current Circumstances' (text in *Izvestiya* 24 Sep. 1989). This included a declaration on the equality of all languages in the Soviet Union, without any discrimination; it acknowledged the status of titular languages in the Union republics, emphasized the role of Russian as a language of communication, and drew attention to the role of the non-Russian and non-titular languages.

The Law on the Languages of the Peoples of the Soviet Union itself was debated for some time in an atmosphere of deep political and economic crisis, and passed only on 24 April 1990 (Maurais 1991; Maurais 1992; text in *Izvestiya* 5 May 1990 and *KP* 6 May 1990), in what Fierman (1995:575) calls 'a last ditch effort to preserve the common Russian linguistic space'. As pointed out by Kreindler (1997:92), this language law made 'Russian the official language of the Soviet Union for the first and last time'. It declared Russian the official language everywhere, but in the circumstances it was a non-starter. Following the breakup of the Soviet Union, the chances of Russian continuing as an inter-nation language were curtailed (Kreindler 1993); the 'Soviet language' was in retreat, its concepts (Zemtsov 1985) eventually ceding their place to national terminology in the new states, sometimes to religious expression or the languages of the West (Thom 1989:203-5; Motyl 1990).

5

LANGUAGE POLITICS: THE INDEPENDENT REPUBLICS

At independence in late 1991, a set of language issues presented itself. The main issue was the status and use of Russian versus national languages. A central goal for the new leaders was to stop the stampede to a higher-value communication language by shifting dominance away from Russian towards the titular language. The attitude of some of them seems to have been that the more people use a language, the more valuable it becomes. Whether to promote other local languages as well and how to do this remained a problem. The difficulties in defining goals and even more so in implementing reforms were enormous: pressing calls for change in other domains; lack of experience and sufficient financial means; the need to cope with a largely russified citizenry and with the demands of articulate nationalists for language reforms versus demands of some non-titular groups for maintaining the *status quo* with Russian as dominant. The language issue, as perceived by nationalists among the titular nations, was only one front (albeit an important one) to assert their own cultural, economic and career expectations.

Since language loss may lead to the erosion of identity, the leading elites of the six newly independent Muslim republics were well aware of the significance of determining language policies. Essentially, these policies were patterned on those of the Soviet Union both in legal formulation and in implementation. In discussing them below (pp. 77-108) we usually refer to the relevant Soviet language policies first, so that some sequence can be perceived. The general education policies in the Soviet Union had created large non-Russian elites, russified and assimilated into Soviet state and society. In a parallel way, however, they had also formed embryos of counter-elites, essentially cultural and economic, but later political, ready for protest due to frustrated expectations. It is mostly the Soviet era elites, however, who are the decision makers in the new ex-Soviet Muslim states. One of the most pressing issues facing them in the changed situation has been the creation of a strong sense of national identity, based on a common national culture. In the process, these leaders are compelled to do a precarious balancing act between continuity and change as well as between nationalist aspirations and minority sensibilities. Well aware of the power of symbols, they are no less conscious that language is a strong symbol of power. These elites have realized that

63

language assumes even greater symbolic significance in ethnically divided societies; it is not merely a matter of convenience, but symbolizes respect for the community it represents, particularly when it is proclaimed as a 'state' or 'official' language (Esman 1992:381). They also think that language is a central marker of their nation and a 'proof of its right to exist', focusing on the titular language as a unifying factor and generally ignoring dialects as a divisive one. As President Karimov declared a few days before Uzbekistan proclaimed its independence, in August 1991, 'A people is its language' (*Literaturnaya Gazeta* 14 Aug. 1991, quoted in Kreindler 1993:266).

Since 'babelization' was there to stay, something had to be done about it. The political leaders of each state strove to obtain and maintain control of language in order to work out a shift towards the titular language. Some elites wanted to have the titular language not only as a state and a national one, but what Calvet (1987:52) called a dominant language in a multilingual society; dominant politically, economically and culturally. After independence, they attempted to change the situation in which Russian, the language of a minority (statistically defined) had been dominant on all these three levels thanks to the powerful support of the Soviet system.

Steps toward changing language policies began to be taken after the adoption of language laws in the final years of the Soviet Union. Such processes went on through the 1990s in the six states, with committees set up on various occasions, then re-staffed or abolished. In most cases, a permanent committee on language has been working on reform in the language situation together with certain cabinet ministers (or their delegates); their recommendations were debated in parliament and, if approved, carried out under a minister's supervision. However, in practically every instance, the state President was the final decision-maker. In most of the states discussed, many agencies were thus involved – too many according to Dr B.Kh. Khasanov, a sociolinguist who heads a Centre for Language Development Strategy of the Ministry of Science and the Academy of Science (*Mysl'* 1997, no.1:73; interview, 13 Sep. 1998) in Almaty.

Nationalist elites within the titular *ethnie* in each of the six states have been striving to consolidate the link between its culture and the state by ascribing official status to its language, promoting national cadres, directing literature (Allworth 1993), rewriting history, reinforcing legends and inventing national symbols and festivals (Akbarzadeh 1996:27-9). Leading groups in the six Muslim states have been attempting to encompass in their conception of nationality all, or as many as possible, of the citizens of their state – minimizing cultural and other differences on the way to nation-building. In any case, over the years the major native languages in Central Asia have been assimilating some of the smaller ones

(Waxman 1973). Along with history, language has been found useful in research – both scholarly and amateurish – attempting to legitimize past and future claims on territory and bolster national identity (examples in Attar and Fedtke 1998). The consequent implementation of preference for the titular language has made less progress in Kazakhstan and Kyrgyzstan – where a large non-titular population group exists – and somewhat more in the four others, although with obvious differences in scope and tempo within each of them (Kangas 1995:282-3; Fierman 1997).

The six independent states have been grappling with many new issues in language policies and politics, as well as with some old ones – but under changed circumstances, the most immediate of which is their being called upon to respond to challenges by making all decisions on their own. We shall attempt to survey these issues briefly, enlarging on them in subsequent chapters, in order to arrive at some comparative observations. Our focus will be to examine certain problems and solutions in language status – how the prestige and use of national languages are increased and defended. This includes, more often than not, political acts, often employed by governments for impression management – but not merely that: language dominance is ethnic dominance, often implying political and economic dominance as well.

De-Russification as a major issue

Russification (by which term we mean linguistic russification) was a fact of life in the Soviet Union. De-russification has been the central issue of language policies in the six independent states, beset by the problem of how to decide on its modality and tempo and implement it without antagonizing the Russians too much. De-russification was only a part, although an important one, of de-sovietization, chiefly in the cultural domain, in the search for a national identity. Rewriting national history and reviving national literature were significant dimensions of this process in the years preceding the independence of the six republics. During the 1960s and 1970s, stories, novels and epic poems in the titular languages had been published, mostly in literary journals, providing historical information disguised as fiction which expressed criticism through the use of symbols, metaphors, parables and allegories. These were followed in the 1980s, mainly in the years of *perestroika*, by historical publications. Numerous works reassessed and idealized the history and culture of local peoples, focusing on early Turkic or Iranian civilization as well as on the pre-Soviet cultural revival, including the political renaissance in the years immediately preceding the Soviet takeover. Many of these publications centred on relations with the Russians, reaffirming Turkic claims countering Soviet theories of the Russian civilizatory mission among the less developed peoples. This study of the Turkic past was perceived as a key to the future (Altstadt 1991; Önder 1993; Kadir 1996).

Side by side with history and literature, language has had a central place in the evaluation of the past and in its de-russification. During *perestroika*, fear of being accused of 'bourgeois nationalism' subsided and all the pent-up resentment towards Russian chauvinism burst forth. *Glasnost'* blew the linguistic scene wide open and language as a political issue became a focal point of public discourse, given the green light from Moscow (*KP* 26 Feb. 1989; 7 Mar. 1989). According to the 1989 Soviet census, in the capital cities, the centres of power, wealth and culture, only a part of the titular *ethnie* claimed to speak its national language as native tongue; 65% in Baku, but only 44% in Tashkent, 22% in Alma-Ata, 23% in Frunze (Bishkek), 49% in Ashgabat and 39% in Dushanbe (culled from Harris 1993:19). National intelligentsias, aware of the people's growing alienation from their own national culture (Naby 1994:40-1), became increasingly alarmed that the much advertised 'language of unity' (Friedgut 1982) was turning into a 'unity of language' at the expense of their native culture – even when considering the benefits of material advancement. Russian was used almost ubiquitously, while the weakness of other languages was highlighted by the inroads of Russian into their vocabulary and grammar. Initiative in language policies was increasingly passing to the nationalities, many of which campaigned for an exclusive or at least a paramount status for their own languages. Some of the first informal organizations set up in the new Muslim republics were established around the language issue; the Foundation for the Tajik Language is one example. Youth organizations argued about language politics, insisting that language was an essential component in their nationalism (or, rather, ethnonationalism). Almost everywhere, the first concrete signs of self-assertiveness were language laws, passed between July 1989 and May 1990, followed by declarations of sovereignty and subsequently of independence. Along with demands for economic and political sovereignty, language was increasingly becoming a political symbol for self-determination and independence (Marshall 1996:7ff), along with other signs. The russification policy of 'overkill' led to an extreme reaction of strong demands for de-russification in the ex-Soviet independent states, comparable perhaps to the arabicization campaign in formerly French-dominated North Africa soon after independence. A difference remains, however: in North Africa independence was attained only after a bitter struggle, while in Azerbayjan and Central Asia it was achieved effortlessly.

Independence unavoidably affected the role of Russian – not so much as a language shared with the other ex-Soviet states (which continued to communicate with each other in Russian), but as a formerly predominant one in the Muslim republics. With independence and the first moves for de-russification, the pervasiveness of Russian among the non-Russians in each of the Muslim states became even clearer. Two scholars from the

Russian Federation investigated this phenomenon in the mid-1990s in selected states of the CIS, with a focus, among others, on Azerbayjan, Uzbekistan and Kyrgyzstan (Belousov and Grigoryan 1996). Heavy ratios of the non-Slavs were speaking Russian at home and at work, using it in their applications to government offices, preferring to read it or listen in to it, and sending their children to Russian schools. Here was a complex situation that, characteristically, demanded a response from the leading elites of the newly independent societies, anxiously searching for identity markers to shape a new self-awareness.

Since the acquisition of Russian by non-Russians in the six republics during the Soviet era had largely been instrumentally motivated, an effort was made after independence by the titular rulers to counter this instrumental element by giving their own language priority in administration, business and schooling. Thus, they aspired to raise its status thanks to the demographic weight of the titular *ethnie* (Kazakhstan excepted) and its cultural distinctiveness versus Russian (Dave 1996b:35-7). The result has been a certain downgrading of Russian in public employment, variable but palpable in the six newly independent Muslim states (Heuer 1998:A 112, A116-7). The other consequence of the same process was the upgrading of native languages, always the titular ones, at the expense of Russian. The need for this was summed up rather sharply by Tleigadzi Esimkhanov, prorector of the Kazakh State University for World Languages, as follows: 'The revival – and, it would not be an exaggeration to say, the rescue – of the Kazakh language was one of the main objectives of our government since the first days of its establishment as independent and sovereign... [to rescue it] from the results of the destructive process of the Soviet period' (*KP* 18 Jan. 1994). What Esimkhanov and others in the newly independent states had in mind was to mobilize the titular language for national state building. His use of the term 'to rescue' in regard to the titular language was echoed by others in Kazakhstan and elsewhere, who used the example of Ireland where Irish still exists but is close to being lost due to the impact of English (Kirchner and Zöller 1996). This approach went along with a certain stigmatization of those non-Russians who continued to use Russian rather than their own language. Concurrently, Central Asia and the Caucasus were being opened up to new linguistic influences, such as English (at the expense of German, French and, sometimes, of Russian) at school and elsewhere.

The problem consequently facing governments, planners and individual citizens has been how to balance unity and diversity in language policies; otherwise phrased, how to bring political and economic benefits to one and all, without simultaneously affecting cultures and languages adversely. In the case of the six new Muslim states, the main rival to native languages (whether titular or not) remains Russian, a favoured and universal language (Norr 1985:89-92) natural to large segments of the local elites and still serving as a language of communication in both external and internal use (Titov 1996). Those in the six states who have taken positions against what they perceive as the exaggerated standing of Russian, have indicated its preponderant use in education, from kindergarten to university and in books, the cinema and the electronic media (Kadyrshanov 1996:19). The Russian press continues to be published, though with a somewhat reduced circulation (due to the emigration of Europeans), as there still seems to be a demand for it (below, tables 5.2, 5.3). Newspapers and periodicals from the Russian Federation are now usually imported in considerably lower quantities, either by governmental design (Uzbekistan and Turkmenistan trying to make their importation more difficult) or because the population in the six states cannot afford to buy them as often as before (details in *NG* 26 Sep. 1996). A partial solution was found by printing Moscow journals in the Caucasus and Central Asia, such as the weekly *Moskovskie Novosti*, reissued in Bishkek since May 1996 (*Moskovskie Novosti* 31 May 1996).

In the independent states, the de-russification of geographical names continues. It was the first to be started, as it is the easiest to accomplish. Kirgiziya has become Kyrgyzstan and has changed the name of its capital city from that of the Red Army commander, Frunze, to a Kyrgyz one, Bishkek; and Kazakhstan altered the name of its then capital, Alma-Ata, to Almaty, which sounds more Kazakh. Other states, too, changed city names, to give them a less non-titular sound and a more local one; thus, in Azerbayjan Kirovabad reverted to Ganja; in Tajikistan, Leninabad again became Khojand. In Tashkent and Baku, many underground train stations changed their names. In Baku alone about 230 street names were altered: Armenian and Soviet heroes were replaced by Azeri poets, artists, musicians, statesmen and freedom fighters (examples in Aslanov 1994:58-9). In Mirza-Ata, an Uzbek village in Kyrgyzstan, the authorities decided to remove the name of the local school, until then named after the Ukrainian poet, Taras Shevchenko (below, ch. 8; Kuleshov a.o. 1997:502).

Another issue was the tempo of reform. Extensive de-russification, particularly if too speedy, held the danger of mass emigration of Russian experts as well as of possible conflict with the Russian Federation, on the one hand; and, on the other, a re-ethnicization of the multiethnic societies in the six states. These might have been among the factors causing the repeated postponement of the date for the full implementation of titular language employment. While declarations-of-intent in the matter abound, achievement of this objective varies from one state to the other. The issue, however, was subsidiary to the main one – deciding upon the state language or languages; which meant, of course, determining the constitutional/legal and practical interrelations between the titular language and Russian (as well as other minority languages). Policy decisions on this crucial issue – indicating both similarities and differences in the six states – have had far-reaching implications.

Evaluation of the situation and trends in the 1990s is rendered difficult by the lack of recent comprehensive censuses after the last All-Union one in 1989. Turkmenistan had a census in 1995, and Kyrgyzstan and Kazakhstan in 1999. Moreover, there are some indications that certain partial investigations may be statistically lopsided: thus, in Baku, in 1995, a large part of the Azeris questioned seemed inclined to deny knowledge of Russian, while submitting that they were avid viewers of Russian-language television channels of the Russian Federation; in Kyrgyzstan very few Russians acknowledged speaking Kyrgyz or listening to Kyrgyz language radio broadcasts, while in Uzbekistan 30% of the Russians claimed to speak Uzbek and to listen to Uzbek radio broadcasts (Alpatov 1997:154-6). One explanation for this response could be that Moscow radio is easily received in Kyrgyzstan but less so in Uzbekistan. Another investigation was carried out by the Committee on Languages at the Council of Ministers in Kazakhstan, in 1994, among 1,169 persons of various *ethnies* in all parts of the state. Asked about preferences for Kazakh and Russian, a heavy majority of the respondents among all professions (students excepted) opted for the latter as the language of their children's education (Arenov and Kalmykov 1995:78). In this instance, again, one would like to know more precisely how many Kazakhs opted for Russian schools.

A complicating factor in inter-language relations was the intervention of the government of the Russian Federation, on political and cultural levels, in favour of the Russians in what was called for a while the 'Near-Abroad'. On the cultural level, this comprised financial assistance for Russian schools and such projects as setting up Russian cultural centres and opening universities (Moiseev 1997:209; Alpatov 1997:157).

Monolingualism, bilingualism, multilingualism

In the area discussed, the number of languages used in pre-Soviet times had been conditioned by history rather than by any decision from the powers-that-be. Monolingualism had existed chiefly in small isolated communities, or among those who simply had no need for a second language. However, even before the Russian and Soviet conquests, people had mastered book knowledge via a second language, usually Arabic or Persian, for religious or cultural purposes. In certain regions, a Turkic/Persian bilingualism was common. In the Soviet Union the situation changed radically and bilingualism became a stage in language shift, chiefly in the towns and cities. Schools and military service, as well as inducements for upward mobility, turned Russian into a second language and, for some, a first one, the language of public discourse, dominant in politics, administration, industry and business – for many purposes, an undeclared, but widely accepted, official language. Soviet Russian thus assumed the functions of the great eastern languages in this bilingualism (Panarin 1994:25-6). Officially, this meant studying and using both the mother tongue and Russian, supposedly at equal levels (Khanazarov 1982a:153-86). However, while bilingualism *per se* is not necessarily political (Spolsky and Cooper 1977:13-15), it was so in the Soviet Union where the term was a euphemism for fluency in Russian, in a lop-sided situation generally favouring Russian – rarely reflecting an equal proficiency in both the native language and Russian (Dave 1996b: 30-1). Soviet publications frequently recommended the adoption of Russian as 'a second mother tongue'; in reality, however, this process did not promote bilingualism, but rather a shift to monolingualism in Russian at the expense of the mother tongues. This situation soon became the rule in many communities in the Soviet Union and was even advocated at official meetings of the Communist Party and other bodies in its last years (details, e.g., in *KP* 23 Feb. 1989).

Emphasis on the need to use Russian as a superior *lingua franca* in a huge multinational empire was perceived by many nationalities as a step towards centralization. Conversely, any call for developing the titular languages of the republics was officially labelled as 'nationalism', in a pejorative sense. If the figures one finds are to be trusted, at the end of the Soviet Union between 74% and 96% of language use in Muslim Central Asia took place within Russian/titular language bilingualism (Savelieva 1997:46-7). In the six Muslim republics, this occurred primarily in the cities and towns, implying a certain degree of language assimilation into Russian. Only since 1986 or 1987, during the *glasnost'* of the Soviet Union's twilight years, was there increased nationalist-oriented advocacy of monolingualism – generally in favour of the titular language (Asankanov 1997:71).

Significantly, bilingualism in the Soviet Union had a marked political and social basis (Krag 1984:73-5) which of course has not vanished of itself in the successor states. The elites who continue to lead the six states in almost all areas of politics, economics, administration, and culture, do not always find it easy to dissociate themselves from the parallel elites which still, to a great extent, managed public affairs in the Russian Federation in the 1990s. These elites are usually – but not always – bilingual; when they are not, they often tend to be fluent in Russian rather than otherwise. Undoubtedly, the political elites are aware of this situation and they know quite well that intensive language loyalty and maintenance exist, expressed in the popular nationalist tendency to foster the national culture rather than assimilate into the Russian. They have to work therefore for national integration and also take into account the demands of the Slav communities in their states as well as the support offered them by the Russian Federation. The representatives of the Russian communities, not daring to attack the titular languages in the newly independent Muslim republics head-on, have spoken up for bilingualism, by which they meant an official status for Russian – in both law and practice. For instance, delegates of Russian cultural centres met in Almaty in late March 1992 and passed a resolution on the rights of man in Kazakhstan, also issuing a declaration on language policy. Both documents demanded equality for all, in particular the cessation of language discrimination as they saw it (*Leninskoe Znamya* 18 Apr. 1992). A demand for bilingualism, for instance, was raised by the Kazakhstan Socialist Party in 1994 (*Krasnaya Zvezda* 12 Jan. 1994). This party, established in 1991 as the successor of the Communist Party, had then about 55,000 members, both Kazakhs and Russians (Petrov and Gafarly 1998: 42-3). Nazarbaev's response to such demands was trenchant (e.g., in an interview in *Argumenty i Fakty* 51:Dec. 1995): the President pointed out that in the 21-member Council of Ministers, seven were non-Kazakhs; 5,000 out of the republic's 8,500 schools were Russian; seven out of the 19 heads of regional administration were non-Kazakhs; no ex-Soviet state except Kazakhstan had a Russian theatre operating in every region; 70% of the mass media used Russian; and only in Kazakhstan had Russian been designated an official language, not merely one of inter-ethnic communication. Actually Nazarbaev's arguments of fair representation are not entirely persuasive: only a third of the Ministers and regional administrators are non-Kazakhs, considerably less than their proportional share in the population. Nazarbaev is trying to promote the Kazakh language, but finds this a frustrating task due to the heavy majority of Russophones.

Language choice, maintenance and shift became one of the first hotly contested issues in the six newly independent states (Hoffmann 1991: 175-92; Mikhal'chenko 1994:221ff). Their cultural elites were not ready to accept unquestioningly the continued dominance of Russian. Insofar as multilingualism is now concerned, the general situation improves slowly and still seems to have similarities to that prevalent in the defunct Soviet Union. Besides the declaratory statements in laws and constitutions, some modest steps are being taken to promote minority languages; they are taught at school in some areas where minorities live in relatively substantial numbers. In this context the case of the third largest ethnic group (after the titular and the Russians) can be mentioned in those places where it is notably concentrated and articulate – like the Tajiks in Uzbekistan or the Uzbeks in Kyrgyzstan and Tajikistan. In these cases, spokesmen of the group argue for their own cause, not for general multilingualism.

The case of the Tajiks in independent Uzbekistan is characteristic. Several nationalist Tajik associations in Samarkand and Bukhara started campaigning for the establishment of Tajik as the official language of their region (Dadmehr 1998:4), while others have been demanding an official status for Tajik as a second language in Uzbekistan as well as legal status for Tajik cultural and educational activities (Novak 1994:47; Subtelny 1994:54-6; Foltz 1996a:19). A social-cultural organization, named *Samarqand*, was particularly noticeable in demanding the increased use of Tajik, the promotion of cultural centres and the publication of press organs in Tajik (Petrov 1998:101). The fact that during the entire year of 1994 only six books in Tajik were published in Uzbekistan (Mesamed 1996:25) did not pass unnoticed. The other side of the same coin is the position of Uzbek in Tajikistan where, although not an official language, it is considered to have the status of an important one, with a good number of publications. While until 1993 Uzbek generally got only a few pages in several regional newspapers, such as *Haqiqati Qūrghon Teppa* (The Truth of Qorghan Teppa), *Haqiqati Khatlon* (The Truth of Khatlon), and *Navidi Vakhsh* (Vakhsh News), from March of that year an Uzbek newspaper, *Dŭstlik* (Friendship), started publication in the Khatlon province, with an alleged circulation of 5,200 (Tadjbakhsh 1996:338). The strained political relations between Uzbekistan and Tajikistan influence – in part, at least – cultural developments.

The other, smaller language minorities, which voice their claims in newspaper and other interviews, apparently without much impact, possess minimal political influence, particularly if they are few in number or dispersed among larger *ethnies*. Nevertheless, while language conflict is already there, as seen above, in bilingual or trilingual competitive situations, multilingual competition for resources also exists, being largely dependent on the decentralized or centralized authoritarian solutions determined by those holding political power (Roig 1985; Baskakov 1994:172ff).

Complete language equality – what Fishman (1996:10-11) calls 'ethnolinguistic democracy' – is very difficult and probably impossible to achieve in full, even if a government wishes it; in the six states there is not much support for the idea. Nevertheless, there is a wide range of options between complete mother tongue implementation and mother tongue substitution in multilingual societies. The option is generally decided by power and demography.

Institutional and public discourse on language policy

It seems that intellectual elites were well aware that language policies and the ensuing language planning were in the domain of the government, the only body having adequate resources to determine the issues and the power to enforce them (Singer 1998). This holds particularly true in the centralized regimes of the six states. Consequently, institutional

bureaucrats, more than public-minded intellectuals, have been prominent in the discourse on language issues and generally were the decision-
makers. The passing of special language laws and decrees, or paragraphs
on language in other laws or in constitutions, was taken care of, accompanied by some public debate; the implementation of the laws varied
from one state to another. Common to all six governments, basically,
was the determination that the titular language was to be revived, developed and improved in status and corpus as a state language common to
all the inhabitants, that is, a national language; this, along with frequent
declarations of the importance attributed to the languages of the other
communities.

Apart from this, there seems to have been limited awareness of the
necessity to invest thought, time and effort in the preparation and adoption of an overall language policy, comprehensive enough to consider
integratively all aspects of language politics in each state: legislation;
implementation; relations between the state language, the Russian language, and minority languages; languages of instruction and of study;
training of teachers and preparation of school textbooks; alphabet reform; language development; and the like. Much of the emotional public
debate dealt with the status of language and its role in determining
national identity in every *ethnie* (e.g. *KP* 5 Sep. 1998). If the press is
indicative of public interest, it seems that this was focused, after language laws had been adopted, on their implementation as well as better
study and wider use of certain languages. The press expressed views on
these issues more in Kazakhstan and Kyrgyzstan, but somewhat less in
Azerbayjan, Turkmenistan, Tajikistan and Uzbekistan – probably because
there were less Slavs in these four, but also because freedom of speech
and of the press are somewhat less restricted in the former. Therefore,
our emphasis in this sub-chapter will be on Kazakhstan and Kyrgyzstan.

Kazakhstan's political and intellectual elites showed rather more
sustained interest in the public discourse about forming some sort of
language policy. This was probably due to its particular demographic
structure as well as to the fact that a large number of Kazakhs were not
fluent in their titular language, even if it was their mother tongue.Some
sociolinguists felt that Kazakhstan had no language policy worthy of
that name (M. Arenov and S. Kalmykov, in *Mysl'* 1995, no. 3: 49-53).
Heated debates went on and still do, according to press reports, in the
Qazaq Tili, the Kazakh Language Society. Other opinions were published
in articles and letters to the editor. For instance, Berik Abdygaliev, a
political scientist in the Kazakhstan Institute of Strategic Studies at
the President's office, contended that the fact that so many Kazakhs
were talking in Russian even among themselves was a disintegrating
factor in the state's body politic (*Ekspress K* 24 Mar. 1995). Another
critic, R. Shaimerdenova, reminded readers that the Jews had revived a

dead language and made it their state language (*Kazakhskaya Pravda* 5[31]:1998).

Probably the most prolific of the Kazakhs writing on language policies has been yet another political scientist, who had already before independence published extensively in Russian on bilingualism, its merits and demerits, B.Kh. Khasanov (1987; 1989; 1990). He has been a consistent proponent of bilingualism everywhere ('the social requirement of our times') and in Kazakhstan proper ('essential for mutual understanding – in both general life and the literary-artistic'); and has urged the improvement of teaching in order to achieve this desirable end. In a more recent work, again in Russian (Khasanov 1992), he addressed the issues of bilingualism and multilingualism. Basing his argument on the factual and legal situation both in Kazakhstan and abroad, Khasanov returned to the assumption in his earlier works, maintaining that, although a national state usually has one state language only, in multi-ethnic Kazakhstan (according to him: 42% Kazakhs, 38% Russians, 20% other nationalities), two are needed on the general level of administration, while other ethnic languages may and should be employed in local administration – the state language and that of the *ethnie* forming at least 20% of the population in that region ought to be used (e.g. German, Uyghur, Ukrainian or Uzbek), or the state language and Russian in regions where Russians made up at least 38% of the local population. However, keeping ethnic concentration in mind, the state language would suffice in certain other districts. Also, the translation of official documents between Kazakh, Russian, and other languages should be regulated. While Kazakh ought to be increasingly encouraged in employment by adequate remuneration, both Kazakh and Russian should be used in foreign relations – while investing even greater efforts in developing the Kazakh language. Thus Khasanov, grappling with language policies in the changed conditions of independence, has somewhat modified his former views on bilingualism – by allocating first place to Kazakh in certain instances, while preserving a significant one for Russian; and by taking into consideration the languages of the larger *ethnies* in Kazakhstan.

In late 1994, Dzhumagali Nauryzbaev, a member of the National Council on State Policy under the President of the Republic, published a long and interesting article entitled 'A new law on languages and a new approach to resolving the language problem are needed' (*KP* 22 Sep. 1994). His views could be considered official and propaganda-minded; consequently, they stirred some reactions in the press. His main points were as follows. The time for convening and debating is over, now the time has come for day-to-day work, without immediate dividends. While Russian was the language of professional and higher education, Kazakh – employed mostly in pedagogical and agricultural institutes – was still considered unsuitable for top administrative positions, and had not developed as a language of science, economics and production. Its prestige was low, so that instructing children in it was seen as a sign of backwardness. Even now it is difficult to assert that all possibilities of development have opened before Kazakh. A well thought out language policy is necessary for Kazakhs and other *ethnies*, in danger of losing their native languages, but it is no less vital for the Russians in Kazakhstan. Consequently, an out-and-out effort is needed, economically and otherwise, to promote languages. School is insufficient to achieve this; the entire society should participate in preparing textbooks, building kindergartens and schools, and using the means of mass information for spreading the native languages. Society should promote the free development of every language as long as it does not prevent the development of others. Language engineering is a task of wide dimensions, to be organized, coordinated and controlled – financially and technically – by a new language law, taking into consideration sociopolitical and socioeconomic changes since 1989 as well as issues of implementation. Kazakhstan must guarantee the flowering of the culture of every single *ethnie*, devoting all possible means to achieve cultural and linguistic pluralism, watching over ethnocultural, and of course linguistic, interests. The government's language policy has a major role in achieving this and thus consolidating society. It should create a symphony in which the language of every *ethnie* reciprocally respects the others. Here was a pluralist appeal for a consensual language policy that, with wide public support and participation, should set up a golden path promoting the culture and language of every *ethnie* in a common interest.

Kazakhstan authorities have apparently invested much time in considering language policies. In November 1996 a new presidential decree on 'The Conception of the Language Policy of the Republic of Kazakhstan' was published (*KP* 6 Nov. 1996; English translation in Black 1997:2, 267-71). This document called for a well-coordinated language policy to ensure effective results. The objectives of the strategies proposed were to guarantee the preservation of the language of each *ethnie* as the basis of its national culture, while defining as the duty of the government the development of Kazakh as the state language according to the constitution. In a multiethnic situation it is important to consult political scientists, sociologists, jurists and linguists about language processes, as more than a hundred languages are in use. The state language status of Kazakh has not yet been achieved in daily life, due to the lack of mechanisms of implementation, e.g., in development and enrichment. The comparative study of the language situation in various parts of Kazakhstan is necessary for this. The state language is used (or should be!) at all official functions everywhere and should tend to become in time the inter-ethnic language – leaving for Russian its current functions in information, communication, technology, and foreign ties. However, special attention ought to be given to the 'population of the state language' – i.e., the Kazakhs – in mass publication and improvement of the methodology of teaching, popular teach-yourself textbooks, conversation manuals, and dictionaries for various levels of study. Civil servants and all public workers should be compelled to learn the state language by determined norms for communication and translation. All official papers and documents should be in the state language. All this should be implemented while maintaining Russian and other languages of Kazakhstan in schools and cultural centres. New terms, technical and others, ought to be coined in the state language. The President's 'Conception' started on the same lines as Nauryzbaev's, favouring all cultures and languages, but makes a special plea for Kazakh while strongly recommending expert consultation and thorough coordination of policies and activities.

This approach was echoed, in part, in an official Kyrgyz document a year later. One should remember that Kazakhstan and Kyrgyzstan have strong ties and many of their language problems resemble one another, so that the document discussed here bears some similarity to the above 'Conception of the Language Policy of the Republic of Kazakhstan'. However, the Kyrgyz text places much more emphasis on the state language. The document is appended to a decree of Akaev, in Kyrgyz and Russian, dated 20 January 1998, 'On the Further Development of the State Language of the Kyrgyz Republic'. The decree established a national commission for the state language at the President's office and charged it with coordinating the activities of all governmental organs and public institutions towards the development and employment of the state language. The decisions of the commission in these matters would be binding. A foundation would be set up besides the commission to provide for the necessary financial and other means, to be allocated by parliament. The commission should present plans relating to the development of the state language for 1998-2007 (*Ėrkin Too* 11 Mar. 1998; *Normativnye akty Kyrgyzskoi Respubliki* 1998, no.3:Feb., 10-14; also in *SK* 27-28 Jan. 1998).

The appendix to this decree, the 'Concept of the Development of the State Language of the Kyrgyz Republic', declares that Kyrgyz, as the state language, is one of the symbols of Kyrgyzstan's sovereignty, a means of consolidating the nation and promoting the political, economic and spiritual progress of the country. However, upon independence, the state language was not yet ready to fulfill all the necessary functions. The proposed conception aims at defining the strategies, problems and priorities of its further development. The state language is to be used in legal documents, by public bodies, and in education, the courts, research, literature and art. The strategy of developing the state language in the coming decade should focus on creating conditions for wide strata of citizens, in particular the youth, to master both writing and speaking in

Kyrgyz. The following priorities are listed: to expand the use of Kyrgyz according to plans worked out by the national commission; to improve the laws relating to the development of Kyrgyz and adapt them to the realities of life; to create the necessary conditions for everybody to master Kyrgyz, via the publication of textbooks, exercise manuals, dictionaries, and teach-yourself books as well as the inauguration of language courses and programmes on radio and television, and in newspapers and periodicals; to guarantee the required level of instruction in Kyrgyz in all schools and resolve administrative, economic and pedagogical difficulties; to develop the language by compiling terminological dictionaries and employing it in scholarly research of all domains; to encourage the development of cinema and the written and electronic media in Kyrgyz; to reward teachers striving to encourage the study of Kyrgyz. Here one has a list of priorities, carefully thought out, for the promotion of Kyrgyz – without however attempting a ranking by importance and urgency.

Azerbayjan

Azerbayjan was in a strong position, since its 1978 constitution stated, as its 1936 constitution had done before, that the titular language was the state one. Azeri was a relatively well developed language by that time and Azeris had only to reckon with the proportionately small number of Russians in their republic. Nevertheless, their April 1978 constitution stipulated that 'Russian and other languages would also be used without any discrimination'. Public involvement in promoting the Azeri language continued. A society named *Qaïghy* (Concern), set up in August 1988, called for stimulating the development of the language and literature by increasing knowledge of them and making them popular in all social strata, chiefly among young people (programme in *BR* 23 Aug. 1988). A year later, in August 1989, a Resolution on Language was passed. Even in those years of Soviet rule – and no doubt later – there was a more determined support for the titular language, Azeri, than in some other republics among the six. If the data of the 1989 Soviet Census are accurate, 99.1% of the Azeris in Azerbayjan knew Azeri as their native tongue, with another 31.7% claiming fluency in Russian.

Ya.V. Karaev, director of the Institute of Literature in the Azerbayjan Academy of Sciences, was probably correct in asserting, in a press interview, that interest in learning Azeri was characteristic of large segments of the population (*BR* 21 Jan. 1989; 4 Mar. 1989). A high-level seminar of the Azerbayjan Communist Party decided that in order to bolster *perestroika*, each nationality ought to be given an opportunity to solve its own social and economic problems and develop its own culture and language (*BR* 10 Feb. 1989). Historians and writers attempted to retrieve

Azeri history and reconstitute cultural identity, using the circumspection imposed by censorship (Vatanabadi 1996:493-7). Under the circumstances, not unexpectedly, the language discussion favoured a bilingual – titular and Russian – solution, with due attention to the languages of even the smallest groups. .

However, with all due lip-service to bilingualism and multilingualism, the trend towards the centrality of Azeri was obvious, then and later. Praise was lavished in the late 1980s on several encyclopedias published in Azeri, and a demand was made that the ten-volume Azerbayjan Soviet Encyclopedia in Russian be issued in Azeri as well (*BR* 21 Apr. 1988). A book published in Baku in 1989 – in Russian – set out to prove that the state language was both required and suitable for use in the courts for all criminal trials (*BR* 1 Sep. 1989). Along with complaints that not enough was being done for Azeri, counter-complaints maintained that salespeople refused to accommodate customers who spoke no Azeri (*BR* 29 July 1989). In short, there was a wave of popular feeling in favour of Azeri (*BR* 27 Aug. 1989). It was also maintained that in the mostly Armenian populated Nagorno-Karabagh much too little had been done for Azeri education, language and theatre among the Azeri population there (*BR* 19 Sep. 1989). By contrast, Armenians also complained of cultural discrimination in Nagorno-Karabagh (Brutents 1998:513-14). As for the 'smaller languages', demands had been voiced since 1988 (if not earlier), for instance in the Commission for Relations between Nationalities and for Inter-nation Education at the Azerbayjan Supreme Soviet, to improve and broaden education as well as radio and television broadcasts in the various minority languages (*BR* 17 Sep. 1988). These demands were repeated later, maintaining, *inter alia*, that 'relations among nationalities start with language' (*BR* 11 Oct. 1989). Such arguments applied also to Azeri and Russian – where the core of the language issue really lay.

In independent Azerbayjan the public language debate continued, but had to face more directly the realities of Azeri-Russian bilingualism, sometimes welcoming its advantages, at other times criticizing its disadvantages, but in a pluralist approach. This attitude fitted well with the official one, as expressed early in 1992 by the then-President, Ayaz Mutalibov, as follows: a. people ought to express themselves in the language of their thinking; b. individuals, not the government, should choose the language of education in school; c. newspapers would be published in whatever language they prefer while government bulletins would be issued in both Azeri and Russian; d. while government policies ought to encourage everybody to master Azeri, no steps should be taken to discriminate against those who do not know this language (*Literaturnaya Gazeta* 5 Feb. 1992). A Committee on Languages at the Council of Ministers and yet another, for the Implementation of Language Policies (set up in September 1993 by a decree of the Council of Ministers), headed by

Elchin Efendiev, a writer and Deputy Prime Minister at the time, have been attempting to plan and carry out language policies.

Official information stated in 1992 that one in four books, one in three magazines and one in ten newspapers printed in Azerbayjan were in Russian (FBIS-SOV-92-113:8 July 1992), despite the small proportion of Russians in the population. This can be explained by the large number of Russophones. For 1996, the ratio changed: According to the State Statistical Committee publication, *Culture* (1997:86), out of 296 newspapers, magazines and periodicals, 273 were in Azeri. In the same year, 542 books and pamphlets were published, of which 446 were in Azeri. Most of the rest were presumably in Russian. A 1994 poll in Baku found that 24% of the respondents read newspapers in both Azeri and Russian, 28% more often in Russian, 48% only in Russian (Belousov and Grigoryan 1996:4-5). This is a high proportion of Russian-language readers. Russian newspapers and periodicals have continued to exist side by side with Azeri ones whose number is on the rise (for a list of the main ones, in December 1993, *Zerkalo* 7 Jan. 1994). In 1996, according to the 1997 Statistical Committee's publication, *Culture*, 257 newspapers were published, of which 237 were in Azeri, along with 39 magazines and periodicals, of which 36 were in Azeri. The most important Azeri newspapers were *Müxalifät, Humanitar, Azärbaycan, Hürriyyät, Azadlıq, Zaman, Yeni Müsavat, 525-ci Qäzet,* and *Cümhuriyyät.* Among the periodicals were *7 Gün Qäzeti* (a weekly), *Azärbaycan Dili vä Ädäbiyyatı Tädrisi, Azärbaycan Müällimi, Araz,* and *Ana Sözü.* In the same year, fourteen Russian periodicals were imported from the Russian Federation (*NG* 26 Sep. 1996).

Formerly, in early June 1992, an open mind on language issues had been exhibited also by Ebulfez Elchibey, before he was elected to the state presidency, strongly emphasizing the significance of Azeri (which he called 'Turkish'), but granting some consideration to every single language employed in the republic's press and otherwise (*BR* 6 June 1992). In a televised speech, President Elchibey expressed pride that the Azeri representative to the 1992 Helsinki Conference had spoken in his own language and promised to strive to make Turkish – according to him, the language of two hundred million people – an official language of the United Nations (speech printed in *BR* 28 Aug. 1992).

The next president, Heidar Aliev, while praising the virtues of the Azeri language and repeating his commitment to 'promoting the language identity of all ethnic groups', generally assumed a more sympathetic attitude toward Russian. He repeatedly pointed out that all Azeris were Russophones and most would prefer to express themselves in Russian rather than otherwise; and he declared that it would be impossible to separate the Azeris from the Russian language (*RG* 20 Aug. 1994). The frequent and continuing employment of Russian in government offices, the media and schools seems to support his stand, at least while he serves as President. An equally moderate attitude was also adopted by *Vestnik* (Herald), the new organ of the Russian Community organization in Azerbayjan, published weekly in Russian in Baku in 6,600 copies since 27 January 1995 and aimed at all non-local minorities in the CIS (*Vyshka* 28 Jan. 1995). The Concord organization publishes its own organ, *Sodruzhestvo* (Cooperation) (Kuleshov a.o. 1997:490). According to their own newspaper reports, the Russian groups in Azerbayjan, smaller in numbers and a little more familiar with native culture than elsewhere among the six states, perhaps meet with less antagonism than in the others on language and other issues (*BR* 23 May 1998). This, however, did not prevent the organization representing the Russians in Azerbayjan from demanding the status of state language or second state language for Russian as well as proportionate representation in the government (reported in *Azadlıq* 4 June 1997; Kuleshov a.o. 1997:488). Most of the leaders of the national minorities in Azerbayjan proclaimed their support for the incumbent President Aliev in the elections of 11 October 1998 (*BR* 26 Sep. 1998). Aliev has shown a deliberate concern with the minorities. This is expressed not only in Article 47 of the new constitution of 1995, the right to use the mother tongue, but also in a noticeable effort to boost the minority languages through the publication of books and textbooks and through instruction in those languages, at least as called for in the published school curricula (ch. 9 below). It might not be an over-interpretation to assume that the government has been trying to attenuate the nationalist Turkic tone of the post-independence years in favour of a more compromise-ready stance of 'the nation of Azerbayjan'.

Uzbekistan

In Uzbekistan, more multiethnic and multilingual than Azerbayjan, public debate in the last decade has focused rather sharply on encouraging Uzbek language and literature (Nazarov 1996); intellectuals were in the forefront of those promoting them as markers of national identity. On 12 July 1991, shortly before independence, some of them founded a language society, *Uzbek Tili*, one of whose objectives was to promote Uzbek as the state language, following the Law on the State Language (*PV* 16 July 1991). Although this society was active throughout Uzbekistan, official language policies remained in government hands. Implementation of the policies remained the duty of the Ministries in their respective areas, with a supervising commission being appointed by the Council of Ministers, assisted by a Terminological Committee; the Linguistics Section of the Uzbekistan Academy of Sciences also gave advice (Fierman 1995:580-2). Meetings of representatives of ministries and commissions, reporting on the progress of implementation, were perceived as important enough to have a Deputy Prime Minister, A. Azizkhodzhaev, chair them in 1998 (*NS* 8 May 1998).

President Karimov has frequently emphasized ideology as 'the flag uniting nation, society and government' (e.g., in Uzbek in *Tafakkur* (Thought) 1998, no. 2; and in Russian, in *Uchitel' Uzbekistana* 32:19 Aug. 1998). Obviously, like the intellectuals, he perceives the Uzbek language as a significant component in this effort. He himself uses both Uzbek and Russian; his Uzbek was reportedly weak, but has improved so much that he is now fluent and even corrects the errors of others.

Seen from the end of the decade, complaints voiced in the early 1990s about slow progress in the implementation of the Law on the State Language (*PV* 12 Mar. 1990; 11 June 1992; 21 July 1994) seem somewhat unrealistic. If earlier local and regional administrative bodies, in the decisions and decrees they issued, did not conform to the language law, but published them in Russian (*PV* 11 June 1992), some change has been achieved since: official organizations increasingly conduct their correspondence and clerical work in Uzbek, and Uzbek and Russian are used in interdepartmental exchange and reports. Even research institutes with a staff of mixed origin are now accustomed to conducting their paper work in the state language and in Russian (information by Aziz Nazirov, May 1999). Business in parliament, also, conducted in Russian during Soviet times, is carried out almost entirely in Uzbek (Fuller 1992:17).

Special efforts were invested in organizing and developing the teaching of Uzbek. A special committee worked on implementing the teaching of Uzbek for adults, employing a new book for schools published by the *O'qituvchi* Press in Tashkent (*PV* 18 Dec. 1993). A new law determining obligatory examinations in Uzbek was passed (Schmidt 1995:25). Later, additional Uzbek language courses were organized throughout the state (*NS* 22 Oct. 1998).

That the whole campaign for the Uzbek language was advancing however at a rather slow pace is clear from a speech of then Prime Minister A. Mutalov, chairman of the official statewide Commission on the Study of Uzbek, in which he complained that only a third of all radio broadcasts were in Uzbek and urged that measures be taken for instructing the mass media to pass to Uzbek (*PV* 17 Mar. 1994). A few months later, he complained that ministries and other government agencies were not using Uzbek sufficiently in their correspondence; and, also, that too many posters in Russian were exhibited throughout the state (Radio Moscow 15 June 1994). Mutalov's reproofs were directed at the language of the media, particularly the press, and were quite accurate, as a comparison of the number and circulation of the various Uzbek and Russian newspapers and periodicals for 1992 shows.

Table 5.1. MAIN NEWSPAPERS IN UZBEKISTAN BY
PRINCIPAL LANGUAGES. 1992

Uzbek		Russian	
	Circulation		*Circulation*
Ishonch	110,560	*Pravda Vostoka*	127,039
Qishloq Haqiqati	52,435	*Tashkentskaya Pravda*	26,514
Ėrk	45,209	*Vechernii Tashkent*	17,840
Toshkent Haqiqati	30,800	*Molodezh' Uzbekistana*	13,968
Ŭzbekiston Oʻvozi	29,711	*Na Postu*	7,374
Turkiston	21,936	*Golos Uzbekistana*	6,807
Oʻila va Zhamiyat	19,850	*Sport*	6,422
Khalq Sŭzi	17,696	*Narodnoe Slovo*	4,259
Ŭzbekiston Adabiëti va San"ati	15,813	*Uchitel' Uzbekistana*	2,403
Postda	13,002	Other	
Ŭzbekiston Tabiiëti	11,856	*Dostyq Tuy*	20,760
Ma"rifat	10,601	*Ovozi Tozhik*	13,732
Sport	10,413		
Toshkent Oqshomi	9,434		
Total	399,316		247,118

Source: *PV* 2 July 1992.
Note: Since the Source is in Russian, it renders the names of non-Russian newspapers and journals without the special signs and sometimes incorrectly. We have made an effort to give the original form.

The importation of several Russian newspapers was banned, time and again (*NG* 26 Sep. 1996); the reason given was a shortage of foreign currency. In 1996, the total number of newspapers and magazines in various languages, including regional ones, seems to have reached 460 (according to *Strany mira*, Moscow: 1996, 483). Russians formed less than 6% of Uzbekistan's population in 1997 but the circulation of the Russian-language press, which had been almost half that of the Uzbek in 1992 (and did not change much), indicates that many Uzbeks and some members of the smaller *ethnies,* with few newspapers of their own, or none, were reading Russian newspapers (Petrov 1998:118).

In the public discussion on the first draft of the 1989 Uzbekistan Law on Languages, commentators emphasized that a special paragraph guaranteed the language rights of all minorities but observed that such guarantees had not been itemized formally, nor had the means for developing those languages been detailed (*PV* 2 Aug. 1989). Already in pre-independence days, public figures repeatedly spoke up in favour of the 'smaller languages', supporting a liberal attitude towards the choice of the language of instruction; special support was demanded for Karakalpak, the language of the minority group living in the Karakalpak Autonomous Soviet Socialist Republic of Uzbekistan (*PV* 12 Apr. 1988). Indeed, there were claims that, in 1990, after the Law on the State Language had been adopted, there was an effort by bureaucrats in the local Communist Party to reply to letters and requests in the language in which they had been written (*PV* 8 Feb. 1990). Another element which complicates the language situation is the demand expressed since 1991 by some circles of the Tajik minority to have their language recognized as a state language, equal to Uzbek (Fuller 1992:23-4). This has not been done, but a chair for Tajik language and literature was established at the State University of Bukhara, and the chair for Tajik language and literature at the State University of Samarkand was converted into a faculty (Rzehak 1995:333).

The promoters of Uzbek strive to support the state language on all administrative and educational levels and proposed to organize an annual Festival of the Uzbek language each October (*Uchitel' Uzbekistana* 21 Oct. 1998). Another measure, government sponsored, is the decision to celebrate in 1999 the ten-year anniversary of the adoption of the Law on State Language: lectures on the history, beauty and significance of Uzbek were slated for all schools, universities, and public organizations (*PV* 6 May 1999). The Russian Centre in Tashkent, also, had already organized, over the years, a Festival of Slav Culture (*NS* 24 May 1997). It was less successful, however, in its attempt to issue a bulletin of its own in Russian, *Vestnik Kul'tury* (Culture Herald), whose publication was forbidden by the authorities (Kuleshov a.o. 1997:500). Most television programmes are in Uzbek and Russian, with a Kazakh channel as well. English, although so much sought after, is still far behind – there is just a weekly broadcast of CNN news.

Kazakhstan

In Soviet Kazakhstan, as we have seen, a special situation prevailed due to the almost equal preponderance of the two largest *ethnies*, which dictated the employment of Kazakh and Russian. Bilingualism was an accepted fact of life, with a preferential standing for Russian; according to the 1989 census, more than 60% of all Kazakhs in Kazakhstan claimed to be fluent in Russian, with many more declaring at least some knowledge. As pointed out by Kaiser (1992:262), this fact was tied to Kazakhstan having a very large Russian population, both in absolute figures and proportionately. About three fourths of the state's population may have problems in employing the state language. The number of Kazakh speakers is smaller than that of Russophones (who include Slavs, Russian-speaking Kazakhs, and many members of minority *ethnies*).

According to Dave's calculation (1996b:217), some 95% of Kazakhstan's inhabitants claim to speak Russian, while only about 20% are proficient in Kazakh. A poll carried out in Almaty in 1993-4 found that 40% of the city's Kazakhs spoke Russian at home and not their native tongue (Haney 1995:15). A Kazakh expert, K.M. Musaev, estimated however in the early 1990s that, statistics notwithstanding, of all the Kazakhs in Kazakhstan about 60% had a good command of Kazakh. Ignorance of Kazakh was more prominent, it seems, in the younger generation; if so, he argued, this bodes ill for the future of the community. The author summed up that 'the correct solution through language policy is a question of to be or not to be' (Musaev 1994:159). Despite the importance of the language issue, Musaev's conclusion seems rather far-fetched in *independent* Kazakhstan.

Another poll arrived at similar conclusions at the same time. To get more data about the language situation and public attitudes, the Informational-Analytical Centre of the Supreme Soviet (*sic*) of Kazakhstan, together with the Committee on Languages at the Council of Ministers, polled a sample of 1,169 people throughout Kazakhstan in July 1994 (published in *Mysl'* 1995, no. 3:49-53). The results indicated that of all the *ethnies* together only 13% were fluent in talking, reading and writing Kazakh, while among the Kazakhs, 71% asserted such fluency, with some others fluent in only one or two of these activities. Of the Russians, 51% had no knowledge of Kazakh at all, only 2.1% were fluent in all activities, and the others indicated partial knowledge in one or two of them. The replies of other *ethnies* displayed a situation not too different from the Russian one concerning knowledge of Kazakh, except for Turkic ethnic groups (Uzbeks, Tatars and Uyghurs), 30% of whom claimed to know Kazakh. This contrasted strongly with fluency (in all three activities) in Russian – 85.5% of all respondents and 74.5% of Kazakhs (among whom another 18% were fluent in one or two activities only). A high percentage of fluency in Russian (in all three activities) was also observed among other respondents: Belorussians (100%), Ukrainians (98%), Koreans (97%), Tatars (91%) and others. Three quarters of the Kazakhs read newspapers in Russian and watched radio and television in Russian, and almost two thirds of the Kazakh respondents read fiction and professional literature in Russian, while only a negligible 1-2% of the Russians read any materials in Kazakh. The results, although different in details from those of Dave's calculation, indicate the same trends of language command.

Indeed, official figures in Kazakhstan, dating from 1995, confirmed that among the Russians, a mere 2% were fluent in Kazakh, another 5.1% used some of it at work, while 92% had no knowledge whatsoever of the language. In comparison, at the same time, about 79% of the smaller *ethnies* had no knowledge (or very little) of Kazakh, while 95.3% of the

Kazakhs themselves had at least a basic knowledge of their native tongue (Eremin 1996:39).

In August 1989, when debates on the first Law on Languages were at their highest point of excitement, Nazarbaev, then First Secretary of the Central Committee of the Kazakhstan Communist Party, was interviewed in *Izvestiya* (25 Aug. 1989). Notably, he did not hesitate to criticize the bilingual situation which gave Russian a preponderant status in administration, politics and education – even in the debates among Kazakhs at Communist Party conventions. In this interview he presented demands of nationalist circles for sovereignty in this and other domains. Since independence, certain movements towards change became perceptible. In a speech in 1992, Nazarbaev, as state President, reasserted that before independence, Kazakh had been 'a language of the kitchen', a situation that was being corrected through education in the new circumstances. However, he wished to see a parallelism between Kazakh and Russian, via consensus (*KP* 23 June 1992). Subsequently, he has affirmed repeatedly that since all Kazakhs spoke Russian, 'a problem of Russian-speaking people in Kazakhstan' could not exist (Dave 1996b:136). Such attitudes were criticized by proponents of Kazakh, who thought that this approach had driven their state language into a *cul-de-sac* (e.g. *KP* 9 Apr. 1996), all its achievements notwithstanding.

In late 1991 a Coordinating Committee had been appointed to control the progress of measures listed in the 'State Program for the Development of the Kazakh Language and Other National Languages in the Kazakh SSR until the Year 2000' (*KP* 2 Nov. 1991). A Committee on Languages at the Cabinet of Ministers was first appointed on 5 April 1993; its first chairman, Sultan Orazalinov, announced that he perceived his main task as being the promotion of the Kazakh language. Other bodies are Commissions for Onomastics, for Terminology and for Statistics at the above Committee (*KP* 27 Apr. 1993), a Department for Languages in the Ministry of Information, the centre headed by Prof. B. Kh. Khasanov (cf. p. 64); and other groups of experts. The Ministry for Education and Culture set up its own Department for Coordination of Language Policy, headed by Sultan Orazalinov who is also a member of the National Council on State Policy at the Presidency of the Republic (*Ogni Alatau* 27 Aug. 1998, 30 July 1997). Orazalinov has complained that achievement fell below expectations. As Khasanov also perceives it, the whole process is thus both politicized and slowed down (interview with Khasanov, Almaty, 11 Sep. 1998).

The language situation is able to change only gradually in independent Kazakhstan, due both to Russian opposition and to the fact that independence is so recent. The Law on Education of 1992 (text in *KP* 5 Mar. 1992) emphasized the importance of studying Kazakh throughout the state. A special commission was set up in April 1993 to ensure that the balance between Kazakh and Russian was not sabotaged by either side (Kolstoe 1995:248). However, well aware of the multiethnic/multilingual situation characteristic of Kazakhstan, its leaders have taken steps (in the 1993 Constitution and otherwise) to enlarge and improve education in the languages of the *ethnies* as well – whenever possible as languages of instruction, or otherwise as one of the languages to be studied in their schools. Still, in the Law on Higher Education of 10 April 1993 (text in *KP* 29 May 1993), both Kazakh and Russian were proclaimed as languages of instruction in colleges and universities. In late 1993, the National Council on State Policy laid down plans for the state's sociocultural development, recommending both the priority of Kazakh culture and language and its harmonious integration with other cultures in Kazakhstan (Dave 1996b:185). The dilemma of preferment has remained an ever-present one.

The language revival campaign has failed to engulf wide strata of society. It is considered 'provincial' by educated Kazakhs who do not consider Russian a 'colonial' language but rather a medium for acquiring information and for communication (Dave 1996a: 56). Kazakhs who have abandoned their native language and traditions and give priority to 'internationalism' or 'cosmopolitanism', as the revivalist intelligentsia see it, have a condescending attitude towards national issues. Their opponents fling the term 'mankurt' at any Kazakh who betrays ignorance of the mother tongue and national values. The word goes back to a mythical character in the Kyrgyz writer Chingiz Aitmatov's (b. 1928) novel *I dol'she veka dlit'sya den'* ('The Day Lasts More than a Hundred Years', Frunze 1981), who was forced to shed any memory of his own past. Therefore, in a situation where prominent public figures like the well-known poet and prose writer Olzhas Suleimenov (b. 1936) advocate two state languages and even propose an economic and cultural union between Russia and Kazakhstan (Dave 1996a: 57), it seems that not only the Kazakh intelligentsia but also the population at large is divided into two camps: one in favour of the preservation of Russian as the cultural and scientific language of the Kazakhs that connects them to the rest of the world; and another which favours beyond all else the revival of the Kazakh language in an attempt to make it eventually accepted nationwide. Some progress has been made in promoting the culture and language of the smaller *ethnies*, as claimed by Nazarbaev again and again (e.g. in *KP* 30 Mar. 1995; see also below, ch. 9, pp. 178ff.).

Nazarbaev and his advisers tend to opt in favour of Kazakh-Russian bilingualism rather than Kazakh monolingualism (not feasible in the present situation) or multilingualism (impracticable). True, one of his advisers, Dzhumagali Nauryzbaev, wrote that the goal should be to develop Kazakh while letting all other languages express themselves freely (*KP* 22 Sep. 1994). B.Kh. Khasanov, mentioned above, opined more forcefully that everybody ought to know Kazakh in addition to their mother tongue (if not Kazakh). Others wrote similarly that Kazakh needed to be reinforced, as Russian was being used in practice as a state language and that Kazakhs suffered in various enterprises for not knowing Russian well enough (*KP* 1 July 1995; 4 June 1998). The leading organization promoting such arguments was the *Qazaq Tili* association founded by a decision of the Council of Ministers on 12 February 1990, together with its newspaper of the same name, which held that there was no need for a second official language, nor even for one of inter-ethnic communication within the state, since everybody should learn and use Kazakh as the sole state language; all documents in governmental bodies should be in Kazakh (*Ana Tili* 26 Nov. 1998), as well as official replies to the public (*Zhas Alash* 15 Dec. 1998). These views were close to those of the association's president, Äbduali Qaydarov, then also Head of the Institute of Linguistics in the Kazakhstan Academy of Sciences (interviewed in 1992 by Dave 1996b:220). The association was active especially in the north, where the Slavs were campaigning for Russian (Bremmer 1994: 621), but strove to increase the use of Kazakh throughout the state (*Vechernii Almaty* 30 Apr. 1998).

Similar attitudes were adopted by other organized groups as well as individuals. A characteristic appeal was published in a Russian-language newspaper, *Aktyubinskii Vestnik* (13 Aug. 1998), under the caption 'Kazakhs Should Talk in Kazakh to One Another!' The sponsors, intellectuals in various fields (writers, journalists, and artists) acknowledged that most were bilingual but committed to the promotion of Kazakh. The gist of their appeal was to persuade all Kazakhs to speak Kazakh not only at home but to start speaking it with one another at work, thus increasing their proficiency. One may assume that the call was also intended to raise the status of Kazakh as a language employed in public.

The champions of Russian naturally took a view diametrically opposed to that of the Language Society, *Qazaq Tili*. In the end, however, it is the President who makes the final decisions. As early as 1992, he expressed himself diplomatically on the matter during public debates about the drawing up of the constitution, saying that the fact that not everybody knew Kazakh reflected a disease to be corrected, while universal mastery of Russian was a *sine qua non* condition (*Izvestiya*: 13 Nov. 1992). Several years later, Nazarbaev, at a meeting with authors and publishers, called on them to write books and textbooks and print them in both Kazakh and Russian (*KP* 30 Aug. 1997). Other pronouncements notwithstanding, Nazarbaev's remains essentially the official position and has numerous supporters (e.g., *Mysl'* 1995, no. 11:47-9). Extreme views, such as harsher judgments of alleged Russian arrogance in continuing to impose the language in Kazakhstan, if printed at all, were accompanied by editorial disclaimers (e.g., *Mysl'* 1993, no. 3:43-8). The situation seems to have changed, but not materially, since G.E. Fuller (1992:48-9) visited

Kazakhstan in 1991 and reported that the Russians there 'were contemptuous of the idea of using even minimal Kazakh', demonstrating little respect for the Kazakh language. *Azat* (Free), a Kazakh political party at the time, complained emotionally of having to use a foreign language in its own country. A few years later, in 1995, official figures conveyed that, among businesses and factories examined, 374 were using Kazakh in full, 891 in part, while 1,027 were not using it at all (Eremin 1996:39). The situation continues to favour Russian somewhat, at least in official publications, which frequently come out in Russian and are then translated into Kazakh – but not all, as in the case of certain statistics. No wonder, then, that few of the Kazakh adults unfamiliar with their tongue – and fewer from other ethnic groups – have taken the trouble to attend courses of instruction in this language.

The *desideratum* of increasing the use of Kazakh in all state offices was being implemented at a slow pace, however: In 1995, there were 55,008 such units; in 70.3% of them only Russian was employed and in 16.6% both Kazakh and Russian, according to official data (Abdygaliev 1995:4). If so, this would mean that in a mere 13.1% of these units was Kazakh used exclusively.

On 10 July 1997, the language situation was discussed and evaluated in a large semi-official gathering in Almaty. Participants included representatives of the President's office, parliament, secretariat of the Council of Ministers, the Committee on Languages (set up on 5 April 1993), various Ministries, social organizations, educational institutions, scholars and linguists. Imangali Tasmagambetov, then Deputy Prime Minister, and Sultan Orazalinov, then Minister of Education, acknowledged in their opening addresses that the implementation of Kazakh as state language was still unsatisfactory, as it was used primarily by certain groups of the Kazakh population, while many others even preferred Russian schools with little study of Kazakh for their children (*KP* 11 July 1997).

Meanwhile, in government offices letters continue to be answered in the language of the writer – Kazakh or Russian (interview with A.K. Akhmedov, Ministry of Education, Almaty, 14 Sep.1998). Both languages are employed in marketing, e.g., in advertisements and labels (*KP* 22 July 1998). Russian is still very widely used in administration as well, since Kazakhs, chiefly urban ones, feel as comfortable in Russian as in Kazakh, or even more so, and still prefer to employ the former in mixed society (Laitin 1998:139). This seems to be the attitude of many in the other *ethnies,* also. The deputy editor of the Korean newspaper *Kore Il'bo* explained that his community used Russian frequently, as many had forgotten Korean and knew little Kazakh (*Ana Tili* 27 Aug. 1998). The various laws enacted, particularly the 11 July 1997 Law on Languages (below, ch. 6) are partly implemented by promoting a parallelism of Kazakh and Russian, with some advantage to the former, and to some extent by encouraging the use of the 'smaller languages' in education (*KP* 21 Jan. 1998; 23 Jan. 1998), although some Kazakhs have been complaining that members of the smaller *ethnies* do not know Kazakh and when they know it, do not use it (e.g., *Saryarqa Samaly,* 25 Nov. 1998). The state President continues to press for middle of the road solutions between the two main languages. Nazarbaev has consistently been demonstrating his desire for continuing cooperation with Russia. In 1997, in a collection of lectures published in Russian in Moscow and entitled *Evraziiskii Soyuz: Idei, praktika, perspektivy 1994-1997* (The Eurasian Union: Ideas, Practice and Perspectives, 1994-1997), he emphasized that his vision for such a union depended on a strategic partnership with the Russian Federation in all domains.

In 1996, newspapers and periodicals appeared in eleven languages, television broadcasts in eleven too, and radio broadcasts in six (*Kratkii Statisticheskii Ezhegodnik Kazakhstana 1997,* Almaty: 1998, 43; Nazarbaev, in *KP* 7 June and 11 July 1997). Still, respondents among the smaller *ethnies* maintained in various polls that they felt discriminated against over language (e.g., for 1994, *Mysl'* 1995, no. 3:52). Most newspapers had only a limited readership (Haney 1995:19-20). The available data about the higher-circulation publications were as shown in Table 5.2.

Table 5.2. MAIN NEWSPAPERS IN KAZAKHSTAN
BY PRINCIPAL LANGUAGES, 1996

Kazakh		Russian		Others	
	Circulation		*Circulation*		*Circulation*
Egemen Qazaqstan	69,144	*Kazakhstanskaya Pravda*	64,186	*Uïghur Avazi*	13,120
Ana Tili	30,967	*Nachnem s Ponedel'nika*	34,914	*Yeni Khayat*	5,497
Zhas Alash	25,801	*Sploshnoi Prikol*	28,818	*Kore Il'bo*	2,271
Qazaq Ädebieti	18,407	*Vechernii Almaty*	20,671	*Deutsche Allgemeine Zeitung*	2,030
Ülan	17,763	*Druzhnye Rebyata*	19,568	*Ukrainskie Noviny*	1,103
Aq Bosagha	13,583	*Ogni Alatau*	18,346		
Almaty Aqshamy	13,027	*Sel'skaya Nov'*	14,827		
Zang	7,608	*Ekspress K*	14,134		
Turksib Tynysy	6,507	*Gorizont*	13,772		
Zhetisu	6,503	*Panorama*	12,884		
Delovaya Nedelya	9,641	*Novoe Pokolenie*	10,186		
Qazaq Eli	5,609	*Turkestan*	7,335		
Vremya-Däuir	5,000	*Nov' Turksiba*	6,556		
Shalqar	2,974	*Yuridicheskaya Gazeta*	6,463		
		Sel'skie Zory	1,000		
Total	241,239		275,966		24,021

Source: Circulation on 1 Apr. 1996, as reported by *KP* 17 Apr. 1996. More details in *Mysl'* 1997, no. 1:2-5. Cf. note below table 5.1.

Table 5.3. MAIN PERIODICALS IN KAZAKHSTAN
BY PRINCIPAL LANGUAGES, 1996

Kazakh		Russian	
	Circulation		*Circulation*
Baldyrghan	28,532	*Zdravookhranenie Kazakhstana*	5,890
Qazaqstan Ëïelderi	25,128	*Ekonomika i Zhizn'*	4,758
Densaulyq	14,373	*Informatika, Fizika, Matematika*[1]	4,637
Parasat	14,094	*Russkii Yazyk i Literatura*[1]	3,325
Aq Zhelken	11,289	*Mysl'*	2,875
Abaï	10,000	*Phönix/Feniks*[2] (German-Russian)	2,000
Araï	8,600		
Bastauysh Mektep	8,365		
Zhŭldyz	6,280		
Qazaqstan Mektebi	4,681		
Qazaq Tarikhi[1]	4,085		
Aqiqat	4,022		
Qazaq Tili men Ädebieti	3,877		
Aï[2]	3,720		
Zerde	3,010		
Ulaghat[2]	2,460		
Otbasy men Balabaqsha[1]	2,438		
Biologiya zhäne Khimiya[1]	2,000		
Total	156,954		23,485

All periodicals are monthly, except for those published every two months (1) and quarterly (2).
Source: Circulation on 1 Apr. 1996, as reported by *KP* 17 Apr. 1996; more data in *Mysl'* Sep. 1996:73
and Taukina 1999. Besides the above, newspapers and periodicals were also imported.
Cf. note below table 5.1.

Compared to the circulation of newspapers in Uzbekistan (table 5.1), where Uzbek titles reached double the number of Russian, in Kazakhstan the situation was different: the circulation of Russian newspapers was somewhat larger and that of periodicals much more so, due no doubt to the much larger proportion of Russian readers in the population and also to the more general knowledge of Russian among the Kazakhs. Massive non-Kazakh emigration was most likely an important factor in the decline in the circulation of the most popular daily newspaper, *Kazakhstanskaya Pravda*, from 64,186 on 1 April 1996 (table 5.2) to 40,500 on 5 February 1998 (*KP* 5 Feb. 1998). Haney (1995:19) reported that in a poll he conducted in Almaty in 1993-4, the Kazakh newspaper with the widest circulation, *Egemen Qazaqstan* (Sovereign Kazakhstan) lagged in popularity after the four most favoured Russian language newspapers even among those Kazakhs in the city who spoke Kazakh at home.

The ratio of Kazakh books approached that of the circulation of newspapers (not periodicals): these rated, out of all books published, 29% in 1990, 35.8% in 1991, 39.8% in 1992, and 45.0% in 1993 (official data, in *Mysl'* Sep. 1996:73). In parallel, between 1992 and 1998 the number and ratio of Russian books published declined year by year (data in Grozin 1998:274-7). However, since Russian books continue to be imported from the Russian Federation, the bookshops are full of Russian-language works, while Kazakh-language ones seem to be less available; English books on sale cover mainly language learning and informatics (visits to bookshops, Almaty, Sep. 1998). The newspapers in Uyghur, Korean, German and Ukrainian have a limited circulation only. Due to emigration, the German daily *Freundschaft* (Friendship) changed to a weekly, *Deutsche Allgemeine Zeitung der Russlanddeutschen* (German General Newspaper of the Russian Germans), published in Almaty. In so far as periodicals are concerned, the limited circulation of Russian ones may perhaps be explained by the competition of such items with imported ones from the Russian Federation. The relatively high circulation of Kazakh periodicals is instructive and may indicate not only genuine interest but also the results of some strenuous efforts to encourage Kazakh readership. Official radio broadcasts use Kazakh much more than Russian. The dozen or so official television channels are almost evenly divided between Kazakh and Russian, but the independent ones use more Russian (Kuleshov a.o. 1997:492). There are also broadcasts in Uyghur, German, and Korean (Haney 1995:18-19; Kan a.o. 1997:216-34), as well as in some other languages: in 1997 there existed, reportedly, 44 television studios, broadcasting in twelve languages, and 18 radio stations, broadcasting in six languages (*KP* 13 June 1997).

In a revaluation of Kazakh culture, one sees that the situation is changing in favour of Kazakh – slowly. The government has also made certain efforts to encourage the cultural development of the 'smaller *ethnies*' to some extent – even though the grandiose projects of promoting their language, literature, music, and film production (*KP* 1 Dec. 1993) have been implemented only modestly, due to lack of funds. One move in this direction was the introduction in September 1998 of what is to be an annual Language Week, featuring musical, folkloristic and literary shows in Kazakh, Russian and several minority languages of Kazakhstan. The celebrations went on throughout the country and were widely reported in both the national and the local press. The week started with a Day of Kazakhstan's Languages on 22 September 1998 (*KP* 22 Sep. 1998; *Aktyubinskii Vestnik* 22 Sep. 1998; *Severnyi Kazakhstan* 28 Sep. 1998; *Zvezda Priirtysh'ya* 3 Oct. 1998; and many other local papers). This effort was at least partly attributable to the national-cultural centres and the Assembly of Nationalities. The former are supposed to regulate ethnicity by promoting inter-ethnic harmony. They started their activity in 1991 and were registered in 1992. In 1994, twenty-five centres were active in Almaty alone (official statistics in *Ekspress K* 24 Mar. 1995). Although they are non-governmental associations, they remain very close to the authorities. Besides their non-political cultural and language-related tasks within their own communities (Holm-Hansen 1997:64-6), they also elect representatives to the Small Assemblies of Nationalities on the district level and others to the 260-member Assembly of Nationalities on the national level. These serve as an advisory structure parallel to the two Houses of Parliament. Active since 1 March 1995 under the state President's guidance, the Assemblies are responsible for certain celebrations and folkloric events, but their main role appears to be depoliticizing ethnicity (Holm-Hansen 1997:77-9; *Vechernii Almaty* 4 May 1998). The activities of the Small Assemblies have included, for instance, joining the *Qazaq Tili* society in certain districts to organize competitions in Kazakh history and language among the local youth, and to bridge cultural differences (Sharif 1999). The national-level Assembly of Nationalities has several roles, the main one being a forum for resolving ethnic and other tensions peacefully (Baigarin 1998:114-16).

Of clearly political impact are the demands of the Association of the Russian Compatriots of Kazakhstan for the full equalization of Russian with Kazakh (e.g. *Kovcheg* 30 Apr. 1998). Many individuals expressed themselves in the matter. M.M. Kopylenko (1997), a professor in the Faculty of World Languages at the Kazakh State University, pointed out that the CIS countries were the only ones in the entire world to employ the two terms of 'state language' and 'official language', giving priority to the former, but without clearly defining them (a statement that ignores the international discussion on this point). Kopylenko suggested that a state or national language should have the function of cultural integration for the entire nation; thus only one would be possible. An official language, in his view, ought to serve political functions; thus two or more could be envisaged. For Kazakhstan, he concluded, the optimal solution was for one state (national) language, Kazakh, and two official ones, Kazakh and Russian.

Another characteristic opinion was expressed in June 1998 in an article in a Russian-language scholarly bi-monthly, edited in Sweden by Central Asian *émigrés*, and typically entitled 'The National Question in Kazakhstan: the View of a Russophone'. The author, Petr Svoik, a member of parliament at the time, maintained that, since Russian speakers were the majority in Kazakhstan, their language should be at least equal to Kazakh (Svoik 1998:30-3). A Kazakh, Burkutbai Ayagan, sent in a rejoinder attacking Svoik's 'Euro-Russocentrism' (Ayagan 1998:40ff).

Kyrgyzstan

On the issue of bilingualism and multilingualism, Kyrgyzstan's public policies to some extent parallel those of Kazakhstan, due to the presence of a proportionately sizable Russian population. While both in absolute figures and in percentages the Slav community has consistently been smaller than in Kazakhstan, it was favoured in many respects, including language instruction: since 1954 Russians were not required to study Kyrgyz at school – thus ensuring that Russian would speedily monopolize elite communication. While many provincial schools continued to use Kyrgyz as the language of instruction, in the late 1980s only three of the sixty-nine schools in Frunze (Bishkek) used it in this way. Bilingualism increasingly assumed a diglossic character, in which urban Kyrgyz were, predictably, employing Russian as a 'high language' in public and Kyrgyz as a 'low language' at home (Huskey 1995:552-4). Kyrgyz was one of the youngest written languages in the Soviet Union; due to the low status of the language, many Kyrgyz preferred to publish in Russian, Uzbek or Kazak. On 15 October 1988, the Central Committee of the Communist Party adopted a Resolution on 'The Further Development of National (i.e., Kyrgyz)-Russian Bilingualism'. This irked the partisans of Kyrgyz and a group of forty-one intellectuals, headed by the well-known writer Chingiz Aitmatov, protested to the Central Committee and other bodies against what they considered limitations upon the functioning of the Kyrgyz language and thus its degradation. They threatened, indeed, to organize a Committee for the Protection of the Native Language and appeal to public opinion (Asankanov 1997:72-3). Concurrently, efforts were made to encourage adults to learn Kyrgyz in courses offered in factories (*SoK* 6 Sep. 1989). After the adoption of the Law on the State Language, workers in various sectors worked additional days, donating their pay for teacher training and the compilation of Kyrgyz-Russian dictionaries (*SoK* 21 Feb. 1990). A political party set up before the disintegration of the Soviet Union and named *Narodnoe Edinstvo* (People's Unity) came out strongly for the renaissance of all local languages in the republic, but mostly of Kyrgyz (*SK* 1 Oct. 1991). Akaev, who maintains that he knows Russian as well as Kyrgyz, or better, has repeatedly promised to watch over the interests of people of all nationalities, including their language rights (*SK* 19 Feb. 1991).

In independent Kyrgyzstan policies have vacillated, with some support for Kyrgyz-Russian bilingualism, but for the smaller local languages as well. A public debate has been going on since independence concerning the demands of the large Russian minority to have their language designated as an official, then as a state language; others, such as the Organization for the Kyrgyz Language (*Asaba* 20 Dec. 1996) took an opposite stand. In the same year and the following one, long public debates were held essentially attempting to have the term 'official language' for Russian in Kyrgyzstan more precisely defined – but the debates led nowhere (*The Central Asian Post*, Bishkek, 20 Mar. 1997).

In Kyrgyzstan, as elsewhere, much depended on the state President. During 1991 and later, Akaev met repeatedly with leaders of various nationalities in the republic to reassure them of his support (*SK* 11 Oct. 1991). Of the smaller *ethnies* in the state, in 1992 he singled out the Germans particularly as 'a worthy minority' with an important language (*SK* 7 Jan. 1992). He called on the press to avoid 'chauvinistic' expressions (e.g., *RG* 30 June 1992) and argued that a multilingual policy was desirable, along with moves to study and develop Kyrgyz – but that 'Kyrgyzstan would never tear itself off from Russian culture' (*SK* 20-1 Jan. 1996), nor would it really be imaginable to cease to employ Russian in technology, economics, and culture (e.g., in *SK* 25-6 Mar. 1997). Already in July 1993, Akaev suffered a setback when German Kuznetsov, then First Deputy Prime Minister and the most prominent Slav in the government, announced that he was considering a move to the Russian Federation, claiming 'isolation' within the Kyrgyz administration. In June 1994, Akaev identified the language issue as the main cause of the large Russian emigration from the state (*SK* 14 June 1994). A Department for Social Development, attached to the President's office, examines and supervises policies on all languages (among other matters). It maintains a bilingual approach: 'Russian will be with us for a long time. Many of us were educated in Russian, and economic ties with Russia go on. Documents will continue to be bilingual' (interview with Mundusbek Tentimishev, *referent* of that department, Bishkek, 17 Sep. 1998). The government also initiated special events in support of a Month of Slavonic Culture in Bishkek. On 24 April 1998 Akaev issued a decree to prepare the commemoration of the 200-year anniversary of the Russian poet Alexander Pushkin's birth (*Vechernii Bishkek* 22 Apr. 1997; *SK* 24-5 Apr. 1998), demonstrating empathy towards Russian sentiments. A monument to Pushkin was constructed near the Kyrgyz-Russian Slavic University in Bishkek and inaugurated with a speech by Akaev on 6 June 1999, who emphasized the close relation of the Kyrgyz people to the Russian language (*SK* 8 June 1999).

Table 5.4 gives an overview of the language use of the main nationalities living in Kyrgyzstan.

Table 5.4. USE OF LANGUAGES IN KYRGYZSTAN, 1994 (%)

	At home			At school or university			At work		
	The language of their nationality	Kyrgyz	Russian	The language of their nationality	Kyrgyz	Russian	The language of their nationality	Kyrgyz	Russian
Entire population	92.4	0.8	6.0	82.5	1.0	15.7	76.4	1.7	21.1
Kyrgyz	97.8	x	1.8	87.4	x	12.3	82.6	x	17.0
Russians	99.6	0.2	x	99.7	0.2	x	99.5	0.4	x
Ukrainians	4.3	0.1	95.2	—	0.3	99.7	0.2	0.9	98.7
Belorussians	0.5	2.4	96.2	—	4.0	88.0	—	—	98.9
Uzbeks	95.8	1.6	2.4	86.4	3.0	10.4	73.1	6.2	20.4
Kazakhs	46.2	26.0	26.1	—	21.2	78.6	2.4	17.8	79.1
Georgians	25.9	20.4	51.8	—	25.0	75.0	—	25.0	75.0
Azeris	51.0	0.2	25.0	—	7.3	69.1	2.1	10.7	71.0
Latvians	—	—	100.0	—	—	100.0	—	—	100.0
Moldavians	5.5	3.6	89.1	—	—	100.0	—	10.7	89.3
Lithuanians	4.5	—	91.0	—	—	100.0	—	—	100.0
Tajiks	67.0	3.7	6.5	20.7	7.2	27.9	13.2	20.8	40.0
Armenians	20.0	—	78.2	—	—	100.0	—	—	100.0
Turkmens	4.3	27.7	59.5	—	25.0	50.0	—	39.1	56.6
Estonians	—	—	100.0	—	—	75.0	—	—	100.0
Tatars	36.5	4.1	55.7	—	3.0	94.4	1.0	5.5	91.1
Jews	2.7	—	95.7	—	—	100.0	—	—	100.0
Germans	6.6	0.1	93.1	—	0.2	99.8	0.2	0.3	99.5
Uyghurs	57.6	7.5	20.6	0.6	10.2	75.7	2.1	9.8	78.1
Dungans	90.5	1.2	5.2	1.6	0.1	95.3	19.9	1.8	75.7
Koreans	18.6	0.4	80.8	—	—	100.0	0.6	1.1	97.9
Turks	72.7	13.8	5.0	2.7	33.3	53.1	2.3	30.2	55.8

Source: Official results of the micro-census in Kyrgyzstan, 1994 (Bishkek 1995:21-2). 'x' means 'not applicable'.

In the early 1990s, officials and parliament members insisted on using Russian rather than Kyrgyz (*Erkin Too* 10 Mar. 1993). In practice, Russian is still employed at conferences and symposia; some Kyrgyz complain that if one Russian is present on such occasions everyone speaks Russian and that all signboards in Ministries and public offices are still in Russian (*Kyrgyz Tuusu* 28-31 Mar. 1997). The use of Russian among many groups in Bishkek is indeed remarkable, chiefly at school and work but also in numerous shops (personal experience, Mar. 1997 and Sep. 1998). An interesting example is the open letter to the mayor of the capital, entitled 'Is Bishkek governed by foreigners?', signed by six Kyrgyz writers who pointed out that shop and restaurant signs are in Russian rather than in Kyrgyz (*Kyrgyzstan Madaniyaty* 1998, no. 9: July, 4). While non-titular groups, including Russians, are expected to learn Kyrgyz, little is done to implement this, and many government offices often employ Russian in their correspondence and some of their publications. University diplomas are issued in both Kyrgyz and Russian, on separate pages.

Kyrgyz newspapers find it difficult to compete with Russian ones in circulation, and several have had to close down (Shamshiev 1996:550). Most newspapers in Bishkek and many outside the capital are in Russian, as so many Kyrgyz can read it. Few newspapers are published in other languages; these appear twice a week, weekly or monthly. However, *Asia Nuru* (The Light of Asia), organ of the writers' union, started publication in Bishkek on 15 May 1999, in Kyrgyz, Russian and Uzbek (*Kyrgyz News*, 16 May 1999. Online. Available: idinov@rferl.org. 17 May 1999). Television broadcasts are generally in Kyrgyz and Russian, although two television stations in Osh (a city inhabited by many Uzbeks) were broadcasting, early in 1999, in Uzbek.

A widespread feeling that not enough is being done to promote Kyrgyz into its deserved place is noticeable, as expressed by Laili Ukubaeva, Dean of the Faculty of Kyrgyz Philology at the Humanitarian University (*Zaman-Kyrgyzstan* 31 Jan. 1997). Perhaps responding to such sentiments, Akaev signed a decree on 20 January 1998, nominating a new 21-member commission to coordinate the use of Kyrgyz in government agencies and public organizations (*CAM* 1998, no. 1:35). One of this commission's meetings, on 22 September 1998, discussed the transition to Kyrgyz of all official documentation in the year 2000 (*CAM* 1998, no. 5: 27). However, the envisaged deadline could not be met. By the summer of 1999 this commission had worked out a draft plan on how to achieve the transition in three stages: a. by 2000, transition completed in the Naryn and Talas regions; b. by 2003, in Issyk-Kul, Osh and Jalalabad; c. by 2005, in Bishkek city and the Chui region (interview with Kazat Akmatov, deputy head of the commission, and Almaz Toktomametov, its secretary, by T. Choroev, as communicated on 24 Sep. 1999).

Polls held in 1996 and 1997 among a representative sample of

Kyrgyzstani politicians found, not unexpectedly, that 63.4% of the Slav respondents were intensely occupied with the question whether Russian ought to continue as the language of inter-ethnic communication, as were 65.4% of the smaller *ethnies* questioned. What was less expected was that 36% of the Kyrgyz, too, shared this concern (Elebaeva and Omuraliev 1998:63); one may assume that these may have been Russophone Kyrgyz. Several other polls showed that many Kyrgyz respondents wished to know both Kyrgyz and Russian, while the local Russians displayed little interest in learning Kyrgyz and complained that the study of English was depleting the class hours formerly programmed for Russian in their schools (*SK* 14-15 June 1996). Even a society like the *Kyrgyz Tili* (Kyrgyz Language) could hardly gather enough support for a monolingual solution – although it tried to do so (*SK* 2 July 1994).

Not only the Russians, but also the other minorities made their language demands known. As elsewhere in the states discussed, numerous minority members were more proficient in Russian than in the titular language, but many of them wished to learn and know their 'own' language as well (*Respublika* 20-6 Oct. 1998). While some representatives of the smaller ethnic groups proclaim on festive occasions that 'the language of my fatherland is my own', it is true that these *ethnies* have not advanced much toward that goal. Nor is the fault entirely their own, as their studying Kyrgyz necessitates considerable government activity and funding, which is still beyond its capabilities.

Of these smaller *ethnies,* the Uyghurs claim to number 200,000 in Kyrgyzstan – according to the chairman of the Uyghur Centre in Bishkek, Nigmat A. Bazakov – but are shown in official statistics to number only about 40,000 (Batalden and Batalden 1997:151). They are divided between the older generation, which immigrated from Sinkiang in the 1950s and 1960s, and is used to the Arabic script, and the younger, employing the Cyrillic (the constitution was translated into Uyghur in the Arabic alphabet). The Uyghurs have a cultural centre in Bishkek and publish two monthlies, *Ittipak* (Concord) and *Vizhdan Avazi* (Voice of Conscience) (interview with the Uyghur Centre's head Nigmat A. Bazakov, Bishkek, 18 Sep. 1998). Similarly, cultural and other complaints were made by the German minority in its own newspaper (*SK* 7 Jan. 1992), as well as by its Member of Parliament, Valerii Dill, who was also the chairman of the German community in Kyrgyzstan in 1997 (*SK* 8-9 Aug. 1997).

A response to claims by the smaller ethnies has been provided by the state-sponsored Assembly of the People of Kyrgyzstan, established in 1994, which encourages cooperation among the country's claimed eighty-six nationalities. It resembles the Assembly of Nationalities in Kazakhstan (above, pp. 91-2) and its slogan could well be the phrase proclaimed by Akaev before the Assembly, viz., 'Kyrgyzstan is our common home!' (*Vechernii Bishkek* 27 Jan. 1994). It sends four representatives to Kyrgyzstan's Legislative Assembly, has opened twenty-eight national cultural centres, and promoted the establishment of schools with instruction in the languages of the minorities wherever they live in compact groups (Uzbeks, Koreans, Uyghurs, Dungans, and others). The Chairman of this Assembly, S.B. Begaliev (interviewed in Bishkek, 16 Sep. 1998) favours schooling in the language of each nationality, with Russian as the language of inter-ethnic communication among them (as is already the case) rather than Kyrgyz. The bulletin published by this Assembly, *Ètnicheskii Mir* (Ethnic Peace) is, not surprisingly, also in Russian.

Demands by the proponents of Russian and other non-titular languages have irked some Kyrgyz considerably. A mouthpiece for these is the *Asaba* Party, set up in October 1990 as an oppositionist ultra-nationalist political grouping. Although small – it has one representative in each of the two houses – it is quite vociferous. Its ideology considers Kyrgyzstan one state, one nation and one language – Kyrgyz, akin to Turkish and the Turkic languages. In the party's view, Kyrgyz should be used everywhere and the Latin script should be encouraged, as a part of Pan-Turkism (interview with Chapirashti Bazarbaev, head of the *Asaba* Party, and Turat Düyshö, deputy head, Bishkek, 17 Sep. 1998). The party's weekly, *Asaba,* published in Kyrgyz, was apparently considered too extreme in its views and was closed down temporarily on 18 August 1998 (*Index on Censorship* 6:1998,100). *Asaba* nicknames those who seem insufficiently dedicated to their native culture and language *Kirgiz* (male) and *Kirgizka* (female) (*Asaba* 20 Nov. 1998); this is how Russians and some others tend to write and pronounce the words. The party continuously proclaims its commitment to the Kyrgyz language. *Asaba* (27 Mar. 1998) roundly attacked those government officials and commission members who were merely wasting public money instead of implementing Kyrgyz as the state language. Later, the fifth general congress of the party, held in Bishkek on 20 February 1999, appealed to the Kyrgyzstan leadership to proclaim the year 2000 the Year of the State Language and, by that year, to carry out the transition from the Cyrillic to the Latin alphabet (*Kyrgyz News* 20 Feb. 1999. Online. Available: tynch.choroev@bbc.co.uk. 22 Feb. 1999).

Facing so many differences of opinion, on 20 January 1998 Akaev issued a decree on 'The Further Development of Language in the Kyrgyz Republic' together with a 'Concept for the Development of the State Language of the Kyrgyz Republic' (*Normativnye Akty Kyrgyzskoi Respubliki* 1998, no. 3: February, pp. 10-14; cf. above, pp. 76-7). Only partly modelled on the 'Conception of the Language Policies of the Republic of Kazakhstan', issued more than a year previously, it reflects Kyrgyzstan's own problems and the efforts of its President to resolve them by compromise.

Turkmenistan

In Turkmenistan, as in the other states, the debate about bilingualism and its alternatives began to attract public attention chiefly since the late 1980s. While some Turkmen intellectuals who were writing in Russian praised the advantages of fluency in this language (*TI* 5 May 1988), others attempted to consider the question more soberly. Some, like O. Nazarov, then director of the language and literature section at the Turkmen Academy of Sciences, maintained that Turkmen-Russian bilingualism had become innate in their republic – although they readily conceded that, according to the 1979 Soviet Census, only some 25.4% (in 1989: 27.8%) of the Turkmens had mastered Russian and a mere 2.1% (in 1989 2.4%) of the Russians living in Turkmenistan knew Turkmen; Nazarov himself acknowledged that the teaching of the mother tongue to Turkmens had been poor (*TI* 14 June 1988). Government spokesmen and others supported Turkmen time and again, recommending an enlargement of its public functions, while insisting on the need to prevent any discrimination against Russian and other languages (e.g., *TI* 22 Oct. 1989). The public discussion on languages in Turkmenistan continued before and after the adoption of the Law on Language (1990) and the obtaining of independence. In early 1990, O. Nazarov and Y. Charyyarov published a book, entitled *Turkmensko-russkoe dvuyazychie na sovremennom ėtape* (Turkmen-Russian Bilingualism at the Contemporary Stage). Intended for linguists, educators and students, the book recommends increased use of Turkmen, including the translation of specialized works from Russian into Turkmen (*TI* 10 July 1990).

Then and since independence, the Russian population was only partly convinced by the promise of non-discrimination in the language issue. Some of its spokesmen pointed out the *de facto* significance of Russian and the length of time the local Slavs would need to learn Turkmen (Anderson 1995:511), while others complained that those who wished to learn it could not find courses or study materials (Chebotareva 1996:18). Throughout the Russians had a lively press of their own, side by side with the Turkmen-language press.

Table 5.5 MAIN NEWSPAPERS AND PERIODICALS IN TURKMENISTAN BY LANGUAGE, 1990

Newspapers				Periodicals			
Turkmen	Times weekly	Russian	Times weekly	Turkmen	Times yearly	Russian	Times yearly
Sovet Türkmenistany	6	Turkmenskaya Iskra	6	Türkmenistan Kommunisti	12	Ashkhabad	12
Yash Kommunist	3			Syyasy Sökhbetdesh	12	Zdravookhranenie Turkmenistana	6
Édebiyat ve Sungat	1	Komsomolets Turkmenistana	1	Sovet Édebiyaty	12	Pioner	12
Mugallymlar Gazeti	3	Vechernii Ashkhabad	5	Yashlyk	12	Russkii Yazyki Literatura v Turkmenskoi Shkole	6
Mydam Taÿyar	1	Reklamnyi Vestnik	1	Körpe	12		
Ashgabat Agshamy	5			Türkmenistan Khalk Magaryfy	12		
				Tokmak	12		
				Ovadan	12		
				Saglyk	12		

Source: TI 31 Aug. 1990:1. In January 1991, a bi-weekly started publication in Uzbek, named *Dŭstlik Bairoghi* (The Flag of Friendship), acc. to *TI* 7 Feb. 1991. The name of *Turkmenskaya Iskra* was changed into *Neitral'nyi Turkmenistan* in December 1995. *Izvestiya* was one of the few foreign Russian newspapers sold in Ashgabat in the 1990s. Cf. note below table 5.1.

The results of the 1995 census in Turkmenistan give us some interesting data about those who claimed to speak Turkmen and Russian freely (these two and Uzbek are the main languages of the population). About 3,400,000 Turkmens and 132,000 members of other ethnic groups named Turkmen as their native language, along with another 200,000 people, approximately, of other nationalities who claimed to speak it freely. Some 297,800 Russians and 51,000 non-Russians gave Russian as their native language, along with another 965,700 of other nationalities who claimed to speak Russian freely. If one adds up these figures, the total of those claiming to speak Turkmen freely was 3,732,000 and Russian 1,214,500 (based on *Brief Results of the 1995 National Population Census of Turkmenistan,* Ashgabat: 1997, 12; details in Robertson 1998:437): these are high ratios, indeed (interview with Dr Juma Durdy Bairamov, President, Union of Economists of Turkmenistan, Ashgabat, 22 Sep. 1998). These data, namely that some 3,732,000 people in Turkmenistan, or 83.2% of the total population, knew Turkmen, did not satisfy the partisans of this language.

Turkmenistan's declaration of independence in 1991 emphasized the need for a revival of Turkmen culture, traditions, and language – the state language. The discourse about multilingualism in Turkmenistan has referred mostly to bilingualism (and, later, to trilingualism), and was somewhat less central in public opinion than among some of the other five new states. One reason was the much lower ratio of Russians, certainly smaller than in Kazakhstan and Kyrgyzstan. A second was the officially declared 'policy of neutrality' promoted by President Niyazov (Turkmenbashy), which was reflected in language policy as well. An instance of this was the strong emphasis on the introduction of English into the educational system. A third might have been the stress laid by the leadership on economic issues and internal stability rather than on language questions.

On 21 May 1991, a Presidential decree announced, in the First Conference of the Turkmen World, the establishment of a Humanitarian Association of the Turkmen World (text in *TI* 2 Sep. 1991). Among its goals were 'the preservation of the Turkmen language, literature, art, culture, national traditions, customs and rites, setting up cultural centres... and printing its own publications in the Arabic, Latin and Russian scripts' (para. 2). One year later, the secretary-coordinator of the association reported (*TI* 18 May 1992) that permanent committees appointed for this purpose had recommended a revival of the Turkmen language, literature and folklore both in Turkmenistan and elsewhere. The association continued its activities for several years (*NT* 12 Mar. 1998). So did poets, like Annaberdy Agabaev, who did not hesitate to declare that bilingualism, if it meant two state languages, was absurd (*TI* 28 Apr. 1994). Promoting Turkmen culture is also the main aim of the

Turkmenbashy National Institute of Manuscripts in Ashgabat (*NT* 24 Oct. 1998) and some dedicated intellectuals (Durdyev 1996).

The final decision-maker since independence has been President Niyazov, who also heads the Supreme Council for Science and Technology, which discusses and decides many issues of language planning and education (interview with Nowruz Kurbanmuradov, Deputy Minister of Education, Ashgabat, 22 Sep. 1998). The President has repeatedly declared that what Turkmenistan needs is a spiritual and intellectual revival to ensure its independence and flowering (*NT* 16 Nov. 1998). This implied not merely the inauguration of a new national museum in Ashgabat, but also, naturally, the development of the Turkmen culture and language. Already on 15 March 1993 Niyazov issued a decree setting up a governmental commission to study the Turkmen people's history and arrive at an 'objective appraisal' of it. To demonstrate the importance he attached to this commission, the President appointed himself chairman, conferred in October of the same year with experts in history, initiated exploratory expeditions and, in October 1998, convoked an international symposium on Turkmen history (*NT* 6 Nov. 1998).

On 28 June 1999, the Turkmen parliament discussed the project of 'the inspiration doctrine' *Milli galkynysh* (National Revival), which is designed to rehabilitate and strengthen high values and traditions (*Extracts* 2 June 1999. Available: http://www.soros.org/turkstan/omri/0138.html. 7 July 1999). This, however, does not preclude the preservation of a special attachment to the Slavonic cultural heritage, e.g. as shown by a week of Ukrainian culture in 1999 (*NT* 15 Mar. 1999) or the celebration of Pushkin's 200th birthday, an occasion for the media to present the Russian poet as a symbol of world culture in one line with Turkmen poets (*Ashgabat* 16 Mar. 1999, 3 June 1999; *NT* 28 and 29 Apr. 1999). Other cultural weeks concerned countries like Iran, India, Pakistan, Germany, and France.

Niyazov dealt with this, as with several other issues, out of his persistent emphasis on neutrality on all counts (such as permitting the translation of the Koran into Turkmen – *TI* 24 Aug. 1995). In language this also meant promoting the status of English which, in a low-key campaign, has been gradually taking over some of the special functions of Russian and is being increasingly studied and used, with the President's encouragement. Niyazov has been quoted as saying that 'a man who knows three languages is worth three men'. Examples of this policy, out of many, are regular television broadcasts, mostly in Turkmen, but also in English and Russian. The latter got seven to ten hours a week broadcast by a Russian company, and 52 hours a week, or 28% of the total broadcast by the national television (Dugarev 1998:174). Local films on life in Turkmenistan are also presented occasionally in all three languages. Turkish cultural influence was introduced by the opening of a TRT (Turkish State Radio and Television) office in Ashgabat on 6 July 1999, the first of its kind in Central Asia (*Extracts* 8 July 1999. Available: http://www.soros.org/turkstan/omri/ 0142.html. 14 July 1999).

Tajikistan

Where language politics are concerned, Tajikistan is in a special situation. It has particular cultural relations with Iran, it has suffered from a recent civil war, a military contingent of foreign forces (chiefly Russian) has been guarding its border with Afghanistan, and a large Uzbek minority is involved in public affairs.

A lively debate was carried on in Tajikistan both before independence and afterwards, despite economic troubles, about the status of the various languages and whether monolingualism, bilingualism or multilingualism should be preferred. While the bill of the Law on Language was being publicly discussed, the President of the Tajik State University and several professors supported 'bilingualism as the norm of our life' (*KT* 22 Feb. 1989; a rejoinder, in favour of Tajik first, 26 Feb. 1989). On 24 February 1989, a demonstration of about 3,000 students of higher education was held in Dushanbe to demand the status of state language for Tajik. It seemed that a grassroots language movement was pressing for the revival and upgrading of Tajik (Perry 1996:573). After the language law had been adopted, there was a further wave of support for Tajik. Time and again, arguments were presented by Tajik nationalists to the effect that Soviet rule had deprived them of much of their cultural heritage.

A representative official view of language policies in the republic was presented by no less than K.M. Makhkamov, then First Secretary of the Central Committee of the Tajikistan Communist Party, in December 1989, in a widely published report (*KT* 8 Dec. 1989). As was to be expected from a person of his standing in the Communist Party of a Tajikistan which was still part of the Soviet Union, Makhkamov adopted a cautious attitude. On the one hand, he bluntly accused Russian of ousting and supplanting Tajik, but, on the other hand, he blamed this on the victims – the Tajiks themselves who had not taken the trouble to enlarge the number of readers in the mother tongue and the quality of their fluency. According to him, one of the objectives of *perestroika* was the equality of languages. Consequently, in the spirit of the time, he supported the promotion of Tajik in many respects, but continued to favour the officially promoted Tajik-Russian bilingualism. He also reminded his listeners that the new language law required that all street and shop signs, the names of official institutions, labels of goods and so on should be made out in both languages, Tajik and Russian.

The multilingual aspect was not totally submerged in public discourse and government decisions, but was repeated rather as lip service (e.g., *KT* 6 June 1989) and mostly thrust into a secondary position by the focus on the monolingual/bilingual issue; after all, most other *ethnies* in Tajikistan – the Uzbeks excepted – are not very important in numbers. Even when the issue of other languages and their public role was mentioned, it was duly relegated to limbo, as in an editorial in *Kommunist Tadzhikistana* (26 Apr. 1989) where the writer, having mentioned multilingualism, quickly returned to discuss Tajik-Russian bilingualism as his main topic. The public discourse reflected considerable support for Tajik; however, one finds people supporting Russian as an important element of social cohesion (*KT* 18 July 1990) and as a valuable element of Tajikistan's culture (*KT* 27 Aug. 1990).

Certain activities as well as speeches and writings were intended to promote Tajik into a position of primacy, especially after the language law had been passed in July 1989. One such instance was the initiative of the poet Zafar Nozimov to set up a public bank account, in April 1989, for a Foundation of the Tajik Language, intended to solve issues connected with its becoming fully the state language (*KT* 26 Apr., 1 Nov. 1989). Private and institutional efforts joined governmental ones to promote Tajik in education and elsewhere.

A special commission under the chairmanship of then Deputy Prime Minister Kh.M. Saidmurodov was appointed in April 1991 to supervise the implementation of the 1989 'Measures for Carrying Out the Law on Language' (*KT* 2 May 1991). It does not seem however to have been very effective, and a Terminological Committee was set up at the Tajikistan Academy of Sciences to complement it.

Aware of the material and financial difficulties in fully implementing the language law, Tajikistan authorities nonetheless took some first steps: courses were initiated and circles set up to learn both Tajik and the Arabic script; the Ministry of Education inaugurated new courses for simultaneous translation; the Ministry of Communications has been accepting telegrams in Tajik readily; Russian speakers would get a bonus for fulfilling their duties in Tajik in the civil service; study hours in Tajik were added in the fourth, fifth, ninth and tenth grades; new curricula, textbooks, dictionaries and conversation manuals were being prepared in Arabic-script Tajik; various newspapers were devoting several columns to the study of Tajik (*KT* 4 Mar. 1990).

Since independence, Iranian influence made itself felt in some areas of state activity. As a response to Turkey's manifest interest in the Turkic states in the Caucasus and Central Asia – addressed also at Tajikistan, which however responded lukewarmly – Iran attempted to increase its own cultural clout in Tajikistan, for instance by setting up, on 19 February 1992, the Association of Persian Languages, together with Tajikistan and Afghanistan (Rashid 1994:213).

The number of Russians in Tajikistan was relatively small and, due to emigration, reportedly dwindled from 388,000 in 1989 to about 60,000-

80,000 in 1996 (Kuz'min 1998:220). The Russian language still called for some respect in government and other circles, despite their inclination to support Tajik as the state language. There was however more discussion than implementation in independent Tajikistan, because of the war and civil unrest. President Rakhmonov had to tread gingerly in his language policies, given the continuing Russian military presence in Tajikistan. In November 1994, he declared that all languages would be used, with Russian being studied at school as the language of communication (*NaG* 19 Nov. 1994).

A few weeks earlier, Rakhmonov's election manifesto for the presidential election did not hesitate to appeal to 'our relations with the countries which share a common language, history and culture with us – Afghanistan and Iran' (*NaG* 19 Oct. 1994). Since Rakhmonov might have felt himself rather isolated in a Turkic environment, he emphasized his own state's relations, in language, at least, with Iran and with the Tajiks in Afghanistan. Rakhmonov's rival, 1994 presidential candidate Abdumalik Abdulladzhanov, argued that Tajikistan's future lay in its ethnic diversity and, in his own election platform, called for granting official status to the Russian and Uzbek languages, along with Tajik (*RG* 19 Oct. 1994). Not unexpectedly, the town of Khojand and its region, heavily inhabited by Uzbeks, gave him strong electoral support. The Iranian connection, as will be described below (ch. 9), has mostly remained a keystone in official Tajikistan cultural policies, chiefly in the supply of language textbooks and similar materials (Mesbahi 1997:144-5) – even if Iran exhibits a certain political coolness towards Rakhmonov and his government.

Following his 1994 election as President, Rakhmonov could devote part of his attention to language issues, particularly as the civil strife was mostly reduced to sporadic occurrences. Only on 31 October 1995 did the government appoint a five-member commission to implement the 1989 Law on Language, which began its work, headed by then Deputy Prime Minister Bashgul Dodkhudoeva. Checks during 1996 and 1997 showed that only 5%-10% of government offices and public organizations were following the prescriptions of the law. In Dushanbe itself, only three Ministries – of Culture, Justice, and Agriculture – were at least trying to supervise the use of the state language. It became clear that the year 2000 deadline for the transfer of all official documents into Tajik would have to be postponed. The main reasons given were financial constraints, lack of modern terminology and the non-availability of typewriters in Tajik (*Tajikistan Economic Review* 52: July 1998, 1-4). In May 1997, we find Rakhmonov admitting that, the Law on Language notwithstanding, government ministries and other departments were not yet employing the state language in their correspondence and other documents (*NaG* 30 May - 5 June 1997).

Meanwhile, the Dodkhudoeva Commission, appointed on 31 October 1995, continued its meetings. Its final report was approved by the government on 21 October 1997 (text in *Omūzgor* 6 Nov. 1997). Entitled 'Programme of the Government of Tajikistan for the Development of the State Language and Other Languages in the State Territory of the Republic of Tajikistan', it comprised two main sections, discussing Tajik and other languages, respectively. As for Tajik, measures were devised to turn it into the state language in all domains of political, cultural and social life – with an emphasis on government offices, business, and education. Courses were to be initiated for learning Tajik and its Arabic-based alphabet. Tajik should be employed in all government offices and in business, in all official documents, with translation in areas where a majority used other languages, from 1 January 1998. Tajik books and newspapers would be sent to Tajiks abroad. Both Tajik and Russian would be used in telegrammes, however; while papers should be written in Tajik in the universities and dissertations defended in it, the records of the defence would be in Russian and dispatched to Moscow. Tajik should be studied in all schools where another language of instruction was employed and a final examination in Tajik required. The Arabic script should be taught in secondary school and university. Broadcasts and films in Tajik should be improved and used for education, too. As for other languages, it recommended the creation of favourable conditions for the use of Russian as the means of communication among the CIS states, as the language of instruction in Russian schools and as a language studied in all others, with a slot allotted to it in the radio and television. Uzbek, Kyrgyz, Pamiri and Yaghnobi languages, too, should get special conditions in education in their areas of concentration (Uzbek in broadcasts as well). Exact dates are spelled out for these measures to be fulfilled by the respective ministries, the Academy of Sciences and the regional and local administrative bodies.

The programme was followed up by a Presidential decree ordering the use of Tajik in all the public services as of 1 January 1998, which worried the Russian community in Tajikistan (*SK* 5 Mar. 1998). The decree, however, does not seem to have been strictly enforced. The languages of the smaller nationalities seem to have remained on the agenda as well, since on 18 February 1998 the government published yet another decree, 'The Concept of Ethnocultural Education in Tajikistan', emphasizing the significance of knowing one's native language for ethnocultural education (*NaG* 20 Mar. 1998). It is not currently known how strictly the decrees are enforced, but it seems that Russian is still largely employed in government business.

Newspapers are published mostly in Tajik and Russian, although the lack of paper hampers their circulation (Perry 1996:573). Most newspapers reasonably sure to appear regularly were in Russian (Tadjbakhsh

1996:339). Recent ones in Tajik have been *Jumhuriyat* (Republic), *Sadoi Mardum* (Voice of the People), and *Istiqlal* (Independence); in Russian – *Narodnaya Gazeta* (People's Newspaper), *Vechernie Vesti* (Evening News), and *Kur'er Tadzhikistana* (Courier of Tajikistan).

Tajikistan's leaders could not ignore for long their substantial Uzbek minority – the largest one in the republic, with about 24.8% of the entire population in 1996. Thus Uzbek, without becoming a state or an official language in Tajikistan, does have a special standing which is expressed to some degree in this country's cultural relations with Uzbekistan (with its own substantial Tajik minority). The special standing of Uzbek is also shown by the fact that the 1994 constitution was officially published in Tajik, Uzbek and Russian.

Already in the late 1980s, several Uzbek literary works had been translated into Tajik; programmes in Uzbek were broadcast on Tajikistan television and radio; and the authorities encouraged newspapers to appear in Uzbek (*PV* 26 Feb. 1989). Uzbek was chosen, along with Tajik and Russian, to be employed in the sessions of the permanent commissions of the presidium of this Soviet republic, being one of the three languages in which the debates were subsequently published. In return, Uzbekistan encouraged several Tajik-language newspapers to appear (*KT* 14 June 1988). There were also exchanges of schoolbooks between the two republics, before and after independence (p. 203). However, these relations changed somewhat over time and, in independent Tajikistan, many Uzbeks became very much involved in the civil war. This war and subsequent civil strife in Tajikistan seem to have rather adversely affected cultural activities, including those relating to language. The Tajik government assumed control of the Uzbek-language newspaper *Khalq Ovozi* (Voice of the People) in January 1999 in order to ensure its 'appropriate coverage of questions of the state's domestic and foreign policies' (*NG* 13 Jan. 1999, quoted in *CAM* 1999, no. 1:37). Significantly, while the chances of Tajik-Russian rivalry over language are minimal – due to the small proportion of Russians in the population – the possibility of Tajik-Uzbek conflict looms larger and may be linked, at some future date, to the same issue in Uzbekistan.

Summing up, one finds similarities in many of the declaratory statements regarding the importance of fostering multilingualism within each of the multiethnic six states, but also a readiness to continue the daily practice of bilingualism inherited from the Soviet Union. A significant change may be perceived, however, in the dominance of language since independence. While Russian was hegemonic in the Soviet Union, titular languages in the newly independent states now strive to assume this position for themselves. There are differences, however, in the attitudes of the states with small Russian minorities and those with large ones. Therefore, the leadership in Azerbayjan, Uzbekistan, Turkmenistan and Tajikistan seems more prepared to move toward a sort of monolingualism of the state language than the leadership in Kazakhstan and Kyrgyzstan. Ultimately, it is less in legal or constitutional documents, important though they are, than in their implementation, chiefly in daily use and education, that language policies of monolingualism, bilingualism or multilingualism in the six states are put to the test. However, an examination of the main legal documents concerned is also essential in evaluating the implementation of language policies and, indeed, the language policies themselves.

6

LANGUAGE LAWS AND DECREES

In the last years of the Soviet Union, language laws assumed great importance; later, other issues loomed larger in the changed situation. In both the Soviet Union and its successor states, legislators have generally understood to what extent it is possible to change language behaviour via constitutions, laws and regulations. However, before the 1980s, neither the Soviet Union nor its component republics had any comprehensive language laws, except for paragraphs in the constitutions of the republics or in laws on education and in certain decrees. This was, also, a policy of sorts, one in which 'small' languages were displaced by 'big' ones, here Russian (Pigolkin and Studenikina 1991:38). Nonetheless, legislators in the last years of the Soviet Union and in the newly independent states have grasped how important the formulation of each such law could be; this applies, evidently, also to regulations, decrees and the like, which have legal force. One should not assume, of course, that words mean the same in differing cultures and environments. Hence one should tread warily when exploring and comparing Soviet and post-Soviet language laws. While the real importance of these laws (and many others) lies in their practical application, their very existence and phrasing since the late 1980s gives us some background on their impact on daily life, on both the individual and the general level.

Some definitions of politico-legal terms should be mentioned. Two terms – which have been coined by UNESCO – continue to be employed as formerly in Soviet parlance. A 'state language' works for integration in all domains and is the symbol of a given state, while an 'official' one is that used for government, administration, legislation, and the courts (Neroznak 1995:6-11). The republics, when they had turned into independent states, focused on de-sovietization and de-russification, and continued to apply these terms, though not always in quite the same sense.

Warmly supported by some nationalist circles as determining national identity, the laws were decried by others as a threat to minority groups (Eckert 1996:43). While in late 1988 and early 1989 nationalists insisted, in the press and at public meetings, on the titular language becoming the state language, the Communist bureaucracy and non-titular residents responded that both the titular language and Russian ought to have this status (*Central Asia and Caucasus Chronicle* 8(3):July 1989, 11-12). In particular, Russians and Ukrainians opposed the entire concept of the titular language becoming the privileged state language (e.g. *Sowjetisches Usbekistan* 1990, no. 4: 12). In essence, the 1989-90 language laws and those which followed initiated several changes, some of them of revolutionary character, a watershed between linguistic russification by command and a policy of self-assertion by the titular languages (Huskey 1995:549). Much of this applied to language status, which was not merely a juridical but a political, social, economic, demographic, and of course a cultural issue. The new laws elevated the status of the titular language above Russian. Thus, the titular language was meant to foster the development of a national culture and the creation of a national identity (Guboglo 1994:5f., 33). Since the main goal of the laws was to raise the status of the language in each titular group, they addressed themselves primarily to language function more than to structure (expanding vocabulary, grammar and orthography). Predictably, the results of language legislation in the six republics could not satisfy every language group; there is no state-language solution acceptable to one and all in multilingual societies. The new laws and decrees required all government employees to learn the titular language. The legislation was perceived as a real threat by many among the millions of Russians living outside the RFSFR, as well as by some members of the non-titular *ethnies*, who began to feel themselves outsiders.

The language laws were prepared and adopted (as was done in post-1947 India and some other new states) without any serious investigation of language competence and usage in each republic's population, nor was there any sociolinguistic or politicolinguistic consideration of the expected results. Rather, the laws mostly reflected *political* decisions from above, accommodating the demands of intellectual circles guided chiefly by what they perceived as nationalist goals. Passed in the Muslim republics (and in others) as signs of self-assertion, they were adopted during *perestroika* and *glasnost'*, shortly before the Soviet Union's dismemberment. In the five Central Asian republics they were put through within a brief span of ten months. The fact that Soviet rule was only slightly less pervasive than before and that the Communist parties were still in control explains the relatively moderate tenor of these laws, prepared, approved (with some changes), and published by the Central Committees of the Party, which however could not but consider the passionate demonstrations supporting the laws or, in some cases, opposing them (Carlson 1994:150).

In all six republics, there were acrimonious debates (which the regime tried to keep under control), often in the daily and weekly press as well as radio and television, in which local intellectuals attacked various paragraphs, some supporting the titular language or Russian as the proposed state language, others demanding enforcement measures in the wording and the setting of definitive timetables for implementation of the titular language in its new central role (e.g., for Kazakhstan, *KP* 26 and 31 Aug. 1989; Tazhutov 1991), or even boldly attacking bilingualism (Critchlow

1991:101-6). In several states, such as Tajikistan, small ethnic groups (non-titular and non-Slav) attacked the drafts of the law as discriminating against their own languages. But the main support in the public debate on the controversial drafts of the laws was for the titular language to become the state language. This had a strong influence on the final decisions.

The laws were passed as follows, in chronological sequence (Maurais 1992:1; Pigolkin and Studenikina 1991:39). Except for the first, all are language laws.

- Azerbayjan, the constitution of 21 April 1978 and a decree published in August 1989 (texts in *BR* 23 Apr. 1978; 19 Aug. 1989).
- Tajikistan, 22 July 1989 (text in *KT* 30 July 1989).
- Kazakhstan, 22 September 1989 (text in *KP* 28 Sep. 1989).
- Kyrgyzstan, 23 September 1989 (text in *SoK* 29 Sep. 1989; *Nationalities Papers* 23(3): Sep. 1995, 631-7).
- Uzbekistan, 21 October 1989 (text in *PV* 24 Oct. 1989; *Nationalities Papers* 23(3): Sep. 1995, 638-643).
- Turkmenistan, 24 May 1990 (text in *TI* 27 May 1990).

Because these laws are relevant for understanding and evaluating later language laws and decrees in the independent states, they should be discussed in some detail separately as well as on a comparative basis (see also Maurais 1991; Guboglo 1994; Malek 1994; Marchenko 1994:141f.) Since the laws were drafted by the respective Central Committees of the Communist Party and put into effect by the Council of Ministers, they had much in common, though with some significant variations. They all discuss, to different degrees, the norms of language use in public office and education (Maurais 1991); none of them, however, attempt to regulate the employment of language in interpersonal relations. All of them contain first general statements and then articles on: a. the rights of the citizen in the selection of language; b. the language of the state organs and public institutions and enterprises; c. language in cultural life, education and science; d. the language of information; e. the protection of language (Pigolkin and Studenikina 1991:42). Most of the texts are drafted in the same order and, indeed, use the same turns of phrase for the same matter, indicating that they were strongly influenced by Moscow.

Each of the six republics was very keen on promoting its titular language as the state language (without however defining this term precisely), with an important role often reserved for Russian as the official language of inter-ethnic communication. There are rather brief mentions of other minority languages, considered of less importance than the titular one.

Looking at similar and dissimilar features, the following stands out. The titles of the laws are not identical. After some changes in the drafts, the Turkmenistan and Tajikistan laws were simply called 'Law on

Language' but the Uzbekistan and Kyrgyzstan laws 'Law on the State Language', thus emphasizing the fact that the titular language had become the state one; while Kazakhstan's was entitled 'Law on Languages', due to the strong standing of both Kazakh and Russian. The headlines had political implications; for example, the first draft of the language law in Uzbekistan was entitled 'Law on Languages', when public outcry brought about the change to 'State Language' instead of 'Languages'. All the laws proclaim the titular language to be the state language, but the organizational details for implementation vary and – as can be said at the end of the decade – are often inadequate and unrealistic in the deadlines set. The laws all start with a sort of preamble. In four of them, this states the main objects of the law – to determine the legal status of the titular language as the state language and regulate its use, emphasizing the equality of all citizens. In the case of Turkmenistan, the preamble is more declaratory. Perhaps because it was drafted later than the others and was meant 'to go one better', it used a more rhetorical style: 'Language is one of the distinguishing characteristics of the national identity of peoples, an inalienable sign of nations; Turkmen, the language of the indigenous population and of the overwhelming majority of Soviet Turkmenistan's citizens, is one of the oldest Turkic languages, in which written monuments of important cultural value were created' (our translation).

Although ambiguities remain, the laws cannot be considered as aiming at monolingualism, but rather at bilingualism or even multilingualism (Maurais 1992:2-9). After having formally declared its titular language as the state language, each of the six republics not only designated Russian, in one way or another, as the language of communication with other republics and communities in the Soviet Union, but allocated it an important place, parallel and almost equivalent to the state language, within the republic. Nevertheless, since the laws raised the status of the respective titular languages, *ipso facto* they heralded a certain downgrading of Russian (Mechkovskaya 1992:89-91). This could not be phrased otherwise in republics which were still part of the Soviet Union, where Russian was in practice the common language. All the laws mentioned the promotion of the state language by research into its old strata and publication of its literary legacy; compilation and printing of dictionaries and textbooks for all levels of schooling; and preparation of films and cassettes to facilitate its spread. The state language was considered the language of instruction, to be studied also in schools teaching in a non-state lan-guage. School examinations in the state language were to be mandatory.

It is obvious that the legislators gave more attention to language status than to language corpus. The laws determined the switch to the state language in government and public administration, as well as in justice, public health, culture and education, commerce, transport, communications, social security and the like. Statistics were to be compiled and published, and documentation prepared in the state language, including those drawn up by notaries and arbitrators. Conventions, meetings and lectures in the state sector, also, were to be held in the state language; the same for scientific reports and dissertations, while all official texts would be issued in both the state language and Russian. Indeed, Russian was seen as an acceptable alternative in almost all cases and, in some republics, minority languages as well were so considered. Provision was made for other languages (in addition to the titular language and Russian) and their use in education and elsewhere. Translations were to be provided for all the above, when needed, 'to promote equal language rights for all citizens'; thus, no discrimination on account of language would be permitted. Communications (posts and telegraphs) within each republic should be in the state language or Russian, with other parts of the Soviet Union in Russian, while international communications would be in the language most suitable for the parties concerned. Commercial labels, instructions on merchandise, and advertisements should be in the state language, with Russian or other translations supplied. Names of regions, towns, villages, settlements, streets, squares and the like would be in the state language, with translation into Russian and, whenever needed, into other languages in areas inhabited by other *ethnies* in sizable numbers. Citizens were free to choose their names and family names, but the current orthography of the national literary languages was to be followed.

Most of the above applied to state institutions and, in some measure, to public bodies. The military was excepted; so was language use among private persons and in religious rites – a somewhat unusual instance of the Soviet Union's non-intervention in religious affairs.

Short instructions for implementation, which was intended to be comprehensive, were annexed to the language laws. A timetable for implementation was set in the majority of instructions: in Kyrgyzstan and Turkmenistan, for instance, the switch to the state language was to be completed by 1999, in Uzbekistan by 1997. Whilst caution was understandable under former Soviet rule, language reform went on slowly, in some of the six republics, after independence as well; new language laws and regulations were passed to suit the changed situation (see below, pp. 114-23), implementation remaining the main stumbling block (Tumanyan 1994:73ff.).

Despite the noticeable uniformity between the language laws and decrees of 1989-90, certain further nuances are worth mentioning. Most laws allow some leeway for employing more than one language in officialdom and correspondence. Those who prepared the law in Turkmenistan recommended the study of Turkmen and the Arabic script. In Kazakhstan, the legislators displayed special concern for developing bilingualism and multilingualism in their republic, and in Uzbekistan the law strongly forbade hostile treatment of any language. In Tajikistan, the law was even more explicit about minority languages and mentioned specifically, side by side with Tajik, also Russian, Uzbek, Kyrgyz and Turkmen as languages having juridical status. In Uzbekistan, again, the law specified that the Karakalpak Autonomous Republic would decide for itself the functioning of this law within its borders.

After independence in all six states, the leaders accorded language its due importance; in Turkmenistan and Tajikistan, the days when the language laws were adopted became public holidays. Language policies were expressed in constitutions and in subsequent legislation, such as laws on implementing language policies or modifying the Law on the State Language. Before the new constitutions were adopted, a strongly worded debate went on, much of it on the language issue. The discussion repeated some arguments discussed in connection with the previous language laws and added others in a fiercer tone, suited to independent polities. As formerly, the focus of the debate was on the status to be accorded to Russian, with arguments becoming more extreme (details in Anderson 1997:307-10). No wonder that there are significant variations in the constitutions adopted. Although all proclaimed equality of rights for all their citizens, irrespective of language, they treated the issues of language, minority rights and citizenship somewhat differently (texts of the constitutions in Bagdasaryan 1997).

Azerbayjan

In Azerbayjan's 1978 constitution, Azeri had been reaffirmed the official language. The August 1989 language decree, based on the 1978 constitution and entitled 'Resolution on Ways to Guarantee a More Active Functioning of Azeri as the State Language' (text in *BR* 19 Aug. 1989) was in some ways more explicit than the language laws of the five other republics, reflecting, perhaps, the general mood of language nationalism, already discussed above. This decree underlined that Azeri was a rich literary and artistic language, attuned to contemporary science and technology – but still not adequately employed in many spheres. It laid down a more active role for Azeri and, towards that aim, called for the coining of terms in the contemporary domains of science and technology, while observing its norms and needs and preserving its nuances to create neologisms and introduce foreign words. The decree also recommended organizing language courses in Azeri and Russian in clubs and groups, along with lectures and competitions. It was even suggested that improved typewriters be introduced for the use of the Azeri alphabet and to learn the Latin alphabet in order to read Azeri works published in it. The declaration of sovereignty on 23 September 1989 (which preceded the declaration of independence) reaffirmed that Azeri was the state language, while guaranteeing the free use of Russian and all other languages employed by the population (text in *Pravda* 6 Oct. 1989).

In independent Azerbayjan, a presidential decree was issued on 16 September 1992 (text in *BR* 19 Sep. 1992), listing measures to encourage the development of the language and culture of national minorities in the state. On 22 December 1992 a Law on the State Language, chiefly reaffirming the status of Azeri, was passed by parliament (*Azärbaïjan Respublikasy Ali Sovetinin Mä'lumaty* 1992, no. 24: 31 Dec.). In a clearly patriotic vein, it insisted that Azeri ought to be employed in all spheres of politics, economics, society, scientific and cultural life, and should be taught to all other nationalities in Azerbayjan – while repeating the text of the 1989 language decree, guaranteeing any other compact group the right to get instruction in its own language. Russian lost its privileged status and became a means of international communication – on a par with English, French and German. In short, while attempting to exhibit liberal pluralism towards other *ethnies,* this law insisted on the primacy of Azeri. This was summarily repeated in Article 21 of the new constitution, adopted by referendum on 12 November 1995 (English translation in FBIS-SOV-95-232-S, 4 Dec. 1995:44-8; Russian text in *BR* 5 Dec. 1995), in which the essence of the 1978 Constitution, the 1989 language decree, and the 1992 language law was summed up, namely that Azeri was the state language, that the state would see to its development, while guaranteeing the use and development of other languages spoken in the republic. No specific reference was made to Russian. The new constitution also stated that everyone had the right to employ one's native language, be educated and display one's creativity in it according to one's wishes.

Uzbekistan

Uzbekistan's Law on the State Language (1989) had been supported by some (Ginzburg 1994-5: I, 280) and bitterly attacked by others in public meetings for having allowed a special standing to Russian (Critchlow 1991:104-6). No alternative existed in the Soviet era, but matters changed after independence. The new constitution, adopted on 8 December 1992 (text in *PV* 15 Dec. 1992; translation in Blaustein 1994-6, release 94-5:July 1994), emphasized that the state language was Uzbek, enjoining a respectful attitude towards it and other languages, without specifically referring to Russian or to the languages of the minorities, not even to the significant Tajik one. While some leeway in language use was left to the lower courts, the Law on the Constitutional Court of the Republic of Uzbekistan determined in May 1993 that Uzbek should be the language of this court (*Tashkentskaya Pravda* 15 May 1993; English translation in Black 1995: II, 241).

On 21 December 1995, parliament adopted a revised version of the Law on the State Language, along with an appendix regulating its coming into force immediately, but deferring the complete switch to the state language in state organs, administration and economy 'until the complete conversion of the alphabet into Latin characters on 1 September 2005' (text in *PV* 29 Dec. 1995). Unlike the 1989 Law on the State Language, the revised version was neither published nor offered for public debate before its adoption by parliament. There was no specific mention of Russian, except that it could be used for notarial purposes. In all other matters, it was treated like any other language except Uzbek (Schlyter 1997:27-9). In regard to Russian, indeed, the 1989 and 1995 Laws on the State Language differ. The former guaranteed the free use of Russian as a language of inter-ethnic communication; the latter did not. The former provided that dissertations could be defended in Russian; the latter had no such provision. The former stated that texts of seals and stamps were to have Russian copies; the latter mentioned only the state language. However, the new law did not insist (as the previous one did) on a sufficient knowledge of the state language for public service jobs (Smith a.o. 1998:200-3), and allowed the use of Uzbek and other languages on radio and television and in postal-telegraphic messages.

On 10 September 1996, in support of the revised Law on the State Language, the Council of Ministers issued a decree, entitled 'The State Programme on the Implementation of the Law of the Republic of Uzbekistan on the State Language'. Its main provisions were: to explain to the population the Law on the State Language; to celebrate the Day of the Uzbek Language annually; to set up programmes for teaching Uzbek with the aid of computers; to introduce automatic translation systems of foreign scientific-technical texts into Uzbek; to expand the study of Uzbek in all schools; to expand the training of teachers of Uzbek for higher education; to organize no-cost study of Uzbek for all Uzbek citizens not yet familiar with the language; and to organize conferences and competitions on learning Uzbek. It is interesting to note that President Karimov has made public statements of varying character. He has had more urgent issues to cope with and, in his book *Uzbekistan on the Threshold of the 21st Century* (1998), his only reference to language was that Uzbekistan's people are multilingual.

Kazakhstan

In June 1990, less than a year after it adopted the language law, the Kazakhstan Council of Ministers issued the 'Government Programme for Developing Kazakh and Other National Languages in Soviet Kazakhstan Until the Year 2000' (text in *KP* 1 July 1990; addenda, ibid. 29 Sep. 1990). However, little was done subsequently for the instruction of civil servants in Kazakh (*Kazakhstan: Ekonomika i Zhizn'* 6:1992). Later, in the Declaration of Independence on 16 December 1991 (text in *KP* 18 Dec. 1991), the main intention was repeated – to develop Kazakh culture and language – and again, in the Law on Education of 18 January 1992 (text in *KP* 5 March 1992), where Kazakh was presented as the state language, to be studied and developed throughout the republic, while guaranteeing the learning of Russian. Prudently, in the Law on the Internal Military Forces of the Interior Ministry of 23 June 1992, both Kazakh and Russian were approved for issuing orders and for documentation. In the 1993 Constitution (text in *KP* 2 Feb. 1993), Kazakh was mentioned as the state language, and Russian as the language of inter-ethnic communication. A guarantee was given for the development of other languages, without any discrimination whatsoever. Kazakh was scheduled to be the language of the state administration as of 1995.

In 1994, a new law project was being discussed (but apparently not passed) by the Council of Ministers, entitled 'The Government Programme for the Development of the Kazakh Language', aiming at full implementation by the year 2000. The project's title notwithstanding, it was meant to encourage not only Kazakh, but also languages of minorities, which at the time were setting up Tatar, Azeri, Kurdish, Uyghur, Dungan and other cultural centres (*Zarya* 28 Sep. 1994). Despite Nazarbaev's request, the Kazakh parliament turned down, on 15 December 1994, a proposal to make both Kazakh and Russian official languages (FBIS-SOV-94-242:45). To soothe claims and counter-claims, in April 1995 President Nazarbaev floated the notion that the requirement for all state employees to speak Kazakh should be postponed for fifteen years.

Kazakhstan's new constitution, approved by a general referendum on 30 August 1995 and published soon afterwards, referred briefly to language (para. 14), declaring that nobody could be discriminated against on grounds of language. The new constitution (text in Blaustein 1994-6, release 96-1:Feb. 1996), Article 7, reads that '1. The state language of the Republic of Kazakhstan shall be the Kazakh language. 2. In state institutions and local self-administrative bodies the Russian language shall be officially employed on equal grounds along with the Kazakh language'. Thus, Russian was elevated from a 'language of inter-ethnic communication' to an 'official' one, equal in use to Kazakh in governmental and public bodies.

The article on language in the new constitution, however, has not allayed the apprehensions of the non-Kazakh inhabitants, nor has it satisfied the wish of Kazakh nationalists to have their language in a dominant position. Nationalist groups (whose slogan was 'no nation without a language') warned that the recognition of Russian as a second state language would pass a death sentence on Kazakh; Russian required no protection from Kazakh, rather the other way around (Dave 1996). Even after the proclamation of this constitution, debates continued, largely on the status of Russian versus Kazakh (Dokuchaeva 1995; Dave 1996a:55; Dave 1996b:219-24). More legislation was needed, apparently, and on 20 December 1995, Nazarbaev issued a presidential decree, saying that both Kazakh and Russian would be official languages in the courts, while in an area with a sizable minority, its own language would also be accepted. On 4 November 1996, yet another presidential decree was issued. Entitled 'Conception of Language Policies of the Republic of Kazakhstan' (*KP* 6 Nov. 1996; translated in Black 1997:II, 267-71), it set up priorities in the study of Kazakh and ways to promote its knowledge and use (while guaranteeing the use of Russian). Some of these views and pressures found expression in the new Law on Languages in the Republic of Kazakhstan of 11 July 1997 (*Qazaqstan Resp. Zangy. Zakon Resp. Kazakhstan. Qazaqstan Resp. Til Turaly. O Yazykakh v Resp. Kazakhstan*, Almaty: Zheti Zharghy 1998; also in *Mysl'* 1997, no. 9: 2-6).

The law was reportedly based on a study of language laws in twenty other states (*Zan Gazeti* 13 Aug. 1997). Its objectives were defined as setting the legal basis for the functioning of languages in Kazakhstan, and the government's responsibility for creating conditions for their study and development. Besides repeating the gist of earlier laws and decrees in this context and the constitution, it contained some additional features. It proclaimed that this law applied to Kazakhstan citizens as well as to stateless residents. It was the duty of every citizen to master Kazakh, the state language, the most important factor for the consolidation of the people of Kazakhstan; the government would take measures for the study of Kazakh, without cost, in Kazakhstan and in the diaspora.

However, the law also specified that both Kazakh and Russian ought to be used in governmental organizations, local government institutions, documentation of state and governmental bodies, constitutional documentation, arbitration courts, the military, education and academia (including defence of dissertations), names of state institutions, texts of seals and stamps regardless of the form of ownership, labels of goods, all texts of visual information, postal-telegraphic messages and customs documentation; and that other languages might be employed in 'localities of compact residence of ethnic groups'. In this manner, a commitment was expressed in the law for preserving and developing *all* languages in Kazakhstan. Virtual equality was institutionalized between the state and the official language; this was the only language law in the six states to put Russian on a par with the titular language in practice. True, the law also stated that in radio and television broadcasting, Kazakh ought to be used no less than all other languages taken together. The law was favourably received by spokesmen of the smaller *ethnies*, such as the Chechen, the Ingush and the Jews (*Oral Oniri* 16 Aug. 1997). Kazakh critics, then and later, complained that this and other laws (barring a few exceptions) had first been drafted in Russian and only later translated into Kazakh (*Syr Boyy* 10 Nov. 1998).

On 15 December 1997, Nazarbaev referred to this law, asserting that he favoured 'careful introduction' of Kazakh as a state language; that he wished everyone in the republic to continue studying both Kazakh and Russian – as well as English (*CAM* 1998, no. 1:35). An official commission was appointed accordingly, in February 1998, to prepare a new law, in two years, concerning the development of languages in Kazakhstan.

Only in August 1998 was a specific decree issued to have all documents processed in both Kazakh and Russian in all government agencies or committees, preparing all the necessary conditions and controls as well as publication of information, letterheads, rubber stamps and signboards – by 1 January 1999 (*KP* 10 Sep. 1998). The decree, named 'On Broadening the Sphere of Use of the State Language in State Organs', was hardly achievable by that date; what has been done, however, is to reorganize the government news agencies so that 50% of all materials are reportedly issued in Kazakh and the other 50% in Russian (some are translated into English as well) (*KP* 7 May 1998). Another decree ordered all government officials to learn Kazakh – or else leave their jobs. Since little progress was being made, apparently, Nazarbaev issued yet another decree, on 5 October 1998 (text in *KP* 2 Mar. 1999), setting a two-year limit on carrying out a new 'Government Programme for Implementing and Developing Languages'. The programme was more comprehensive than most earlier ones and more insistent on implementation. The discussion of its goals was divided along five lines: a. forming the normative legal basis; b. guaranteeing a scholarly linguistic approach; c. applying language in the spheres of information, science, culture and education; d. promoting the state language; e. undertaking terminological and onomastic research. Altynbek Sarsenbaev, Minister of Culture, Information and Social Consensus correctly evaluated this programme as resolving many problems, if implemented energetically (*KP* 2 Mar. 1999).

Kyrgyzstan

In Kyrgyzstan, the adoption of the 1989 Law on the State Language had been preceded by a lively public debate (Huskey 1995:555-7), in which representatives of the Slavs in Kyrgyzstan maintained that the law was divisive, costly, unethical and impracticable, while its supporters argued that it was a necessary corrective to an unjustified neglect of Kyrgyz linguistic and cultural development (e.g., in *Sovettik Kyrgyzstan* 24 Aug. 1988). The debate continued, at times acrimoniously, after the law's adoption and after a supplementary law had been passed, on 27 October 1989, on the measures of implementing the Law on the State Language of Soviet Kirgiziya.

The controversy was not lost on policymakers after independence. They realized that language was a symbol of statehood and nationhood, but were aware of the Russian stand on the matter, both in Kyrgyzstan and the Russian Federation. The 5 May 1993 Constitution (text in Blaustein 1994-6, release 94-5: July 1994) contained several articles spelling out citizens' rights to employ the language of their choice at work and in education. It also reaffirmed Kyrgyz as the state language and the functioning of Russian, 'the language of inter-ethnic communication', and of all the other languages used by the republic's population. However, reacting to Russian complaints, it was proposed in a project for the change of article 5 on language in the constitution (text in *SK* 13 Jan. 1995) to raise Russian to the position of official language because it was essential to the progress of the state's industry, technology, science and public health. However, only the Lower House of Parliament approved the changes in June 1996 (*NG* 1 July 1996). The matter was subsequently brought to the Constitutional Court by members of parliament, who asked whether this revision conformed to the 1993 constitution. The court replied, in early January 1997, that Russian could be designated in the constitution specifically as an official language, side by side with Kyrgyz as the state one (text in *Vechernii Bishkek* 8 Jan. 1997). A number of Kyrgyz members of parliament did not accept this ruling, maintaining that the 1996 parliamentary vote and the 1997 court ruling were contrary to the 1993 constitution, hence claiming that they were invalid. Upon Akaev's special request, the Lower House of Parliament voted in June 1997 again to change the Kyrgyz constitution. *Nasha Gazeta (*27 June 1997) celebrated the vote in the Lower House as a victory, claiming that Russian was hence virtually a second state language. Opponents argued that the voting had not been regularly passed and therefore illegal.

Finally, after years of dispute, the legislative assembly passed 'The Law on the Official Language of the Kyrgyz Republic' on 25 May 2000, according to which Russian is the official language of Kyrgyzstan and should be used at all levels of the administration, the legislature, the judiciary and other spheres of public life. Members of parliament expressed the hope that the law would help to decrease the emigration of the Russians (*Kyrgyz News* 25 May 2000. Online. Available: idinovn@rferl.org. 25 May 2000). There cannot be any doubt that the representatives of the Russian community would now like to see a corresponding amendment to the constitution.

To bolster the status of Kyrgyz, a new law on language was being considered in early January 1998 (TÜRKSAM 1999:90). A 21-member National Commission on the State Language was appointed, on 20 January 1998, to coordinate the enforcement of the use of Kyrgyz in government agencies and public organizations, to create special conditions for its study by the population at large, particularly the youth, and to support it in broadcasting and publication. The secretary of the National Commission, Almaz Toktomambetov, ended its work in early August 1999 and submitted to the government the draft of a new law on language. The draft enhanced the role of Kyrgyz as state language to be employed in all official documentation. After being discussed by the government, the draft law was to be sent to parliament (*Kyrgyz News* 4 Aug. 1999. Online. Available: idinovn@referl.org. 4 Aug. 1999). It seems that language legislation in Kyrgyzstan is gaining momentum.

Turkmenistan

Turkmenistan's government, also, took the language issue very seriously. The regulations on the status of the languages spoken in Turkmenistan are contained in the 1990 Law on Language, in a short article in the constitution and in the laws on alphabet change and education. Turkmenistan adopted a constitution on 18 May 1992 (text in *TI* 19 May 1992; English translation in Black 1994: II, 452-62 and Blaustein 1994-6, release 94-5: July 1994), which in sum repeated the paragraphs referring to language in the 1990 Law on Language and in the Declaration of Independence of 27 October 1991 (text in *TI* 29 Oct. 1991). The Law on Language had made Turkmen the state language. This was institutionalized in the constitution (Clark 1998:12), whose Article 13 was extremely laconic in the matter: 'The state language of Turkmenistan is Turkmen. All citizens are guaranteed the right to use their native language'. No mention was made of Russian. President Niyazov defended this on 19 May 1992 in a meeting of the Turkmen parliament, as follows: 'Rumours are being spread that the fact that a law is missing which defines the Russian language as a language of inter-ethnic communication might violate the rights of the Russian population [in Turkmenistan]. The same article was also missing in the previous [i.e. Soviet] constitution. We see no need to include such an article in the new constitution, because we have the Law on Language which states that Russian is a language of interethnic communication. Doubts in this regard are unfounded. Those who use these facts for veiled insinuations seem to forget that the constitution guarantees equal rights for Russians, Turkmens, Kazakhs, Uzbeks and people of other nationalities' (Nijasow 1994:44). In Turkmenistan, as in Kyrgyzstan, knowledge of the state language was perceived as mandatory, although not with a definite deadline. A bill of law to this effect, debated in parliament in 1996, was incorporated into the Constitution (art. 13). President Niyazov has seen to it, however, that all laws are published both in Turkmen and in Russian.

Tajikistan

Tajikistan was one of the first to adopt a language law, in July 1989. Notably, the name of the state language was rendered as '*tojikī (forsī)*' – Tajik (Persian) (Fragner 1995:48; Perry 1996a:289). In the immediately preceding years, intellectuals complained of the decline of their culture and demanded the restoration of Tajik national dignity by elevating the status of the Tajik language. These complaints prompted K.M. Makhkamov, then First Secretary of the Central Committee of the Tajikistan Communist Party, in May 1988, to advocate the improvement of Tajik schooling and encourage Russians to learn Tajik (Akbarzadeh 1996a: 1108-9). The Law on Language, adopted on 22 July 1989, established Tajik Persian as the official state language and Russian and Uzbek as other languages of the administration (Tadjbakhsh 1996: 337; text in *Qonuni Zaboni Jumhurii Tojikiston*, Dushanbe: Irfon, 1993). Russian, being the language of communication between the nationalities of the Soviet Union, was a language frequently used in Tajikistan. Uzbek, Kyrgyz, Turkmen 'and other languages' as well as the languages of Gorno-Badakhshan received guarantees of free use in all spheres of society, including official institutions. The final draft of the law was prepared by the well-known specialists of Tajik language and literature, Prof. Tolib Khaskashev, Prof. Muhammadjân Shukûrî, Prof. Bahriddin Kamoliddinov and Prof. Mahmadullo Lutfulloev. Muhammadjân Shukûrî, one of the initiators of the law and the person charged with editing it, assures us that he and others had a feeling that they were saving Tajik from disappearing and that their basic intention was to return it to general literary and administrative use (Shukûrî 1994:173-8). The law was perceived as discriminatory by certain non-titular residents of Dushanbe and mass demonstrations were organized in the capital, inducing Makhkamov to pledge a struggle against all manifestations of chauvinism (*KT* 2 Feb. 1990, quoted in Gleason 1997:63).

In the spring of 1992 a redraft of the 1989 Language Law was presented to the public for debate and finally adopted (for a thorough analysis of the new version, see Perry 1996a:300ff). The name of the state language, Tajik, is now rendered as *forsī (tojikī)*, thus reversing the 1989 terminology. There is less reference to the use of Russian and other languages. English is particularly mentioned as a language of communication with foreign states and for academic and scientific purposes. A revival and teaching of the Arabic-based Persian script are recommended.

On 27 December 1993, Tajikistan adopted a Law on Education, which entered into force on 15 January 1994 (text in *NaG* 15 Jan. 1994). The law, after proclaiming the principle of accessibility to education without any discrimination whatsoever, set Tajik as the language of education, however allowing instruction in other languages as well in compact settlements of minority groups (article 5-6). Still in 1994, at a time when an anti-Persian mood was prevalent, the Tajik parliament passed an amendment to the 1989 Law on Language, stating that the name of the state language was now called only *tojikī* (Mesbahi 1997:145). The constitution of Tajikistan, adopted on 6 November 1994 by popular referendum (text published in Tajik, Russian and Uzbek, Dushanbe: Irfon, 1995; translation in Blaustein 1994-6, release 95-7:Nov. 1995), reiterated in article 2 the gist of the 1989 language law, briefly declaring that Tajik was the state language, Russian the language of inter-ethnic communication, and that every national group in the republic might employ its own native language freely (Hunter 1996:44-62).

While the language laws were unanimous in their aim to promote the titular language to the status of state language, in the issue of alphabet change – one of the symbols of the search for a new identity – differences in approach and achievement in the six states are noticeable, as is explained in the next chapter.

7

ALPHABET CHANGE AND ITS IMPLEMENTATION

The issue of alphabet change

Alphabet selection and use have often been decided on political grounds. Alphabets can be an important unifying or divisive factor. Serbs and Croats, divided on religious and historical grounds, had one common language, Serbo-Croatian, from 1954 to 1991, written in two alphabets, a factor which may have deepened the chasm between them. Champions of Pan-Arabism have been quick to single out the Arabic script as a basic and important part of their case, as against the diversity of Arabic dialects, in what a French scholar has called 'linguistic Pan-Arabism' (Carré 1993:71-90). Some propagandists of Islam have also argued that the Arabic alphabet serves as an important bond between Arabs, Persians, Afghans, Pakistanis and others (Landau 1994). Over the years, arguments and counter-arguments have parallelled those of the Turkish and the Persian proponents, respectively: the Latin script is a bridge to modern civilization, while Arabic is the alphabet of the cultural heritage and of the community of Islam.

Against the background of Russian imperialist expansion into the Kazakh steppe, the Caucasus region and Central Asia, the question of alphabet selection and use was a major one for the few literate people involved in both the formation of national awareness and the articulation of demands for cultural autonomy. In the late Russian Empire, government involvement in alphabet creation and some attempts at alphabet change were sometimes considered a tool in the service of assimilation and russification; and much more so in Soviet times. In the early twenties, the question of alphabet was, for Azeris and some other Turkic peoples, a sensitive matter that the national elites tried to regulate according to the individual needs of their respective languages. From the late 1920s onward, however, directives from the Central Committee of the Communist Party in Moscow determined the course that was to be taken (Baldauf 1993:471ff.). The discussions in the 1980s and 1990s on alphabet change, and together with it, language development, remind us of certain experiences and debates in the first quarter of this century.

The *ethnies* in the Soviet Union offered then a mosaic of scripts: some had no alphabet whatsoever, while many others – including those in the Caucasus and Central Asia – possessed sophisticated ones (Ergin 1976:

348-9; Akiner and Sims-Williams 1997:vii-viii). The Soviet leadership was well aware of the political significance of alphabet selection. One of the considerations of the specialists dealing with nationality politics, when switching alphabets from the Arabic to the Latin script ('the alphabet of the Revolution') in the 1920s, was their fear of Pan-Islam (Landau 1994:ch. 3). Another was a certain readiness among Muslims of the former Russian empire – as also in Turkey – to open towards western science and values, in short to modernization, an outlook which had been building up in the early years of the twentieth century. The Latin alphabet was discussed by these modernizing circles as a means to break away from what they saw as the obscurantism, tyranny and backwardness of the past. In Soviet parlance, the shift from the Arabic to the Latin script expressed opposition to Islam and carried the commitment to world revolution, the Latin script symbolizing internationalism (Comrie 1996a:781). Later, one of the factors impelling the Soviet leadership to change from the Latin to the Cyrillic script in 1940 was its search for a unified alphabet through most of the Union as well as its suspicion of the Pan-Turkism liable to emanate from Turkey, which had adopted the Latin alphabet in 1928 (Landau 1995:17-18). Thus the alphabet change was perceived as driving a political wedge between the Muslim, Turkic and Iranian communities in the Soviet Union and their relatives abroad, with the Cyrillic script intended simultaneously to unite them all in the struggle against illiteracy and bring them closer to the Russians and others in the Union (Bruchis 1984) – another move towards russification (Adler 1980:192), but also towards the standardization dictated by modernization (Dave 1996b:108). In the end, the Cyrillic script became a symbol of commitment to Sovietness. It is notable, however, that some communities with old cultural traditions, which possessed their own distinctive script, unconnected with alphabets across the borders, such as the Armenians and Georgians, were not affected by these changes.

In response to the intensified linguistic russification of the 1970s and 1980s, symptoms of increased national awareness became evident in the six Muslim republics among the cultural elites. In their search for a particularist ethnic or national identity, members of these elites focused on their own linguistic traditions, devoting some attention, also, to a discussion of the Cyrillic alphabet as a symptom of Soviet rule.

The language laws passed near the end of the Soviet Union's existence either did not mention alphabet change at all or referred to it in a vague, not too binding way (Maurais 1991:86-8). After the adoption of language laws in the Muslim republics in 1989-90, and achieving independence in late 1991, it was possible for the first time to contemplate change without fear. The alphabet issue was perceived by some as an aspect of 'decolonization' (Tishkov 1997:104) or de-sovietization (Mesamed 1999:10). It was debated energetically, usually under two headings – whether to change the Cyrillic script and, if so, into what other. While the Russians and other Russophones in the new Muslim states generally opposed any change, interpreting it as yet another symptom of Russophobia (Mesamed 1999:10), so too did not a few local intellectuals who had been educated in Russian and found it easier to express themselves in it than in their native tongue. In those states, moreover, as B.E. Behar discovered in her fieldwork in the mid-1990s, average people interviewed seemed to oppose any change of alphabet: 52.5% in Azerbayjan, 82.6% in Uzbekistan, 80.6% in Kazakhstan, and 79.95 in Kyrgyzstan. Of those interviewees supporting a change, 89.6% in Azerbayjan and 37% in Kyrgyzstan favoured the Latin script. But 61.4% in Uzbekistan and 49% in Kazakhstan favoured the Arabic script (Behar 1995:51).

Such attitudes notwithstanding, the prevailing mood of the elites was for a change that would help create a new identity, dissociated from the Russian language and culture imposed by the Soviets. The circles advocating a switch to Latin script argued that it would help students, businessmen and others to learn Western languages, meeting the challenge of the times, and make for easier communication with Turkey, which some of them saw as the model of a westernized, secularized and democratic society. An additional and widely accepted argument was that the Latin script provides more vowel signs than the Arabic one to suit the sounds of the Turkic languages. Advocates of the Arabic alphabet, chiefly in Tajikistan, in contrast, maintained that it would enable everyone to read the rich pre-1923 Central Asian literature, as well as the Koran and other religious sources, and create a bridge to Iran and other Islamic neighbours which they perceived as culturally related (Naby 1994:47).

Hardly anyone remarked that, following a script change, overall illiteracy would be the rule and most writings of the Soviet period would become unreadable (Mikhal'chenko 1994a:23-4). A switch to another alphabet meant the re-education of adults as well as a huge investment in new printing machines, typewriters, computers, curricula, textbooks and teaching aids, in short, everywhere where script is used. Moreover, educators like the then Azerbayjan Deputy Minister of Education Ahmad Abdinov (1996:18, 84) pointed out that not only new textbooks in another alphabet were needed, but also new contents to suit the shaping of a new identity – another costly enterprise. But financial considerations have rarely been a decisive factor in nationalist ideology. The apprehension of the probable adverse effects, however, visibly slowed down the implementation of alphabet change, both in Tajikistan, which had opted to promote the Arabic script, and in Azerbayjan, Uzbekistan and Turkmenistan, which had opted for a switch to the Latin one. In Kazakhstan and Kyrgyzstan, the question whether to switch to the Latin alphabet or not is still being debated.

The campaign for a common language and script

The idea of a Turkish-Turkic *lingua franca* with a common alphabet for Turkey and the Turcophone populations elsewhere, already aired in the nineteenth century (Gökdağ 1997), gained ground in the early 1990s. After the Muslim states had obtained independence, the staunchest supporters of the idea could be found in the Republic of Turkey (Ercilasun 1993:65-75), but even here, some scholars warned of such difficulties as serious differences between an artificial common literary language and the existing spoken languages (Türkmen 1994:89-90). The idea of a common Turkic language went back to the last quarter of the nineteenth century, when the Crimean Tatar intellectual Ismail Gaspyraly (Gasprinskii, 1851-1914) found a large readership among the Turkic community of Russia for his newspaper *Tercüman* (Interpreter), written in a widely understood literary version of Turkic and a modified Arabic alphabet (Fisher 1988). After Gaspyraly's death, the concept was adopted by others, such as a Kazakh, Magzhan Zhumabaev, who propagated it in a book entitled *Pedagogika*, published in Orenburg in 1922, then in Tashkent a year later (Usta 1999). His main proposition was that Kazakh should serve as the basis for a common Turkic language. Suggestively, the book was reprinted in Almaty in 1992. However, the idea was mainly fostered by Pan-Turkist circles in the Republic of Turkey and it was finally taken up by certain intellectuals and some officials after the Soviet Union's dismemberment (Yetkin 1992:298-301).

In the cultural domain, Turkey has initiated cooperation between its own institutes of higher education and those in the newly independent states (*TI* 2 Dec. 1993); it has annually offered grants for thousands of students from Turkic regions to come and study at its universities and has also initiated courses in Turkish for teachers and students in the new states. It has repeatedly donated large numbers of textbooks in Turkish to schools in the Turkic states, printed textbooks in the languages of the new republics as aids to development and even created universities as joint ventures. Turkey also began, as early as April 1992, to televise programmes to Azerbaycan and Central Asia, often in simplified Turkish with Latin script subtitles (Landau 1996:140). A Hoca Ahmet Yesevi International Turk-Kazakh University was established in the city of Turkistan in Kazakhstan on 1 February 1993 by a bilateral agreement.

For a few years, political and academic circles in Turkey hoped that a common Turkish-Turkic language could be put into shape quite soon. In 1992, with official support, a new body was established, the Turkish Republics Educational, Scientific and Cultural Organization, or TURESCO (most probably modelled on UNESCO's name), among whose projected components were centres for compiling dictionaries and carrying out research into the written language and the alphabets (Duman 1993:54-6).

That was also the year when Elchibey, then President of Azerbayjan, was reputed to support the idea; and, in Uzbekistan, a pamphlet on *Orta-Türk*, published in Tashkent in 1992, advocated the idea of 'Common Turkish' (Alpatov 1997:166).

Turkey became particularly active on the issue of a common alphabet – a basic aspect of an eventual *lingua franca*. This seems to have been treated on four levels: a. donations of books, textbooks (FBIS-SOV-92-116:16 June 1992), typewriters and printing machines, together with instructions for their use (*Cumhuriyet* 28 March 1993:17); b. research by Turkish and Turkic experts on how to make up a common Latin alphabet of 33 to 34 characters (Ercilasun 1996:XIII-XIV); c. special credits for cultural assistance (Twining 1993:142); d. official meetings between scholars and government officials.

In the early 1990s, a number of meetings between political representatives and scholars from Turkey and the new Turkic states took place. The first conference convened in the Institute of Turkic Studies at Marmara University in Istanbul, on 18-20 November 1991, and recommended the adoption of a common Latin alphabet, basically consisting of the 29-letter alphabet currently used in Turkey supplemented by an additional five letters (Devlet 1992:1-3, 67; text of the resolution in Şimşir 1995: 119; Ercilasun 1993:63ff.; Seegmiller and Balım 1998). This was followed by a meeting of highly-placed government representatives of Turkey and the five Turkic states in Istanbul between 19 and 21 June 1992. For the first time, the Ministers of Culture of Azerbayjan, Uzbekistan, Kazakhstan, Kyrgyzstan and Turkey met to discuss the issue of a common alphabet, as they did again in Ankara between 8 and 10 March 1993. They agreed on a resolution urging the governments of the five Turkic states to adopt officially a slightly revised version of the alphabet proposed by the 1991 conference of linguists (*Cumhuriyet* 28 Mar. 1993; Artam 1993:136; Seegmiller and Balım 1998). In subsequent years, various attempts at similar official meetings to reach a binding agreement on a common alphabet failed.

Parallel meetings of scholars from Turkey and the new states, such as one in Ankara between 4 and 8 May 1992, and others in Munich on 22 June 1992, in Ankara on 26-7 November 1992, and in Antalya on 21-3 March 1993, reached agreement on a common alphabet and orthography (*Milli Kültür* 92: June 1992, 1-80; *Türk Kültürü* 31(360): Apr. 1993, 193-215; T.C. Dışişleri Bakanlığı 1993; Şimşir 1995: 122-4), but these decisions were not officially binding (Toker 1992:227-35; Mütercimler 1993:208-12).

Yet another Turkish Language Conference met in Ankara on 4-8 May 1992, under the aegis of a newly-founded forum entitled The Permanent Turkish Language Conference (Sürekli Türk Dili Kurultayı). Although no practical consequences ensued, the meeting was widely acclaimed.

This international gathering considered all the varieties of the Turkic languages as one language. Its work was carried out by three commissions, respectively, on the alphabet, the written language, and questions of the literary language. Delegates from Turkey, Azerbayjan, Kyrgyzstan, Uzbekistan, Kazakhstan, Turkmenistan, the Kazan Tatars, and the Turkish Republic of Northern Cyprus stood up and recommended the reintegration of all their languages into one, with a common alphabet (Kültür Bakanlığı 1992, summarized by Bellingeri 1999:345-60).

The same organization convened another meeting in Ankara on 22-26 September 1993. More than one hundred delegates came from Turkey, the new ex-Soviet states and elsewhere and debated the advantages and disadvantages of a common script. The participants agreed on the following points (Bodrogligeti 1994:55):

– The most appropriate writing system for the languages and dialects of the Turkic group is one based on the Latin alphabet. Within the framework of a common alphabet, the Turkish-language republics and the autonomous republics can apply an appropriate Latin-based alphabet to their languages.

– The National Assemblies of the Republics of Azerbayjan, Uzbekistan, and Turkmenistan have decided to change over to the Latin alphabet. Moreover, Azerbayjan has already started to implement a Latin-based alphabet.

– Conference members from Bashkortostan, Kazakhstan, Kyrgyzstan, and Tatarstan reported that – for political and economic reasons – they may delay the change to the Latin-based writing system. However, they expressed the strong hope that these countries would follow the same path in the near future.

– The increase in the number of words and technical terms, same or similar in the written or spoken languages of the Turkic-language countries, will strengthen communication and mutual understanding.

One of the more concrete results of these encounters has been the increase in academic cooperation. The process can be gauged by the bilingual and multilingual grammars and dictionaries published since the early 1990s, e.g. in a scholarly dictionary of the nine main Turkic languages (*Karşılaştırmalı Türk lehçeleri sözlüğü 1991- 2*, ed. by Ercilasun a.o.) and a new dictionary of the Turkic languages, published in London and New York in 1996 (Kurtuluş Öztopçu a.o. 1996).

In the years since, many individual scholars have made practical suggestions how to pursue further the goal of a Turkic common language and alphabet (Karaörs 1994:146-7; Öner 1997; *Turkish Daily News* 4 Apr. 1998). Meanwhile, the issue has ceased to be at the centre of public attention outside Turkey. In Turkey articles on the subject are still being published sometimes in periodicals which discuss language issues (Bellingeri 1999:360). However, since 1996, approximately, scholars in Turkey itself have acknowledged that the idea of a common language and script belongs to the realm of fantasy and, if at all achievable, is a matter for the distant future only (Gürsoy-Naskali 1997) – although some writings in favour of a common alphabet are still published there, occasionally (e.g., Kocaoğlu 1993; Mahmudov 1997; Zülfikar 1999). Several official and unofficial Turkish groups continue to campaign for a common language, as at a meeting organized by the Turkish Language Society, in Ankara, on 13 March 1998 (*Türk Dili* 565: Jan. 1999, 71), or for a Universal Turkish Alphabet. In Azerbayjan, which is closest to Turkey, some interest persists. With time, the newly introduced Latin scripts are being increasingly accepted and used, with their own peculiarities, in Azerbayjan, Uzbekistan and Turkmenistan; in Kazakhstan and Kyrgyzstan the alphabet question is still an exercise for scholars and officials.

Azerbayjan

In Azerbayjan, the leader in Latinization, the discussion within intellectual circles on the reform or change of the Arabic-based alphabet dates back to the second half of the nineteenth century. In the early 1920s, the partisans of a Latin-based alphabet finally carried the day and from 1924 onwards, the new alphabet was the official and obligatory one, as directed by Moscow. Its introduction into schools followed and from 1 January 1929 all official correspondence, schooling and the press had to follow the new script (Ordoubadian 1977:304; Aslan 1990:55; Baldauf 1993:364-86). A new directive imposing Soviet integration from above led to the introduction, in 1940, of the Cyrillic alphabet and was largely motivated by the wish to have an alphabet common to most of the Soviet peoples and to separate even further Soviet from Iranian Azerbayjan (which was using an Arabic-based script) and Turkey (which had switched in 1928 to the Latin one) (Şimşir 1991:29-30; Yazdani 1993:70-1).

After Gorbachev acceded to the leadership of the Soviet Union in 1985 and the policy of *glasnost'* was adopted, a large number of articles appeared in the Azeri press, criticizing the colonialist nature of the Cyrillic script and calling for the reinstatement of the pre-Soviet Arabic one. The poet Bakhtiyar Vahabzade was one of the prominent supporters of this demand (interview in *Azärbaïjan Müällimi* 12 Dec. 1990), while another intellectual, Ziya Bunyadov, was among the first to call, in 1989, for the adoption of the Latin alphabet. Demonstrations were held in Baku during 1989-90, supporting these respective stands. Azeri intellectuals were soon divided on the issue (Mehmedov 1992), which tied up politically with the Iran-Turkey controversy in the matter, each side pulling its own way and presenting itself as a role model. Iran's spokesmen maintained that the Arabic script was a key to Azeri literature and scholarship before the 1920s; Turkey's argued that the Latin alphabet was a bridge to the West and modernization; while local Communists warned that a hasty rejection of Cyrillic characters would exacerbate an already painful transition (Lester 1997:26-7).

At the same time, readers' letters in newspapers and discussion groups as well as conferences on the pro and contra of the Latin script point to great public interest and participation, as recorded in the newspaper *Azärbaÿjan Müällimi* which over many months offered a forum for all kinds of opinion (7 Feb., 22 Aug., 14 Sep., 23 Nov., 12 Dec. 1990; the topic was taken up again in a retrospective interview with Nasib Nasibzade in *Müxalifät* 21 Dec. 1996 on the occasion of the fifth anniversary of the 1991 alphabet decision). In May 1990, the Supreme Soviet of Azerbayjan set up a commission of well-known writers, linguists and philologists, to prepare the Latinization of Azeri. Once the change in script had been decided upon, public support for the Latin script clearly prevailed over that for the Arabic (which was favoured by the new Islamist organization *Tövbä* (Penitence), in opposition to the Popular Front government of the time [Helly 1998:256]) or even over the preservation of the Cyrillic (*Azärbaÿjan Müällimi* 22 Aug., 23 Nov. 1990).

In a poll conducted in August 1990 among primary school teachers in Baku, 58 out of 59 persons were in favour of the transition to a new alphabet; 57 out of the 59 advocated the Latin alphabet. The partisans of Latin script assessed the time needed to prepare a class for the new Latin script as one classroom hour, while the proponents of the Arabic script assessed it as five hours (*Azärbaÿjan Müällimi* 31 Oct. 1990). The matter was still being discussed in 1992 (*Yeni Müsavat* 25 Apr. 1992) and, to a lesser extent, also later (Bayatli 1997). Nonetheless, in 1996 a 72-page textbook for studying the pre-Soviet alphabet (Rüstämova 1996) was published in Baku, with well thought out rules, examples, exercises and selected reading texts – apparently for adults. The introduction recommended the study of the Arabic script, used for Azeri literature until 1929. Azeri arguments parallelled those of Turkish and Iranian proponents. In the Azeri case, two additional arguments were frequently heard: those favouring the Latin script pointed out its value in a rapprochement with Turkey, while those supporting the Arabic one emphasized commonality with the large Azeri community in Iran (Mehmedov 1992:169). However, the Latin script seems to have won. Looking back in 1997 on the Elchibey era, Firidun Zhälilov, then Minister of Education, congratulated himself on the great achievements of that period, particularly the alphabet change that he claimed to have initiated with an article published in March 1990 in the newspaper *Azärbaÿjan* (*Hürriyyät* 30 May 1997).

After preparatory work by a commission (*BR* 28 Feb. 1991), the parliament of Azerbayjan adopted a law replacing, on 25 December 1991, the Cyrillic alphabet with a modified version of the Latin Azeri script of the 1920s and 1930s (Lester 1997:26) gaining the votes of the Communist majority (*525-ci Qäzet*: 20 Nov. 1996). Earlier, the public had been consulted consistently, e.g. the draft had been prepared for public discussion (*Azärbaÿjan Müällimi* 1 March 1991). The law described the Soviet imposition of the Cyrillic script as 'a repressive measure' and formally abolished it. The 32-letter Latin alphabet adopted resembled, but was not identical to the Turkish one (published in *Xalq Qäzeti* 1 Jan. 1992; *BR* 11 Jan. 1992; Seegmiller and Balım 1998: 639; see also ill. 2.), although it adhered to the Common Turkic Alphabet proposed in Ankara in 1993. Different from the Turkish alphabet are the additional letters Ә ə (=ä), X x (=kh) and Q q (=q), three sounds particular to Azeri (Bahadori 1993; *BR* 11 Nov. 1993). However, the discussion about the individual shapes of the letters continued even after the alphabet law had been passed (*Azärbaÿjan Müällimi* 5 Feb., 6 Mar. 1992). The decision reached can be judged by the *Orfoqrafiya-Orfoepiya lüğäti* (Orthographic and orthoepic dictionary) by Äziz Äfandizadä (Baku: Azärbaycan Dövlät Näşriyyatı, 1996).

The law of 25 December 1991 had also spelled out the programme of measures to be taken in 1992 and 1993 in schools and public places. This programme was far from modest. Beginning with the school year 1991-2, the Latin script was to be introduced in the first grade in general education schools; in the upper grades of these schools, in vocational schools and in universities, optional classes were to be offered for the new script; teachers of all institutions were to introduce the alphabet in special courses; all people employed in the publishing sector were to take appropriate steps for change; in newspapers and periodicals, both the Cyrillic and the Latin script were to be used in parallel, as a first stage; public institutions were to revise their seals, stamps and letter forms and to begin changing them; maps, town and street names, as well as street signs were to be transposed into Latin graphics; the same applied to all other types of official documents; in state television, special courses in the Latin script were to be offered and written announcements were to be changed into the Latin script; social institutions were to offer courses to those who wanted to learn the new alphabet; all cultural and scientific institutions were expected to change to the Latin alphabet; a new Latin script orthographic dictionary was to be printed. For 1993, the programme envisaged the printing in Latin script of all textbooks for secondary, vocational and academic education; the whole press and all general, scientific and political books were to be issued in Latin script (*Xalq Qäzeti* 1 Jan. 1992).

Even after the adoption of the Latin alphabet some opponents continued to advocate a move to the Arabic alphabet as a unifying factor between independent Azerbaijan and the Azeris living in Iran, across the border, and using the Persian script (which is Arabic-based). A Turkish-language broadcast from Iran, on 13 January 1992, claimed that a crowd had gathered in Baku to demand that the decision to adopt the Latin alphabet be rescinded and replaced with another, adopting the Arabic one. According to this broadcast, the demonstrators had chanted slogans such as 'Our alphabet is the alphabet used in the Koran'. President Mutalibov was said to have received Islamic clerics after the demonstration, who insisted that the transition to Latin script in schools, universities and government offices be halted (FBIS-SOV-92-012: 17 Jan. 1992). Many of the new state's intellectuals, led by Ebulfez Elchibey (president between June 1992 and June 1993), warmly supported Latinization, despite criticism by the Russian community and an articulate group of Islamists (Goltz 1994:311-12). The government of Turkey proved itself willing to help (Stadelbauer 1996:189). One instance was the supply of a printing press in Latin characters to the autonomous region of Nakhichevan, in Azerbayjan, where no such press could be found at the time (FBIS-SOV-92-116:16 June 1992).

Following the 25 December 1991 law, the Latin alphabet (*Älifba*) was introduced into the first grade (*BR* 22 May 1992) and then into upper ones (*Müxalifät* 9 Apr. 1997; Behar 1995a:397) in a textbook issue of 50,000 copies. In 1994, single textbooks and atlases printed in the new script began to be available in secondary schools. The first newspapers featuring articles in both Cyrillic and Latin script started to appear (Behar 1995a:397) – only to disappear again from the newsstands due to financial problems.

Six years later, with the leadership visibly less committed to alphabet change and in the face of considerable economic pressures, it is clear that the extensive programme envisaged for alphabet change has been carried out in part only. The Azeri press is still largely in Cyrillic characters with Latin script banners. The number of Latin script books available in shops is still restricted. Paper money and stamps are now in Latin characters, while in some other cases the situation is ambiguous: At least in Baku, street name plates can be found in both Cyrillic and Latin script; vehicle license plates and bus destinations are at times in Cyrillic characters, at others in Latin, occasionally in both; the plates on the doors of government offices, universities, schools and other institutions, advertisements and political slogans are frequently in Latin characters with Cyrillic equivalents (Tütüncü 1998; personal visit to Baku, Sep. 1998; see also ill. 2.1-5). It is remarkable, however, that more or less all school books up to the eighth grade are by now available in the new script. A small number of academic and political books and brochures have likewise come out in it (personal visit, Sep. 1998). A minority of official documents and texts are by now written in Azeri, in Latin script, but Russian maintains its place in the diplomatic and economic sphere (information by M.M. Aliev, director of the Foreign Relations Department, Ministry of Education, 29 Sep. 1998).

The pace of change continues to be characterized as too slow; e.g., in 1997, newspapers drew attention to the fact that not even the inscriptions on the monument to Azerbayjan's war heroes had been changed (*Müxalifät* 9 Apr., 23 Apr. 1997; *525-ci Qäzet* 20 Nov. 1997; *7 Gün Qäzeti* 27 Nov. 1997). At a seminar on 'Our new alphabet – our old family names', organized by the New Writers and Artists Society in Baku in February 1999, participants regretted that newspapers and books are still published in the Cyrillic script and placed this problem in the larger context of the general neglect of the Azerbayjan Turkish language. They passed a resolution to the effect that the responsible authorities of the state should be approached in this matter (*Turkistan-N. Azeri: Chaghdas Azerbaycan*, vol. 99: 11, 2 Mar. 1999, 2 pp. Online. Available: turkistan-n@nic.surfnet.nl. 2 Mar. 1999).

Uzbekistan

Uzbekistan has a long literary tradition (preserved in the Arabic-based script) which was affected, as in all other cases discussed here, by Soviet rule. The debate on the choice of alphabet dates essentially from the 1920s. First steps for Latinization were taken in 1927-8, and in 1929-30 the new Latin-based alphabet became effective in the spheres of official correspondence, education and the press (Baldauf 1993:703-7). In 1940, a modified Cyrillic alphabet was introduced under the influence of Soviet integrationist policy.

The arguments about the relative merits of the various alphabets went on both before and after independence much along the same lines as in Azerbayjan (Mahmudov 1997:31). *Birlik*, the most important political force besides the government before independence (it was later banned), came out, although not unanimously, in favour of the Arabic-based script (Schlyter 1997:31). It seems that the Tajiks in Uzbekistan, an important minority, sentimentally inclined to Iran through their cultural heritage, also supported this change.

The argument that returning to the Arabic-derived alphabet would permit both Uzbeks and Tajiks access to their cherished literary and hence cultural heritage should not be taken too much at face value. As the literary elite knew all too well, access to the medieval texts would only become possible if the whole population were instructed – along with the alphabet – in the classical language of Central Asia, Chaghatay or, in Soviet terms, 'Old Uzbek'. In essence, the question is not so much marked by love of the cultural heritage as by the political need to engage in a path different from that prescribed by the Soviet rulers, in other words, derussification and the shaping of a new identity, which could as well be constructed from elements of the past.

Even before the language law was adopted in Uzbekistan (October 1989), the foremost literary journal *Sharq Yulduzi* (Star of the East) started offering a complete course in the Arabic-based Persian script (Sep.-Dec. 1989 issues). The literary journal *Ŭzbek Tili va Adabiëti* (Uzbek Language and Literature) offered text samples in 1990. The 1989 Law on the State Language of Soviet Uzbekistan, without mentioning the alphabet issue, contained an article providing for the study of the vocalized Arabic-based script (the 'old' Uzbek script) for all Uzbek schoolchildren and students getting instruction in Uzbek. One sign of the interest in this script after independence is an Arabic-letter textbook, issued in 1991 in an edition of 550,000 copies. One wonders who paid for it. The Arabic-based alphabet books for schools distributed in 1995-7 were published in editions of only 50,000. In the following years and to this day, booklets on how to learn the Arabic alphabet as well as brochures in Arabic script have remained a standard feature of popular street bookstalls. There were signs of an 'Islamic boom' in Uzbekistan in the early 1990s, while the civil wars in neighbouring Tajikistan and Afghanistan added to the fear of growing fundamentalism. President Karimov regards militant Islam as a threat to state and society (Khalmukhamedov 1998) and such considerations may have helped to tip the balance against the Arabic alphabet and in favour of the Latin one (Zülfikar 1992; Mesamed 1997: 152-3). It is interesting that three years later the 'State Programme on Implementation of the Law on the State Language' (above ch. 6, p. 116) again decreed the creation of conditions for the learning of the 'Uzbek alphabet in Arabic script'.

Yet, other considerations influenced policymaking concerning alphabet choice in favour of the Latin script. Arguments often adduced for the need to switch to the Latin alphabet were that Uzbekistan had to adapt to sophisticated computer programmes and lay the bases for studying Western languages; but the concern for national identity may well have played a role. In this path, the President could even count on the support of the opposition party of the time, *Erk* (Freedom), a political movement which had split from *Birlik* and registered as a party in 1991, whose followers stressed more the proximity to Turkey and the opening towards the West (Ginzburg 1994-5: I, 213ff; Uhres 1996:8). One observer argued that the Latin script would not prevent one from being a good Muslim and that both alphabets could be used, as in Turkey (*Sharq Yulduzi* 1992, no 10:120). A public debate about the symbols to be adopted in the new Latin script developed in 1989 (*Sharq Yulduzi* 1990, no. 5:199-201) and gained momentum in 1992-3, preceding the official decision (Kuchkartayev 1993:37-8; our interview with the head of the Institute of Languages, Uzbek Academy of Sciences, Prof. Azim Hojiyev, Sep. 1998. For readers' letters, interviews, opinions, reports on official meetings, *Ŭzbekiston Ovozi, Khalq Sŭzi, Ŭzbekiston*

Adabiëti va San"ati, Narodnoe Slovo, Toshkent Oqshomi, Guliston 1992, *Ma"rifat* 1993).

The 'Law on the Introduction of the Uzbek Alphabet Based on Latin Graphics' was adopted by the Uzbekistan parliament on 2 September 1993, after a governmental campaign in the media calling for support. Published in Uzbek and Russian (*Ŭzbekiston Respublikasining qonuni Lotin ëzuviga asoslangan Ŭzbek alifbosini zhorii etish tŭghrisida*, Tashkent: Ŭzbekiston, 1993; *Vatanparvar* 19 Oct. 1993; FBIS-SOV 18 Dec. 1993:105), this law was very brief, but widely and repeatedly publicized (e.g. *Ma"rifat* 13 Oct. 1993 with a list of the members of the State Language Commission; *Ŭzbekiston Adabiëti va San"ati* 15 Oct. 1993; *Saodat* 12 Dec. 1993).

The introduction to the new law declared that it was based on the experience gained with the Latin script in 1929-40 and on the wishes of the public's representatives. Its first paragraph stated that a Latin-based new alphabet, consisting of thirty-one letters and one apostrophe as shown in an accompanying list, was to be introduced. The second paragraph said that conditions would be preserved for retaining mastery and use of both the Arabic and the Cyrillic characters in which the spiritual legacy of Uzbekistan had been created. A decree in ten paragraphs, appended to the law, laid down the details of implementation, the main ones being the following: a. first-graders would start to learn and read the Latin script as from 1 September 1995 and so continue, with each year introducing it in one further grade; b. the rest of the population should acquire the new script gradually, in a process to be completed by 1 September 2000; c. a state commission was to be appointed to work out programmes and details, e.g., new orthographic rules (with a list of the various institutions represented in the commission appended); the state publishing committee was called upon to print by 1 August 1995 the necessary kindergarten and schoolbooks and other teaching aids. The Ministry later issued directives for special sixty-hour courses in the new alphabet for all educational institutions, starting in 1994-5 (Schlyter 1997:32-3).

By the end of 1993, the *Alifbo* was printed in 100,000 copies and distributed (Behar 1995a:398). Schoolbooks, manuals for teachers and other works started to come out only since 1994 (*Boshlanghich Ta"lim*, 1994, no. 2; Behar 1995a:398). Examples of manuals for the use of the new alphabet and orthography are Yo'ldosh Abdullayev's *Hamrohim* (Companion) and *Sovg'a* (Gift), Tashkent: O'qituvchi 1996. Some of the primers teach the new alphabet by parallel texts in both Cyrillic and Latin, like Tursunboy Adashboyev's *Topishmoqli alifbe* (The alphabet in riddles) (Tashkent: Cho'lpon, 1997), but most employ the new alphabet alone, such as *Harflar chamani* (Garden of letters) (Tashkent: O'qituvchi, 1997) for first graders. Eventually, full teaching of the new alphabet in pre-school and primary school education started in the school year beginning on 1 September 1996 (interview with Mr Ghairat Shomanov, director, Republican Educational Center, 2 Sep. 1998).

The largest publishing firm of schoolbooks in Uzbekistan, Ŭqituvchi/ O'qituvchi, announced in August 1996 that for the school year about to start, it had prepared the necessary textbooks in Latin characters for the first graders and will prepare more for other grades each year (*PV* 7 Aug. 1996; for a list of primary schoolbooks published and in press as of 1996, *Til va Adabiët Ta"limi* 1996, no. 4). Uzbek language textbooks in the new script for second and third graders were to be printed by July 1997, for fourth and fifth graders by July 1998 (copy of decree no. 82, 'Implementation of the Uzbek alphabet based on the Latin script' of the Ministry of People's Education, 16 April 1996). In fact, in spring 1997, several such primers for first graders were available at schoolbook outlets, while in September 1998 Uzbek language and literature readers up to the fifth grade were on the market (own experience, Apr. 1997 and Sep. 1998).

For the higher grades, two hours a week are set aside for the teaching of the 'Lotin grafika', while at the universities, the attendance of lessons for the Latin script is optional (interview with Mr Akram Akmolov, director, Tashkent Teachers' Training Centre, 3 Sep. 1998). A series on how to learn the new script in small doses was published in *Khalq Sŭzi* (2 Nov. 1994 ff). A special course for adults was proposed in *Til va Adabiët Ta"limi* 1994, no. 2-3, and also in *Guliston* 1994, no. 2. A course on state television was demanded in *Khalq Sŭzi* (22 July 1994). This started in 1995 under the title 'Let's learn the new alphabet' (Balcı 1996:719). As of September 1998, two television channels continue to broadcast half-hour alphabet courses for adults per week. Television educational programmes have usually employed the Latin alphabet, while a few varied between the Latin and Cyrillic scripts. Parents of young children expressed their readiness to learn the new alphabet in order to be able to help their children with their homework.

Within less than two years a revision of the new alphabet signs was announced. On 6 May 1995, the parliament of Uzbekistan (*Oliĭ Mazhlis*) issued a law to this effect (*PV* 7 June 1995; *Novye Zakony Uzbekistana* 1996, no. 11), distancing the alphabet even farther from those of Turkey, Azerbayjan and Turkmenistan. The new law had been preceded in the press and in interested circles by some discussion on the shape and necessity of single letters or signs (e.g. *Saodat* 1994, no. 2). On 24 August 1995, the Council of Ministers issued a decree explaining how to use the revised alphabet and giving exact spelling rules for every sign (*Til va Adabiët Ta"limi* 1996, no. 2). While the alphabet introduced in 1993 had comprised 31 signs (six of them special characters corresponding to special Uzbek sounds) and in addition the apostrophe indicating a glottal stop, the revised form of 1995 contains only 26 signs (two of which are combined with a special sign), three sign combinations (diagraphs) and again the apostrophe (see ill. 3). Discarded were now the specific Uzbek characters, thus making the alphabet more practical and bringing it closer to the Anglo-Saxon sign repertoire. In this way, the diagraphs 'Sh sh', Ch ch' and 'ng' representing one sound each (the latter only appearing within a word) replaced the former 'Ş ş', Ç ç' and 'ñ', while the signs 'Ō ō' and 'Ḡ ḡ' – also standing for one sound each (roughly 'Ö ö' and 'Gh gh') – obtained a new variant for their printed form: 'O' o'' and 'G' g''. An impression of the differences between the 1993 and the 1995 versions of the alphabet can be obtained by comparing I. Qŭchqortoev and M. Tozhiboev, *Lotincha Ŭzbek Alifbosi* (The Uzbek Alphabet in Latin Script) (Tashkent: Ŭqituvchi 1994) with Shavkat Rahmatullayev and Azim Hojiyev, eds., *O'zbek tilining imlo lug'ati* (Orthographic Dictionary of the Uzbek Language) (Tashkent: O'qituvchi 1995). Both books are in Uzbek, but the former in Cyrillic, the latter in Latin script (cf. also Schlyter 1997:34-5, and a comparison of the two alphabets in Balcı 1996).

Essentially, the new Uzbek Latin alphabet represents a transliteration of the Cyrillic; no analysis of the present state of the Uzbek language was made before the alphabet reform was carried through. Thus, a number of the phonetic deficiencies of the Uzbek Cyrillic alphabet are also noticeable in the new Latin one (Balcı 1995; Balcı 1996; Uhres 1996:8); e.g., in spite of the effort at transparency, its signs do not correspond in each case to one sound or, in other words, several signs represent more than one sound. Further, in spite of all the zeal demonstrated by some representatives of the Turkic republics at the language conferences convened by Turkey in the years 1991-3, the new Uzbek alphabet shows no sign of any effort to make it congruent with the alphabets of Turkmenistan and Azerbayjan or with the Common Turkic alphabet (as discussed on pp. 127-30).

Latin characters were introduced into Karakalpak, too, with slight variations. The Republic of Karakalpakstan – as part of Uzbekistan – has followed the language and alphabet reforms launched by the Tashkent government over the years. On 29 December 1995, four months after the revised alphabet had been adopted by parliament in Tashkent, the Karakalpak legislature in Nukus, the capital of this autonomous republic, passed a law on a revised version for Karakalpak as well (*Latyn grafikasyna tijkarlangan Qaraqalpaq alfavitin engiziw haqqynda*, cited in Schlyter 1997:15, 35). For Karakalpak, which is closer to Kazakh than to Uzbek, an orientation towards a future Kazakh Latin alphabet can be considered as more reasonable, hypothetically; but it is doubtful whether Uzbekistan – competing with Kazakhstan for regional leadership – would tolerate it. On the other hand, the production in Karakalpak linguistics in the first half of the 1990s, including dictionaries, grammars, works on dialectology, and others is presented as making the point that Uzbek and Karakalpak should each preserve their characteristics (Dauletov 1996:112).

By the Alphabet Law of 6 May 1995, the overall deadline for the final transfer to the Latin script was postponed until 1 September 2005, to conform to the Law on the State Language, revised in 1995 as well. This called for full implementation in 2005, when the switch to the new script should be completed. A 'step by step' transition was considered more desirable than a short-term switching period (interview with Mr. Ghairat Shomanov, 2 Sep. 1998).

Since the mid-1990s, the Latin script can be seen increasingly, but unevenly, spread in the old (1993) and in the revised (1995) version on logos of institutions and firms, on commercial products, in shop windows, billboards, street signs, place name signs and in various slogans. In order to speed up change, new toponymic commissions were appointed and, by May 1998, about 2,000 street signs in Latin characters were prepared for Tashkent, many with new names (*NS* 8 May 1998). A few newspapers have been printing articles in both Cyrillic and Latin script. The biweekly *Ma"rifat* (Knowledge), intended for teachers, uses both Latin and Cyrillic characters on facing pages (Fierman 1995; Landau 1996:144; own experience in Sep. 1998). The new money, introduced since July 1994, was printed in Cyrillic characters (unlike in Azerbayjan and Turkmenistan, where money has been issued in the official Latin ones), but stamps in Uzbekistan show the Latin script. Road signs on the inter-city routes were still exclusively in Cyrillic in 1995 (Uhres 1996: 10), but have since been partly replaced by signs in Latin script.

Kazakhstan

In the last third of the nineteenth century, Cyrillic letters were introduced into government schools among the Kazakhs (who traditionally used the Arabic script) together with the alphabetization and education programme of the Russian missionary and orientalist Nikolai I. Il'minskii (1822-91) (Kappeler 1993:215-16). A reformed Arabic-based script successfully adapted to the needs of Kazakh is the reason that in the 1920s the advocates of Arabic script lost ground only slowly, a phenomenon unique to Kazakhstan. Eventually, the Kazakhs – like the other Turkic peoples – had to follow the directives of the Party in adopting the 'New Alphabet' (i.e., the modified Latin script). Latinization, introduced in 1929, was soon well on its way (Baldauf 1993:279-87). A Kazakh alphabet on the basis of the Cyrillic was imposed in 1940.

Although in the last few years of Soviet dominance there was a relatively free public discourse about language and alphabet – as an expression of the need to recover national self-esteem – Kazakhstan's leaders displayed caution in such matters, then and up till now. Alphabet reform was a delicate issue in a country with more Slavs than Kazakhs and with more Russophones than Kazakh-speakers; and, after independence, they were faced with the implicit (and sometimes explicit) threats of chauvinists in Russia and northern Kazakhstan to annex that part of the republic to the Russian Federation. It was a relatively simple matter to change place and street names (and some personal ones) from Russian into Kazakh, or issue banknotes in Kazakh only – in Cyrillic script. The Law on Languages adopted in August 1989 had not mentioned the alphabet. Newspaper articles argued for this or that script. Those favouring Latinization mentioned computer compatibility (*KP* 31 July 1992; *Novoe Pokolenie* 20 Aug. 1997; *Turkestan* 25 Nov. 1998) and superior suitability in the technological age (*Irtysh* 18 Mar. 1997), or argued that it would facilitate foreign language study (*Panorama* 9:4 Mar. 1995), or the cultural rapprochement of the Turkic peoples (*Qazaqstan Sarbazy* 31 Mar. 1998) – summing up a widespread sentiment for political and cultural reorientation.

In any event, Kazakhstan participated in the meetings of high-ranking representatives from the five Turkic republics convened in Turkey in 1992 and 1993, in which it was eventually agreed in principle to adopt the Latin script (above, pp.128-9). Kazakh linguists and turkologists showed a sustained interest in the matter (*KP* 31 July 1992; *Zaman-Qazaqstan* 12 Jan. 1996). Among these specialists, Äbduali Qaydarov, then director of the Institute of Linguistics of the Academy of Sciences of Kazakhstan and chairman of the Kazakh Language Society (*Qazaq Tili*), argued for the introduction of the Latin alphabet in an important initiative taken in 1992. In 1993, he went a step further by proposing a revised version oriented towards the Common Turkic alphabet. Another important move came in 1995 from the well-known turkologist K.M. Musaev who advocated a combination of elements of the Kazakh Latin script used in the 1930s and the Turkish Latin script (references in Kirchner 1999). The campaign for developing a new Latin alphabet has been well received by specialists at the Institute of Linguistics of the Kazakh Academy of Sciences (conversation with Prof. Kobei Khusainov, Almaty, 28 March 1997; notes by Professor Äbduali Qaydarov, e.g. in *Egemen Qazaqstan* 6 Jan. 1996) and continues to occupy the minds of language specialists in other institutions in the country (*Qazaq Ädebieti* 24 Feb. 1998) and abroad. A current scientific project sponsored by a programme of the European Union for cooperation with scientists from the New Independent States and the Academy of Sciences of the Republic of Kazakhstan is evaluating the suitability of the current Kazakh script and plans to make recommendations for a Kazakh alphabet and orthography reform (cf. INTAS website).

Others spoke up for the Cyrillic alphabet, in which important Kazakh works had been published (*KP* 6 June 1995). In fact, it is estimated that more than 90% of the available literature in Kazakh is printed in the current Cyrillic-based Kazakh script (Kirchner 1999). Another argument, not shared by many, pointed out the satisfactory adaptation of the Cyrillic script to the Kazakh language, and the fact that Russian served perfectly well as a 'bridge' between the nationalities, especially in the face of an admitted slowdown in the development of Kazakh scientific and technological terminology (*Russkii Yazyk i Literatura v Kazakhskoi Shkole* 1995, no. 7-8:35).

Latinization is largely a matter for political decisions, part of the wider language policies adopted. Sultan Orazalinov, a Kazakh who has chaired various public committees for the coordination of language policies, emphasizes that, despite all difficulties, Latinization, in its larger perspective, would be a bridge to join Kazakhstan to world civilization in the future (*KP* 19 Feb. 1998). This was also the view of Olzhas Suleimenov, a famous author who himself writes in Russian (*KP* 13 Mar. 1996).

A basic decision on whether to reform the current Kazakh alphabet or to switch to the Latin script still seems far away. One or the other decision requires a thorough study of the Kazakh language on the basis of modern linguistic research. Since the shortcomings of the present script are even said to hamper the reading and writing abilities of schoolchildren and students alike, the question plays an eminent role for educators and politicians who see their goal in making Kazakh a sophisticated modern language for future generations, capable of replacing Russian in all fields of science and technology (Nazarbaev 1998). As Kazakh continues to play a minor part in Kazakhstan society, the switch to the Latin script might increase the danger of further marginalization of this language (Kirchner 1999). This state of affairs can best be judged by the fact that even though in 1996 the State Committee for Nationalities Policy took a first official decision towards the introduction of the Latin script, backed by President Nazarbaev (*NG* 5 July 1996; Kuleshov a.o. 1997:492), it is remarkable that the programme *Kazakhstan 2030* has no provision on the question of alphabet (Nazarbaev [1998]). At the state level no progress in this matter has been made since (Kirchner 1999).

Kyrgyzstan

Alphabetization developed relatively late among the pastoralist Kyrgyz (Huskey 1995:549). In the 1920s their modified Arabic-based script gave way to the Latin-based script favoured by the local and central Soviet leadership. Already in 1929, a five-year plan for Latinization in a move for a more general alphabetization had come into effect and, by 1931, the transition to the new alphabet was largely achieved (Baldauf 1993:691-3; Bohr and Crisp 1996:387; a positive Kyrgyz view of the process in *Kyrgyz Tuusu* 9 Apr. 1992). From 1940 onward, Kyrgyz had to be written in a modified Cyrillic script. Some Kyrgyz argued that the number of letters in use could be reduced (details in Asankanov 1997:83).

In 1992 and 1993, Kyrgyzstan – like Azerbayjan, Kazakhstan, Uzbekistan and Turkmenistan – attended the meetings in Turkey at which an agreement in principle was reached to adopt the Latin script (*Bishkek Shamy* 18 Mar. 1993; above, pp. 128-9). However, the debate over the Latin script continued at a moderate pace, apparently for three main reasons: first, to avoid irritating further the important Russian community in Kyrgyzstan; secondly, because of the lack of sufficient teachers and funds (*Kyrgyz Tuusu* 9 Apr. 1992); thirdly, because many Kyrgyz are convinced that the current Cyrillic alphabet is well adapted to the phonetic characteristics of their language and they cannot see any advantage in severing ties with a written heritage of more than 70 years (*Nasha Gazeta* 31 Jan. 1998). Meanwhile, on 8 September 1998, the organizers of a computer project for the Latinization of Kyrgyz applied for official registration at the Ministry of Justice (information by Dr T. Choroev, 29 Sep. 1998).

The National Commission on the State Language under the President, appointed on 20 January 1998 (above, p. 96), started to reconsider the issue of a switch to the Latin alphabet, although this task had not been formulated in the decree setting up the Commission (*Normativnye Akty Kyrgyzskoi Respubliki* 1998, no. 3: Feb., 10-14; *Ėrkin Too* 23 Sep. 1998; interview with Prof. A.D. Toktomametov, secretary of the National Commission on the State Language, Bishkek, 16 Sep. 1998). However, the commission's work is proceeding slowly and, due to opposition to Latinization, no decision seems to have been reached (letter from Dr Choroev, 11 December 1998). By the end of 1999, scholars, intellectuals and officials continue to be interested in alphabet switch, while the government procrastinates.

Turkmenistan

Like the other republics with a predominant Turkic population and like Tajikistan, Turkmenistan had to switch under Party directives from its Arabic-based alphabet to the modified Latin one in 1929, when the new alphabet became the official state script and was introduced into schools (Baldauf 1993:699-702). With the imposition of a Cyrillic-based script in 1940, the drive for alphabetization of the preceding ten years had to be started anew.

The public discussion of alphabet change had begun in Soviet Turkmenistan with the general discussion concerning the bill for the Law on Language (*TI* 16 May 1990). Soon after the declaration of independence on 27 October 1991 and following the Istanbul alphabet conference of the Turkic peoples in November 1991, the Turkmen press began to articulate more insistently a debate on the transition to the

Latin alphabet. Turkmenistan differed from other states insofar that there were hardly any advocates of the Arabic script, while the number of partisans of Latin in contrast to Cyrillic was constantly rising (Şimşir 1995: 118). A new periodical, *Türkmen Sesi* (The Turkmen's Voice), which started to appear in Ashgabat in October 1991, had the first issue in Cyrillic characters, soon followed by others in Arabic and Latin (*TI* 9 Oct. 1991). Later, three collections of Turkmen poetry were published in Latin script in Turkey (*TI* 12 August 1992).

The debate over Latin versus Cyrillic script continued throughout 1992, reflecting also a discussion on how the letters representing special Turkmen sounds should be formed (e.g., *TI* 17 Sep.,16 Oct., 20 Oct. 1992). When Turkey's then President, Turgut Özal, visited Ashgabat on 12 April 1993, Niyazov offered him an original gift – a presidential decree instituting the Latin script, here called New Turkmen Alphabet – *Täze Türkmen elipbiü* – which was to serve as the graphic basis of standard Turkmen (*Türkmenistan* 13 Apr. 1993; discussed by Behar 1995a:397; Clark 1998:86). The Turkmenistan parliament adopted this decree in May 1993 (Blacher 1996:11; *PV* 15 May 1993), setting 1 January 1996 as the date from which the Latin script of 30 letters should be employed everywhere (a list of the new script: *TI* 10 Jan. 1995; see ill. 3). By a further presidential decree of 25 June 1993, a programme for achieving this goal was set in motion (text in Söegov and Rejebov 1993:16-26).

On 23 April 1993, another presidential decree instituted a 14-member State Organizational Committee in charge of the transition to the new Turkmen alphabet under the chairmanship of the President himself (Söegov and Rejebov 1993:15). In June, Prof. Myratgeldi Söegov, director of the Institute of Linguistics of the Academy of Sciences of Turkmenistan, and N. Rejebov published some documentation on the adoption of the alphabet, along with lessons and sample texts (Söegov and Rejebov 1993). It is obvious, however, that the precarious financial situation of the country has prevented the smooth transition envisaged in the decree. Following a further presidential decree of 29 September 1994, 'On the Transition to the New Alphabet in the Educational Institutions of Turkmenistan', schools started to teach the Latin alphabet, on the basis of a printing of 22,000 primers, beginning with the 1995-6 school year (Behar 1995a:397). It is not surprising that the first book published in Turkmen in Latin characters, in early 1995, was about the state President. Entitled *Türkmenbaşy – Türkmenlering ykbaly* (Turkmenbashy – Destiny of the Turkmens), it was written by Akbibi Yusubova, a journalist (reviewed in *TI* 22 Feb. 1995). In spite of the alphabet switch, some teachers continued to debate the advantages and disadvantages of the new script, comparing it with the Cyrillic alphabet or Latin letters as used in English.

The decrees of 29 September 1994 and 1 January 1997, calling on all Turkmen citizens to start using the Latin alphabet, have not been very successful, a reflection of pedagogical and financial difficulties. However, the Latin alphabet has been recently introduced for the study of Turkmen in the first school grades. Also, books, dictionaries and textbooks for Turkmen in the Latin script have been published, some with help from Turkey (*Turkish Daily News* 24 May 1997) and the Turkmen state television broadcasts lessons on the new writing system. Television in Turkmen employs captions in Latin script. It also appears in street names and road signs, on most government and other public buildings, as well as on the new currency, *manat*. Shop signs are partly in Cyrillic, partly in Latin script – or both. Those at the Ashgabat International Airport are in Turkmen (in Latin script), Russian and English (own experience, Sep. 1998). The Ashgabat daily *Neitral'nyi Turkmenistan* is in Russian; another, *Ashgabat*, is half in Russian and half in Turkmen in Cyrillic characters. In summer 1999, *Ashgabat* offered its readers a course in the new alphabet, comprising regularly a corrected (but still not correct) table of the letters in printed and handwritten forms and – as a reading exercise – a poem. Turkmen periodicals often carry Latin-script title captions, while the news and articles remain in Cyrillic characters – as not many adults are fully familiar as yet with the Latin alphabet. On 27 October 1994, the Ashgabat newspaper *Gün* (Day) was the first to appear entirely in Latin script – but remained a short-lived experiment. *Türkmen Sesi* was still appearing in mostly Cyrillic letters as of autumn 1996 (report in *Milliyet* 27 Dec.1994:18; Şimşir 1995:128; Landau 1996:144-5).

It cannot escape the observer that the commission in charge of the creation of the new Turkmen alphabet adhered to the principle agreed upon at the conferences in Istanbul and Ankara suggesting 'one letter for one phoneme', but ignored the principle of 'one letter for those phonemes that are common to all Turkic languages'. In this way, the new Turkmen alphabet (1999 version), now of 30 letters, although allegedly aiming at simplicity, was a far cry from both the Turkish model and the Common Turkic Alphabet of 1993, as it used some letters that differ from that proposed list and are not easily found in an international computer programme (computer compatibility has always served as a ready argument for the transition to Latin graphics), such as 'Ä ä', 'Ƒ ƒ' (= zh), or 'Ɏ ÿ' (= y) (*Ashgabat* 6 July 1999; see ill. 4). Another set of changes was reported by *Türk Dili* (579: March 2000, 286-7): as of 1 Jan. 2000 the printed letter 'Ƒ ƒ' was replaced by 'Ž ž', 'Ñ ñ' by 'Ň ň', and 'Ɏ ÿ' by 'Ý ý'. Further, the Russian hard and soft signs are discarded, thus 'Turkmenizing' Russian loanwords in the Turkmen vocabulary. As in Uzbek, the Russian character Ц ('ts') was disregarded. Instead, this sound is rendered in Russian loanwords or foreign words adopted via Russian by the letter 's'. Russian 'shch' has been reduced to mere 'sh'. Moreover, it is noteworthy that the new Turkmen Latin letters – as in Uzbek – do not reflect the phonetic realities of the contemporary standard language, but constitute rather a transliteration from the Cyrillic counterparts (Şimşir 1995:129-34; Blacher 1996: 11; Tryjarski 1998:116; Clark 1998:86).

Tajikistan

The Tajik language or Tajiki, one of the South-Western Iranian languages, developed since the sixteenth century as the Persian vernacular of Central Asia, its written form using the Arabo-Persian script. In the hope of solving the problem of illiteracy and of spreading modernizing European ideas more easily, Soviet rule introduced a modified Latin script in 1929 and replaced it in 1940 with a modified Cyrillic alphabet with six additional letters (Lorenz 1994:172-3; Perry 1997:5-12; Steblin-Kamensky 1998). With this cultural and political background in mind, it comes as no surprise that after independence a majority of Tajiks have opted for the return to the Arabic-based Persian alphabet, at least in the long run. A return to the pre-Soviet Arabic-based alphabet was in line with the search for identity (Guboglo 1994:3).

In 1989, teachers of Russian and Tajik language and literature were invited to participate in the public debate in preparation of a new language law. At this point, it was suggested that the Arabic-based Persian script be included in the teaching program of schools with Tajik language instruction (*KT* 6 May 1989). The Law on Language of 22 July 1989 stated (article 7, paragraph 27) that the necessary conditions would be created for studying the Arabic-based Persian alphabet and for publishing literature in this script. This was popularly understood as an intention of alphabet change (Perry 1992:4). The first textbook for learning this script was published in Tajikistan a few weeks later (*KT* 8 Aug. 1989). Several books in the script have been published in Tajikistan subsequently and many more have been provided for schools and the general public by Iran, which also supplied them to Tajiks living in compact groups in Uzbekistan and elsewhere. The government of Iran has been helping with printing and other facilities. Several established journals, such as *Adabiët va San"at* (Literature and Art) and new ones such as *Somon* (Order) and *Adab* (Belles Lettres) published articles in Persian script by 1992 (Perry 1992:4). Nevertheless, a local intellectual estimated that, three years after the enactment of Tajikistan's Law on Language, no more than 1% of the state's population was literate in the Persian script (reported by Atkin 1994:94).

A government committee in charge of the implementation of the language law of 1989 was also given the task of encouraging the spread of the Arabic-based Persian script, with the aim of enabling young Tajiks to read and write it with ease. In the early 1990s, a large number of class hours was to be allotted in schools (*KT* 15 June 1991; *NaG* 20 June 1992) and introduction into universities was slated for 1996 (Roy 1991:31; Atkin 1994a:131-3; Landau 1996:145-6). Three-month courses in the

Persian alphabet were organized for various groups of professionals, such as teachers and engineers (*KT* 15 June 1991; 20 June 1992). As of 1999, the Persian script is being taught in schools from the third year onwards and at universities in the first year. It can also be seen in shops and in advertisements, along with its local Cyrillic variant.

The civil war raging in this country has clearly had an impact on the government's political and economic ability to implement the language law of 1989 (Asimov 1996). Insofar as the alphabet is concerned, the original intention of Persianizing it by 1996 (Mesbahi 1997:156, fn. 23) has not been achieved. The population does not expect the transition to the Persian script to materialize, at least not within the next fifteen to twenty years. A change to the Latin alphabet is no longer on the agenda (personal information by H. Saifulloev, 4 Apr. 1999).The Cyrillic alphabet continues to be the predominant script in the country.

On 3 March 1998 a revised version of the Cyrillic alphabet was adopted to replace the 1940 version with the intention of better adapting the alphabet to Tajik phonetics (information by H. Saifulloev; *Omūzgor* 23 Sept. 1998; *Jumhuriyat* 12 Jan. 1999). Tajikistan is thus the only state in Central Asia so far that has revised its Cyrillic alphabet after independence (see ill. 5; Rzehak 1999:1-5). A government committee presided over by Gaffor Juraev is charged with controlling the realization and implementation of the language law of 1989 and of the new revised alphabet. Since its introduction, combined with a revised corpus of orthographic rules, it has been used in newspapers, periodicals and all books published. The 39 letters of the old alphabet were reduced to 35, arranged in a slightly different sequence. Four letters that are considered typically Russian – Ц, Щ, Ы, Ь – were discarded to conform to the trend of de-russianizing orthography that started immediately after the Law on Language had been passed. Thus, Russian loanwords in Tajik now acquired an orthography more in line with Tajik pronunciation: e.g., the single Russian letter and sound Ц (ts) as in '*tsement*' (cement) was replaced either by 's' as in '*sement*', or by a combination of the two letters 't' and 's' as in '*dotsent*' (lecturer). The single Russian letter Щ (*shch*) was replaced by 'sh' and Ы (y) by 'i'. The Russian soft sign disappeared altogether (*Omūzgor* 23 Sep. 1998).

With independence, the impetus of alphabet change was perceived as an instrument of de-sovietization and at the same time as a means of individual nation-building, westernization, and modernization. This impetus had mainly seized the three new states with a smaller Russian population – Azerbayjan, Uzbekistan and Turkmenistan. In Kazakhstan and Kyrgyzstan, by contrast, each with a considerably higher percentage of Slavic speakers, the question of alphabet change remained an aim discussed largely by intellectual circles and individuals. In Tajikistan, on

adı	çap şəkli	əlyazma şəkli	adı	çap şəkli	əlyazma şəkli
a	Aa	*Aa*	ге	Qq	*Qq*
бе	Bb	*Bb*	ел	Ll	*Ll*
че	Cc	*Cc*	ем	Mm	*Mm*
че	Çç	*Çç*	ен	Nn	*Nn*
де	Dd	*Dd*	о	Oo	*Oo*
е	Ee	*Ee*	ə	Öö	*Öö*
ə	Əə	*Əə*	пе	Pp	*Pp*
фе	Ff	*Ff*	ер	Rr	*Rr*
ке	Gg	*Gg*	се	Ss	*Ss*
ге	Ğğ	*Ğğ*	ше	Şş	*Şş*
хе	Hh	*Hh*	те	Tt	*Tt*
хе	Xx	*Xx*	у	Uu	*Uu*
ы	Iı	*Iı*	ү	Üü	*Üü*
и	İi	*İi*	ве	Vv	*Vv*
же	Jj	*Jj*	је	Yy	*Yy*
ке ka	Kk	*Kk*	зе	Zz	*Zz*

2. The new Latin-based alphabet of Azerbayjan (1991). The first and fourth columns give the name of the letter, the second and fifth its printed form, the third and sixth its equivalent in handwriting. *Source*: School poster (Baku, September 1998).

ЛОТИН ЁЗУВИГА АСОСЛАНГАН ЎЗБЕК АЛИФБОСИ							
Босма шакли	Ёзма шакли	Ҳарф номи	Кириллча шакли	Босма шакли	Ёзма шакли	Ҳарф номи	Кириллча шакли
Aa	*Aa*	a	Aa	Qq	*Qq*	qe	Ққ
Bb	*Bb*	be	Вв	Rr	*Rr*	er	Рр
Dd	*Dd*	de	Дд	Ss	*Ss*	es	Сс
Ee	*Ee*	e	Ээ	Tt	*Tt*	te	Тт
Ff	*Ff*	ef	Фф	Uu	*Uu*	u	Уу
Gg	*Gg*	ge	Гг	Vv	*Vv*	ve	Вв
Hh	*Hh*	he	Ҳҳ	Xx	*Xx*	xe	Хх
Ii	*Ii*	i	Ии	Yy	*Yy*	ye	Йй
Jj	*Jj*	je	Жж	Zz	*Zz*	ze	Зз
Kk	*Kk*	ke	Кк	O'o'	*Õõ*	o'	Ўў
Ll	*Ll*	el	Лл	G'g'	*G̃g̃*	ge	Ғғ
Mm	*Mm*	em	Мм	Shsh	*sh*	she	Шш
Nn	*Nn*	en	Нн	Chch	*ch*	che	Чч
Oo	*Oo*	o	Оо	ng	*ng*	nge	нг
Pp	*Pp*	pe	Пп				

3. The new Latin-based alphabet of Uzbekistan (1995). The first and fifth columns give the printed form of the letter, the second and sixth its equivalent in handwriting, the third and seventh columns its name, the fourth and eighth its form in the Cyrillic script. *Source*: Kh. Bobobekov, T. Mukhtorov, A. Sulaĭmonov, S. Badalboev, *Alifbo*. Tashkent: Ёzuvchi 1998.

Басма-часы	Язма-часы	Ады	Аңладышы сеси	Мысаллар
Aa	_Aa_	a	а	Aşgabat, arkadaş, nama
Bb	_Bb_	бе	б	Biribar, bereket, käbe
Çç	_Çç_	че	ч	Çaryýarlar, gerçek, jäç
Dd	_Dd_	ге	g	Dürli, dag, adat
Ee	_Ee_	э	э	Erkin, kerem, wesýet
Ää	_Ää_	э	э	Älem, äht, Mälik
Ff	_Ff_	фе	ф	Faraby, Afzal, aryf
Gg	_Gg_	ге	г	Garyndaş, aga, bag
Hh	_Hh_	хе	х	Howes, alham, çarh
Ii	_Ii_	и	и	Iman, giyar, ilçi
Jj	_Jj_	же	ж	Jahan, seljyk
£ſ	_Łł_	же	ж	Ezdat, wyzdan
Kk	_Kk_	ка	к	Kelam, gorkyt halyk
Ll	_Ll_	эл	л	Lebiz, leyli, bilbil
Mm	_Mm_	эм	м	Maglymguly, namys
Nn	_Nn_	эн	н	Nagym, pent, nan
Ññ	_Ññ_	эн	н	Weýeňňaм, jenňel, aaň
Oo	_Oo_	o	о	Omar, Osman, don
Öö	_Öö_	ө	ө	Öwlüyä, Sögüt, töwir
Pp	_Pp_	пе	п	Periзde, topràk, sogap
Rr	_Rr_	эр	р	Resul, çarbad, serdar
Ss	_Ss_	эс	с	Suhangoy, nesil, Kayys
Şş	_Şş_	ше	ш	Saşenem, çeşme, syrdaş
Tt	_Tt_	ме	т	Türkmenistan, tut, gudrat
Uu	_Uu_	y	у	Ulama, Dawud, musulman
Üü	_Üü_	y	у	Ülke, sünnet, dünýä
Ww	_Ww_	бе	в	Watan, dewlet, dewür
Yy	_Yy_	ы	ы	Ylam, yklym, haly
Ýý	_Ýý_	ые	и	Yyldyz, Lebrayyl, toy
Zz	_Zz_	зе	з	Zyýarat, gazal, duz

4. The new Latin-based alphabet of Turkmenistan (1993). The first column gives the printed form of the letter, the second its equivalent in handwriting, the third its name, the fourth its form in the Cyrillic script. The fifth column gives examples of full words in handwriting. *Source: Aşgabat* 3 June 1999.

А а	О о
Б б	П п
В в	Р р
Г г	С с
ғ Ғ	Т т
д Д	У у
Е е	Ӯ ӯ
ё Ё	Ф ф
Ж ж	Х х
З з	Ҳ ҳ
И и	Ч ч
Ӣ ӣ	Ҷ ҷ
Й й	Ш ш
К к	ъ
Қ қ	Э э
Л л	Ю ю
М м	Я я
Н н	

5. The revised Cyrillic-based alphabet of Tajikistan (1998). *Source*: Copied from *Omūzgor* 23 Sept. 1998 (which only has the Cyrillic-based letters and no equivalents).

AZERBAYJAN

6, 7. Baku 1998. Presidential campaign posters hailing incumbent President Heidar Aliev. Top (Cyrillic-based script): *Khalq h.ä. deïr* – 'The nation says h.ä. [Heydär Äliyev]' (a play on the word hä – 'yes'); bottom (Latin-based script): *Heydär Äliyeve säs verin!* – 'Give your vote to Heydär Äliyev!'

8, 9. Baku 1998. Street sign 'Academician Äbdülkärim Älizadä Street', above in Azeri (Cyrillic), below in Russian, and small company sign in Russian 'plasterer's workshop'.

10. Baku 1998. Entrance plates of the H. Z. Tağiyev College of Finance and Economics of Azerbaijan; left side: in Azeri in Latin-based script, right: in Russian; above the door: 'You're welcome' in Azeri (Cyrillic) and Russian.

UZBEKISTAN

11. Tashkent 1998. Inscriptions on monument to Amir Timur (Tamerlane) on central Independence Square: 'Strength – in justice' (in hybrid Uzbek/Latin-based script, Russian, English and hybrid Uzbek/Arabic-based script).

12. Bukhara 1998. Above, official name-plate of a general secondary school (Uzbek in Latin-based script); below, slogan in Uzbek (Cyrillic-based script) *Bilimlar kuningiz qutlugh bŭlsin, qadrli ŭquvchilar!* (May your *"Day of Sciences"* be happy, dear pupils!).

13. Tashkent 1998. Name-plate of a ministry (above, Uzbek in Cyrillic-based script).

TURKMENISTAN

14, 15. Ashgabat 1998. Slogans on public buildings *Halk – Watan – Turkmenbaşy* (!) – 'People – homeland – Türkmenbashy', above in Latin-based script and below in Cyrillic-based script.

16, 17. Ashgabat 1998. Signs of state-owned companies: Turkmengaz and Turkmennebitgaz – left in Russian, right in Turkmen (Latin-based script).

18. Ashgabat 1998. Street slogans and posters in Turkmen (Latin-based script). Left, *'Türkmen halkynyň geljegi – eşretli gündür!'* – (The future of the Turkmen people – a blissful life!). Right, *'Agzybirlik, asudalyk, jebislik'*. (Harmony, tranquillity, unity). On the roof: 'People, homeland, Türkmenbashy'.

KAZAKHSTAN 19. Almaty 1998. Street slogan in Kazakh and Russian – 'My homeland – Kazakhstan'.

the other hand, where at first alphabet change also received a considerable public response, other concerns gained priority due to the civil war and its aftermath. Nevertheless it is remarkable that in 1998 Tajikistan acquired a revised Cyrillic alphabet. In the three countries that officially introduced Latin-based alphabets, the results achieved by the end of the decade were somewhat limited, but because of the gradual introduction of the new alphabets in schools, the younger generation is in fact growing up with two versions each of the Cyrillic and the Latin alphabet: the Cyrillic for Russian, the Cyrillic-based one still very widely used for the state language, the new Latin-based one also for the state language, and finally, the Latin alphabet for the western languages required in the school curricula.

8

LEXICAL AND ORTHOGRAPHIC
INTERVENTION

Language intervention – be it in the form of standardization, purification, modernization – is often a politically motivated reform process,
essentially intended to correct a perceived asymmetry. The motivations
usually have a collective significance in shaping the identity of certain
members or groups within the community, thus serving the processes of
identity politics. The basic assumption is that language is not merely a
neutral medium of communication, that is, an instrument, but also a social and political discourse, for languages comprise socio-ideological as
well as politico-ideological components. Policies aimed at standardizing
a society's language system are in themselves political acts since they
tend to delegitimize or at least narrow forms of otherness. Language
purification enhances a controlling tendency on the part of the state's
central authority which may well consider it one of its resources of power
(Shapiro 1989).

Purification represents an effort to purge the language of elements
perceived to be non-native or non-standard and their replacement with
others, borrowed from local dialects or written sources (and sometimes
the creation of completely new words); thus, an increase in vocabulary
rather than a decrease is the result. A modern vocabulary cannot be created immediately, of course. Anyway, language purification is frequently
a defensive measure against what is considered an external attack expressed in excessive import of vocabulary or grammatical forms. This is
sometimes seen as endangering the language or at least as a threat by a
rival to its role as a national unifier. Efforts at language purification are
consequently made by those devoted to the cause of nationalism, either
with or without support of the powers that be.

In many Western states, such as Germany, language purism is not a
real issue (Ammon 1997a:175-7). In others, speakers of a prestigious
language in a long-established state adopt policies of purism to defend
its status, as in French nowadays against 'the danger of English'; the
state authorities support Francophonie morally, organizationally and
financially (Têtu 1988; Weinstein 1989). This was the case of Persian,
too, in removing Arabic accretions, chiefly under Reza Shah Pahlavi
(reigned 1925-41) (Karimi-Hakkak 1989: 89 ff). Much more frequently,
this is the situation of an *ethnie* or a nation opting for purism as one of

148

the means to promote its nationalist goals, as occurred in the Ottoman, Austro-Hungarian and Russian empires in the nineteenth and early twentieth centuries. Thus, in the Jewish community of Palestine under late Ottoman rule, Eliezer Ben-Yehuda and his associates, in a conscious effort at cementing Zionism, strove to revive Hebrew as a spoken language by the concentrated invention of Hebrew words (or, at least, adoption of Semitic words) to supply lacunae in the old literary tongue (Fellman 1973). Slav ethnic groups in the Austro-Hungarian empire did the same kind of thing.

Most instances of collective efforts at language intervention and reform ride on the waves of a nationalist awakening preceding or following the achievement of statehood. In practically every case, some steps towards achieving language reform had been evident before independence and statehood. But in almost every instance, the campaign for language reform was better coordinated and more effective in the new state, not least because the political leadership took a lively interest in it. In the Republic of Turkey, established in 1923, its founder and president, Mustafa Kemal Atatürk (1923-38), moved by the wish to create a new Turkish nation, secularized and westernized, guided the Turkish Language Society, which he had set up, to act for the purification of the language from Arabic and Persian vocabulary and syntactical elements, a purification which basically implied its turkification (Heyd 1954; Lewis 1961:433-6; Lewis 1984; Landau 1993; Brendemoen 1998). The new Arab states in North Africa, which achieved independence during the 1950s and early 1960s, struggled in a similar way for the purification and modernization of Arabic as part of their national decolonization. True, their arabicization (Grandguillaume 1983) achieved different levels of language purification in the separate cases of Morocco, Algeria and Tunisia.

Language intervention in the six new states

In the six new states, language intervention can be observed particularly in the sphere of purification, but also to a certain extent in modernization, standardization and development of the lexicon. Topographical renaming occurs here as a characteristic phenomenon of de-sovietization (Bacık 1999:98-102). In a symbolic act of breaking with the past, the presidents of the five Central Asian states agreed in January 1993 to rename their region by replacing 'Srednaya Aziya' (Russian: Middle Asia) with 'Tsentral'naya Aziya' (Russian: Central Asia), along with its parallel in the titular languages (Mangott 1996:1).

In the Soviet period, thousands of Russian words had been introduced via school textbooks, dictionaries, military manuals, translations from world literature – generally carried out via the medium of Russian – and otherwise (Bruchis 1984:137-42; Bruchis 1987:250-1). Many of these imported terms 'swallowed up' existing ones in the native languages, in a process named *glottophagie*, or 'language cannibalism' by Calvet (1974) when describing French colonialism. Since the 1930s, the lexical interference of Russian as a prestige language in other tongues was very extensive. Due to sovietization and industrialization, numerous international terms were introduced via Russian (Kozlov 1988:167), employing Russian phonetic and orthographic paradigms in transcription. Data vary as to the precise size of the interference, but it appears that this was frequently linked to subject matter, so that general books and newspapers showed it less, while scientific ones were much more affected. While scholarly and academic discourse, as well as officialese, were more markedly influenced, even conversation on everyday matters often displayed the penetration of Russian vocabulary – but also of accidence and syntax. The Russian interference was greater in the standard languages than in their dialects and widened the formal/informal language split (Bruchis 1982:31-41; Ivanov 1990; Schlyter 1997). Generally, the Turkic languages are characterized by a highly stable grammatical structure and considerable resistance to change in this domain (Sjoberg 1993); not so, however, in the lexical domain. It was in the general area of lexical purification, or rather de-russification, as part of national reidentification, that nationalist motivated activities, consistent at times and sporadic at others, were noticeable during the late 1980s. The six Muslim states have initiated language reform chiefly since the early 1990s, largely as a struggle for status and prestige. From the start, committees on language were appointed to debate and decide usages, largely in the domain of vocabulary. The alternatives selected were from Chaghatay, the standard literary Turkic language before the Soviet era, or from Arabic and Persian, but very little from local dialects (which had served language purification in Turkey in the last seventy years) (Rzayev 1992).

The issue of language purism also concerns changing the names of localities, streets and persons to conform better with the titular language. The language laws of the Muslim republics refer to this. Later decrees (governmental or municipal) spelled out the details of change in place and street names, generally leaving changes in personal names to individual discretion, even while recommending them (details spelled out in Pigolkin and Studenikina 1991:67).

Azerbayjan

Azerbayjan has a literary history dating back to the thirteenth century. By the sixteenth century, Azerbayjan Turkish was at its zenith, when the famous poet Fuzuli (d. 1556 in Baghdad) wrote in a language which can be considered close to Ottoman Turkish and an earlier stage of the language Azerbayjan Turks write today. *Dede Qorqud* (probably written down in the late fifteenth century), regarded as a national epic by Turks in Turkey, as well as by Azeris, who also share a common eponymous ancestor, the mythical hero Oghuz Khan, leader of the Turkmen tribes, is written in a language connected to modern Azerbayjan Turkish and Turkish dialects spoken in the Eastern Anatolian parts of the Republic of Turkey.

This linguistic history led to an eminently political contemporary question – unique to Azerbayjan – which divides the republic of Azerbayjan of the 1990s into essentially two camps, one represented by the ruling government of Aliev, the other by the opposition. The question asked, not for the first time, is: 'What should we call the language we speak? Should we call it "language of Azerbayjan" (*Azärbaÿjan dili*) or "Turkish of Azerbayjan" (*Azärbaÿjan türkjäsi*) or simply "Turkish language" (*Türk dili*)?' This question, like the issue of the alphabets, is a variant of the question 'Who are we?' and seems to be of much more relevance to the public as well as to politicians and scholars than any attempt at language purification and the like (*Ana Sözü* 1-4, 1992; *Yeni Müsavat* 24 Dec. 1992, 7 Jan. 1993; *Cümhuriyyät* 20, 27 Mar. 1993; *Azadlıq* 25 Apr., 4 Nov. 1995; *Millät* 14 Nov. 1995; *535-ci Qäzet* 30 Oct. 1996; *Müxalifät* 21 Dec. 1996; *Araz* Oct.-Dec. 1996; *Azärbaycan Dili vä Ädäbiyyatı* no. 2, 1997; *Hürriyyät* 20 May 1997; Närimanoğlu 1995).

Under Elchibey's government (June 1992-June 1993), the answer was 'Turkish language', meaning at the same time 'we are the cousins of the Turks of Turkey', and stressing the close cultural and historical bonds with that country which was still considered a model and support in the early 1990s. This stand was also underlined by the law on language, adopted on 22 December 1992, renaming the state language 'Turkish'; this had been the official name of the Azerbayjan state language from 1918 to 1936. The Aliev government which seized power in June 1993 insisted on the public use of the term 'language of Azerbayjan', to boost the young state's self-assurance and emphasize its independence. Before the referendum over the proposed constitution, held on 12 November 1995, Aliev made a speech flatly rejecting the suggestion that the new constitution's calling the state language 'language of Azerbayjan' was a 'political message', stressing: 'Our language is the Azerbayjani language ... From historic ... and philological perspectives, the Azerbayjani language has its source in the Turkic languages ... The Turkic language world is very large. Some 23 Turkic languages existed in the former Soviet Union. Each has its own name ... One of them is the 'language of Azerbayjan' (text in *Azärbaycan* 2, 7, 9, 10 Nov. 1995; FBIS-SOV-219: 14 Nov. 1995; also *BR* 6 Aug. 1998). In the late 1990s this question is still a favourite topic of debate in the press and also strongly contested in private circles (oral communication by Haläddin Ibrahimli, Baku,

September 1998; Kellner-Heinkele 2000). In official circles, however, the issue was considered as settled: in August 1998, for instance, the Ministry of Justice refused to register the Labour Union of Azerbayjan Journalists, on the grounds that its name and charter 'were not written in the Azeri language' – apparently a code for the use of too many Turkish words (*Index on Censorship* 4:1999, 120).

Although the question can be primarily understood as a political one, public discussion over the years had usually been conducted in a linguistic-Turkological tone (e.g. Seidov 1982; Melikli 1999). But the fact that the term 'Turkish language' ('Tyurkskii yazyk'; literally 'Turkic' rather than 'Turkish', in Russian 'Turetskii'), which figured in the language law of 22 December 1992, was replaced in the new constitution of 1995 by the term 'language of Azerbayjan' ('Azärbaïjan dili', article 21), represents not only a linguistic-philological correction. The main argument of the proponents of 'Turkish' is that it was Stalin who first used the term 'Azerbayjani language' in 1936 (FBIS-SOV-92-238:10 Dec. 1992; *Azärbaycan Dili* 23 June 1995), instead of 'Turkish language'. While it is true that Stalin established the usage as official, he certainly was not the one who coined it. International scientific literature of the nineteenth and twentieth centuries demonstrates that the term 'Azeri' or 'Azerbayjanian' was a convenient way to distinguish topographically the strands of a bundle of Turkish dialects spread over a large area with differing political backgrounds. Anyway, Aliev's return to the former name of the state language was widely understood as a move not only intended to highlight independence, but also to satisfy the Russian neighbour and to distance himself from the Republic of Turkey (e.g. Behar 1995:7). Undeniably, the Aliev government, whose main figures are old hands from Soviet times, started to steer a course much closer to Russia's political preferences than Elchibey's government had cared to do.

Both sides evidently have a worthy cause and dispose of arguments that not only reflect political predilections but also have a historically sound basis. It is exactly this double situation of common roots, hence closeness, but distinct historical development, that makes it so difficult for the Turks of Azerbayjan to determine their national linguistic identity. According to one Baku professor of philology, the Azeri language was phonologically much purer and closer to a primary Turkic ideal than Turkish (of Turkey) (Grocer 1997:5). It is not important here to what extent the statement is correct; what matters is that the professor perceived his own language in this manner and hence arrived at the demand for independence in every respect: 'We do not want to be subsumed under any nation, be it politically, socially or linguistically, ever again' (Grocer 1997: 5). This is obviously a statement against any kind of 'big brother' (for an example of this attitude, frequently encountered in Turkey, Zülfikar 1999), a repudiation of any shade of Pan-Turkism and a definite farewell to russification, in short, the expression of a will to find one's own national road. This aim, which is supported by a wide section of the population, refers also to what can be termed 'regaining the mother tongue' or, in other words, purification of Azerbayjan's Turkish.

During Soviet times, linguistic research on the Azeri language had been made possible in every way, especially on the level of the Academy of Sciences, although before *perestroika* academic limits were clearly drawn, as a profusion of books and conference volumes demonstrates (reports on such activities: *BR* 12 May 1988; 9 Dec. 1988; 3 Nov. 1989; Babaïev 1996; Tenishev a.o. 1997:171f.). In the light of this literature the general complaint of the 1990s about the neglect of the Azeri language cannot be readily understood or should be interpreted as a lack of language modernizing efforts. The most likely explanation seems to be that the results of such scientific pursuits were not made available to the general readership, but remained the purview of scholarly circles.

The poet Bakhtiyar Vahabzade (b. 1925) regretted, in 1989, that Russian instead of Azeri Turkish had been used to conduct state business since the Second World War. It is often claimed that it was with the beginning of Soviet rule that Russian words began to invade the Azeri vocabulary, especially in the ideological and technical sphere. However, it should be remembered that Russian terms began to play a role in everyday speech in Northern Azerbayjan (as opposed to the province of 'Southern' Azerbayjan within Persia/Iran) ever since Russia acquired most of the territory of contemporary Azerbayjan by the 1828 Peace of Turkmanchay with Persia (details in Azarsina and Mamedova 1993).

The quest for linguistic autonomy, a major concern with Azeri writers and intellectuals in the late nineteenth and early twentieth centuries, is repeated at the dawn of the twenty-first within the wider framework of shaping a national identity. While the choice used to be between coining a new terminology with the help of the traditional language versus adopting the European terminology of modernity which kept pouring in with the oil boom, today the choice is basically between a clean-out of Russian vocabulary for ideological reasons and its partial replacement by new terms, usually American, for practical reasons, on the one hand, and the revitalization of traditional (Turkic, Persian, Arabic) vocabulary by ascribing new modern meanings to it, on the other. In reality, a mixed process of language development can be observed. An example is a 1993 *Dictionary of Market Economy* of 80 pages by S. Sultanova and Ch. Mämmädzadä (Baku 1993). Two parallel columns on each page, in Russian and Azeri (in Cyrillic script), respectively, explain international business terms, generally borrowed from American usage via Russian (e.g., 'know-how', 'overdraft', 'rating'). Another instance is a three-language dictionary of financial and economic terms, prepared by Rasul Rahshanli, Anatolii Renkin and Lyubov' Dokuzanskaya, published in

Baku in 1998. Comprising about 12,000 terms in Russian, English and Azeri, it seems intended mainly for translators (*BR* 8 July 1998; *Vyshka* 6 Nov. 1998).

Moderate and practical application of language-developing goals seems to draw the broadest backing. A good example of this standpoint is the dictionary of orthography and pronunciation of 'the language of Azerbayjan' (i.e., Azerbayjan Turkish) by Äziz Äfändizadä (Baku: 1996), which offers a good number of international loanwords transmitted via Russian, and even Russian words displaying either their original Russian orthography or a spelling adapted to Azeri phonetics. The criteria for such a distinction are not explained in the dictionary.

The shortcomings of language intervention in the Azeri case are caused by economic and organizational deficits. In contrast to Turkey in the 1930s and later, Azerbayjan today does not possess a person or body authoritative enough to enforce puristic measures. Even Turkey under Atatürk could not easily achieve the language revolution from above, because language usage cannot be rapidly influenced by government imposed norms. The Soviet example was complex and did not succeed solely on the strength of decrees and laws. It was accompanied, rather, by the monopoly of superior technological, administrative, financial and ideological authority. Today creative minds from literary and scholarly circles, readily supported by opposition politicians jumping on this seemingly objective intellectual train, may display a variety of national and patriotic choices in replacing the popular and familiar albeit Russian vocabulary, but the population might not pick them up and get used to them unless persuaded to do so by a heavy campaign in all the media or by a convincing handiness, as in the case of Western terms. At least in September 1998, on the state television Channel 1, there was no more than one programme, lasting half an hour to one hour every other day, on Azerbayjan language and literature.

The variety of political goals in the different camps aside, the way to national identity cannot be disconnected from financial considerations. It is in this field that a major effort at language purification and development meets its limitations. Here, as in the question of the alphabet, it can be observed that the lack of resources hinders any progress from becoming publicized nation-wide, i.e., beyond scholarly and literary discussion.

The discussion on the name of the state language seems to have obscured the fact that not much has actually been achieved in the way of modernizing and purifying Azerbayjan Turkish, or at least in making the results of such efforts available for the general public. A rather secondary issue, the form family names could or could not take, is widely considered a question of personal taste (Garibova and Blair 1996). On 2 February 1993, parliament approved a decree stipulating that family names of all citizens be adapted to the state language and that the state set the appropriate conditions. While the bureaucracy did indeed try to adjust to individual citizens' wishes concerning the replacement of a Russian-type name-forming suffix (-ov/-ova, -ev/-eva) attached to the family name by a Persian (-zade) or Turkish suffix (-li/ly, and in extension -oglu/-qyzy), Soviet practice remains popular, even though this is deplored in some circles (*Müxalifät* 16 Nov. 1996; 8 Jan. 1997).

Uzbekistan

Like the Azerbayjan Turks, Uzbeks have a long literary history that goes back to the fifteenth century. The language this literary heritage was written in, Chaghatay, shows the strong impact of Persian; and, besides Uzbek, other modern Turkic languages – like Kazakh, Turkmen, Modern Uyghur, and Tatar – can claim a linguistic relationship with Chaghatay (Boeschoten and Vandamme 1998:166-9). When in 1924 new nations were created in Central Asia, the pre-Soviet writings were left behind as 'relics of a feudal past' and expressions of outdated language usage, as the new borders also meant that new national languages were being created in the allotted territories on the basis of local idioms. With time, Uzbekistan's new literary and state language became far removed – both in vocabulary and in grammar – from the idiom that had formed the literary *lingua franca* of the Turkestan area and beyond (Critchlow 1991:101).

The efforts of the Soviet regime in the 1920s to create standard literary languages for the numerous nationalities of the Union meant in the Uzbek case singling out one of the dialects spoken by Uzbeks within the new borders drawn in 1924. The – phonologically speaking – half-Iranized dialect of the Tashkent area was chosen and ever since used exclusively in official transactions, education, publications and radio, if Uzbek was used. At the same time, this dialect, in its new role, rapidly adopted the vocabulary and modern terminology of Russian or as transmitted through Russian. The ideological and political structure of this act of language planning cannot be attributed merely to the Soviets' use of the means of power, but must also be seen within a fairly widespread concept of the time, namely the idea that people can be transformed globally to fit a political programme of the future by implanting in their minds not only new ideas, but also deepening their familiarity with Russian as part of sovietization. Essentially, what happened was a kind of language intervention, in the service of an unlimited belief in the idea of progress and a future classless society.

Together with the alphabet changes before the Second World War, the measures just described resulted in a culture shock comparable to the one experienced in the Turkish Republic in the same period. The cast-off language of the few literate Uzbeks, Chaghatay, thus came to assume the role of a dead language that could be of interest only to the small group of orientalists and philologists whom the Soviet state was prepared to preserve as an academic elite. Modern Uzbek itself, however, emerged in the late 1980s as a vehicle for opposition to linguistic russification (Critchlow 1991:99-105). Uzbek elites started debating how to eliminate from their language words of foreign – generally, Russian – origins, along with promoting the values of their own national culture through their 'national literary language' (*millĭ adabiĭ til*) (*ŬTA* 1990, no. 5:75-80; *Sharq Yulduzi* 1990, nos. 3, 4, 10; 1992, no. 1).

The attitude of the contemporary Uzbek state is pragmatic. Language is again to serve the goals of the future, namely to become a tool which permits the people to unite in the feeling of being one nation responding to the demands of the modern age. This includes and requires that the titular language be developed, expanded in its tasks and applicability, particularly in official use, and that it also become firmly rooted as the everyday medium of communication among all citizens. One way to expand language is to comb the popular language for expressions that might also serve in other fields. At the same time, language planners of today seem to be ready to accept common international and universally acknowledged terms while at the same time demanding their uzbekization (*Ŭzbekistonda Izhtimoiĭ Fanlar. Obshchestvennye Nauki v Uzbekistane* 1993, no. 7:75-6; oral communication by Prof. Dilarom Rashidova, Nov. 1996).

Already in the late 1980s, Uzbek intellectuals severely criticized the fact that towns, villages, streets and other geographical marks within Uzbekistan bore non-native names (for a unionwide conference on the subject in 1989 *ŬTA* 1989, no. 5). With *glasnost'*, the topic rapidly became one of the major concerns of the re-nativization movement which was carried on not only by intellectuals but also by the people in general. The wave of topographical re-naming, typical of tsarist and Soviet times in Central Asia, rolled back and changed the maps again (Critchlow 1991: 109-11). In 1992, the revision of topographical and historical names became a regular concern at meetings of the Council of Ministers, attended by scholars, writers, journalists and government officials (*PV* 11 June 1992). Lately it can be observed that Uzbeks have become used to Uzbek terms in addresses ('mahalla' instead of 'kvartal' and 'rais' instead of 'predsedatel''). In June 1996, Karimov issued a decree on the renaming of designated administrative-territorial objects by 1 September of that year (Smith a.o. 1998:147). In January 1998 the Committee for Coordinating the Implementation of the Law on the State Language at the Council of Ministers made another significant move on this issue, determining to appoint new local commissions in the various quarters of Tashkent and elsewhere to regularize the names of streets, alleys, squares, cinema-halls and schools – keeping also the earlier signs in special cases, however (*PV* 16 Jan. 1998; 28 May 1998). Much of this has been carried out.

according to reports presented at the meeting in May 1999 of the high-level commission supervising this activity (*PV* 6 May 1999). It appears that Uzbekistan and Kazakhstan have made more headway than the other states in their toponymic overhaul.

The language issue is a different matter. The Law on the State Language of 1989 (and its revised form of 21 Dec. 1995) proclaim that Uzbek must be revised, meaning de-russified and enriched, and that a state committee responsible to the Government Language Commission (which in turn depends on the Council of Ministers) is to supervise the implementation of the law, guided by a state programme passed by the Council of Ministers (*ŬTA* 1990, no.5:45-8). The first Terminology Committee was in fact created shortly afterwards (26 Dec. 1989).

The most pressing task clearly consisted in following out the foremost intent of the language law and creating a set of Uzbek terms that would permit people to express in Uzbek what had been expressed mainly in Russian, i.e. in administrative and scientific contexts, in situations where primarily Russian used to be spoken. In March 1991, a conference was convened in Tashkent by the State Terminology Committee and the Institute of Linguistics of the Uzbek Academy of Sciences to deliberate on the Law on the State Language and Uzbek terminology. The conference agreed on twelve recommendations for steps to be taken if the goal to enrich, unify, purify and modernize Uzbek was to be achieved (*ŬTA* 1991, no.3:29-30). Subsequently, government commissions, linguists in academia and members of the Uzbek Writers' Union continued to make proposals in the press and in scholarly journals. But consensus concerning the practical meaning, contents and method of such a task was and remains difficult to reach. Since the language law had not spelled out how the language was to be changed and implemented or how far this should go, the committees' work met with public and private criticism (interview with Prof. Azim Hozhiev, 8 Sep. 1998; with Mr. Zhemal Kemal, Uzbek Writers' Union, 7 Sep. 1998; *ŬTA* 1996, no. 3:3-7; proposals for the replacement or orthographical reform of Russian, international and Arabic/Persian terms: *ŬTA* 1991, no. 3:65-7, no. 5:51-3; 1995, no. 3:27-31, no. 4: 34-8; 1996, no. 3:26-30).

One aspect of the matter was the question of how to deal with loan-words. Not before 1992 did the State Terminology Committee publish *Principles for the Choice of Uzbek Counterparts to Russian-International Loanwords,* which was commented upon by the well-known linguist A. Hozhiev in his *Termin tanlash mezonlari* (Criteria for the Choice of Terms) (Tashkent: Fan, 1996). As summed up by Schlyter (1997:37f), he recommended the following approach to Russian loan-words:

– Russian words that have been truly integrated into Uzbek should be retained.

– Russian words that are intelligible on an international level should also be retained and written according to international standards, not according to Uzbek phonetics.

– Necessary substitutions can be found resuscitating 'Old Uzbek' words or Uzbek dialectical forms or coining new terms. While no particular emphasis is given to the Turkic origin of such new terms, semantic isomorphism is a requirement. In fact, the tradition of discussing the enrichment and improvement of the Uzbek language continues in popular and academic journals and in newspapers as well (*Ëshlik* 1998, no. 2:56).

Already in 1994, the Terminology Committee had proudly announced that in the course of the past year, new Russian-Uzbek terminological dictionaries had been published for mathematics, biology, chemistry, botany, linguistics, and military affairs. The new terms were to be employed in official documents, business papers, in the press and in school books. At the same time, orthographical dictionaries of Uzbek personal names and of toponyms and short Russian-Uzbek dictionaries of sociopolitical, bureaucratic and geological terminology were published in small numbers, though it was hoped that the size of editions could be increased in the future. The small socio-political dictionary also contained socio-economic and cultural vocabulary (*PV* 21 July 1994).

As the situation stands now, no proof of a consistent language reform has as yet been offered to the public. The few examples that can be given so far, like the modest orthographic dictionary with *ca.* 14,000 entries published in 1995 (Sh. Rahmatullayev and A. Hojiyev, *O 'zbek tilining imlo lug'ati,* Tashkent: O 'qituvchi) only highlight the complexity of this issue. That author opposed an 'exaggerated' zeal in the replacement of international terms with traditional ones (mostly of Arabic or Persian origin) or newly coined Uzbek vocabulary (*ŪTA* 1995, no. 2:26-8). On the other hand, neologisms like 'grant' and 'komp'yuter' that came mainly with the fast growing interest for English (if they are not anglicisms imported via Russian), can readily be found in everyday conversation and academic and popular publications as well. The discussion reflected in periodicals of language and literature like *Sharq Yulduzi* and *Ŭzbek Tili va Adabiëti* in the 1990s seems rather conservative and not very creative, often hardly more than a reiteration of pre-independence concerns (e.g. *ŪTA* 1989, no. 3).

The replacement of Russian vocabulary with a revitalized pre-Soviet Uzbek one, usually termed Chaghatay and consisting predominantly of Persian and Arabic words, can be observed, as well as the parallel existence of modern Uzbek and traditional vocabulary, e.g. Arabic 'muqaddima' (introduction) for modern Uzbek 'sŭzboshi' can be seen in publications of the last few years, but this is no systematic phenomenon (*ŪTA* 1995, no. 3). On the other hand, there were some views supporting also the elimination of Persian and Arabic words from Uzbek (*PV* 16

July 1991). More often, however, merely orthographic adaptation to Uzbek pronunciation is suggested (*ŬTA* 1991, no. 6). It is still too early to determine to what extent such usage will be accepted by the public.

Following the Uzbek example, in the Karakalpak Autonomous Republic a special committee for terminology was set up on 1 March 1990 and invested some time and work in enlarging the vocabulary (Nasyrova 1994:237).

Kazakhstan

Although less affected by the post-independence fever of alphabet change than Azerbayjan or Uzbekistan, Kazakhstan has nevertheless tried its hand at language development. But it is obvious that Kazakhstan is less free to deal with its own language than the other states mentioned, because whatever language change is envisaged, it is bound to influence the status of the second official language in the state, Russian, and the sentiments of the Russian-speaking population. The state-supported *Qazaq Tili* language revival society with its president Äbduali Qaydarov consequently campaigns mostly for the proper use of the state language, e.g. by verifying the translations into Kazakh of public signs, announcements, and product labels which are often issued with grammatical or orthographical errors (Dave 1996a:55; *Delovaya Nedelya* 6 Nov., 11 Nov. 1998; *Aqtöbe* 10 Sep. 1998). Kazakhs also feel free today to criticize their fellow countrymen's incorrect (i.e. inspired by Russian phonology) pronunciation of Kazakh names and words (reader's letter in *KP* 2 July 1996).

The State Terminology Commission set up by the government with the particular aim of developing the language does not seem to have attracted general interest. Moreover, the commission is divided in opinion, thus representing two main tendencies that can be found among those Kazakh citizens who take a close interest in the language question. The following standpoints were expressed by two highly-placed administrators who, in one case, advocated that the Kazakh language needed to preserve the 'international vocabulary' it already possesses, especially in the sciences, otherwise it would not be able to serve on an international level; and, in the other, that equivalents must be found in the national language, Kazakh, for all scientific and technical terms (*KP* 6 Aug. 1998).

A reader's letter complained that neither the members of the commission nor the way it works are known to the public, although the terms it innovates are published in the press. Citing the great representatives of Kazakh literature, arts and sciences of the nineteenth century and of the Soviet period, this reader stresses the long and close friendship of the Kazakhs with the Russian people in order to underline the usefulness of the international vocabulary transmitted into Kazakh via Russian.

Severe criticism is levelled at efforts to replace the international vocabulary thus acquired ('arkhitektura', 'transport', 'redaktor', 'finansy' and many others) with Kazakh terms or neologisms, arguing that these in no way cover the same semantic ground (*Novoe Pokolenie* 1995, no. 12). Similarly, Berik Abdygaliev (1995:4), a political scientist in the Kazakh Institute of Strategic Studies at the President's Office, complains about 'the children's disease' in the purification of Kazakh – both its extreme approach and its hasty elimination of international terms, without due replacement except by archaisms. Others agree with this argument, saying that some of the words used for this type of replacement can easily be recognized as old Arabic or Persian loanwords in Kazakh.

Some scholars propose the enrichment of the Kazakh literary language by adopting into it a vocabulary from its dialects which allegedly often conveys modern meanings (*Mysl'* 1995, no. 10:83-4). The limitations of this proposal are evident. Moreover, the sixty terminological dictionaries said to have been prepared between 1990 and 1995 have not always been compiled in consultation with the State Terminology Commission and have been criticized as inadequate by many. Among these critics were Altynbek Sarsenbaev, then Minister of Information, and Vladimir Shkol'nik, then Minister of Science and President of the Kazakh Academy of Sciences. In a joint article, intended to set the right course, they announced, for 1998-2000, a programme for the publication of terminological dictionaries under the supervision of two prominent Kazakh scholars, A.K. Khusainov, director of the publishing house *Rauan* of the Ministry of Information, and K.Sh. Khusainov, education science specialist and director of the Institute of Linguistics of the Ministry of Science and the Academy of Sciences – in close cooperation with the State Terminology Commission (*KP* 11 July 1998).

The State Onomastic Commission set up by the government was empowered to change the geographic and administrative-territorial names on the map of Kazakhstan, 'which dated from the time of tsarist colonization, from the period of collectivization in the 1930s, personality cult, arbitrary rule and stagnation' (*KP* 20 Sep. 1991). The above-mentioned Sultan Orazalinov (p.85) pointed out that too many places had been named after Soviet personalities and concepts: 181 for Lenin, 71 for Kirov, 53 for Kalinin, the term 'October' 105 times, 'Bolshevik' 53, and 'socialism' 35 (Orazalinov 1995; *KP* 19 Feb. 1998). The commission changed many of these appellations (list in Karasik 1993:297). Another of its tasks was to check whether the spelling of topographical names suited the rules of Kazakh phonology (*Irtysh* 18 Mar. 1997). It is noteworthy that of the *ca.* 2,500 names of the capital's boulevards, streets and squares only 15-16 % were in Kazakh, in most cases named after people who had nothing to do with the history and culture of the republic (*KP* 29 Nov. 1990). The work this commission is doing has brought to the public's attention the imbalance that characterized the situation of geographical names in Kazakhstan (*Segodnya* Mar. 1995).

Quite a number of topographical renamings may be noticed even in the international media, like the change of name of Gur'ev to Atyrau or Tselinograd to Akmola and then to Astana, which means 'capital city' – Nazarbaev's own innovation (according to an interview he gave *Izvestiya* 4 June 1998). This process was not always unanimously welcomed by the Kazakh citizens concerned. Some of them thought that in difficult times, the government should attend to other, more pressing matters (*KP* 8 July 1992). In other cases, only the russified orthography of place names was officially exchanged for the existing Kazakh equivalent, as e.g. in the case of Alma-Ata to Almaty (Constitution of 28 Jan. 1993; FBIS-SOV-93.027: 11 Feb. 1993), Chimkent to Shymkent, Zhanykurgan to Zhanaqorgan, Chu river to Shu river (for a list of renamings, *KP* 17 Sep. 1992). The campaign reached even small towns, villages and all twenty oblasts (provinces) (*The Current Digest of the Post-Soviet Press* 47(10):15 Apr. 1995). On the village level, however, much renaming needs yet to be done (*Aktyubinskii Vestnik* 31 Oct. 1997; *Akmolinskaya Pravda* 16 Apr., 21 Aug. 1998).

The craving for change extended also to the renaming of streets. In spring 1993, twenty street names in Almaty lost their Soviet flavour: the names of political figures of the Soviet Union or of heroes of the Civil War were replaced by names of prominent Kazakh figures and heroes (*The Current Digest of the Post-Soviet Press* 47(10): 15 Apr. 1995). The same happened in multi-national Akmola, but without asking the non-Kazakh inhabitants their opinion (*KP* 29 July 1996). The campaign went on and in 1998 extended to the renaming of bus and trolleybus stops in Almaty's streets (*Vechernii Almaty* 11 Mar., 14 Sep. 1998).

Non-Kazakh citizens of Kazakhstan do not feel comfortable with the Kazakhization of topographical and other terms, some even rating this process as 'russophobia' or 'apartheid' (*KP* 6 Apr. 1994). As the chairperson of the Slavic movement *Lad* put it: 'When I go to my own housing area and I do not see one sign in the Russian language, I cannot understand why in a state which says that I am an equal citizen here I cannot find my way around even in a housing area' (FBIS-SOV-95-146:31 July 1995).

New legislation has finally permitted what many Kazakhs have long felt to be a necessity to facilitate national identity building, that is, to shed, if they wish, the Russian ending (-ov/ -ova, -ev/-eva) of their family name and replace the Russian suffixes of fathers' names (-ovich/-ovna, -evich/-evna) with -ūly and -qyzy (*KP* 8 Nov. 1996). The practical costs of this change in documents and passports are enormous, and not all citizens feel that they are justifiable.

Kyrgyzstan

In June 1934, the local Communist party ordered that the Kyrgyz language be developed 'by the maximum use of sovietisms and international terminology through the Russian language' (Huskey 1995:552). This process continued unabated. Already in 1986, the Kyrgyz poet Aali Toqombaev (1904-88) published an article calling for the reform of Kyrgyz orthography and the purification of the language.

One of the first decisions taken in independent Kyrgyzstan was to change place names given by the Russians and Soviets back into Kyrgyz-style ones (Moldokasımtegin 1995-6). This started with the re-naming of its capital: 'Good-bye Frunze, hello Bishkek!' as the newspaper *Slovo Kyrgyzstana* headlined at the time (7 Feb. 1991). It reported that in the concluding debate the national parliament had decided after long discussions and consultation with experts that the capital should not be given some name like Ala-too or Manas, but that it ought to revert to its historical name, Bishkek, thus committing the garbled Russian and early Soviet form Pishpek to oblivion (information on 19 Mar. 1999 from Dr T. Choroev, a Kyrgyz historian who campaigned actively for the restoration of the name Bishkek). Along with it, the names of twenty other towns were changed. Some towns and villages were named after historical figures or people active in science and art. In choosing these names and those of streets, Kyrgyz personalities were selected first, then those of neighbouring peoples – such as Uzbeks, Kazakhs, Turkmens, or Tajiks – then others. General concepts ('freedom') or borrowings from nature ('sun', 'moon') were also employed (Asankanov 1997:144-55).

A special governmental Commission for Terminology, cooperating with the Academy of Sciences, is preparing lists of terms in economics and various fields of work. Replacement of Russian terms by Kyrgyz ones is also progressing (*Asaba* 7 Feb. 1993; *Ėrkin Too* 18 Sep. 1998; *KT* 22 Sep. 1998; *Kyrgyz Tuusu* 25-27 Sep. 1998). Committed nationalists, however, such as those writing in the weekly *Asaba*, maintain that work on terminology is proceeding too slowly and that more dictionaries and lists of Kyrgyz terms are urgently needed (*Asaba* 18 Dec. 1998).

Turkmenistan

Similarly to Kazakhstan, Turkmenistan's government undertook its efforts at language change in moderate terms, though for other reasons: the Turkmen language can be considered only superficially 'russianized' (Clark 1998:86). It remains open to discussion to what extent Turkmen was less 'russianized' than the titular languages in the other five states. Russian terms continue to be used in Turkmen, with modest efforts to translate or supplant them. However, a special commission has started looking for old Turkmen terms to replace Russian ones, and plans eventually to publish a standard dictionary; meanwhile, provisional lists of medical, economic and other terms are being prepared for publication. Terminology is being developed and supervised by the Supreme Council for Science and Technology under the president. In July 1998, the Institute of Language and Literature was transferred from the Turkmen Academy of Sciences to this presidential council in order to improve its working conditions and efficacy, especially in preparing the many-volume dictionary of the Turkmen language from its early history to the present, and a new eight-volume *History of Turkmen Literature* (*NT* 11 July 1998).

Sub-commissions of the Supreme Council attend to education (curricula and textbooks, chapter 9 below) and to geographic names. Its innovations have become more immediately visible in the latter case. On 17 April 1992, the Presidium of the Supreme Soviet (*sic*) of Turkmenistan issued a decree that changed, in accordance with the Law on Language of 1989, the spelling of two oblasts (provinces), thirty rayons (districts), and thirteen towns, i.e. the Russian spelling was officially replaced by the Turkmen equivalent. In this way, e.g., the spelling of the former Chardzhou oblast was changed to Chärjev, the Kizyl-Arvat rayon became Gyzylarbat and the city of Tashauz is now spelled Dashkhovuz (*TI* 29 Apr. 1992). In 1993, further changes in topographical and administrative names took place (*TI* 11 Aug. 1993). This time, place names mostly of Russian origin also were changed, and provinces and districts were no longer designated by the Russian terms 'oblast'' and 'rayon', but by the Turkmen terms 'velaet' and 'ètrap'. The former Kirov, Krasnovodsk, Leninsk, Kalinin, Tel'man, Oktyabr', and Parakhat districts were renamed Babadaikhan, Turkmenbashy, Akdepe, Boldumsaz, Gumdag, Saparmurat Turkmenbashy and Niyaz, respectively (*TI* 11 Aug. 1993; Karasik 1993:442-3).

In June and July 1999, by presidential decree, further changes on the map of Turkmenistan took place. The town, district and region of Tashauz were renamed Dashoguz – possibly inspired by a popular etymology hinting at Oghuz Khan, the hero eponymous of the Turkmens. Further, the President renamed Charodzhou/Chärjev Turkmenabad, 'to ensure that the names in the country reflect its rebirth' (*Extracts* 16 June, 21 July 1999. Available: http://www.soros.org/turkstan/omri/0132 and 0149.html. 16 Sep. 1999).

In contrast to some other states, Turkmenistan's search for identity seems to focus much less on linguistic de-russification than on constructing Turkmen self-confidence around certain national symbols, the most expedient of which seems to be the person of its President. Another is the concept of 'Turkmen neutrality', an idea that is used to navigate more safely in a geopolitically sensitive position and to distance the state from any insinuations of obligations towards its Turkic neighbours. Under these circumstances, any attempt at language change can be understood as a distinctive marker in both home and foreign politics.

Tajikistan

As in the other new Muslim states, independence has initiated a certain degree of language intervention. Most visible is again the change of names of districts, towns, streets and public institutions which started immediately after independence (Perry 1992). Some examples may illustrate this: The former district of Proletar was renamed Gafurov (after the former First Party Secretary and orientalist) and Leninabad went back to its traditional name Khojand. In Dushanbe, central streets formerly carrying the names of Lenin and Sviridenko acquired that of Rudaki (a Persian poet of the tenth century) and Bukhara (the symbol of irredentist aspirations). The former Shevchenko University in Dushanbe became Juraev University (after a former rector of that university) and Kirov University in Khojand was renamed Rahim Jalil University (after a twentieth-century author from this city).

Another psychologically important change was the possibility of sheding Russian-style endings in family names like -ov/-ova or -ev/-eva in favour of Persian formatives like -zod, -zoda, -i, as provided in the Law on Language (Perry 1992). However, due to the chaotic political situation during most of the 1990s, this provision came into force only after 1 January 1998 ('Programme for the Development of the State Language ...', 21 Oct. 1997, publ. in *Omūzgor* 6 Nov. 1997; cf. p. 106). Therefore, even in 1999 Russian-style names are ubiquitous.

On the level of language purification, by the second anniversary of the Law on Language certain changes had taken place that indicated a concern to reduce Slavic loanwords or words considered Soviet imports, replacing them with words mostly employed by Persian speakers in Iran and Afghanistan: e.g., 'Soveti Olī' (Supreme Soviet), 'gazeta' (newspaper), 'zhurnal' (periodical) were replaced by their Tajik equivalents 'Majlisi Olī', 'rūznoma' and 'mohnoma'. Vocabulary considered international, however, such as 'telefon', 'komp'yuter' and the like, continues to be acceptable (information by H. Saifulloev, 4 Apr. 1999).

There is some debate, however, in selecting new words – whether from the Persian used in Iran nowadays or from older materials surviving in Eastern Iranian or other regional languages (Atkin 1994:94). Not all neologisms created by the then newly appointed Terminology Commission, headed by the leading Tajik lexicographer Muhammadjân Shukurov, (Shukûrî), found general approval. Concern was expressed about the fact that the majority of recent neologisms corresponded to the usage of Iran. Shukurov justified this procedure by pointing out that Iran had made significant progress in creating native scientific-technological terminology (Perry 1992:4).

As of 1999, the Institute of Language and Literature of the Tajik Academy of Sciences is the official institution in charge of the development and purification of the Tajik language. In particular, its Department of Lexicology and Lexicography has shouldered the task of studying the vocabulary and making proposals for change. Basically, all university departments and chairs of Tajik language and literature are expected to participate in this effort. The question of language development also has its forum in the media. Newspapers like *Omūzgor* or scientific journals like *Ma"rifat* provide space for such contributions, while radio and television stations broadcast discussions on language reform on a regular basis (information provided by H. Saifulloev, 4 Apr. 1999). Language purification, however, seems to have proceeded slowly, due to the civil war and its consequences.

9

LANGUAGE OF INSTRUCTION AND LANGUAGE INSTRUCTION

Scholars such as the Kazakh K.E. Kusherbaev (1996:209) have pointed out that in multiethnic states and societies education encouraging respect and empathy for the culture of other *ethnies* is the best prescription for inter-ethnic consensus. However, in the six newly independent states, the centricity of the titular culture and language has been paramount in public opinion and hence in education. Current loyalties are frequently focused on the political units whose boundaries are often perceived as being defined by the language of the educational system. Education is a major instrument in nation building and in the inculcation of societal values, and the case of the six republics is no exception (Schmidt 1995:21ff). Education may be an even more potent factor in the six new states than elsewhere due to the fact that close to half of their entire population is of school age or younger and that school attendance is almost universal (in the Soviet-initiated tradition).

Language instruction and the changes introduced into it during the 1990s are a useful indicator of language policies and language politics in the newly independent states, even if the information one has is sometimes incomplete or not detailed enough, chiefly because the official departments of statistics in several of these states have not yet caught up with the heavy work load involved, while some other government agencies have not dealt fully with the plethora of problems facing them. However, enough data and opinions are available to attempt an exposé of the relevant situation in each state, together with some comparative and contrastive remarks. One should remember that the debates and decisions concerning language instruction are only one aspect of the change in course stemming from the de-idealization of the Soviet past and its replacement with other objectives and methods, stressing – to various degrees within the six states – 'heritage respecting' and 'heritage creating' within more nationalist-minded parameters.

The standing of Russian in Soviet education was typical of unequal bilingualism. In 1938, its study was made compulsory in all non-Russian schools. The general situation was characterized by the fact that the brighter the student and the higher one went, the greater the use of Russian. Other languages were approached variously: in each of the fifteen republics studying the titular language was compulsory, although not always enforced. In the twenty autonomous republics, the eight autonomous regions and the ten autonomous districts it was optional. Considerable efforts, both administrative and pedagogical, went into the teaching of Russian (Shorish 1976).

The system was divided into Russian schools and national schools. In most cases, since 1984, there were eleven-grade schools teaching all subjects in the Russian language (in the following Russian schools) and others offering instruction in the non-Russian native languages of the republics (in the following Azeri schools, Uzbek schools, etc.). The former offered certain courses in the titular language, the latter in Russian with more class hours and more systematically. General education schools had parallel classes in the same school, in which the language of instruction was either Russian or a local one (usually the titular). In joint activities, Russian was employed. In the national-language classes, Russian was studied, often from the first grade to the last. In the Russian-language ones, the local language was introduced later, fewer hours were devoted to it, and its study was much less productive. 'Smaller languages' generally had few or no schools offering full instruction, except in areas with heavy concentrations of their *ethnies* (Anderson and Silver 1990:98-130; Suny 1996:390).

Despite all the talk about change, the general patterns during the first years of independence were still modelled on the Soviet precedents, except in trying to discontinue the marginalization of the titular language and raise its prestige, while striving to start the study of a foreign language earlier (in second grade, usually) – generally English, German or French. The language laws and decrees of the six states introduced no specific details concerning the language of instruction besides proclaiming in principle that the state language should be employed in education, along with a commitment to freedom of choice in the language of instruction and a ban on discrimination on a language basis (Pigolkin and Studenikina 1991:68-9). There seems to be a contradiction in this when referring to the problematic instruction in the 'smaller languages'. The imbalance was only partly corrected later by new education laws and decrees. The absence of significant change in education is due to a variety of reasons: a. lack of financial resources; b. shortage of teachers and experts; c. difficulty in reaching some outlying regions.

There are several types of school in the republics discussed, with curricular variations difficult to describe in detail. In the six states, Soviet administrative practice continues: primary (grades 1-4) and middle schools (grades 5-9), are all compulsory and free of charge; grades 10-11 are optional in the same schools or in technical ones – with a tendency to extend obligatory study to all 11 grades, as had been the practice in the Soviet Union. Some upper grade special schools are closely connected to an institute of higher education and therefore their students are sometimes absolved from college or university entry examinations. Certain secondary schools specialize in specific disciplines. Graduates of the 11th grade may enroll in a university or higher institute. Such institutes are of two kinds, state and private. The former are either free (as in Uzbekistan) or charge tuition but dispense gifted students from this payment. The latter charge tuition, which can be very expensive by local standards, reaching, e.g., $5,000 a year in the recently founded Western University in Baku.

In the universities as well as in technical, medical, military and other higher institutes (or colleges), teaching in Russian had been compulsory. A sophisticated system of higher education existed at the end of the Soviet Union. Several universities had been founded in earlier years: Tashkent (1918), Baku/Baky (1919), Samarkand (1927), Alma-Ata/Almaty (1934), Stalinabad/Dushanbe (1948), Ashkhabad/Ashgabat (1950), Frunze/Bishkek (1951), Karaganda (1972) and others (Balland 1997:231). Counting all higher education institutes (including universities), there were, in 1980, 17 in Azerbayjan, 43 in Uzbekistan, 53 in Kazakhstan, 10 in Kyrgyzstan, 7 in Turkmenistan, and 11 in Tajikistan. These figures increased in the independence years, largely due to various institutes being turned into universities and the establishment of many private ones (Vasil'ev 1998:17). With the growing popularity of, and demand for, English and other foreign languages, several institutes offered full programmes in them. Thus, e.g., the Institute of Foreign Languages in Baku continued its traditions from Soviet times, when it had prepared translators and consular officers, but now limits instruction mostly to English, German and French, training teachers and translators (four years of *ca.* 30-35 hours per week) (interview with Michael Gaebel, a lecturer in German at this Institute, 25 Sep. 1998). The Asia University in Baku offers courses in Japanese, Indonesian and other languages (information from N. Nasibzade, intellectual and statesman, Baku, 29 Sep. 1998).

An important indication of the diminished status of Russian in the six new states was the decrease in the number of students enrolling in universities which offered instruction in Russian. Of course, this was partly due, also, to the emigration of Russophones. The Russian Federation is investing in efforts to increase the number of universities teaching in Russian within the ex-Soviet states. In a parallel manner, special efforts were made by the Turkish government and private organizations in Turkey to assist education in all six states. According to Turkey's Minister of Education at the time, Mehmet Sağlam (1997), teachers and students from the six states were awarded numerous grants to study in Turkey and Turkish schools were opened in those states, for the children not only of local Turks and Meskhetians, but also of those Turks who arrived from Turkey to the six states for business and work (Osipov and Savurov 1992:105ff). By 1996, 11 Turkish schools had been inaugurated in

Azerbayjan, 18 in Uzbekistan, 30 in Kazakhstan, 11 in Kyrgyzstan, 13 in Turkmenistan, and 5 in Tajikistan. Turkish was a language of instruction in all of them. Personal encounters in Azerbayjan and Central Asia indicate that some knowledge of Turkish is indeed spreading among the Turkic populations thanks to increased mutual travelling, the presence of a Turkish business community and not least the Turkish broadcasts.

Common educational issues in most of the Soviet Union's successor states caused the CIS members to sign an agreement on cooperation in education, on 15 May 1992, and to set up a standing consultative body, the Conference of Ministers of Education (*NG* 17 Mar. 1993), which however has not been very effective in problem-solving in each state.

Table 9.1. STUDENTS IN SPECIALIZED SECONDARY SCHOOLS AND INSTITUTIONS OF HIGHER EDUCATION IN AZERBAYJAN AND CENTRAL ASIA, BY LANGUAGE OF INSTRUCTION, 1990

	Specialized Secondary Schools		*Institutions of Higher Education*	
	No. (x 1000)	*% of students*	*No. (x 1000)*	*% of students*
Azerbayjan				
in Azeri	51.0	87.7	81.0	77.3
in Russian	7.0	12.3	24.0	22.5
Uzbekistan				
in Uzbek	186.0	71.1	222.0	65.1
in Russian	58.0	22.2	110.0	32.3
in Karakalpak	16.0	6.1	6.0	1.9
in Kazakh	1.0	0.4	1.0	0.3
in Tajik	0.4	0.2	2.0	0.4
in Turkmen	0.1	0.02	–	–
Kazakhstan				
in Kazakh	21.0	8.7	39.0	13.6
in Russian	226.0	91.1	248.0	86.3
in Uzbek	0.1	0.5	–	–
in Uyghur	0.1	0.4	0.2	0.1
in German	0.2	0.1	–	–
Kyrgyzstan				
in Kyrgyz	8.0	18.0	14.0	23.4
in Russian	35.0	81.1	45.0	76.3
in Uzbek	0.3	0.8	0.2	0.3
Turkmenistan				
in Turkmen	6.0	17.1	10.0	23.6
in Russian	28.0	82.9	32.0	76.4
Tajikistan				
in Tajik	16.0	38.2	33.0	48.2
in Russian	23.0	56.8	30.0	44.1
in Uzbek	2.0	4.9	5.0	7.7
in Kyrgyz	0.03	0.1	–	–

Source: *Vestnik Statistiki* 12(1991):53-4, quoted in Khazanov 1995:249-50.

Table 9.2. STUDENTS, BY LANGUAGE OF INSTRUCTION
IN CENTRAL ASIA, 1990-3
(% of total student population in state)

	Studying in the titular language				Studying in Russian			
	1990	*1991*	*1992*	*1993*	*1990*	*1991*	*1992*	*1993*
Uzbekistan	65.1	65.4	69.2	71.6	32.3	30.6	26.8	23.4
Kazakhstan	13.6	17.6	21.6	28.9	86.3	80.5	78.4	75.0
Kyrgyzstan	23.4	25.8	29.4	34.0	76.3	73.8	69.1	65.4
Turkmenistan	23.6	38.4	50.7	59.5	76.4	61.6	48.6	40.5
Tajikistan	48.2	n.d.	66.9	17.9	44.1	42.8	10.9	34.3

Source: Katagoshchina 1996:80. The rest were studying in other languages of instruction.

Azerbayjan

In pre-independence Azerbayjan, as elsewhere, much of the discussion
in both official and unofficial circles revolved around instruction in the
titular language and Russian at various levels, e.g., their respective roles
as the language of instruction in school. As long as the Soviet Union still
functioned, the premise of a bilingual education in Azeri and Russian
continued to be axiomatic. Probably due to local demands, Azeri became
a required subject of study in Russian schools; in general, Azeri was in a
relatively stronger situation than the indigenous languages of Central
Asia, also due to the relatively higher percentage of the local Azeri-
speaking Russians.

Glasnost' opened up discussion of various opinions. A long article by
a philologist, V. Mirzoev (*BR* 23 Jan. 1988), advocated the need for an
intensive development of bilingualism and reported on a programme
worked out at the M.F. Akhundov Pedagogical Institute of Russian Language and Literature in Baku. In 1988 the Institute recommended the
study of Russian language and literature as a core curriculum in Azeri
schools, from the first to the eleventh grade, following the current school
curriculum in the Soviet Union. At the same time, there was a growing
interest in spreading Azeri in the republic. Special efforts were invested
by public and private bodies in encouraging the learning of this language
– still limited in scope but with considerable enthusiasm. For instance, in
June 1988 it was reported that those attending *Dom Tekhniki*, the Technological Centre in Baku, largely non-Azeris, were studying Azeri. The
provision of such language courses aroused interest among others in
Baku – Azeris in various establishments, institutions and schools – who
wished to join (*BR* 22 June 1988).

After Azerbaijan had passed the language decree in August 1989 and
declared sovereignty in September 1989, the government's language

policies became more explicit. In a lengthy interview, which appeared under the title 'National Permanent Education: Today and Tomorrow', the then Minister of Education R.B. Feyzullaev outlined his far-reaching plans (*BR* 13 Nov. 1990). Not only was the study of Azeri to be promoted both in his own republic and among the Azeris in Kazakhstan, but he emphasized also the training of teachers for the 'smaller languages' – Lezghian, Talysh, Kurdish, Avarian, and others. In independent Azerbayjan efforts were directed towards diffusing and improving popular knowledge of modern literary Azeri throughout the state. In addition to government activities, some newspaper sections and certain television programmes were earmarked towards furthering these goals. Considering the short time involved, these efforts have enjoyed some success. It is important, however, to note that as late as 1994 complaints were being aired that Azeri was still neglected in many Russian schools, as students approaching graduation failed to speak it correctly (*BR* 1 Apr. 1994). One of the reasons for this situation may have been the brief time that had elapsed since independence. Another was the popularity of Russian and the relatively large number of Russophones (Kuleshov et al. 1997:489). The Russian ambassador to Azerbayjan, A.V. Blokhin, praised the fact that *ca*. 180,000 Russians could send their children to Russian schools, a number which was not reduced, unlike in other CIS states; he also mentioned the local publication of twenty Russian-language newspapers. But all in all, a marked swing to Azeri is evident, also notable on Azeri television, in general education schools, and in higher education institutes, of which there were twenty-five in 1997. Most of these institutes offered instruction increasingly in Azeri, except in the departments of Russian language, literature and history (information by Prof. Nizami Jaferov, Dean of the Philological Faculty at Baku State University, 25 Sep. 1998).

Russian still holds its own, for the time being, as a language of culture and interethnic and international significance, which Azeris well know. When a congress of Muslims from the Caucasus convened in Baku, on 30 September 1998, Russian was employed almost throughout. The M.F. Akhundov Pedagogical Institute of Russian Language and Literature in Baku, founded in 1946, still trains teachers for Russian schools, with a good grounding in Russian (*Business* 1997:167; *Vyshka* 14 Feb. 1997). Since 1947, it has been publishing the quarterly *Russkii Yazyk i Literatura v Azerbaidzhane* (Russian Language and Literature in Azerbayjan), taken over in January 1997 by the Ministry of Education in Azerbayjan. A recent book on the institute's history (Guseinov 1996) informs us that in 1995-6 it still had about 4,500 students enrolled in three faculties. Some of its professors continue to devise new ways of improving the curricula and methodology of teaching Russian. The latest figures available for education illustrate the standing of Russian versus Azeri. At the start of the 1997-8 school year, out of 1,574,113 schoolchildren, 92.7% were in

Azeri schools, 7.1% in Russian, and 0.2% in Georgian. The 79,800 students in higher education were then registered as follows: 76.3% in Azeri institutions and 23.7% in Russian, while of the 32,600 students in professional schools 86.8% were enrolled in Azeri schools and 13.2% in Russian (official data of the Institute of Statistics, Baku).

Provisions were made to offer instruction during the first four years of school in minority languages, too, in their areas of concentration, such as Georgian in the village of Goragan (*BR* 4 July 1989), as well as Lezghian and Avarian elsewhere (*BR* 2 Sep. 1989; 11 May 1990). Curricula for teaching Kurdish and Talysh were published in Baku in 1990. Others came out for Tat, Lezghian and Udin in 1992; for Sakhur in 1993; and for Khynalyg in 1997. Works like a grammar of the Tat language (1995) comprising 222 pages, show that a scholarly interest in minority languages is upheld.

English has already been mentioned as potentially competing with Russian in Azerbayjan and elsewhere. At least one English newspaper, a weekly called *Azernews,* has been published since 1997 in Baku. As results in regular classes are not always satisfactory, all sorts of institutes offer – for a fee – courses in English lasting two or three months or more (*Zerkalo* 13 May 1995). One of the most effective, the Institute of Foreign Languages in Baku, established in 1973 to train teachers, interpreters and translators, now has five faculties: English, French, German, Spanish and Korean. About 50% of its student body of 3,000 study English (visit to the Institute, 21 May 1997). At the Baku State University, named after M.E. Resulzade (the President of the independent Republic of Azerbayjan, 1918-20), the students are offered programmes of study in English, French and Italian (*BR* 15 Aug. 1998). Increasingly, universities are not merely teaching English, but also using it as a language of instruction.

The case of Khazar University in Baku is edifying, even if not yet characteristic. Its founder and President, Prof. Hamlet Isakhanly, planned a small-size quality university (of about 1,000 undergraduates and graduate students). Courses started in the fall of 1991. English is the compulsory major discipline, with a minor in German, French or Spanish. In addition, most B.A. courses are taught in English in the Schools of Law and Social Sciences (where the focus is on International Relations) as well as the Master courses in Business Administration. Although the annual tuition of $1,600 is steep by local standards, many compete to enroll as students (interview with Prof. Isakhanly, Baku, 30 Sep. 1998; *Khazar University Catalog 1996-1998*). On the other hand, there seem to be English speakers eager to acquire the Azeri language. Khazar University has met this by publishing *The Azerbaijani Language/Azärbaycan dili*, by H. İsaxanlı, E. Ismayilova, Firangiz Nasirova (1997).

Equally renowned, but smaller (around 900 students) is Baku's Western University (founded in 1991) with its Schools of Western philologies and Western area studies. Some of its financing is derived from the special English courses it offers to firms and organizations in Baku (information by Michael Gaebel, 25 Sep. 1998). This is yet another indication of the swiftly rising importance of English in language choice. In addition to courses, public interest has encouraged the publication of textbooks and conversation manuals in English, as well as the enlargement of the frequently visited library of the British Council in Baku (*Vyshka* 13 Sep. 1996).

Uzbekistan

Education issues in Uzbekistan are tied up with the particularly high population growth which this republic has experienced since the 1970s, along with Turkmenistan and Tajikistan (Kaiser 1994a:232). Owing to insufficient planning to cope with this phenomenon, educational facilities have fallen behind earlier standards. This affected all areas of education, including language education – whether in the titular language, in the Soviet *lingua franca*, Russian, or in the minority languages.

By 1940, twenty-two languages were being studied in Uzbekistan's schools (*PV* 19 Aug. 1988) compared to seven in the 1959-60 school year. The authorities recommended the study of the languages of all nationalities, but the main argument in public discourse remained, as elsewhere, about the titular language versus Russian. The division, by student numbers and language of instruction, in 1991 is shown in Table 9.3 (Schmidt 1995:32; slightly different figures in *The Europa World Year-Book 1998:* II, 3694).

As long as the Soviet regime continued, most of those complaining of inadequate knowledge of Uzbek ('two hours a week of the native

Table 9.3. PUPILS IN UZBEKISTAN, BY LANGUAGE OF INSTRUCTION, 1991 (%)

Uzbek	79.0
Russian	12.2
Kazakh	2.9
Tajik	2.8
Karakalpak	2.6
Turkmen	0.3
Kyrgyz	0.2
Total	100.0

language could hardly produce satisfying results') offered methodological rather than structural suggestions for reform (*PV* 16 Jan., 17 Mar., 24 Mar., 5 Apr. 1988).

Aware of the growing debate about language instruction, concerned Uzbeks had already increased their involvement. During the 1987-8 school year, a group for the promotion of Uzbek was founded at the Kori-Niyazi Pedagogical and Scientific Institute in Tashkent which, together with the regional Department of Public Education, elaborated a general curriculum for the study of Uzbek at Russian schools and kindergartens. At the same time, this department also established a Council for the Methodology of Learning Uzbek in the Russian schools along with a teachers' seminar for the same purpose. The council and seminar started preparing materials and examining ways for bringing the teaching of Uzbek in Russian schools to a satisfactory level of competence. Separately, countrywide competitions in Uzbek for teachers and pupils of Russian schools, with cash prizes, were instituted in 1987 (Savelieva 1997:49-60). With time, support for Uzbek versus Russian grew more articulate, and experiments were made with introducing Uzbek into Russian-language schools in the first grade (instead of the second or third) and adding one class-hour per week (three instead of two) – a significant change (*PV* 12 Apr. 1990).

Complaints about unsatisfactory achievements in Uzbek at Russian schools and in Russian at Uzbek ones continued due to lack of textbooks and inadequate teacher training (e.g. *PV* 20 Nov. 1991). But efforts were made to teach the state-language to non-Uzbeks. In 1991 the Ministry for Amelioration and Water Management, for example, invested 12,000 rubles in teaching an 80-hour course of Uzbek to some 150 adults. Plans were afoot to enlarge the scope of these studies and considerably strengthen the use of Uzbek in official work (*PV* 14 Dec. 1991).

Since independence, public interest in the teaching of Uzbek has visibly increased. A Permanent Assembly on the Improvement of the Teaching of the Uzbek Language, set up in 1991, has convened in a major city every two years to discuss methodological questions (*Ma"rifat* 32:21 Apr. 1999). School hours were added to the study of Uzbek language, literature and history, and the curriculum was changed so as to give a 'better appreciation' of the Uzbek past (Nettleton 1992:19-20). Some progress was indeed made in subsequent years (*PV* 8 Apr. 1993).

The Law on Education of July 1992 set up firmer rules concerning objectives, structures and curricula – all intended to improve teaching and social formation (Yuldashev 1994). However, it was only on 1 July 1993 that the commission appointed to implement the 1989 Law on the State Language met in Tashkent, under the chairmanship of then Prime Minister Mutalov. Its first duty was to improve the study of Uzbek in

Russian schools and kindergartens. The Ministry of People's Education was charged with seeing to an increase in the study of Uzbek, planning it and preparing suitable teaching materials (*PV* 3 July 1993). Later the total number of class hours assigned to the study of Uzbek language and literature in Uzbek schools was made equal to that for Russian language and literature in Russian schools. In addition, the titular language was listed first in priority among subjects needing new curricula for grades 1 through 9 in all general schools (decree by the Council of Ministers, text in *PV* 15 May 1998).

The relative number of children in Uzbek schools also grew (Fierman 1995:583-5; Fierman 1995a:212-14). In the school year 1996-7, there were 4,200,241 pupils in Uzbek schools and only 384,128 in Russian schools (official data of the Ministry of People's Education, Uzbekistan 1997). The decline in numbers in the Russian schools, however, is partially explained by the emigration of Russian families from Uzbekistan (above, ch. 3) among whom there were reportedly *ca.* 55,000 Russian teachers (Kuleshov a.o. 1997:501).

University students may choose to study either in Uzbek or Russian as the language of instruction, except in the natural and technical sciences which continue to be taught in Russian. Back in 1994, 90% of all dissertations at universities and institutes were still presented and defended in Russian (Rzehak 1995:332). Subsequently, Uzbek has been making advances at the expense of Russian at many of the higher education institutions, of which there were 58 in Uzbekistan in 1997 and 60 in 1998 (*PV* 17 June 1998; details in Megoran 1997). A decree of 25 May 1998 (*NS* 26 May 1998) allotted grants to cover 50% of all tuition fees, starting with the 1998-9 academic year.

Issues of language instruction were being tackled throughout the 1990s, but were seemingly not solved. A difficult issue which found no immediate solution remained that of the standing of Russian in the curriculum. It undoubtedly continues to be an important subject in the curriculum, but its formerly central place in education is weakening to some degree in practice, due to the emphasis on Uzbek. Russian still receives more attention in school than other languages, Uzbek excepted. New curricula and a special methodology were worked out during 1998 for the study of Russian in Uzbek language schools. Although it was proclaimed that Russian 'would be treated like any other foreign language', in fact this is not quite so, as Russian is taught in *all* Uzbek schools from second grade onward and is given many more hours per week than 'other foreign languages'. New methods were tried as a pilot project in selected schools throughout Uzbekistan during the first semester of the 1998-9 school year. Its main points were learning the languages in themes (to assist with the vocabulary) and a communicative approach (chiefly verbal) – apparently with some success (*Uchitel' Uzbekistana* 3 Feb. 1999).

Judging from available materials, the following issues have continued to be publicly discussed in Uzbekistan in recent years: the need to stimulate the study of Uzbek among the national minorities, such as Koreans (*PV* 24 May 1996); encouraging it in Russian-language schools (*PV* 16 Oct. 1996); and promoting successful bilingualism or even multilingualism in the schools (*PV* 18 Feb. 1997).

Permitting Tajiks from Uzbekistan and elsewhere to take final examinations in Tajik in Samarkand – and reciprocally allowing Uzbeks in Tajikistan to sit for parallel examinations in Uzbek – was apparently the exception rather than the rule, as was the case for Kazakhs and Kyrgyz.

As to education for the minorities, by the mid-1990s the situation for the Tajiks and Kazakhs, the largest groups after the Russians, was as follows: 2.7% of the Tajik and about 3% of the Kazakh schoolchildren received instruction in their mother tongue (Schlyter 1997:13). Earlier, in 1988, there had reportedly been 4,184 school classes using Tajik as the language of instruction in the Tajik-inhabited regions of Uzbekistan, with teachers trained at the State University of Samarkand (*PV* 27 Oct. 1988). In 1997, 138,200 pupils in Uzbekistan obtained instruction in Kazakh (*KP* 6 Sep. 1997). An agreement was reached in 1998 between the Prime Ministers of Uzbekistan and Kazakhstan to open Kazakh and Uzbek schools, respectively (*NG* 11 Mar. 1998). Up till now, Uzbekistan has been importing schoolbooks for its minorities from the respective neighbouring country. But more recently, Uzbek school authorities have expressed their intent to produce schoolbooks with a more Uzbek content.

In the early 1990s, there were already classes using Crimean Tatar and Bashkir, altogether 35 classes, as the language of instruction (*PV* 11 Jan. 1991) and another 350 pupils were being taught in Kazan Tatar in the oblasts of Dzhizak and Tashkent and in the capital. In Tashkent, 55 pupils were studying in Greek; in Ferghana oblast, 42 were studying German, their mother tongue (*PV* 27 Dec. 1991). The teaching of other national languages, like Turkmen, Uyghur and Korean, continues to be encouraged. In spite of all this, it was claimed that out of 200,000 Koreans in Uzbekistan, a mere 1% could read and write in their native tongue (*PV* 20 Aug. 1994). The Government of South Korea opened a special centre in Tashkent which, in 1998, could accommodate up to 800 Uzbekistani Korean students (*PV* 30 May 1998).

Various cultural centres continued their activities during the 1990s in Tashkent: Russian, Uyghur, Tajik, Tatar, Kazakh, Azeri, Turkish, Karakalpak, and Armenian, some of which offered instruction in their respective language (*PV* 25 Nov. 1989; 31 Jan. 1990). Other centres operated elsewhere (Ginzburg 1994-5:II, 40-273; *NS* 9 June 1998; *PV* 30

July 1998). All these are modest undertakings but they indicate a readiness by the authorities to cope with multilingual instruction problems, although some Uzbeks were quick to complain that in schools offering instruction in minority languages, Uzbek was neglected, e.g., by a shortage of textbooks and teaching aids for it (*NS* 21 May 1997).

Increasing political and economic relations with foreign countries have created a growing awareness of the population in Uzbekistan of the importance of foreign language command. This sentiment was expressed by a journalist on the occasion of the ninth anniversary of the passing of the Law on the State Language. Knowledge of foreign languages permits us, he writes, '...to communicate our peaceful intentions towards other peoples and to absorb the wealth of universal ideals into our own culture' (*NS* 22 Oct. 1998). Generally, the teaching of foreign languages starts in the fifth grade.

English is now introduced at an earlier stage into schools and even into select kindergartens, with professional American advice and financial grants (*PV* 21 May; 30 July 1998). In many Uzbek schools Russian-language class hours were reduced in number in order to introduce English. Like English, other foreign languages receive more emphasis now than they used to in the Soviet period, depending on the availability of teachers: usually German (more than 100,000 pupils between the fifth and the eleventh grade) or French (in selected schools); sometimes Arabic, Chinese or Japanese (in Tashkent, for instance). English, however, remains a favourite in foreign language re-orientation, and pupils make great efforts to learn it on an extracurricular basis, practically everywhere (Kinzer 1997:A4). A weekly lesson in English is offered in a thirty item cycle of a TV educational series (Dollerup 1998:149).

In universities as well, English has an increasing share in the curriculum. For instance at the Tashkent State University, in the departments of economics, management, international relations and sciences, intensive courses in English (and sometimes another foreign language, generally French or German) are compulsory. The Uzbek State University of World Languages in Tashkent had 3,801 students in the 1997-8 academic year, enrolled in the Faculties of English Philology, German Philology, Romance Philology, Russian Philology, as well as of Education – for upgrading teachers' skills. About 60% of its students major in English (Dollerup 1998:150). The four year B.A. curriculum comprises linguistics, literature, and history (interview at the university, 3 Sep. 1998). The Tashkent Polytechnic teaches in English (*NS* 25 May 1997). The Samarkand State Institute for Foreign Languages offers, in addition to English, French and German, such languages as Japanese, Chinese, Spanish, Arabic, Urdu, Persian and Hindi (*Uchitel' Uzbekistana* 9:1998). Other universities and institutes require a sizeable number of curriculum hours for the study of Uzbek (and/or Russian) as well as of a foreign language in most disciplines, in addition to having departments of both Uzbek and Russian philology, except in technical institutes (for details, *PV* 28 June 1995).

A specialized journal in Russian, *Prepodavanie Yazyka i Literatury* (The Teaching of Language and Literature), features articles about the methodology of teaching foreign languages, such as English (e.g., 1996, no.1:88-91). It should be noted, however, that this periodical and others urging readers to study foreign languages (e.g. *NS* 1 Apr. 1997; *Uchitel' Uzbekistana* 33:1997) emphasized the importance of learning Russian, particularly in Uzbek schools (*Uchitel' Uzbekistana* 22:1996; 47:1996; 6:1998) and, no less, Uzbek as thoroughly as possible everywhere.

All things considered, the competition for centrality between Uzbek and Russian still remains relevant, although Uzbek increasingly appears the winner. Foreign languages add a new dimension to the competition. President Karimov phrased this in his own way, speaking in parliament in February 1995, as follows: '... it is necessary to remember always that the study of foreign languages should not be carried out at the expense of oblivion to the mother tongue. It is hard to understand and justify a specialist, especially one holding a high post, who is unable to choose fine and appropriate words to express his idea, concisely and precisely, in his mother tongue. In our recent past, in most cases the Russian language but not the mother tongue served as mediator in the study of foreign languages... Students should leave school with the Uzbek language as a language of instruction experience while studying foreign languages' (Karimov 1998:9).

Kazakhstan

In the last generation which grew up in the Soviet Union, instruction in Russian had been very widespread in most kindergartens; urban and well-educated Kazakh families opted for Russian school education, while peripheral ones sent their children to Kazakh-language schools (Naumova 1992:30-3). In March 1987, a joint meeting of the Central Committee of the Kazakhstan Communist Party and the Republic's Council of Ministers decided to improve instruction in Kazakh, focusing in the rural areas – but also in Russian areas (text in *KP* 5 Mar. 1987) with some promotion for the languages of other groups as well. A frequently voiced criticism was that the teaching of Kazakh in Russian schools and of Russian in Kazakh schools was unsatisfactory – the former even more so (*KP* 26 Apr. 1988). In 1989, 2,021,596 schoolchildren were attending Russian-language schools, while only 923,990 were at Kazakh-language schools (Khazanov 1995:159). By student numbers and language of instruction, the general division in the 1988-9 school year was as follows (Schmidt 1995:32), indicating an overwhelming imbalance:

Table 9.4. PUPILS IN KAZAKHSTAN, BY LANGUAGE
OF INSTRUCTION, 1988-9 (%)

Kazakh	30.2
Russian	67.4
Uzbek	1.9
Uyghur	0.4
Tajik	0.1
Total	100.0

Aware of the imbalance, the Ministry of People's Education in Kazakh-stan passed a formal decision, on 31 January 1991, to establish a new faculty for the speedy training of teachers of Kazakh in Russian schools.

With its array of *ethnies* (above, table 2.5), independent Kazakhstan has constantly faced problems in planning education policies and then carrying them out even after an agreement had been achieved. In 1994 eighteen languages were being taught in school (*KP* 22 Sep. 1994). Language status seems dictated largely by the fact that the titular *ethnie*, the Kazakhs, numbered in 1993 only *ca.* 43.2% of the entire po-pulation, followed by the Russians (36.4%) and the Ukrainians (5.2%) (*KP* 19 June 1993). In 1998, according to official data, there were 52.0% Kazakhs, as against 31.4% Russians, 4.4% Ukrainians, and 12.2% others – in a total population numbering *ca.* 15,642,000 (data given by Dr Y.K. Shokamanov, Institute of Statistics of Kazakhstan, in an interview on 11 Sep. 1998).

In independent Kazakhstan, the language debate gained in intensity, as the results of several polls indicate (see below). As already said, con-cerned Kazakhs had established a Kazakh language (*Qazaq Tili*) society in 1990 with government support, to mobilize public demand for teach-ing Kazakh in schools, including Russian ones (*Vechernii Almaty* 16 May 1997), and increasing its prestige. While generally agreeing with the motives of such enthusiasts and others for the promotion of Kazakh in education, officials – such as V. Voevod, adviser to the Ministry of Education – warned against rash measures which could stir up ethnic strife (*KP* 26 Mar. 1992).

The warning was apposite, considering that public opinion was sharply divided. Replies, according to a 1994 poll (above, p. 84) were divided as follows: 50% of all respondents – and 86% of the polled Kazakhs – opined that children should study Kazakh. Large percentages of other *ethnies* expressed a wish to have their children study in their own native languages in kindergarten and primary school; but many of these gave preference to instruction in Russian in the secondary school.

As to higher education, 28% of those polled wished their children to have instruction in Kazakh, 46% in Russian, and 9% in their native languages. For technical institutes, 62% of Kazakh respondents preferred instruction in Kazakh and 20% in Russian. Russians and other groups preferred Russian; only among the Uyghurs 50% chose instruction in Kazakh and 35% in Russian.

It is interesting to compare the results of this poll with the situation in the 1990s, indicating progress in numbers of Kazakh schools and students, but also in Russian ones (some Kazakh parents were reported to have moved their children from Kazakh to Russian schools, which were reportedly better equipped (Pilkington 1998:137). Anyway, Kazakh seemed to hold its own in the education system and even to make some progress: in 1994, there were reportedly almost fifty Kazakh schools in Almaty, as against only one in 1991 (Dave 1996:24).

A more recent poll was taken by two sociologists connected with the Kazakhstan Academy of Sciences, in November-December 1997. They polled 1,149 people in nine different provinces, 42.87% of them Kazakhs, 39.04% Russians, 4.26% Ukrainians, 3.83% Germans, 2.96% Tatars, 0.78% Uzbeks, 6.26% other *ethnies.* To a question about the school language parents preferred for their children, the results were as follows: Kazakh 25.2%, Russian 49.0%, the language of their *ethnie* 9.4%, another language (i.e. a foreign language) 10.3%, no reply 6.1% (Zakaeva and Sarsenbaeva 1998:55). It is noteworthy that the parents preferred Russian to Kazakh as the language of school instruction at a rate of almost 2:1, while the number of Kazakhs polled roughly equalled that of the Russians and Ukrainians together. Of course, some respondents from the smaller *ethnies* might have opted for Russian instead of their native language. Still, the results support those of the 1994 poll and indicate that a sizable proportion of the Kazakhs preferred their children to be taught in Russian rather than Kazakh.

English is penetrating, too; not only in Almaty but elsewhere, as in East Kazakhstan province, where eighteen schools offer intensive English courses and there is an active centre for learning English (*Rudnyi Altai* 19 Sep. 1998). A Kazakh-American school was scheduled to be inaugurated in Astana on 1 September 1999 and others in Almaty and elsewhere later; instruction in English was to be compulsory in the upper grades, on the assumption that pupils had already mastered both Kazakh and Russian (*Oxus* 2:1999, 62). The focus on English undoubtedly received a boost from Nazarbaev himself who, in a book and lectures presenting his vision of Kazakhstan in the year 2030, foresaw a people fluent in Kazakh, Russian and English. A National Association of Teachers of English was founded in Almaty in late 1997 (*Rudnyi Altai* 14 Nov. 1998). French is lagging behind English, although it gets some special attention on the 'Days of Francophonie' at the end of March each year (*KP* 6 Apr. 1993). It is studied in some schools, but there have been cases of parents insisting on English instead of French for their children (*Kustanaiskie Novosti* 7 Oct. 1998). The Republic of Turkey has helped to establish 29 Kazakh-Turkish *lycées* (*Uchitel' Kazakhstana* 31 Jan. 1998; *KP* 24 Nov. 1998).

School instruction is offered in eight 'smaller languages' in areas where other nationalities live in sizable numbers: Ukrainian, Uyghur, Uzbek, Meskheti Turkish, Korean, German, Dungan, and Polish (interview with A. K. Akhmedov, Ministry of Education, Almaty, 14 Sep. 1998). There are even a few classes in Azeri, Armenian, Hebrew and Chechen (*KP* 22 Sep. 1998). It seems that German is favoured, probably as a result of the interest displayed by the authorities in Germany and the presence of a sizable German minority in Kazakhstan. According to the 1998 data supplied by Sophia Wenzel, *referent* for culture of the Council of Germans in Kazakhstan, 400 special courses, of 160 hours each, and 415 courses, of 80 hours each, were catering to 13,600 Germans, besides 57 Sunday schools for 2,600 children. 28 September 1998 was declared 'Day of the Germans' in Kazakhstan, to be celebrated as a cultural occasion (*KP* 24 Sep. 1998). The Uyghurs have 64 schools offering instruction in Uyghur, out of which 15 employ only Uyghur in class. Additional classes in mixed schools offer some Uyghur. Close to 21,000 school children study Uyghur (*Ana Tili* 27 Aug. 1998). In contrast, the Tatars complained, in 1997, that they had only one school and one kindergarten in the whole of Almaty (*KP* 23 Aug. 1997).

In general, daily school practice followed the 1992 Law on Education (text in *KP* 5 Mar. 1992). This stated that the Law on Languages ought to be observed and implemented in all educational institutions, which should create conditions suitable for the active study, use and development of Kazakh. The law also guaranteed the study and employment of Russian as a language of inter-nation use. Thus the Law on Education struck a balance between the two languages.

In the mid-1990s, anticipating the publication of a revised constitution and a new law on language, numerous newspaper articles and readers' letters complained about the unsatisfactory status of Kazakh in language learning (e.g., *Zarya* 17 Sep. 1994; *Yuridicheskaya Gazeta* 30:1995, 13). The points made in a press interview by Bulgan Shinibaeva, president of the Council of Kazakh Teachers in Almaty, in June 1995, were characteristic. She estimated that the teaching of Kazakh was in a catastrophic state in which the Law on Languages was not applied. The classes had too many pupils, more than in other language groups; there were no adequate language laboratories for Kazakh; teachers of Kazakh were poorly paid and were moving away; textbooks were few in number and outdated; and no literature was available on the methodology of teaching Kazakh (*Gorizont* 16 June 1995). To this one may add that, according to official figures in 1995, the entire state did not have more than 2,350 teachers of Kazakh (Eremin 1996:40), although efforts had been invested in training more, as well as teachers of Russian, Polish, German, Uyghur, Azeri, Turkish, Kurdish, Uzbek, and Korean (Nauryzbaev 1993:48).

There is no end to complaints: K.E. Kusherbaev, then Minister for Education, has officially complained of the lack of teachers of Kazakh (*Uchitel' Kazakhstana* 31 Jan. 1998:5), despite efforts to train such teachers (*KP* 23 Oct. 1997).

By official data, in 1998 there were in the entire state 3,291 Kazakh, 2,406 Russian, and 2,138 mixed schools (with another 77 using Uzbek for instruction and 13 Uyghur) (*National Policy in the Republic of Kazakhstan* [1998]. Available: http://www.president.kz/. 2 July 1998). Another point worth noting is that, while Kazakh schools are almost exclusively attended by Kazakhs, Russian schools have a multiethnic pupil population – which partly explains their majorization in both percentages and absolute numbers.

Table 9.5. EDUCATION IN KAZAKHSTAN, BY LANGUAGE
OF INSTRUCTION, 1990-4

	% of schools			% of students in	
	Kazakh	Russian	Mixed	Kazakh schools	Russian schools
1990/1	34.0	44.7	20.2	32.4	65.0
1991/2	35.3	41.7	21.9	34.3	63.1
1992/3	37.1	36.7	25.2	37.0	60.3
1993/4	38.3	33.9	26.8	40.1	57.2

Source: Kazakhstan Ministry of Education, quoted by Kaiser 1995:105. The few missing percentage points referred to schools with other languages of instruction.

Table 9.6. PUPILS IN GENERAL SCHOOLS IN KAZAKHSTAN, BY
LANGUAGE OF INSTRUCTION, 1990/1 -1997/8 (at start of the school year)

	1990/1	1993/4	1994/5	1995/6	1996/7	1997/8
Kazakh	1,008,100	1,232,700	1,302,600	1,358,400	1,421,800	1,475,000
Russian	2,027,000	1,772,000	1,655,500	1,584,900	1,558,300	1,498,400
Uzbek	64,600	64,900	67,000	69,100	72,800	75,300
Uyghur	13,800	17,000	19,500	20,700	21,100	21,600
Tajik	2,300	2,300	2,200	2,200	2,200	2,300
Turkish	—	—	—	500	800	900
German	—	—	—	100	600	400
English	—	—	—	100	100	n.d.

Source: Statisticheskii Ezhegodnik Kazakhstana, Almaty: 1997, 103; additional details for 1992, *KP* 9 June 1992; for 1995, Abdygaliev 1995; for 1996, *Mysl'* Sep. 1996: 65-75; for 1997-8, information from Dr. Y.K. Shokamanov, Deputy Chairman of the National Statistics Agency, Almaty (interviewed on 11 Sep. 1998).

These two tables indicate that since independence there has been a fairly clear although moderate trend for Kazakh and other languages to advance numerically at the expense of Russian as language of instruction in general schools. The margin between the number of pupils studying in Kazakh/Russian is continually narrowing. In 1995-6, according to table 9.6, 53.8% of all pupils were taught in Russian versus 46.2% in Kazakh (*The Europa World Year-Book 1998*:II, 1938, suggests 51.2% versus 44.8%). Russian was losing its edge almost completely by 1997-8 (*The Economist* 15 Feb. 1997:58 even surmised that by then more schools used Kazakh than Russian). A specialized periodical in Russian, named *Russkii Yazyk i Literatura v Kazakhskoi Shkole* (Russian Language and Literature in the Kazakh School), founded in the Soviet period, is still published regularly to promote and assist the teaching of Russian in Kazakh schools. In private schools, both Kazakh and Russian are offered, according to the student's preference.

It seems that some teachers are still undecided about the relative merits of Kazakh and Russian. A poll among 149 secondary school teachers, carried out in October-November 1996 by the University of Kentucky, found that the respondents were divided regarding the place of Kazakh, versus Russian, language, culture and history in their schools (DeYoung and Valyayeva 1997:27-9). Considering this situation, there was a stronger need to see how the teaching of Kazakh could be improved and better results obtained more quickly.

In 1997, the Kazakh State National University in Almaty, together with the Ministry of Education, convened a 'scholarly-methodological conference'. Various papers recommended the use of computers and multimedia, but it is not known whether the suggestions were put into practice in the schools. An official Centre for Learning the State Language, headed by Prof. Sh. Shayakhmetov, has recently been set up to try and computerize the study of Kazakh in school (*Akmolinskaya Pravda* 16 Apr. 1998).

Kazakh as language of instruction has also advanced somewhat during the 1990s in institutes and universities (Gömeç 1996:95; Dave 1996b:204-11). Reportedly, in only 20 out of 65 institutions of higher education are there departments that use Russian as the language of instruction (Kuleshov a.o. 1997:492). However, student numbers in higher education indicate that many still prefer instruction in Russian. Thus, in the 1995/6 academic year, by official figures, out of 260,043 students, 69% studied in Russian and only 31% in Kazakh (*Mysl'* Sep. 1996:71); the ratio has not changed in the 1997/8 academic year (*Delovaya Nedelya* 29 Jan. 1999). This is hardly surprising, considering the standing of Russian science. It seems that only one technological institute in the entire state, the East Kazakhstan Technological University, is now offering all its courses in Kazakh (*Rudnyi Altai* 24 Sep. 1998); other technical institutes offer a choice between Russian and Kazakh as the language of instruction. In other university departments, too, Russian is still used frequently as the language of instruction. Since 1997, the government has also been looking for ways to set up intensive courses for adults in the Kazakh language. There are several reasons the teaching of Kazakh to adults has not been up to expectations: a mistaken methodology, lack of experts with suitable linguistic knowledge, and financing. But the main reason is that Kazakh cannot compete with Russian in providing information about many domains of life – while Russian does not need any incentive to have people learn it. The status of Kazakh and the need for it are still regarded dubiously by non-Kazakhs and even by some of the Kazakhs themselves (*Mysl'* 1995, no. 3:49-53). The study of English, too, is attracting students at school, college and special courses.

The Hoca Ahmet Yesevi University, founded in the town of Turkistan in Kazakhstan in February 1993, was renamed in December of that year The Turkish-Kazakh University and became the first international Turkish university established for all speakers of Turkic languages. Teaching in Turkish, Kazakh and Russian, it reached a student body of 17,000 in 1996 and served as a model for the Manas Turkish-Kyrgyz University in Bishkek (İsen 1997:703).

In 1999, there were in Kazakhstan 150 universities and institutes, attended by about 314,000 students (Damitov and Kirillova 1999:159). Various reforms in higher education were being planned or carried out. One was a bold measure based on a proposal of Nazarbaev to allocate 10% of the places in all institutions of higher education – without participating in competitive examinations – to students of the smaller, non-Kazakh nationalities. This measure, practised since 1995, increased the share of minority students to 17.7% in 1997 (*KP* 13 June 1997).

The results in higher-level language acquisition may be affected by an important change in the availability of university education. The rather speedy increase in the number of university students has laid a heavy financial burden on the state. In May 1999, it was officially announced that, as from the 1999-2000 academic year, university instruction would be free no more – except for the exceptionally gifted students, while others would have to pay the equivalent of $700-1,000 annually (*Extracts* 3 May 1999. Available: httpt:www.soros.org.Kazakhstan/omri/049 html. 17 Aug. 1999).

Kyrgyzstan

Much of the public discussion on language in Kyrgyzstan in the 1980s focused on bilingualism, a term frequently employed in the local press and elsewhere, which elegantly hinted at peaceful coexistence rather than competitive rivalry between the two main languages in public use and education. A large section of public opinion insisted on allotting a greater share to Kyrgyz, its culture and traditions, at school and elsewhere. Aware of this situation, the Central Committee of the Kyrgyzstan Communist Party approved, in August 1988, a bill on 'The Continuing Development of National-Russian Bilingualism and the Improvement of the Study and Teaching of Kyrgyz, Russian and Other Languages of the Peoples of the Soviet Union in the Republic' (text in *SoK* 6 Aug. 1988). The bill's essentials concerning language instruction were as follows. Noting that Kyrgyz had become a literary language in the Soviet Union, its further study was recommended, as well as the learning of Russian (defined as a language of science and technology, of domestic and international culture) and of the languages of various peoples living in the republic, like the Uzbeks, Dungans, Germans, and Tajiks. The bill then stated that there were in Kyrgyzstan almost 1,400 schools teaching in various languages: 983 in Kyrgyz, 274 in Russian, 116 in Uzbek, 12 in German, 11 in Dungan, and 2 in Tajik as the language of instruction. Every fourth pupil was learning a second language, and the acquisition of both Kyrgyz and Russian at school was recommended. Much had to be done to foster the study of Kyrgyz, chiefly in schools offering instruction in Russian, as many Kyrgyz young people did not know their native tongue, not having been sufficiently exposed to it at home and in kindergarten. The teaching of Russian, too, should be much improved, particularly in schools offering instruction in Kyrgyz. The teaching of the languages of other *ethnies* ought to be strengthened as well. Better teaching and methods and richer school libraries in both Kyrgyz and Russian were needed. The Ministry of Education should prepare curricula, textbooks, dictionaries and conversation manuals, readers with parallel pages in Kyrgyz and Russian, teach yourself books, and study methods for both these languages as well as others; it should also train suitable teachers. Deadlines were specified for carrying out the various projects between 1988 and 1995. Here was a document acknowledging unequivocally the need for parallelism at school between Kyrgyz and Russian and recommending bilingualism based on the development of both.

More detailed data were soon added and in September 1988 it became known that about 53% of all schoolchildren were being taught in Kyrgyz, 35% in Russian, 12% in Uzbek and 0.8% in Tajik. At that time, every third schoolchild receiving Russian instruction was a non-Russian (*SoK* 2 Sep. 1988). The Law on the State Language, adopted in September 1989 (above, ch. 6), was widely perceived as directed at encouraging the spread of Kyrgyz, and the local press published numerous articles on how to implement the law in favour of the Kyrgyz language (e.g., *SoK* 31 March 1990).

With independence, differences of views continued concerning the relative merits of Kyrgyz and Russian. One example was the opinion of Sadyrbek Cherikov, who wrote in the Kyrgyz newspaper *Erkin Too* (30

Dec. 1992) calling for the speedy promotion of Kyrgyz schools to prepare cadres for this language. Such opinions and others found expression
in the Law on Education of 16 December 1992 (amplified later, 29 November 1997). Chapter 5 dealt with the language of instruction in school.
Probably aiming at some compromise, it declared that the state language,
Kyrgyz, was the basic language of study, but that in all schools Kyrgyz,
Russian and English were compulsory. The public drive towards strengthening Kyrgyz in general, including in education, went on – both at
school and among adults (*SK* 11 Apr. 1992). Among the Kyrgyz themselves the study of their language advanced, albeit slowly at first.
Naturally, language socialization depends both on state efforts and on
individual choices. By 1992, the number of Kyrgyz schools in the entire
state had increased by 10.2% since 1989 and that of Russian had decreased by 39.3%. Six years later, the number of Kyrgyz schools had
risen by another 9.8%, while that of Russian schools had remained un-
changed (below, table 9.5). This trend, encouraging to Kyrgyzophones,
does not, however, reflect the fact that a majority of the teachers had had
their university training – chiefly in the technological disciplines – in
Russian and could find it difficult to teach them in Kyrgyz (Oruzbaeva
1994:168).

Table 9.7. SCHOOLS IN KYRGYZSTAN, BY LANGUAGE OF
INSTRUCTION, 1989-98

	Total	Kyrgyz	Russian	Uzbek	Tajik	Mixed
1989	1,702	1,018	234	116	2	332
1992	1,796	1,122	142	120	2	409
1998	1,899	1,232	143	133	2	389

Source: Head of Department of State Language, Ministry of Education, quoted by Huskey 1995:562;
Interview with R.Zh. Bakhtyarov, Deputy Minister of Education, Bishkek, 17 Sep. 1998. A few German
and Dungan schools should be added. For 1988 compare the bill on 'The Continuing Development of
National-Russian Bilingualism' (p. 185).

A special situation can be observed in the capital, Bishkek. Few schools
used Kyrgyz as the instrument of instruction versus Russian (Kaser and
Mehrotra 1996:289-90). According to the data supplied by the Bishkek
Municipality's Department of Education, in the 1990-1 school year, out
of 77 schools of general education, only 7% offered Kyrgyz as language
of instruction, 39% parallel Kyrgyz and Russian, and 54.5% Russian. In
the 1996-7 school year, out of all schools of general education, 12.5%
were Kyrgyz, 62.5% parallel, and 25% Russian (reported by Asankanov
1997:69). All these data are not fully satisfactory, as the number of schools
is not necessarily a precise indication of the number of students, nor of
the quality of teachers, nor of the availability of learning materials. In the

entire state, by comparison, in 1993-4, 63.6% of all pupils in primary and secondary schools in Kyrgyzstan studied in Kyrgyz and 23.4% in Russian (another 12.7% in Uzbek and 0.3% in Tajik) (*The Europa World Year-Book 1998:*II, 2031). In addition, we have some official data about the number of language teachers in the general education schools at the beginning of the 1996-7 school year: 7,158 teachers of non-Russian tongues, 1,831 teachers of Russian in schools with Russian as the language of instruction and 6,213 teachers of Russian in schools with other languages of instruction (Russian schools excepted) (*Obrazovanie v Kyrgyzskoi Respublike. Statisticheskii sbornik,* Bishkek:1996, 25). While full details are not yet available, it would seem that, although instruction in Kyrgyz has advanced in quantity, interest in learning Russian is still high not only among Russian but also among non-Russian schoolchildren and their parents. This is probably one of the reasons why the government still supports financially a pedagogical periodical, *Russkii Yazyk i Literatura v Shkolakh Kyrgyzstana* (Russian Language and Literature in Kyrgyzstan's Schools) (*SK* 24-25 Apr. 1998). This move led to criticism from the proponents of Kyrgyz, chiefly in the Kyrgyz-language press, which described Uzbekistan as their model for promoting the national language (*Atazhurg* 1998, no. 2:21-30 Nov. 1998).

Among minority languages, Uzbek has a special place, chiefly in the region of Osh. There are also some Dungan schools in the villages of this community in the Chui Valley of Kyrgyzstan and Kazakhstan (letter from T. Choroev, 11 May 1999). The Uyghurs complain about the small number of their schools and about only three subjects being taught in Uyghur – language, literature and history. They acknowledge however that, since 1994, the National State University has a Faculty for Uyghur philology (*SK* 6 Aug. 1998).

In higher education, students in independent Kyrgyzstan could for the first time take entrance examinations in Kyrgyz – a measure benefiting rural candidates who thus improved their chances of careers in government service and elsewhere. The more experienced university teachers, however, continued to use Russian and thus attracted more students. Moreover, in several institutions Russian was the only language available – as in the Medical School and the newly established (1992) Bishkek International School of Management and Business (Huskey 1995:562).

In September 1993, Akaev inaugurated a Slavic (Kyrgyz-Russian) University, offering instruction in Russian on the basis of an existing curriculum. Despite protests by nationalist Kyrgyz groups in Bishkek (Huskey 1995:562-3; Pannier 1996), Akaev, in his speech inaugurating the new university, defined it as 'a symbol of our hope and belief that [it will be] a centre for preserving and developing Russian language and culture. This is of interest not only to Russians and other Slavs in

Kyrgyzstan. The Russian language... is part of the spiritual world of the Kyrgyz' (*SK* 10 Sep. 1993). In its first academic year (1993-4) the university enrolled only 185 students (*NG* 24 Feb. 1994). However, by the beginning of the 1997-8 academic year it already consisted of seven faculties: science-technology, humanities, economics, law, medicine, international relations, and external studies, along with several research centres, with a total enrolment of 2,567 students and another 600 external ones (*SK* 14 Oct. 1998). A pedagogical centre and library, also, had been set up with the avowed aim of organizing meetings and discussions on Russian culture in Kyrgyzstan (*Sankt-Peterburgskie Vedomosti* 10 Jan. 1998). On the five-year anniversary of the university's foundation, Akaev could proudly call it 'a symbol of eternal friendship' between the two countries financing the university (*SK* 20 Oct. 1998).

The success of the university and the wish of the two governments to foster cultural relations prompted them to found a Kyrgyz-Russian Academy of Education in October 1997 (*Utro Bishkeka* 22 Oct. 1998), which follows the practice of using both Kyrgyz and Russian for instruction. This was no innovation, for it had been customary in some of Kyrgyzstan's thirty-nine universities and higher institutes to offer instruction in two languages, enabling people to study in the language of their choice: Kyrgyz/Russian, Kyrgyz/Uzbek, Kyrgyz/Turkish, and more recently Kyrgyz/English (interview with R. Zh. Bakhtyarov, Deputy Minister of Education, Science and Culture, Bishkek, 17 Sep. 1998).

Special attention is due to the Kyrgyzstan State University in Bishkek, whose official name was changed by a Presidential decree on 11 August 1993 to National State University (Toktomyshev 1997:4). The following year a Centre of Kyrgyz Studies was set up for research and preparation of materials for this discipline. In 1996, a chair for the theory and practice of the state language was added, to equip Kyrgyz with the vocabulary needed for technology and informatics, on the one hand, and, on the other, to introduce some new notions on society and government for the benefit of the university's students and of people in general throughout the state. Simultaneously, a new chair was established in Russian Studies to assist its study everywhere, computerize it, write textbooks, and prepare suitable conditions for its use in the defence of philological dissertations.

Also in 1996, a French Language and Culture Centre was founded at the same university to increase Kyrgyzstan's contacts with French universities, to improve methods of teaching French and prepare suitable textbooks, and to translate literary works from French into Kyrgyz and vice versa (Toktomyshev 1997:80-3). Turkish, too, has had some success in the educational landscape of Kyrgyzstan. By 1999, fifteen *lycées* were offering instruction in Turkish, which was also taught at the Ala-Too Kyrgyz-Turkish University in Bishkek. At the Bishkek Humanitarian

University, Turkish lecturers teach not merely Turkish courses, but also in the social sciences (visit to the university, 31 Mar. 1997). English, however, has made the most notable impact in higher education as well as in lower levels, too, partly funded by the Soros Foundation (interview with a representative of the Foundation, local office, 17 Sep. 1998).

Outside the capital, for instance in the district of Osh, the country's second largest town, progress in Kyrgyz was less noticeable by 1997 than in Bishkek, some eight years after the adoption of the Law on the State Language. This is partly explained, however, by Osh being largely inhabited by Uzbeks, whose language of instruction at school is Uzbek. Still, at the state university there, tens of books and textbooks on various aspects of teaching Kyrgyz were prepared, some of which were designed for instructing the Russian and Uzbek population in the state language. Moreover, at the Kyrgyz-Uzbek University in Osh, founded in 1996 (with a pedagogical faculty added in 1998), parallel instruction in Kyrgyz, Uzbek, or Russian was offered for the student's choice (interview with Alisher Sabirov, an Uzbek representative in the Kyrgyzstan Legislative Assembly, Bishkek, 16 Sep. 1998). Thus Kyrgyz was advancing in the Osh district. In 502 schools and many kindergartens in this district, it was employed as the language of instruction – although the Ministry of Education had apparently done but little to prepare adequate materials for teaching Kyrgyz in the Uzbek and Tajik schools. Nevertheless, in numerous enterprises in the district – industry, building, and public health – most activities were still carried out in Russian (*SK* 25-26 March 1997).

Turkmenistan

Public discourse on language and language policies within the educational system and outside it was never absent, even if it seems to have been less passionate – both in the era of *perestroika* and subsequently. About 100 national groups live in this state, but Turkmens number *ca.* 77% of the entire population.

Quantitatively, school instruction in Turkmen was satisfactory: in 1988, 76.9% of all pupils at general day-schools were studying in Turkmen, versus 16% in Russian, 6% in Uzbek and 1% in Kazakh (*The Europa World Year-Book 1998*: II, 3396).

As in some neighbouring Soviet republics, but somewhat later, a 'Government Programme for the Development and Diffusion of the Turkmen Language and the Improvement of the Teaching of Russian and Other Languages' was prepared and published in late October 1989 (text in *TI* 31 Oct. 1989). The Programme stated, among other points, that a part of the population knew Turkmen only scrappily, so that this language had to be strengthened, particularly in the general education schools. Hence the bill proposed an increase in the teaching of Turkmen

– as well as of Russian, Uzbek, Kazakh and other languages – as part of an effort toward bilingualism and multilingualism. A worthy goal was to preserve the purity of literary Turkmen. Other means envisaged were to set up language courses wherever feasible, also employing the electronic media and other audio-visual tools; to publish numerous teaching aids (dictionaries, anthologies, textbooks, grammars, popular literature, guides, and maps); to see to it that Turkmen was studied in all school grades, from the first to the eleventh; and to train teaching staff.

The Programme immediately received press support (e.g., *TI* 5 Nov. 1989; 25 Nov. 1989; 31 Jan. 1990). Among the educational reforms suggested in the press were the imposition of Turkmen-language requirements for entry into and graduation from institutions of higher learning and the abolition of the regulation that dissertations had to be presented in Russian (Nissman 1993:391). The increase in the study of Turkmen was widely acclaimed, although other views were heard, too, such as that Turkmen had developed thanks to the Russian language (*TI* 24 Nov. 1989), and that knowledge of Russian was low in the Turkmen village schools (*TI* 25 Oct. 1989, based on *Druzhba Narodov* 10:1988) – views which give a sorry image of the expected bilingualism. By the time of the 1995 census in Turkmenistan 4.9% of Russians claimed to know Turkmen, while 22.2% Turkmens claimed to know Russian (Robertson 1998:437).

The Law on Language, adopted on 24 May 1990, was largely based on the above bill and was discussed, much in the same vein, not least in its bearing on language instruction. Among the reactions, there was significant support for full bilingualism, with requests to give both Turkmen and Russian sufficient scope at school (*TI* 10 July 1990); to permit other groups to be educated in their own languages, e.g., in Uzbek, Kazakh or German (*TI* 14 Apr. 1990; 24 June 1990; 1 Dec. 1990); or to study in school 'smaller languages' like Kurdish or Beluch – the latter already possessed an instruction manual (*TI* 25 May 1991). A special agreement was signed, in August 1991, by state leaders Niyazov and Makhkamov, for Turkmenistan and Tajikistan respectively, granting Tajiks in the former and Turkmens in the latter the right to get instruction in their respective language in their own schools and institutes, with special textbooks, as needed (*TI* 14 Aug. 1991).

After independence in December 1991, education was given high priority by the state leadership, at least in public speeches (*TI* 19 Nov. 1993; *NT* 14 Oct. 1998). Problems of language learning were discussed and partly tackled, such as the production of films to improve learning and speaking ability in Turkmen (*TI* 30 June 1992) and the development of new didactic methods for achieving this ability (*Mugallymlar Gazeti* 1 Feb., 5 Feb. 1999); the official introduction of both Turkmen and Russian into higher education (FBIS-SOV-92-146: 29 July 1992); or the preparation of a large Russian-Turkmen dictionary (*TI* 16 Oct. 1992).

That Turkmen still lagged behind Russian in 1992 was evident from data about the school year beginning on 1 September 1992, at least in Ashgabat: out of 57 general education schools, 39 used Russian as the language of instruction, 15 Turkmen, and 3 English (*TI* 31 Aug. 1992). The phenomenon is partly to be explained by the relatively large non-Turkmen population in Ashgabat. The official approach to the issue of language of instruction had been expressed as early as October 1992 by President Niyazov himself, whose views on this point (and most others) were decisive: 'In Turkmenistan, the Turkmen language ought to be the state one. Together with the Turkmen schools, there function others, too, where Russian, Uzbek and other languages are studied. Because of this, we are covering all costs of language study. Scholars should prepare curricula for language study' (*TI* 27 Oct. 1992). This policy continued to be supported by Niyazov during the following years (*NT* 3 July 1997).

The teaching of Turkmen and other languages received continued official encouragement over time in independent Turkmenistan (*TI* 5 Jan. 1994), although Turkmen-Russian bilingualism officially remained the order of the day in education and elsewhere. In practice, many schools had to decide on instruction with an emphasis on *one* language – while, again, preaching bilingualism or even multilingualism. Thus, in the 1997/8 school year, according to official data, the main languages of instruction of more than 800,000 pupils were as follows: Turkmen in 1,938 schools, Russian in 250, Uzbek in 90, and Kazakh in 40 (Kuleshov et al. 1997:507). For 1999 the figures given are as follows: Russian in 170, Uzbek in 100, Kazakh in 40 (*NT* 15 March 1999). Efforts continued to improve the study of Turkmen in Russian schools by allotting more hours to it (interview with N. Kurbanmuradov, Deputy Minister of Education, Ashgabat, 22 Sep. 1998).

Special attention was paid during the independence years to preparation of better curricula for the study of Russian language and literature at school (*Mugallymlar Gazeti* 7 Nov. 1997; *Ashgabat* 29 Jan. 1998). A recent case was the inauguration in 1997 of a school offering instruction in Russian for the Russian border guards' children (*Turkmenistan News Weekly* 179(35):1 Sep. 1997). However, some Russians felt that the education of their children was suffering by the over-emphasis on Turkmen and perhaps on English as well, which, they claimed, had reduced the number of schools and classes available to them (Chebotareva 1996:19).

It seems that Turkmenistan, as presided over by Niyazov, is moving towards trilingualism, perhaps a little more determinedly than some of the other states, striving to give its young generation an education in three languages – Turkmen, Russian and a second foreign language. Niyazov, indeed, has frequently returned to this theme; on 2 May 1996, he addressed a meeting of teachers and education officials, announcing the formation of a special council at the Ministry of Education to coordinate the teaching of Turkmen, Russian and English throughout the state and the preparation of experts in these languages. He declared that the Council would issue teachers' certificates, draw up curricula and planning, see to the writing of textbooks, and initiate radio and television programmes on the government's language policies (*NT* 28 Oct. 1996).

A comprehensive school reform aiming at a more general trilingual education (in Turkmen, Russian and English), envisaged since 1996, seems an over-ambitious goal. It resembles the trilingual drive in Kazakhstan (for Kazakh, Russian and English). The Turkmen National Institute of World Languages, which offers instruction in several languages, has also been in charge of preparing curricula, textbooks, dictionaries, and audio and video materials for trilingual education, while a Coordination Council, appointed by the Council of Ministers, has maintained supervisory responsibility (*Turkmenistan News Weekly* 162(18):5 May 1997; *NT* 1 Sep. 1998).

A significant reorientation in language education policies can be observed beginning with the 1997/8 school year. The basic approach was to focus on foreign language instruction in special schools and educational institutions for especially gifted pupils. This was intended to train specialists for professions needing foreign language expertise. Overall instruction in foreign languages (in most cases English) in such specialized schools and institutions is part and parcel of this structural reform (*NT* 2 Sep. 1997; 19, 27 Jan. 1998). For students who could not get into these courses but still would like to be proficient in a foreign language, extracurricular courses and centres for the study of English (and other foreign languages) against payment of fees were introduced. This situation was apparently criticized by some parents, who worried that the quality of foreign language instruction would consequently decline at school (*NT* 11 Aug. 1997).

The Turkmen National Institute of World Languages coordinated the centres. Such a centre in Ashgabat, called *Dil* (Language), offered foreign language instruction to everybody, intensively and with an emphasis on speaking – apparently achieving good results (*NT* 28 Aug. 1997). Four other centres for teaching, respectively, English, French, German and Turkish were opened in Ashgabat in 1997 with the support of the four embassies there (*NT* 12 Aug. 1997), and others were opened in provincial towns like Tashauz and Lebap (*Ashgabat* 1 Nov. 1998). In the former, this was an American-supported centre for the study of English; two-year courses, on twelve levels of language proficiency, aimed at oral-aural fluency (*Ashgabat* 19 Jan., 5 May 1998).

According to the first Deputy Minister of Education, A.R. Annaeva, efforts will be invested in teaching foreign languages from kindergarten and up in all schools (*NT* 1 Sep. 1997). Many schools offered foreign languages: English or German (in that order of prevalence), or more rarely

Persian or French (1 school each), or Turkish (1 boys' school) (*NT* 12 Mar. 1998). In 1998, special classes in English were introduced into 23 schools and in German into 10 (*NT* 11 Apr. 1998). The British Council in Turkmenistan organized courses in English required by specialized officials, such as frontier guards and customs officers (*NT* 10 June 1998). From the 1999/2000 school year a new subject – Arabic – was offered at eight Turkmen-language schools in Ashgabat (*Extracts* 2 Sept. 1999. Available: http://www.soros.org/turkstan/omri/0184.html. 16 Sept. 1999).

In 1998, Turkmenistan had two universities and twelve institutes of higher education. The Makhtumkuli Turkmen State University in Ashgabat is considered the flagship of higher education; the other is the University of Agriculture, promoted to this status (1998) from an institute founded about seventy years earlier. Both Turkmen and Russian are employed in universities and institutes, in a realistic approach: the humanities are taught in Turkmen; the technological disciplines, as well as the study of international relations, usually in Russian. In 14 establishments of higher education and 18 technical schools, only 7% had Russian as the language of instruction (Kuleshov a.o. 1997:507). Whatever the department, the students have to study some Turkmen, too. In the Faculty of Foreign Languages, all students have to take a four-year major in English; they may take a minor in another language, such as German or French – but not the other way round (visit to the Department of English, 22 Sep. 1998). German is preferred to French for business reasons, as Germans have more companies working in Turkmenistan. A network of other institutions provides, against payment, courses in various foreign languages (*NT* 21 Jan. 1998). As of now, English prevails numerically over other foreign languages and will probably continue to do so.

Tajikistan

In the Republic of Tajikistan, the main groups are Tajiks, Uzbeks, Russians, and Kyrgyz. Tajik nationalists have maintained for some time that their people included all those who spoke an Iranian language, thus blurring the fact that the so-called mountain Tajiks speak languages belonging to the east Iranian group. In order to promote Tajik identity in Tajikistan and elsewhere, emphasis was laid on language as a unifying element (Jahangiri 1998:19-20). Political conflict was more between Tajik and Uzbek than between either of these and Russian, reflecting rivalries between the two communities in Central Asia. The Russian Federation and its army, after all, have been supporting the newly independent Tajik government against militant Islamic incursions from Afghanistan. Moreover, the economy of Tajikistan, already in the Soviet period one of the poorest republics, has suffered greatly during the civil war and subsequently. In such an atmosphere, language education has held only a modest ranking in independent Tajikistan's agenda of priorities.

Earlier, however, in the late 1980s, as in all non-Russian Soviet republics, language occupied a place in public discourse, and the status of Tajik in education was debated. Tajik history and Persian-language literature were given short shrift, arousing criticism among some Tajik intellectuals (Atkin 1997:282). But, due to Soviet dominance, such basic conflictual issues kept a low profile for some time. As elsewhere, Russian had been promoted at the expense of other languages at school, with rather mixed success. In 1988, 66% of all pupils in general day schools studied in Tajik as the language of instruction, 22.9% in Uzbek, 9.7% in Russian, 1.1% in Kyrgyz, and 0.3% in Turkmen. Only a year later, following the adoption of Tajik as the state language, pupils in Russian schools were supposed to study some Tajik through all eleven grades (*The Europa World Year-Book 1998*: II, 3266).

The Law on Language of 22 July 1989 (above, ch. 6) had a special section on education, science and culture, in which the state promised to guarantee, whenever possible, that every citizen should get instruction in his or her own language – Tajik, Russian, Uzbek, Kyrgyz, or others. The state would also guarantee that the Tajiks learned Russian and the Russians learned Tajik, from kindergarten throughout all grades and in all forms of school; also that Tajik should be studied in all non-Tajik establishments. Special guarantees would be given for the equal employment of Tajik, Russian and Uzbek in all domains of science. The state would also produce films, television films, videos, etc. in Tajik with a translation of the text into other languages.

Public debate continued, with such arguments and suggestions as the following: better qualified teachers should be trained; public leaders should know Tajik fluently (*KT* 16 Apr. 1989); the level of teaching Tajik language and literature in Russian schools ought to be improved by better curricula, textbooks and methods (*KT* 21 Apr. 1989). In June 1989, the Ministry of Education underlined that in the 2,931 schools of all sorts in Tajikistan, constant efforts were being made to improve the teaching of Tajik language and literature. According to the official curriculum projected for 1989-90 (published in *KT* 20 July 1989), in principle the same number of hours was allocated to learning Russian in Tajik schools as Tajik in Russian ones in grades 1-11. An exception was the addition of one more hour for Tajik in grades 3 and 4 of the Russian schools. The curricula, also, were soon modified to lay more emphasis on the Tajik language, adding, since 1990, another class hour in Tajik in grades 4, 5, 9 and 10 and preparing suitable textbooks and dictionaries (*KT* 4 Mar. 1990); and on literature, including classical Persian texts in the Arabic-based alphabet (Payne 1996:378), some supplied by Iran (below, ch. 9, p. 202). 8,645 teachers were said to be working then in all of Tajikistan's schools, 90.4% of whom had had higher education. Starting with the 1980s, Tajiks have been studying a wide range of subjects in Tajik in their institutions of higher education, where reportedly some departments have even weighted their courses to favour Tajik by teaching mathematics, physics, early-childhood education, labour economics, and history of pedagogy in this language (Atkin 1992:54).

Due to destruction and displacement during the civil war and its ensuing economic crisis, the functioning of the educational system was severely disturbed. Schoolchildren received considerably less study hours. Nevertheless, in the second half of the 1990s, the provisions of the Law on Education of 27 December 1993 (*NaG* 15 Jan. 1994; above, ch. 6) were set in motion and the use of Tajik as the language of instruction seems to have made some progress.

In October 1997, a new start was made with the decree on the 'Programme of the Government of Tajikistan for the Development of the State Language and Other Languages... of the Republic of Tajikistan' (*Omūzgor* 6 Nov. 1997). Its section on education specifies directives for the improvement of language education and language of instruction on all school levels, in universities and in adult education. The state language is to be taught in all schools, including non-Tajik schools. Special programmes are to be developed for special secondary schools. Instruction in the state language is compulsory in all disciplines at the university level, philological, social, technical and natural sciences alike. From the 1998-9 academic year onward, a complete transition to instruction in the state language was envisaged for all secondary and university education groups studying the technical, agrarian, medical and economic sciences. All pupils sitting for final examinations on the secondary, specialized and university levels have to pass a test in Tajik.

Russian has retreated in education, probably as a result of war, insecurity and emigration: In the years 1991-5, the number of Russian schools decreased from 22% to 11% (Kuleshov a.o. 1997:509). The above-mentioned Government Programme clearly provides for Russian to be taught in all secondary and professional schools as well as in higher education, where Tajik and other national languages are used as language of instruction.

The amount of detail in the Programme seems to reflect the government's concern with the minority groups: The large Uzbek community is assured support for its language from kindergarten to university level. In regions with compact settlements, the Kyrgyz are granted their own classes and schools. Exchange of schoolbooks, students and teachers with Kyrgyzstan is on the agenda. Children whose mother tongue is one of the Pamiri languages (Yaghnobi, Shughni, Yazghulami, Vakhi, and others) are guaranteed instruction in their own language, along with Tajik, on the elementary school level.

According to the evidence of foreign visitors, however, the universities as well as the academies of science have been weakened by both civil strife and the emigration of many non-Tajik teachers and scholars. The sharp drop in the number of women students also bodes ill (Rzehak 1995: 333-4; Kuleshov a.o. 1997:509). In a public address, in May 1998, President Rakhmonov spoke of twenty-five universities and institutes with some 80,000 students (*NaG* 8 May 1998). The (Slavonic) State University in Dushanbe, founded in September 1996 with 1,200 students, to bring about a reduction in European emigration, may have been established too late for the purpose (*NaG* 15-22 May 1997; Payne 1996; Kreindler 1997:101); this university trains teachers of Russian language and literature. At other universities, both Tajik and Russian are studied, with special courses training translators for these languages and English (Government Programme, above, p. 195).

Textbooks

Book publishing in Azerbayjan and Central Asia is beset by the lack of paper production and availability. Indeed, throughout the Soviet period, the entire area was paper-dependent on the centre's allocations, which went in a larger part to Russian language publications. The situation could not change overnight – and it did not (Naby 1993). The paper shortage inherited from Soviet times and the restructuring of the printing and publishing sector after independence have hampered the realization of ambitious education programmes.

Textbooks (together with handbooks for teachers) are, of course, a crucial instrument of language instruction. Their suitability and availability condition progress, indeed success, in education. For the six states discussed, all financially constrained, the nature and use of textbooks has become a touchstone of their education policies, which aim at introducing new textbooks, different from the Soviet ones, to promote their own ideologies. This approach is expressed to no little degree in language instruction. In many cases, language textbooks (particularly for foreign languages) are more plentiful for the lower grades than the upper, that is, they are more adequate for teaching the core courses. In this context, several issues are significant, such as whether the textbooks used are still the old ones, modelled in the Soviet style and often imported from Russia, or new ones, adapted to suit the changed situation in each independent state, and whether they are printed in the newly-introduced alphabets. In every case, the government, the only agency with financial resources, has been involved, but to a different degree in every state. Some of these issues have already been briefly alluded to; here we shall attempt to group some of the relevant data and evaluate them.

Azerbayjan. The Azerbayjan government provides schoolbooks without cost to the first four grades, but from the fifth the pupils' parents have to buy them, as the state cannot yet bear the cost. Many textbooks for the

Russian schools are still imported from Russia, as are those for studying English, in both the Russian and Azeri schools, since they are considerably cheaper there. The same applies to textbooks for German language instruction, although the contents are frequently outdated (*Azärbaican Müällimi* 30 Oct. 1997). However, considerable efforts are being invested in preparing all textbooks for Azeri schools locally, with those in Latin script having been introduced into the first grade on 1 September 1992, and with every passing year one grade higher. During the five years 1992-7, more than 120 new schoolbooks were published in Azeri in Latin characters for grades one to eleven, with government allocations (Turkey assisted financially with some textbooks for the lower grades). In 1998, the schoolbooks which we saw for almost all subjects in the seventh grade in Azeri schools were in Latin script. In the languages of the minority groups (such as Tats, Talyshes, Kurds, Lazes, Sakhurs, Udins, and Khynalygs) the Cyrillic alphabet is being preserved; textbooks were prepared for the early grades; six came out in 1996 alone, at the Maarif Press in Baku. In the humanities the books were written anew, their authors distancing themselves from Communist ideology; those in the sciences were usually translated from the Russian (interviews with Mahir M. Aliev, Head of the Foreign Relations Department, Ministry of Education, Baku, 22 May 1997 and 29 Sep. 1998). Azeri schoolbooks prepared in Azerbayjan are also sent to Azeri schools in Georgia and elsewhere (interview with Prof. Hamlet Isakhanly, Baku, 30 Sep. 1998).

Textbooks for learning Persian, which is studied in a number of schools, like a series prepared by N.M. Hatemi and Sh.I. Shiroliev (published in Baku by Maarif Press), were still in the Cyrillic script in 1992 but later in the Latin one, side-by-side with the Arabic/Persian alphabet. Since most available literature in Azeri, including numerous translations of world classics, is still in the Cyrillic alphabet, the children study it, too. Many children's books are, of course, in Russian. Some are bilingual (or even trilingual), such as a periodical entitled *Nävä: Detskii Zhurnal na Azerbaidzhanskom i Russkom Yazykakh* (Children's Magazine in Azeri and Russian), of which the first issues appeared in Baku in 1996, each consisting of 18 pages. The text was in both Azeri and Russian, with translations into one another and sometimes into English. This seems to have been intended for both Azeri and Russian children. In the opinion of local parents, the number of children's books in Azeri printed in Latin script has been growing.

Uzbekistan. Like Azerbaijan, Uzbekistan imports textbooks for its Russian schools from Russia, but has been investing efforts to prepare its own materials for the Uzbek schools. Its educators are attempting to present Uzbekistan's culture and history 'as it really was'. In the Uzbekistani schools, emphasis in language instruction has usually been on the conversational skills in grades 1-9 and on reading and writing skills in grades 10-11. This applies to Uzbek, but also to the other languages taught. New textbooks are being prepared and the advice of experts is sought. For those wishing to learn a 'western' foreign language, especially English, a large variety of textbooks is in the market; some of these are prepared locally, others are imported from Russia or the respective country. For instance, S. Musaev and others have written a *Guide parlé français-uzbek-russe,* probably for adults, published in Tashkent by Ŭqituvchi Press in 1994, soon followed by an *English for Businessmen,* in two volumes, 1997-8, of which the first was printed in Tashkent and the second in Moscow.

For most school books in Uzbek the Latin script is being increasingly introduced, but Cyrillic is still employed in Tajik, Kazakh and Turkmen ones, at least for the time being. During the first half of the 1990s, 300 textbooks and exercise books – 33 of them for first graders – have been published in about 30 million copies, a growing number printed in Latin characters (*PV* 7 Aug. 1996). For the school year 1996/7, the Ministry of National Education published 50,000 copies of a handbook in Latin script for first-grade school teachers by Q. Abdullayeva, K. Nazarov and Sh. Yo'ldosheva, entitled *Savod O'rgatish Metodikasi* (Method of Teaching How to Read and Write), Tashkent: O'qituvchi, 1996. In the spring of 1997, another Latin script teaching instrument for first-grade teachers was published by the same Ministry, again in 50,000 copies: Q. Abdullayeva, M. Yusupov, D. Abdullayeva: *Diktantlar To'plami* (A Collection of Dictations, Tashkent: O'qituvchi, 1997); and, later that year, a primer by V. Lipatov, entitled *Izuchaem Uzbekskii yazyk* (We Study Uzbek, Tashkent: Ŭqituvchi), intended for Russian schools.

Most effort was invested in preparing textbooks for the pupils in Uzbek schools. These comprised, up to and including the fifth grade, textbooks in the sciences and in history, and of course in literature – like *O'zbek adabiyoti* (Uzbek Literature, Tashkent: O'qituvchi, 1998) – and in language, like *Ona tili* (Mother tongue), a series for various grades (Tashkent: O'qituvchi, 1998).

The preparation and provision of the necessary schoolbooks, teachers' manuals and methodological help for teaching the state language in schools with Russian, Kazakh, Tajik, Kyrgyz, Turkmen and Karakalpak language of instruction seems still far from satisfactory, as the State Commission for the Implementation of the Language Law stated at one of its regular meetings (*Uchitel' Uzbekistana* 7 Apr. 1999). On the one hand, much had been done in this field and work was going on actively, but on the other hand there were shortcomings: schools were not receiving the amount of already published schoolbooks and teachers' manuals they needed; there was also a lack of dictionaries and conversation manuals for self-teaching as well as breaks and delays in the publication of new schoolbooks, manuals and teachers' handbooks; and the task of helping teachers with methodical problems was not well organized. The commission strongly underlined the necessity to overcome these shortcomings as soon as possible.

For adults wishing to learn Uzbek, there are a number of manuals in Cyrillic characters, which they know better. Equally, the first issue of a new journal for language and literature teachers published early in 1998 was again completely in Cyrillic script, *Til va Adabiët Ta"limi* (Language and Literature Instruction – Scientific-Methodical Journal of the Ministry of National Education of the Republic of Uzbekistan, Tashkent). Another journal for primary school teachers, *Boshlanghich Ta"lim* (Primary Education, Tashkent: first published in 1992) included in its July-August 1997 issue six articles, out of fourteen, in Latin script. As for university textbooks, an effort is being made to increase the production of Uzbek publications, although many Russian ones are still in use.

In the Soviet Union it was customary for the republics to exchange school books, when necessary; e.g. in 1988, 391,000 textbooks in Uzbek (96 titles on various topics) were received in Tajikistan from Uzbekistan for schools using Uzbek as the language of instruction; in return, Tajikistan sent to Uzbekistan 477,000 textbooks in Tajik (62 titles on various topics) for schools in which the language of instruction was Tajik (*PV* 30 Aug. 1988). Textbooks for studying Uzbek are still being sent to Uzbek schools in Tajikistan, but less than previously, probably due to political tensions between the two states and to the fact that Uzbek textbooks are increasingly produced in Latin characters (not employed in Tajikistan). The parallel arrangement for importing textbooks from Tajikistan for the numerous Tajik schools in Uzbekistan does not seem to be working any more, due to the difficult economic conditions in Tajikistan. Consequently, preparations have started in Uzbekistan to prepare its own textbooks for its Tajik schools. By 1997, twenty-three titles for teaching in Tajik schools were already in use, practically all translated from Uzbek into Tajik, thus spreading the ideological outlook of new Uzbekistan (interview with a Western correspondent based in Tashkent, 9 Sep. 1998).

Kazakhstan. In Kazakhstan, the issue of textbooks is more urgent than in the other independent Muslim states, since a proportionately large section of the population does not know the titular language. This has necessitated special efforts in the preparation and publication of language textbooks for both schoolchildren and adults as well as teachers' manuals in Kazakh. While the situation can still be improved (for complaints, *Gorizont* 16 June 1995), textbooks for Kazakh have been recently prepared for workers' circles at factories and for the military (*Zvezda Priirtysh'ya* 15 Nov. 1997; *Aktyubinskii Vestnik* 6 Oct. 1998). Not only video cassettes, but computer programmes are increasingly prepared, along with manuals for self-study (*Kustanaiskie Novosti* 15 Apr. 1997; 8 Oct. 1998; *KP* 15 May 1998).

The main effort of the education authorities in Kazakhstan seems directed however at promoting Kazakh at school. One such instance is a much-praised textbook by R.A. Abuzyarova and K.T. Ugenova, entitled *Uchimsya i uchim govorit' po-kazakhskii* (Let us learn and teach to speak Kazakh), published in 1997 (*Priural'e* 18 Nov. 1997). Unfortunately, the distribution of language textbooks is not always well administered.

The authorities have organized deliveries of textbooks to school libraries; parents could borrow them against a small fee (and at the end of the school year bring them back to the libraries). Since the 1994-5 school year, these fees have risen, however, even for the lower grades. Textbooks for grades 9-11 are on sale in the bookshops. Every year, new textbooks, dictionaries and conversation manuals are published in Kazakh, Russian, Uyghur and other languages (Nauryzbaev 1993:48; for an Uyghur primer, *Ana Tili* 37:1998). However, language textbooks for children, students and others cover a part of the ground only. This seems to be characteristic of the general situation of printing in Kazakh: in 1995, only 600 titles in Kazakh in all fields were published, compared to 762 in 1940 (*KP* 23 Apr. 1996). Also, some are too expensive (Eremin 1995:41). The education authorities, however, are intent on having many more school books in all domains prepared, in due course, by Kazakh authors (interview with A.K. Akhmedov, Almaty, 14 Sep. 1998).

Kyrgyzstan. Kyrgyzstan suffers, more than some others of the states discussed, from a dearth of school textbooks. No less an authority than Sovetbek Toktomyshev, Minister of Education, Science and Culture, frankly acknowledged this in a press conference in August 1998, just before the start of the school year, saying that the budget for textbooks was woefully inadequate for the needs of the whole country. Many classes in the Uzbek schools would have only a few textbooks to use, including those for language; books for the study of foreign languages would be entirely unavailable (*Kutbilim* 29 Aug. 1998). The government, like Kazakhstan's, has adopted a system whereby parents can rent school books for their children; in cases of economic hardship and large families, these are given away at no cost. Before independence, practically all textbooks were imported from Russia; following it, they are gradually being written and published in Kyrgyzstan, at a national centre for textbooks, emphasizing the Kyrgyz viewpoint (interview with S.B. Begaliev, chairman of the Assembly of the People of Kyrgyzstan, Bishkek, 16 Sep. 1998). At this centre and elsewhere in Kyrgyzstan, textbooks are prepared in Kyrgyz for the disciplines of language, literature, history, and geography. Examples are Zh. Mametov and M. Atakisheva's *Kyrgyz Tili* (The Kyrgyz Language), published in Bishkek by Kyrgyzstan Press in 1996 for the seventh grade of the Russian schools, or a *Russkii yazyk* (Russian Language) manual, published in Bishkek by Kyrgyzstan Press in 1997 for the second grade of the Kyrgyz schools. The writing and printing of more than 120 Kyrgyz school books was financed by the George Soros Foundation (*Novoe Vremya* 20: 25 May 1997, 20-1) in editions of 1,000-2,000 copies in the expectation that the Ministry of Education would then reprint the number required in the schools. This procedure has had a limited success only, due to the Ministry's lack of funds (interview with a collaborator at the Soros Foundation Centre, Bishkek, 17 Sep. 1998).

Since the school year 1996-7, a group of younger Kyrgyz historians started to publish history books for school use, reassessing the history of the Kyrgyz people. The books were also translated into Russian and Uzbek (Čorotegin 1997).

An interesting task is the preparation of the necessary Uzbek textbooks for Uzbek schools in Kyrgyzstan. Formerly, these were imported from Uzbekistan. More recently, however, they had to be written in Kyrgyzstan, as Uzbek textbooks increasingly use Latin script, while those in Kyrgyzstan schools still adhere to Cyrillic. The Kyrgyzstan Press in Bishkek, already mentioned, has been publishing a wide range of textbooks in several fields for all school grades, in Kyrgyz and Russian, including language ones for English, French, German, and others. Although it is not a government firm, it collaborates closely with the Ministry of Education in the preparation of school materials (interview with Prof. Kadirali Konkobey Uulu, General Director of Kyrgyzstan Press, Bishkek, 18 Sep. 1998).

Turkmenistan. Turkmenistan manages to donate textbooks without cost, for all grades, via the schools. The textbooks (except those for the first grade) are returned at the end of the school year, to be re-used. Turkmenistan has started publishing Russian textbooks for Russian schools and Turkmen ones for Turkmen schools, although most Russian books as well as many English ones still come from Russia. The former are increasingly printed in the new Latin alphabet, like one by Myratgeldi Söegov and Nyyazberdi Rezhebov, teaching the new alphabet, *Täze Türkmen Elipbii*, Ashgabat: Rukh, 1993. A recent *English-Russian-Turkmen Phrase-book* by R. Mustagov and Zh. Mustagova, Ashgabat: 1997, still uses the Cyrillic script for Turkmen, perhaps because it is intended for adults, not yet familiar with the new alphabet. All curricula and schoolbooks have to be approved by the Supreme Council of Science and Technology at the President's office, which works via sub-commissions for the various subjects at the schools. The Council selects authors for the textbooks requested by the Ministry of Education, in which an Institute of Education deals with textbooks. Scholars from the Academy of

Sciences and the Makhtumkuli National State University are also involved.

The Turkish government, too, had 29 schoolbooks for Turkmen schools printed in Latin script in 1997, in 3 million copies altogether. Textbooks are published by the Magaryf Press in Ashgabat, which is a state publishing house. A paper mill was in construction near the city in 1998 to resolve the paper shortage for schoolbooks and other works. This also enables the authorities to photocopy certain textbooks instead of buying them abroad, but the introduction of the Latin alphabet in Turkmenistan schools implies that many books would have to be written anew, or at least transcribed into Latin characters (interview with Nowruz Kurbanmuradov, Deputy Minister of Education, and Tagan Bekdjaev, Faculty of Turkmen Philology at the Makhtumkuli National State University, Ashgabat, 22 Sep. 1998).

Tajikistan. Soon after independence, scholars in Tajikistan were already busy preparing schoolbooks with Tajik instead of Russian terms in different areas of study. Tajikistan has its own problems in supplying the necessary textbooks, even though the government has been accepting Iran's help. In 1992, extensive cultural agreements were signed between the two states: in addition to cooperation between the governments of Tajikistan and Iran in the areas of student exchanges, educational grants and book exhibitions, textbooks have been given for Tajik schools; in addition to 120,000 Persian alphabet books, 250,000 Persian textbooks for elementary and high school students were donated in 1993 and another 400,000 in 1996 (Mesbahi 1997:144-5).

Evidently, such gestures cannot supply all the needs, and it seems that Tajikistan's main problem in the matter is the scarcity of its financial resources. A special Foundation for the Tajik Language, set up in 1992, with ample means in old Soviet rubles, lost its holdings overnight in 1995, as L. Sherali, the Foundation's chairman, declared (*Tajikistan Economic Review* 52:July 1998, 3-4). Nevertheless, Tajik language specialists pointed out that a number of manuals for learning the Tajik language were published: The *Tajik language* for students of Russian-language universities, *Tajik language textbook* by S. Arzumanov, *Tajik language textbook* by A. Karimov and U. Obidov, *Tajik language textbook* by M. Mahadov, and *Tajik-Russian speech manual*, edited by R. Dodikhudoev.

Yet another issue relates to the Uzbeks, Tajikistan's largest minority *ethnie*. In a November 1996 interview, Kurbon Sattarov, chairman of the Association of Uzbeks in Tajikistan (Attar and Fedtke 1998a: A 206-A 208), maintained that, while the Uzbeks had their own schools offering instruction in their own language, their greatest problem was the non-availability of textbooks, which at the time they could neither find the money to produce in Tajikistan, nor get from Uzbekistan as they did before (Uzbek informants contradict the latter).

Summing up, it seems that the problems connected to language textbooks in the six independent states present certain similarities. They all need new textbooks suited to their changed status but find it difficult to finance their production or importation. Not all have quite determined how the contents and style of new textbooks should effectively assist in shaping a changed awareness of national identity. In the few years since independence, most of their efforts have been directed towards emphasizing the titular language, generally without an avowed downgrading of Russian.

10

CONCLUSION

NEW SOLUTIONS, OLD PROBLEMS

In the present state of our knowledge, when we discuss phenomena less than a decade old, a substantial part of our presentation must necessarily be descriptive and evaluative – with analytical-comparative comments wherever possible – without presuming to formulate general theoretical deductions, premature at this stage.

Bearing in mind, then, that it is rather presumptuous to reach any finite conclusions when attempting to sum up an ongoing process, one may still try to estimate certain of its features. Among these, a dilemma common to the leading elites in the six newly independent states stands out, namely, how to achieve and maintain policy primacy over ethnicity. The problem is more acute in new states and societies, most particularly so in multiethnic ones. The majority group usually encounters difficulties in formulating and delivering a generally acceptable political message of nationalism, often expressed in terms of patriotism as a norm of loyalty shared by all citizens towards their state. The message of commonality in the case of the six republics ties up with the assimilationist objectives of the majority group in reducing the impact of a potentially fissiparous multi-ethnic situation. Yet another consideration is the desire to minimize the danger of the disruption of national unity in the new states, although language differences do not necessarily lead in themselves to such disruption, unless combined with other factors that are not always present in the new situation of independence. The moulding of *ethnies* to nation, however, is not merely a matter of manipulation by leaders, but also a historical process which takes time. While the new-old elites in the six states are responsible for the former, they cannot hasten the latter.

Promoting the homogeneous character of what is intended to be the identity of a new nation counters the aspirations of other *ethnies* – chiefly the largest minority group – which consider themselves adversely affected by the titular majority's measures towards nation-building, in a process perceived as imposing the titular group's identity on all others. The Russians have not been mollified in their opposition to majorization by the titular language even by renewed assurances, like that of President Karimov of Uzbekistan who, in March 1998, declared that 'the Uzbeks will not tear away from the Russian people, culture and civilization' (*NG* 27 Mar. 1998). Ethnic conflicts are hardly ever resolved by official proclamations. The common denominators of identity politics, in our case, have been conflictual rather than consensual in the domain of culture and language. The language issue has served as a centrifugal, no less than a centripetal, factor.

Nation-building seems to follow certain patterns conditioned by the legacies of these states which are heirs to an empire that collapsed through non-revolutionary means. Among the legacies are demographic and ethnic situations, social and economic structures, some state institutions, an overall inheritance of political culture, and certain sets of elites (Barkey 1997:101-3). One of the contradictions of Soviet history was that a Communist elite which once preached an internationalist agenda ended by shaping nations within its body politic. In the six states discussed, the nations still have the character of *ethnies*. Their political elites are largely those of Soviet times, matured in a definite world view and continuing in office at top leadership levels; thus, they are hardly the best-suited to offer a civic vision of nationhood to their multiethnic and multicultural societies. Following the Soviet models in which they themselves had been trained, they have usually opted for an authoritarian assimilationist version, multiethnic and multicultural in rhetoric but exclusive in practice. Two goals are noticeable in the process: to articulate a distinct national culture and address a collective memory, on the one hand, and to promote ethno-linguistic political consciousness, on the other. Many declarations notwithstanding, policies according advantages to the members and the language of the titular *ethnie* are manifest, along with the exclusion of members of non-eponymous groups from the public sector. In this matter, as in some others, broadly speaking, there is a lack of fundamental change in the area's political, social and cultural character. In the absence of a strong independent tradition in the six states, Russian influence in education and language use has persisted to a great extent. The enthusiasm for Western material and ideological values has largely remained a veneer.

The Soviet policy of linguistic russification had been only partly successful in the six Muslim republics. While knowledge of Russian, particularly after the end of the Second World War, spread rapidly, chiefly in urban areas, it did not preclude continuing loyalty to the native tongues in a great number of cases, with Russian becoming a second language, continually enlarging its hold and functioning as *lingua franca* throughout the entire area. The advantages that the mastery of Russian implied resulted in alienating many *ethnies* from their native heritage. In the six independent states certain elites set out to correct this and establish a firm relation between language choice and national identity. As a current slogan in Kazakhstan goes, 'Respect for the language – respect for the country'.

Nationalism has frequently been, although in various degrees, an influential factor in language planning, as a link with the past and with authenticity (Fishman 1972:xiii, 39ff). In the new situation discussed, a national language, while not equated with national identity, is often perceived by the elites as its clearest attribute; thus, it is seen as a major instrument of consolidation as well as a powerful symbol of nationhood. As elsewhere, conflict about the state language reflects competition for power and prestige (O'Barr 1984). Nationalist circles in the six states frequently identify language with patriotism, so that the promotion of language is one of their favourite slogans. Their choices for language priorities and language use are made in order to direct and shape their nations via the call for cultural solidarity. Government decision makers are still in the process of determining a crucial issue – how to raise *de facto* the language of the titular *ethnie* to the status of state language, with certain provisions for Russian and for all other languages spoken in the republic.

The leading elites in each of the newly independent states have reconsidered some of the rules of language policy, well aware that few issues stir such passions as language, a marker of collective identity (another such issue could have been religion, which the ruling elites had mostly discarded, probably due to their Soviet upbringing). In order to reverse the language processes of the Soviet era, the role ascribed to the titular language versus Russian became the focal element in determining language policy in each of the six new states – but with varying emphases. The common denominator of the policies pursued in the six republics was that, while formerly the non-Russians had had to learn Russian in order to enjoy social mobility and economic benefits, in the new situation the Russian and other groups were confronted with the need to learn the titular language if they wished to maintain their social and economic level.

In the case of the six new states, one wonders whether the entire process of awarding the titular language a special status may not have been somewhat hasty. Its official status as state language was proclaimed and its wider communication promoted, with emphasis laid on its standing in the capital city and in school education; however, sensitivity has not always been shown towards the status demands voiced by speakers of Russian and minority languages. Implementation was also quickly carried forward in legislation, but less so on the administrative and educational levels, good intentions notwithstanding. This was due to various factors, such as lack of trained staff or of financial resources (reserved for pressing economic needs) and, in Kazakhstan and Kyrgyzstan, due (in part, at least) to articulate Russian opposition which the two governments could hardly afford to ignore.

One reason for what appears to be rather hurried planning and hasty attempts at implementation is attributable to nationalists who argued that the principle of 'one territory, one language' ought to be applied urgently so as to provide society in each of the six states with an awareness of its own identity as rapidly as possible. This approach indicated designs for the pursuit and maintenance of power – policies to which other linguistic groups reacted accordingly. The Slav communities as well as some other large minorities (like the Tajiks in Uzbekistan or the Uzbeks in Kyrgyzstan and Tajikistan) protested, arguing that majorization by the titular language hindered the process of legitimizing cultural and linguistic minorities. Nevertheless, the representatives of practically every titular *ethnie* in the six independent states, while claiming to profess a real interest in all languages employed within its own borders, have been perpetuating to a great extent one aspect at least of Soviet linguistic policies, viz., the promotion of a policy aimed at the eventual overall integration of the minorities into the culture and language of the dominant *ethnie*.

Language policies in multilingual states are frequently designed to minimize complex aspects of societal multilingualism since such complexity is inconvenient for the workings of modern states. There is however another important motivation in our case. The leading elites of the titular *ethnie* have used the language issue to strengthen their own community. For this purpose they raised the status of the titular language (by legislation and increasing its role in education and its visibility in public life). Modification and treatment of the corpus in the titular language (by purification and invention of new terms) was also deemed necessary for de-russification in favour of what was considered national identity. A serious attempt was made in several of the six states, to varying degrees, to turn the titular literary language into one capable of nuanced functioning in all domains of modern life. Alphabet change and even more so language enrichment with new words are intended to maximize standardization and modernization of the language. Authentication seems to be one of the preferred methods in trying to de-russify the titular language. Planners often remain at odds as to what to do with international terms which were introduced via Russian. Indeed, it has been argued that the uprooting of Russian and international words from the titular languages would render it even more difficult for the titular *ethnies* to learn Russian and for the non-titular inhabitants to learn the titular languages. Language engineering has been and remains a difficult enterprise. Work in language corpus is not easy; what has been achieved in half a dozen years falls short of expectations.

Unwilling to support monolingualism at the present time, political leaders in the six independent states have striven to adopt a new vision of bilingualism, where de-russification is expressed in promoting the titular language to the first place and downgrading Russian to the second. Legislation has raised the titular language to the status of a state language; official record keeping is managed increasingly in it; the number of Russian schools has somewhat decreased and class hours are being transferred to the state language and culture. The political leadership in

Azerbayjan and Central Asia is carefully watching reactions both in the Russian Federation, which is charging discrimination, and within the Slav diaspora in each independent state – especially so in Kazakhstan and Kyrgyzstan with their proportionately large Slav communities, but elsewhere as well. As for the language laws, it might well be that some of them were modified, because the Russian diasporas reacted with out-migration, and were only partly implemented in the public service and education, due to financial circumstances (and, sometimes, Russian opposition).

It is remarkable that the non-titular communities in the six states, inexperienced in initiating political action, have merely protested, without regularly resorting to organized political reactions (except, to a minor degree, in Kazakhstan) and even less so to militant opposition. The identity of Russian diasporas in the six states is by no means simple. Some of the ethnic Russians are third or fourth generation, with deep roots in the republic and a higher standard of living than they could now expect in Russia. Many emigrate to the Russian Federation, nonetheless, but some of them return. Those who remain are left with an identity problem – to adapt to some degree to the new circumstances and attempt to create for themselves a new identity and new loyalties. In Kazakhstan, and to a lesser degree in Kyrgyzstan, their numbers, their professional positions, and the vicinity of the Russian Federation have lent the Russian diasporas considerable weight.

Another aspect of the new version of the bilingualism campaigned for by leaders of the titular *ethnie* has been to induce members of the smaller groups to study and employ their native language along with the titular one – rather than Russian – not necessarily an easy undertaking of persuasion. Government policies towards the 'smaller languages' have shown slight variations. While in some parts of Europe legal and political protection for the 'smaller languages' has been defended in both theory and practice (Veiter 1990), in the six states less real concern for this issue has been exhibited by the powers that be, despite solemn pronouncements and some limited activity in providing schooling in their languages for some of the smaller *ethnies* in areas of higher demographic concentration. A distinction, however, exists between two categories of the smaller *ethnies* – those who have their own titular states elsewhere, such as the Uzbeks, Kazakhs, Tajiks and others; and those who do not and are numerically few, such as the Kurds, Tats, Dungans and others. The former have sometimes rated better treatment, in schools and textbooks. To paraphrase George Orwell, official spokesmen and others who have proclaimed language equality may well think that some languages are more equal than others.

The smaller groups themselves have been cautious in their language demands. Spokesmen of the smaller minorities have generally presented two main issues: first their wish to prevent loss of culture and language, important components of their ethnic identity, through constant interaction with the majority *ethnie*, which is more interested in promoting an overall national identity than otherwise; and secondly their uncertainty over whether to choose as second language at school the titular language, whose importance has been gradually growing as the government-supported state language, or – as formerly – Russian, an international language of considerable potential for inter-ethnic communication both at home and abroad. Yet another problem for the smaller minorities is their almost general use of the Cyrillic script in their languages, differing from the Latin script increasingly introduced for the titular languages. Exceptionally, several of the larger 'smaller language' groups (like Tajiks in Uzbekistan or Uzbeks in Kyrgyzstan and Tajikistan) have adopted – like the Slav minorities – moderate policies of cultural resistance as a counter-strategy to what they consider enforced homogeneity and uniformity by the titular *ethnie*. Their policies have consisted chiefly in complaining and asking for improvements, mostly in education.

Reverting to the four questions at the end of our introduction to this study, our findings may help to explain *why* the new governments thought that raising the titular language to the status of state language was imperative – not only to ensure maintenance of the language that symbolized cultural and ethnic survival, but also to assist nation-building by emphasizing in the titular *ethnie* the element of language commonality, which would then cement a wider national identity – Uzbekistani, Kazakhstani, and so forth. For the leaders of the newly independent multilingual states, what Ulrich Ammon (1997) has called 'language spread' – in this particular case, the titular language seen as the national one – became a primary objective.

As to *how* the leading political and intellectual circles asserted the primacy of their titular language, this was carried out on several levels of what some sociolinguists call 'language development' (Mackey 1979:51-2): by legislation; administrative measures; education; de-cyrillizing the alphabet (in three cases out of six) and, in some states, readjusting orthography; preparing and publishing textbooks and reading materials; and purifying the language of Russian-Soviet accretions, including the altering of place and street names as well as offering the possibility of changing the form of personal names. Not surprisingly, a number of deadlines set for the implementation of provisions of the language laws and decrees have had to be postponed. Propaganda, usually moderate in tone, in the press, on the radio and television, and elsewhere, accompanied these moves. Well-known intellectuals, public figures and practitioners, as well as ordinary people participated in the debate – at least in some of the states.

It is difficult to say at this stage how this is working out and what results have been achieved. This depends on the state discussed and on one's vantage point and expectations. It is evident that within such a small number of years, only a part of the above policies could be implemented – but on the surface it appears to have been done more successfully on behalf of the titular language in Azerbayjan, Uzbekistan and Turkmenistan; the pace has been more measured in Kazakhstan, Kyrgyzstan and Tajikistan. Most language policies were laid down by the state presidents or within their immediate circles. These circles accepted only selectively the recommendations of their officially appointed committees of experts, and most perceived themselves as responsible for an institutional long-term intervention in altering the status and functions of language. Of course, cultural, political, demographic and socioeconomic conditions have dictated not merely policy, but also implementation. Many issues of language policy were similar in all six states, but not necessarily identical; nor were they perceived everywhere as equally urgent. While all six governments have proclaimed their commitment to the titular language within a framework of multiethnicism and multilingualism, they have applied themselves differently to language planning and implementation.

Regarding the promotion of the titular languages and the implementation of policies, the six states may be divided roughly into two groups, as suggested above. The first comprises Azerbaijan, Uzbekistan and Turkmenistan, the second – Kazakhstan, Kyrgyzstan and Tajikistan. The first group has progressed more visibly in promoting the titular language in administration and schooling, including the preparation and introduction of new textbooks in the Latin alphabet. The fact that they have, proportionately, smaller European minorities within their republics may partly account for this. In the second group, Kazakhstan and Kyrgyzstan, inhabited by proportionately large Slav minorities, have invested more organizational efforts in language planning, but have achieved less, although the former's authorities have encouraged Kazakh studies in school at the expense of Russian ones, while promoting Russian to an 'official status'. Presidents Nazarbaev and Akaev have both pressed for a civic agenda in language issues, with a definitely pluralistic, rather than monoculturalistic aspect. The leaders of both states have adopted relatively pluralistic policies in order to marginalize the impact of extreme nationalists in both their societies – another reason for the caution displayed in alphabet change and language intervention. Tajikistan, slowly recovering from civil strife and unrest, has devoted serious attention to issues of language policy and planning only since 1998. All the governments involved have shown more interest in promoting the titular language at school than among adults, for whom less has been done, either to instruct them in the language or in a new script. Regarding school textbooks, rethinking their contents to suit the new situation is an ongoing process.

Since there are so many contextual uncertainties, it would be premature to speculate on the success of the language reforms undertaken and on future scenarios of development in the six independent states. While the leaders of all six governments proclaim their commitment to the multiethnic and multilingual character of their societies, they act to strengthen the status (and, to some extent, the corpus) of their titular languages. But in the ten years since the adoption of the language laws, the hold of the Russian language has not yet been affected to the extent that some political leaders would have wanted. The process of obtaining full primacy for the titular language will take some time to achieve, perhaps an entire generation.

As for the Slav diaspora, its politics of alarmism, and sometimes of refusal to acknowledge the expected consequences of the new language policies, have failed, *grosso modo*, and its members seem increasingly resigned to the new situation. Some acceptable accommodation of language pluralism will probably prevail, in time, although its nature will vary from one state to the other. However, the chances for this diaspora's cultural assimilation into the titular society are rather low, due to the cultural-religious chasm between Slavs and Muslims. Language switch would mean that all inhabitants would speak the state language. This seems far-fetched, at least for the foreseeable future. Some adjustments by the Slavs (Laitin 1998:243-60) are however possible, over time, in acculturating to the titular nation and learning its language, probably on a limited scale – which could however grow if the Slavs conclude that they will obtain more attractive, better paid jobs when conversant with the titular language and as long as they believe that this advantage is accessible to them through a fair school system. Such a process of adaptation applies also to members of the smaller *ethnies* at the expense of Russian. Cultural and language shift remains a lengthy process and largely depends on everybody learning to adopt and implement adaptive strategies instead of isolationist policies which have serious potential for conflict. Until such strategies are worked out, it is doubtful whether the public debate on language consensualism or language competition and conflict will disappear. Despite some new solutions, most of the old problems remain.

REFERENCES

Abazov, Rafis 1999. 'Central Asia's Conflicting Legacy and Ethnic Policies: Revisiting a Crisis Zone of the former USSR', *Nationalism and Ethnic Politics* 5(2): summer, 62-90.

Abbas, Najam 1999. 'Search for the Motives behind the Recent Blasts in Tashkent', *CAM* 2:21-4.

Abdinov, Ahmad 1996. 'Education in Azerbaijan: The Challenges of Transition', *Azerbaijan International*, 4(4): winter, 16-18, 84.

Abdygaliev, Berik 1995. 'Ėtnolingvisticheskaya situatsiya v Kazakhstane', *Ėkspress K* 24: March, 4.

Achylova, Rakhat 1995. 'Kırgızıstan dış politikasındaki öncelikler ve politik kültürü', *Avrasya Etüdleri*, 2(1): spring, 2-29.

Adler, M.K. 1980. *Marxist Linguistic Theory and Communist Practice*. Hamburg: Helmut Buske.

Akbarzadeh, Shahram 1996. 'Nation-Building in Uzbekistan', *CAS* 15(1): 23-32.

—— 1996a. 'Why Did Nationalism Fail in Tajikistan?', *Europe-Asia Studies* 48(7): November, 1105-29.

Akhmedov, Said 1997. 'Konflikty v Tadzhikistane: prichiny i posledstviya' in A. Malashenko a.o., eds, *Ėtnicheskie i regional'nye konflikty v Evrazii. 1. Tsentral'naya Aziya i Kavkaz*. Moscow: Ves' Mir, 75-93.

Akiner, Shirin 1995. *The Formation of Kazakh Identity: From Tribe to Nation-State*. London: Royal Institute of International Affairs.

—— 1996. 'Uzbekistan and the Uzbeks' in Graham Smith, ed., *The Nationalities Question in the Post-Soviet States*. London and New York: Longman, 334-47.

—— ed. 1991 *Cultural Change and Continuity in Central Asia*. London and New York: Kegan Paul International.

—— and Nicholas Sims-Williams, eds, 1997. *Languages and Scripts of Central Asia*. London: School of Oriental and African Studies.

Alimov, K.Z. 1994. 'The Rediscovery of Uzbek History and Its Foreign Policy Implications' in S.F. Starr, ed., *The Legacy of History in Russia and the New States of Eurasia*. Armonk, NY: M.E. Sharpe, 217-36.

Allworth, Edward 1989. 'The New Central Asians' in Edward Allworth, ed., *Central Asia: 120 Years of Russian Rule*. Durham, SC: Duke University Press, 527-72.

—— 1993. 'A New Tone in Writings for the 21st Century' in B. A. Nazarov and Denis Sinor, eds, *Essays on Uzbek History, Culture and Language*.

213

Bloomington: Indiana University Research Institute for Inner Asian Studies, 15-37.

Alpatov, V.M. 1996. 'Yazykovye problemy v sovetskom i postsovetskom prostranstve', *Nauchnyi Al'manakh Tsivilizatsii i Kul'tury* 3:293-317.

—— 1997. *150 yazykov i politika 1917-1997: sotsiolingvisticheskie problemy SSSR i postsovetskogo prostranstva*. Moscow: Ivran.

Altstadt, A.L. 1991. 'Rewriting Turkic History in the Gorbachev Era', *Journal of Soviet Nationalities* 2(2): summer, 73-90.

—— 1992. *The Azerbaijani Turks: Power and Identity under Russian Rule*. Stanford, CA: Hoover Institution Press.

Ammon, Ulrich 1997. 'Language-Spread Policy', *Language Problems and Language Planning* 21(1): spring, 51-7.

—— 1997a. 'National-Variety Purism in the National Centers of the German Language' in Martin Putz, ed., *Language Choices: Conditions, Constraints and Consequences*. Amsterdam and Philadelphia: John Benjamins, 161-78.

Anderson, B.A. and B.D. Silver 1990. 'Some Factors in the Linguistic and Ethnic Russification of Soviet Nationalities: Is Everyone Becoming Russian?' in Lubomyr Hajda and Mark Beissinger, eds, *The Nationalities Factor in Soviet Politics and Society*. Boulder, CO: Westview Press, 95-130.

—— 1996. 'Population Redistribution and the Ethnic Balance in Transcaucasia', in R.G. Suny, ed., *Nationalism and Social Change: Essays in the History of Armenia, Azerbaijan and Georgia*. Ann Arbor: University of Michigan Press, 481-506.

Anderson, John 1995. 'Authoritarian Political Development in Central Asia: the Case of Turkmenistan', *CAS* 14(4):509-27.

—— 1997. 'Constitutional Development in Central Asia', *CAS* 16(3): 301-20.

Anweiler, Oskar 1982. 'Russifizierung durch Unterricht. Fakten und Hypothesen', *International Journal of the Sociology of Language*, 33: 41-51.

Arenov, M.M. and S.I. Kalmykov 1995. 'Sovremennaya yazykovaya situatsiya v Kazakhstane', *SI* no. 12:76-81.

—— 1998. 'Ėtnonatsional'naya deistvitel'nost' Kazakhstana', *SI* no. 3: 45-58.

Artam, Atila 1993. *Türk Cumhuriyetlerinin sosyo-ekonomik analizleri ve Türkiye ilişkileri*. Istanbul: Sabri Artam Vakfı.

Asankanov, Abylabek 1997. *Kyrgyzy: rost natsional'nogo samosoznaniya.* Bishkek: Muras.

Asimov, M.S. 1996. 'Rewriting Tajik History' [Paper presented to European Society of Central Asian Studies Conference V: Copenhagen 1996]. 3 pp. Online. [International Institute for Asian Studies.] Available: http://iias.leidenuniv.nl/iiasn/iiasn6/central/tajik.html. 25 May 1999.

Aslan, Yasin 1990. *Bugün Azerbaycanda Pantürkizm ve Panislamizm.* Istanbul: Baysan.

Aslanov, Vagif 1994. 'Name Changes in Azerbaijan: Evidence of the Passing of an Era', *Azerbaijan International* 2(2): spring, 58-9.

Atkin, Muriel 1992. 'Religious, National, and Other Identities in Central Asia' in Jo-Ann Gross, ed., *Muslims in Central Asia: Expressions of Identity and Change.* Durham, NC: Duke University Press, 46-72.

—— 1994. 'Tajikistan's Relations with Iran and Afghanistan' in Ali Banuazizi and Myron Weiner, eds, *The New Geopolitics of Central Asia and Its Borderlands.* London and New York: I.B. Tauris, 91-117.

—— 1994a. 'Tajiks and the Persian World' in B.F. Manz, ed., *Central Asia in Historical Perspective.* Boulder, CO: Westview Press, 127-43.

—— 1997. 'Thwarted Democratization in Tajikistan' in Karen Dawisha and Bruce Parrott, eds, *Conflict, Cleavage, and Change in Central Asia and the Caucasus.* Cambridge University Press, 277-311.

Attar, Ali and Gero Fedtke 1998. 'Die nationale Abgrenzung im Rückblick', *Osteuropa* 48(5): 500-4.

—— 1998a 'Vermächtnis der "Freundschaft der Völker"', *Osteuropa-Archiv* 48(5):A 200 - A 208.

Auch, E.-M. 1995. 'Die politische Entwicklung in Aserbaidshan' in Boris Meissner and Alfred Eisfeld, eds, *Die GUS-Staaten in Europa und Asien.* Baden-Baden: Nomos, 153-76.

Ayagan, Burkutbai 1998. "'Russkii vopros" v Kazakhstane: istoricheskie paralleli', *Tsentral'naya Aziya* 15:39-46.

Azarsina, Habib and Naida Mamedova 1993. 'Azerbaijani: Language of a Divided Nation: The Differences Between the North and the South', *Azerbaijan International* 1(3): September, 20-1.

Babaĭev, Adil 1996. *Azärbaijan dilchiliiinin tarikhi.* Baku: Baky Universiteti Näshriiiaty.

Babak, Vladimir 1996. *The Concept of an Eurasian Union: Roots, Essence, and Prospects.* Jerusalem: Leonard Davis Institute.

Babazhanov, Bakhtiyar 1999. 'Vozrozhdenie deyatel'nosti sufiiskikh grupp v Uzbekistane', *Tsentral'naya Aziya i Kavkaz* 1(2):181-92.

Bacık, Gökhan 1999. 'Türk Cumhuriyetleri'nde kimlik sorunu' in M.K. Öke, ed., *Geçiş sürecinde Orta Asya Türk Cumhuriyetleri.* Istanbul: Alfa, 61-127.

Bagdasaryan, A.V., ed. 1997. *Konstitutsii stran-chlenov SNG.* Yerevan: Mkhitar Gosh.

Bahadori, Abulfazl 1993. 'Alphabet in the Boiling Pot of Politics', *Azerbaijan International* 1(3): September, 10-13.

Baigarin, Ravshan 1998. 'Natsional'nyi vopros v poliétnichnom gosudarste (Kazakhstanskii opyt)', *Rossiya i Sovremennyi Mir* 20:113-17.

216 *References*

Balcı, Sami 1995. 'Özbek Latin alfabesi'nin problemleri', *Türk Kültürü* 33(389):552-5.

—— 1996. 'Özbek Latin alfabesi'nin yeni problemleri', *Türk Kültürü* 34(404):717-22.

Baldauf, Ingeborg 1993. *Schriftreform und Schriftwechsel bei den muslimischen Russland- und Sowjettürken (1850-1937). Ein Symptom ideengeschichtlicher und kulturpolitischer Entwicklungen.* Budapest: Akadémiai Kiadó.

Balland, Daniel 1997. 'Tachkent, métropole de l'Asie Centrale?', *CEMOTI. Cahiers d'Etudes sur la Méditerranée Orientale et le Monde Turco-Iranien* 24: July-December, 219-50.

Barkey, Karen 1997. 'Thinking About Consequences of Empire' in Karen Barkey and Mark von Hagen, eds, *After Empire: Multiethnic Societies and Nation-building: The Soviet Union and the Russian, Ottoman and Habsburg Empires.* Boulder, CO: Westview Press, 99-114.

Baskakov, A.N. 1994. 'Tipy yazykovykh konfliktov v regione Srednei Azii i Kazakhstana' in V.M. Solntsev and V.Yu. Mikhal'chenko, eds, *Yazyk v kontekste obshchestvennogo razvitiya. Language in the Context of Social Development.* Moscow: Russian Academy of Sciences, 171-80.

Batalden, S.K. and S.L. Batalden 1997. *The Newly Independent States of Eurasia: Handbook of Former Soviet Republics.* Phoenix, AZ: Oryx.

Baud, Michiel and Willem van Schendel, 1997. 'Toward a Comparative History of Borderlands', *Journal of World History* 8(2):211-42.

Baum, Renate 1999. *Integrationsprobleme von Spätaussiedlern aus der GUS. Sozialisation – Rollenbilder – Wertevorstellungen.* Berlin: Osteuropa-Institut der Freien Universität Berlin.

Bayatli, Tamam 1997. 'The Latin Script: A Chronology. Symbol of a New Azerbaijan', *Azerbaijan International* 5(2): summer, 22, 24, 49.

Bazarov, Ablakul 1997. 'Islamskii fundamentalizm i obshchestvenno-politicheskaya stabil'nost' v Uzbekistane' in *Ètnicheskie i regional'nye konflikty v Evrazii.* 1: *Tsentral'naya Aziya i Kavkaz.* Moscow: Ves' Mir, 112-29.

Behar, B.E. 1995. *Türk Cümhuriyetleri kültür profili araştırması.* Ankara: Kültür Bakanlığı.

—— 1995a. 'Türk cumhuriyetlerinde Latin alfabeleri', *Cumhuriyet dönemi Türkiye ansiklopedisi.* Istanbul: İletişim, vol. XII:396-8.

Beissinger, M.R. 1993. 'Demise of an Empire-State: Identity, Legitimacy, and the Destruction of Soviet Politics' in Crawford Young, ed., *The Rising Tide of Cultural Pluralism: The Nation-State at Bay?* Madison: University of Wisconsin Press, 93-115.

Bellingeri, Giampiero 1999. 'Questioni di Turco di Turchia e *ORTAK DIL* ("Lingua Comune")' in Emanuele Banfi, ed., *Percorsi socio- e storico-linguistici nel Mediterraneo.* Trento: Dipartimento di Scienze Filologiche e Storiche, 333-64.

Belousov, V.N. and E.A. Grigoryan 1996. *Russkii yazyk v mezhnatsional'nom obshchenii v Rossiiskoi Federatsii i stranakh SNG.* Moscow: Russian Academy of Sciences.

Benner, Katrin 1996. *Der Vielvölkerstaat Kazachstan: Ethnische Heterogenität in friedlicher Koexistenz?* Hamburg: LIT Verlag.

Berezin, F.M. a.o. 1992. *K probleme natsional'no-yazykovykh otnoshenii v SSSR i drugikh stranakh: istoriya i sovremennost'.* Moscow: Russian Academy of Sciences.

Biryukov, S.V. 1997. 'Respublika Uzbekistan: model' avtoritarnoi modernizatsii', *Vostok. Oriens* 1: 85-96.

Blacher, Philippe 1996. 'La langue turkmène et son écriture à l'aube du XXIème siècle', *Observatoire de l'Asie Centrale et du Caucase* 1:9-11.

Black, J.L., ed., 1994. *Russia and Eurasia Documents Annual 1992*, vol. 2, Gulf Breeze, FLA: Academic International Press.

—— ed., 1995. *Russia and Eurasia Documents Annual 1993,* vol. 2, Gulf Breeze, FLA: Academic International Press.

—— ed., 1997. *Russia and Eurasia Documents Annual 1996*, vol.2, Gulf Breeze, FLA: Academic International Press.

Blank, Stephen 1994. 'Soviet Reconquest of Central Asia' in Hafeez Malik, ed., *Central Asia: Its Strategic Importance and Future Prospects.* New York: St. Martin's Press, 39-64.

Blaustein, A.P., ed., 1994-6. *Constitutions of the Countries of the World.* Dobbs Ferry, NY: Oceana Publications.

Bodrogligeti, Andras 1994. 'Turkish Language Conference September 22-26, Ankara', *Azerbaijan International* 2(1): winter, 54-5.

Boeschoten, Hendrik and Marc Vandamme 1998. 'Chagatay' in Lars Johanson and É.Á. Csató, eds, *The Turkic Languages.* London and New York: Routledge, 166-8.

Bohr, Annette 1996. 'Turkmenistan and the Turkmen' in Graham Smith, ed., *The Nationalities Question in the Post-Soviet States.* London and New York: Longman, 348-66.

—— and Simon Crisp 1996. 'Kyrgyzstan and the Kyrgyz' in Graham Smith, ed., *The Nationalities Question in the Post-Soviet States.* London and New York: Longman, 385-409.

Borovali, Fuat 1992. 'Azerbaijan: From Trauma to Transition' in Miron Rezun, ed., *Nationalism and the Breakup of an Empire: Russia and Its Periphery.* Westport, CT: Praeger, 113-23.

Bregel, Yuri 1995. *Bibliography of Islamic Central Asia.* Bloomington: Research Institute for Inner Asian Studies.

Bremmer, Ian 1994. 'Nazarbaev and the North: State-Building and Ethnic Relations in Kazakhstan', *Ethnic and Racial Studies* 17(4): October, 619-35.

Brendemoen, Bernt 1998. 'The Turkish Language Reform' in Lars Johanson and É.Á. Csató, eds, *The Turkic Languages.* London and

New York: Routledge, 242-7.

Breton, R.J.L. 1991. *Geolinguistics: Language Dynamics and Ethnolinguistic Geography*. University of Ottawa Press.

Breuer, Margrit 1995. 'Kasachstan wird kasachisch: Emigration der russischsprachigen Bevölkerung', *Osteuropa-Archiv* 45 (6):A 341.

Brown, B.A. 1998. 'The Civil War in Tajikistan, 1992-1993' in Muhammad-Reza Djalili, Frederic Grare and Shirin Akiner, eds, *Tajikistan: The Trials of Independence*. Richmond (UK): Curzon Press, 86-96.

Brubaker, Rogers 1994. 'Nationhood and the National Question in the Soviet Union and Post-Soviet Eurasia: An Institutionalist Account', *Theory and Society* 23(1): February, 47-78.

—— 1997. 'Aftermaths of Empire and the Unmixing of Peoples' in Karen Barkey and Mark von Hagen, eds, *After Empire: Multiethnic Societies and Nation-Building: The Soviet Union and the Russian, Ottoman and Habsburg Empires*. Boulder, CO: Westview Press, 155-80.

Bruchis, Michael 1982. *One Step Back, Two Steps Forward*. Boulder, CO: East European Monographs.

—— 1984. 'The Effect of the USSR's Language Policy on the National Languages of its Turkic Population' in Yaacov Ro'i, ed., *The USSR and the Muslim World: Issues in Domestic and Foreign Policy*. London: Geo. Allen and Unwin, 129-48.

—— 1987. 'The Language Policy of the Soviet Communist Party. Comments and Observations', *East European Quarterly* 21(2): June, 231-57.

—— 1988. *The USSR: Language and Realities: Nations, Leaders and Scholars*. Boulder, CO: East European Monographs.

Bruhn, Peter 1968. *Russisch für Bibliothekare*. Wiesbaden: Harrassowitz.

Brusina, O.E. 1992. 'Russkie v Srednei Azii: natsional'noe men'shinstvo s proshlym "starshego brata"' in *Rossiya i Vostok: problemy vzaimodeistviya*. Moscow: Nauka, 46-9.

Brutents, K.N. 1998. *Tridtsat' let na staroi ploshchadi*. Moscow: Mezhdunarodnye Otnosheniya.

Buckley, Cynthia 1996. 'Exodus? Out-Migration from the Central Asian Successor States to the Russian Federation', *CAM* 3: 1996, 16-22.

Business 1997. Business – Baku Informatsionnyi Spravochnik. Baku.

Buškov, V.I. and G.Ju Sitnjanskij 1997. *Russen und Russischsprachige in Zentralasien. Eine russische Sicht*. Cologne: Bundesinstitut für ostwissenschaftliche und internationale Studien. February 1997.

Calvet, L.-J. 1974. *Linguistique et colonialisme. Petit traité de glottophagie*. Paris: Payot.

—— 1987. *La guerre des langues et les politiques linguistiques*. Paris: Payot.

Capotorti, Francesco 1991. *Study on the Rights of Persons belonging to Ethnic, Religious and Linguistic Minorities*. New York: United Nations.

Carley, P.M. 1995. 'The Legacy of the Soviet Political System and the Prospects for Developing Civil Society in Central Asia' in Vladimir Tismaneanu, ed., *Political Culture and Civil Society in Russia and the New States of Eurasia.* Armonk, NY: M.E. Sharpe, 292-317.

Carlson, C.F. 1994. 'Language Reform Movements in Central Asia' in Ingeborg Baldauf and Michael Friedrich, eds, *Bamberger Zentralasienstudien. Konferenzakten ESCAS IV. Bamberg 8-12. Oktober 1991.* Berlin: Klaus Schwarz, 133-52.

Carré, Olivier 1993. *Le nationalisme arabe.* Paris: Fayard.

Carrère d'Encausse, Hélène 1993. *The End of the Soviet Empire: The Triumph of the Nations.* New York: Basic Books.

Chebotareva, V. 1994. 'Rossiiskie nemtsy: novye problemy v Rossii i blizhnem zarubezh'e', *Obozrevatel'*, no. 2:61-7.

—— 1996. 'Turkmenistan segodnya: ètnopoliticheskaya situatsiya', *Obozrevatel'*, no. 9:17-21.

Chinn, Jeff and Robert Kaiser 1996. *Russians as the New Minority: Ethnicity and Nationalism in the Soviet Successor States.* Boulder, CO: Westview Press.

Chvyr, Ludmila 1993. 'Central Asia's Tajiks: Self-Identification and Ethnic Identity', in Vitaly Naumkin, ed., *State, Religion and Society in Central Asia: A Post-Soviet Critique.* Reading (UK): Ithaca Press, 245-61.

Clark, Larry 1998. *Turkmen Reference Grammar.* Wiesbaden: Harrassowitz.

Clem, R.S. 1993. 'Inter-ethnic Relations at the Republic Level: The Example of Kazakhstan', *Post-Soviet Geography* 34(4): April, 229-32.

Clement, Peter 1994. 'Prospects for Political Pluralism in Central Asia' in C.R. Civets and Anthony Jones, eds, *In Search of Pluralism: Soviet and Post-Soviet Politics.* Boulder, CO: Westview Press, 86-108.

Comrie, Bernard 1996. 'Adaptations of the Cyrillic Alphabet' in P.T. Daniels and William Bright, eds, *The World's Writing Systems.* New York: Oxford University Press, 700-26.

—— 1996a. 'Script Reform in and after the Soviet Union' in Daniels and Bright, eds, *The World's Writing Systems*, 781-4.

Conermann, Stephan 1994. 'Tadžikistan auf der schwierigen Suche nach einer eigenen Identität' in Peter Nitsche, ed., *Die Nachfolgestaaten der Sowjetunion.* Frankfurt am Main: Peter Lang, 147-76.

Coulmas, Florian 1984. 'Linguistic Minorities and Literacy' in Florian Coulmas, ed., *Language Policy Issues in Developing Countries.* Berlin: Mouton, 5-20.

Crisp, Simon 1991. 'Census and Sociology: Evaluating the Language Situation in Soviet Central Asia' in Shirin Akiner, ed., *Cultural Change and Continuity in Central Asia.* London and New York: Kegan Paul International, 84-123.

Critchlow, James 1991. *Nationalism in Uzbekistan: A Soviet Republic's Road to Sovereignty.* Boulder, CO: Westview Press.

References

Čorotegin, T.K. 1997 [Chorotegin]. 'Neue Curricula und Lehrbücher zur Geschichte Kyrgyzstans', *Berliner Osteuropa Info* 9:23.

Dadmehr, Nasrin 1998. 'Tajikistan – Inevitable War? Inevitable Peace?', *CAM* 1:1-6.

Damitov, Bazar and Galiya Kirillova 1999. 'Osnovnye napravleniya razvitiya vysshego obrazovaniya v Respublike Kazakhstan', *Tsentral'naya Aziya i Kavkaz* 4(5):159-63.

Dani, A.H. 1993. *New Light on Central Asia*. Lahore: Sang-E-Meel Publications.

Dauletov, A. 1996. 'Qoraqalpoq tilshunosligi – yangi bosqichda', *Uzbekistonda Izhtimoiĭ. Fanlar Obshchestvennye Nauki v Uzbekistane* no. 6:112-5.

Dave, Bhavna 1996. 'Kazaks Struggle to Revive Their 'Language of Folklore' ', *Transition*, 24: 29 November, 23-5.

—— 1996a. 'National Revival in Kazakhstan: Language Shift and Identity Change', *Post-Soviet Affairs* 12(1): 51-72.

—— 1996b. 'Politics of Language Revival: National Identity and State Building in Kazakhstan', unpubl. Ph.D. diss., Syracuse University.

Davis, Sue and S.O. Sabol 1998. 'The Importance of Being Ethnic: Minorities in Post-Soviet States – the Case of Russians in Kazakstan', *Nationalities Papers* 26(3):473-91.

Desheriev, Yu. D. a.o., eds. 1980. *Russkii yazyk v natsional'nykh respublikakh Sovetskogo Soyuza*. Moscow: Nauka.

Devlet, Nadir 1992. *Milletlerarası Türk alfabeleri sempozyumu*. Istanbul: Marmara Üniversitesi.

DeYoung, A. J. and Galina Valyayeva 1997. 'Post-Soviet Secondary School Reform in Kazakstan: The Views of 149 Classroom Teachers', *CAM* 3: 22-34.

Djalili, Mohammad-Reza a.o., eds, 1998. *Tajikistan: The Trials of Independence*. Richmond (London): Curzon Press.

Dokuchaeva, A. 1995. 'O gosudarstvennom yazyke, i ne tol'ko o nem', *Etnopolis* 2(8):155-61.

Dollerup, Cay 1998. 'Language and Culture in Transition in Uzbekistan' in Turaj Atabaki and John O'Kane, eds, *Post-Soviet Central Asia*. London: I.B. Tauris 144-56.

Dudoignon, S.A. 1998. 'Communal Solidarity and Social Conflicts in the Late 20th Century Central Asia: The Case of the Tajik Civil War'. Tokyo: Islamic Area Studies Project.

Dugarev, K.P. 1998. 'Postkommunisticheskii avtoritarnyi rezhim', in *Postsovetskaya Tsentral'naya Aziya: Poteri i obreteniya*. Moscow: Russian Academy of Sciences – Vostochnaya Literatura, 160-90.

Duman, Hasan 1993. *Türk Cumhuriyetleriyle kültürel işbirliği*. Ankara: Enformasyon ve Dokümantasyon Hizmetleri Vakfı.

Dunlop, J.B. 1994 'Will the Russians Return from the Near Abroad?', *Post-Soviet Geography* 35(4): April, 204-15.

Durdyev, Khudayberdy 1996. Turkmenistan: Toward a New Maturity', *World Literature Today* 70(3): summer, 590-2.

Eckert, J. M. 1996. *Das unabhängige Usbekistan: Auf dem Weg von Marx zu Timur. Politische Strategien der Konfliktregulierung in einem Vielvölkerstaat.* Münster: LIT Verlag.

Eisener, Reinhard 1991. *Auf den Spuren des tadschikischen Nationalismus. Aus Texten und Dokumenten zur Tadschikischen SSR.* Berlin: Das Arabische Buch.

Elçi Bey, Ebülfez 1993. *Azadlık ve demokrasi.* Istanbul: Veli Yayınları.

Elebaeva, Ainura and Nurbek Omuraliev 1998. 'Mezhètnicheskie otnosheniya v Kyrgyzstane: dinamika i tendentsii razvitiya', *Tsentral'naya Aziya* 15:60-74.

Enokh, Reuven 1998. 'Yazykovaya politika v Gruzii', *Tsentral'naya Aziya i Kavkaz* 1:142-6.

Entessar, Nader 1993. 'Azeri Nationalism in the Former Soviet Union and Iran' in Crawford Young, ed., *The Rising Tide of Cultural Pluralism: The Nation State at Bay?* Madison: University of Wisconsin Press, 116-37.

Ercilasun, A.B. 1993. *Türk dünyası üzerine incelemeler.* Ankara: Akçağ.

—— 1996. *Örneklerle bugünkü Türk alfabeleri.* Ankara: Kültür Bakanlığı.

——a.o. , eds, 1991-2. *Karşılaştırmalı Türk lehçeleri sözlüğü, Kılavuzkitap,* I-II.' Ankara: Kültür Bakanlığı.

Eremin, A. 1995. 'Kto s kamnem za pazukhoi?', *Mysl'* 5: 54-8.

—— 1996. 'Khotyat li russkie ovladet' kazakhskim yazykom?', *Mysl'* 1:35-42.

Ergin, Muharrem 1976. 'Türklerde yazı ve alfabeler', in Türk Kültürünü Araştırma Enstitüsü, ed., *Türk Dünyası el kitabı,* Ankara: TKAE, 340-73.

Eschment, Beate 1997. *Hat Kasachstan ein "russisches Problem"? Revision eines Katastrophenbildes.* Cologne: Bundesinstitut für ostwissenschaftliche und internationale Studien. Sonderveröffentlichung. February.

Esenova, Saulesh 1996. 'The Outflow of Minorities from the Post-Soviet State: The Case of Kazakhstan', *Nationalities Papers,* 24(4): December, 691-707.

Esman, M.J. 1992 'The State and Language Policy', *International Political Science Review* 13(4): October, 381-96.

The Europa World Year-Book 1998, vols 1-2. London: Europa Publications.

Fartin, Gerald 1982. 'Les mots pour le dire', *Recherches Sociologiques* (Québec) 23(3):357-60.

Fellman, Jack 1973. *The Revival of a Classical Tongue: Eliezer Ben-Yehuda and the Modern Hebrew Language.* The Hague: Mouton.

Fierman, William 1989. 'Glasnost in Practice: The Uzbek Experience', *CAS* 8(2):1-45.

—— 1995. 'Problems of Language Law Implementation in Uzbekistan', *Nationalities Papers* 23(3):573-95.

—— 1995a. 'Independence and the Declining Priority of Language Law Implementation in Uzbekistan' in Yaacov Ro'i, ed., *Muslim Eurasia: Conflicting Legacies.* London: Frank Cass, 205-30.

—— 1997. 'Language, Identity, and Conflict in Central Asia and the Southern Caucasus'. *Perspectives on Central Asia* II(5), August. 4 pp. Available: http://www.cpss.org/casianw/perca0897.txt. 10 December 1998.

—— 1997a. 'Political Development in Uzbekistan: Democratization?' in Karen Dawisha and Bruce Parrott, eds, *Conflict, Cleavage, and Change in Central Asia and the Caucasus.* Cambridge University Press, 360-408.

—— 1998. 'Language and Identity in Kazakhstan: Formulations in Policy Documents 1987-1997', *Communist and Postcommunist Studies* 31(2): 171-86.

Fisher, A.W. 1988. 'Ismail Gaspirali, Model Leader for Asia', in Edward Allworth, ed., *Tatars of the Crimea. Their Struggle for Survival.* Durham, NC: Duke University Press, 11-26.

Fishman, J.A. 1972. *Language and Nationalism: Two Integrative Essays.* Rowley, MA: Newbury House.

—— 1996. 'Ethnolinguistic Democracy: Varieties, Degrees, and Limits' in K.E. Müller, ed., *Language Status in the Post-Cold War Era.* Lanham, MD: University Press of America, 7-21.

Foltz, Richard 1996. 'The Tajiks of Uzbekistan', *CAS* 15(2): 213-16.

—— 1996a. 'Uzbekistan's Tajiks: A Case of Repressed Identity', *CAM* 6:17-19.

Forced Migration Projects 1999. Language Politics in Central Asia. 19 pp. Available: http://www.osi.hu/fmp/laws/index/html. 30 April 1999.

Fragner, B.G. 1995. '"Glasnost" in einem fernen Land. Die tadschikische Literaturzeitschrift *Adabijot ve San'at* als Meinungsforum' in Christoph Herzog, Raoul Motika and Anja Pistor-Hatam, eds, *Presse und Öffentlichkeit im Nahen Osten.* Heidelberg: Heidelberger Orientverlag, 45-57.

—— 1998. 'Tādjīk', part 2, *Encyclopaedia of Islam*, new edn., vol. X. Leiden: E.J. Brill.

Friedgut, Th. H. 1982. 'The Unity of Language and the Language of Unity', *International Journal of the Sociology of Language* 33:79-89.

Fuller, Elizabeth 1996. 'Azerbaijan at the Crossroads' in Roy Allison, ed., *Challenges for the Former Soviet South.* Washington, DC: Brookings Institution, and London: Royal Institute of International Affairs, 117-53.

Fuller, G.E. 1992. *Central Asia: The New Geopolitics*. Santa Monica, CA: Rand.

Gadzhi-Zade, Khikmet 1998. 'Novaya identichnost' dlya novogo Azerbaidzhana', *Tsentral'naya Aziya* 14:60-7.

Gaebel, Michael, and Carsten Jürgensen 1996. 'Die politischen Parteien in Aserbaidschan' in Eva-Maria Auch, ed., *Lebens- und Konfliktraum Kaukasien. Gemeinsame Lebenswelten und politische Visionen der kaukasischen Völker in Geschichte und Gegenwart*. Großbarkau: Edition Barkau, 130-50.

Galieva, Zairash 1998. 'Civil Society in the Kyrgyz Republic in Transition', *CAM* no. 5:7-10.

Garibova, Jala and Betty Blair 1996. 'Names: History in a Nutshell. 20th Century Personal Naming Practices in Azerbaijan', *Azerbaijan International* 4(3): autumn, 54-5.

Garkavets, A.N. 1990. *Printsipy natsional'noi politiki i yazykovogo stroitel'stva*. Alma-Ata: Akademiya Nauk Kazakhskoi SSR.

Ginzburg, A.I. 1992. 'Russkoe naselenie v Srednei Azii' in A.N. Zhilina and S.V. Cheshko, eds, *Sovremennoe razvitie étnicheskikh grupp Srednei Azii i Kazakhstana*. Moscow: Russian Academy of Sciences, vol. II, 38-66.

—— ed. 1994-5. *Uzbekistan: Étnopoliticheskaya panorama. Ocherki, dokumenty, materialy*. Moscow: Russian Academy of Sciences - Institut Étnologii i Antropologii, vols I-II.

Giroux, Alain 1997. 'Kazakistan: Asya devinin potansiyeli ve ekonomik modeli', in Semih Vaner, ed., *Unutkan tarih: Sovyet sonrası Türkdilli alan*. Istanbul: Metis, 318-33.

Gitelman, Zvi 1992. 'Ethnopolitics and the Future of the Former Soviet Union' in Zvi Gitelman, ed., *The Politics of Nationality and the Erosion of the USSR*. New York: St. Martin's Press, 1-25.

Gitlin, Semyon 1998. *Natsional'nye otnosheniya v Uzbekistane: illyuzii i real'nost'*. Tel Aviv: publ. by the author.

Gleason, Gregory 1993. 'Uzbekistan: from Statehood to Nationhood?' in Ian Bremmer and Ray Taras, eds, *Nation and Politics in the Soviet Successor States*. Cambridge University Press, 331-60.

—— 1997. *The Central Asian States: Discovering Independence*. Boulder, CO: Westview Press.

Goldenberg, Suzanne 1994. *Pride of Small Nations: The Caucasus and Post-Soviet Disorder*. London: Zed Books.

Goltz, T.C. 1994. *Requiem for a Would-be Republic: The Rise and Demise of the Former Soviet Republic of Azerbaijan: A Personal Account of the Years 1991-1993*. Istanbul: Isis Press.

Gökdağ, Bilgehan Atsız 1997. 'Türk Dünyasında iletişim dili meselesi', *Yeni Türkiye* 3(15): May-June, 216-20.

Gömeç, Saadettin 1996. *Türk cumhuriyetleri tarihi*. Konya: Köymen Yayınları.

Götz, Roland, and Uwe Halbach 1996. *Politisches Lexikon GUS*. 3rd, revised edn, Munich: C.H. Beck.

Graffy, Julian 1993. 'Russian Language Journals in the Central Asian Republics' in Marco Buttino, ed., *In a Collapsing Empire: Underdevelopment, Ethnic Conflicts and Nationalisms in the Soviet Union*. Milan: Feltrinelli, 161-72.

Grandguillaume, Gilbert 1983. *Arabisation et politique linguistique au Maghreb*. Paris: Maisonneuve et Larose.

Grigoryan, Vartan 1992. *Nasil'stvennaya assimilyatsiya musul'manskikh natsional'nykh men'shinststv v Azerbaidzhane*. Erevan: Barandean.

Grocer, Jennifer 1997. 'The Politics of Language Reform in Azerbaijan', paper presented at the 31st Annual Meeting of the Middle East Studies Association of North America, San Francisco: 24 November. Mimeo.

Grosjean, François 1982. *Life with Two Languages: An Introduction to Bilingualism*. Cambridge, MA: Harvard University Press.

Grozin, Andrei 1998. 'Knigoizdanie v nezavisimom Kazakhstane', *Vestnik Evrazii* no. 1-2(4-5):273-8.

Guboglo, Michail 1994. *Sprachengesetzgebung und Sprachenpolitik in der UdSSR und in den Nachfolgestaaten der UdSSR seit 1989*. Cologne: Berichte des Bundesinstituts für ostwissenschaftliche und internationale Studien, 32.

Guboglo, M.N. 1990. 'Factors and Tendencies of the Development of Bilingualism among the Russian Population Living in the Union Republics' in M.B. Olcott a.o., eds, *The Soviet Multinational State: Readings and Documents*. Armonk, NY: Sharpe, 258-81.

Gurr, T.R. a.o. 1993. *Minorities at Risk: A Global View of Ethnopolitical Conflicts*. Washington, DC: US Institute of Peace Press.

Gürsoy-Naskali, Emine 1997. 'Türk dünyası ve ortak dil', *Yeni Türkiye* 3(15): May-June, 196-8.

Guseinov, F.G. 1996. *Azerbaidzhanskii Pedagogicheskii Institut Russkogo Yazyka i Literatury im. M.F. Akhundova (1946-1996)*. Baku: Mutardzhim.

Haarmann, Harald 1985. 'The Impact of Group Bilingualism in the Soviet Union' in Isabelle Kreindler, ed., *Sociolinguistic Perspectives on Soviet National Languages: Their Past, Present and Future*. Berlin: Mouton de Gruyter, 315-44.

—— 1992. 'Measures to Increase the Importance of Russian within and outside the Soviet Union. A Case of Covert Language-Spread Policy (A Historical Outline)', *International Journal of the Sociology of Language* 95:109-29.

Haase, C.-P. 1994. 'Uzbekistan – Von der Staatsbildung zum National-staat?' in Peter Nitsche, ed., *Die Nachfolgestaaten der Sowjetunion*. Frankfurt am Main: Peter Lang, 131-46.

Haghayeghi, Mehrded 1995. *Islam and Politics in Central Asia*. New York: St. Martin's Press.

Halbach, Uwe 1995. 'Eigenstaatlichekeit in Kasachstan und Mittelasien' in Boris Meissner and Alfred Eisfeld, eds, *Die GUS-Staaten in Europa und Asien*. Baden-Baden: Nomos, 199-211.

—— 1997. 'Zentralasien. Eine Weltregion formiert sich neu', *Internationale Politik und Gesellschaft* 3:305-22.

— 1997a. *Zentralasien als Auswanderungsregion*. Cologne: Berichte des Bundesinstituts für ostwissenschaftliche und internationale Studien, 44.

Haney, Michael 1995. 'Media and Ethnicity in Almaty', *CAM* 2:15-22.

Harris, C.D. 1993. 'The New Russian Minorities: A Statistical Overview', *Post-Soviet Geography* 34(1): January, 1-27.

—— 1994. 'Ethnic Tensions in the Successor Republics in 1993 and Early 1994', *Post-Soviet Geography* 35(4): April, 185-203.

Hazard, J.N. 1990. 'Codification of Soviet Nationality Politics' in H.R. Huttenbach, ed., *Soviet Nationality Policies: Ruling Ethnic Groups in the USSR*. London: Mansell, 47-61.

Helly, Damien 1998. 'Le paysage politique du nouvel Azerbaidjan', *CEMOTI, Cahiers d'Etudes sur la Méditerranée Orientale et le Monde Turco-Iranien* 26: July-December, 243-70.

Helton, A.C. 1998. 'The 1998 CIS Conference Steering Group Meeting, June 1998', *The Forced Migration Projects News and Views*, 1 July, pp. 1-4. Available: http://www.soros.org/fmpviews/0024.html. 2 July 1998.

Henze, P.B. 1984. 'The Significance of Increasing Bilingualism Among Soviet Muslims' in Yaacov Ro'i, ed., *The USSR and the Muslim World: Issues in Domestic and Foreign Policy*. London: Geo. Allen and Unwin, 117-28.

—— 1991. 'The Demography of the Caucasus According to 1989 Soviet Census Data', *CAS* 10(1-2):147-70.

Heuer, Brigitte 1998. 'Exodus der Russen aus Uzbekistan', *Osteuropa-Archiv* 3:A112-21.

—— 1999. 'Schmelztiegel Zentralasien. Perspektiven für ein friedliches Zusammenleben', *Internationale Politik* 54(9):35-40.

Heyd, Uriel 1954. *Language Reform in Modern Turkey*. Jerusalem: Israel Oriental Society.

Hiro, Dilip 1994. *Between Marx and Muhammad: The Changing Face of Central Asia*. London: HarperCollins.

Hoffmann, Charlotte 1991. *An Introduction to Bilingualism*. London and New York: Longman.

Holm-Hansen, Jørn 1997. *Territorial and Ethno-Cultural Self-Government in Nation-Building Kazakhstan*. Oslo: Norwegian Institute for Urban and Regional Research.

Hough, J.F. 1996. 'Sociology, the State and Language Politics', *Post-Soviet Affairs* 12(2):95-117.

Hunter, S.T. 1993. 'Azerbaijan: Search for Industry and New Partners', in Ian Bremmer and Ray Taras, eds, *Nation and Politics in the Soviet Successor States*. Cambridge University Press, 225-60.

—— 1994. *The Transcaucasus in Transition: Nation-Building and Conflict*. Washington, DC: Center for Strategic and International Studies.

—— 1996. *Central Asia since Independence*. Westport, CT: Praeger.

Huskey, Eugene 1995. 'The Politics of Language in Kyrgyzstan', *Nationalities Papers* 23(3):549-72.

—— 1997. 'Kyrgyzstan: The Fate of Political Liberalization' in Karen Dawisha and Bruce Parrott, eds, *Conflict, Cleavage and Change in Central Asia and the Caucasus*. Cambridge University Press, 242-76.

Huttenbach, Henry 1992. 'Raspad – The Political Crises in Post-Soviet Transcaucasia', *Nationalities Papers* 20(2): 89-96.

—— 1995. 'Post-Soviet Crisis and Disorder in Transcaucasia' in Vladimir Tismaneanu, ed., *Political Culture and Civil Society in Russia and the New States of Eurasia*. Armonk, NY: M.E. Sharpe, 337-68.

Huttenbach, H.R. 1998. 'Whither Kazakhstan? Changing Capitals: From Almaty to Aqmola/Astana', *Nationalities Papers* 26(3):581-7.

Hyman, Anthony 1996. 'Post-Soviet Central Asia' in Roy Allison, ed., *Challenges for the Former Soviet South*. Washington, DC: Brookings Institution Press/London: Royal Institute of International Affairs, 7-67.

Iontsev, V.A. 1998. 'Mezhdunarodnaya migratsiya naseleniya: Rossiya i sovremennyi mir', *SI* no. 6:38-48.

Isaev, M.I. 1978. *O yazykakh narodov SSSR*. Moscow: Nauka.

—— 1979. *Yazykovoe stroitel'stvo v SSSR: Protsessy sozdaniya pis'mennostei narodov SSSR*. Moscow: Nauka.

Isayev, M.I. 1977. *National Languages in the USSR: Problems and Solutions*. Moscow: Progress.

Ivanov, V.V., ed. 1990. *Grammaticheskaya interferentsiya v usloviyakh natsional'no-russkogo dvuyazychiya*. Moscow: Nauka.

İsen, Mustafa 1997. 'Türk Dünyasının yeniden şekillenmesinde eğitimin rolü ve bunun bir uygulaması olarak Ahmet Yesevi Üniversitesi deneyimi', *Yeni Türkiye* 3(15): May-June, 701-3.

Jachnow, Helmut 1982. 'Sprachpolitische Tendenzen in der Geschichte der Sowjetunion', *International Journal of the Sociology of Language* 33:91-100.

Jahangiri, Guissou 1996. 'The Premises for the Construction of a Tajik National Identity, 1920-1930' in Mohammad-Reza Djalili a.o., eds, *Tajikistan: The Trials of Independence.* Richmond (London): Curzon Press, 14-41.

Kabuzan, V. 1996. *Russkie v mire.* St. Petersburg: Blits.

Kadir, Djelal 1996. Searching Asia', *World Literature Today* 70(3): summer, 489-92.

Kadyrshanov, Rustem 1996. *Die ethnopolitische Situation im multinationalen Kasachstan.* Cologne: Berichte des Bundesinstituts für ostwissenschaftliche und internationale Studien, 4.

Kagedan, Allan 1991. 'Nationalism, Language and Culture', *Nationalities Papers* 19(1): 59-62.

Kaiser, R.J. 1992. 'Social Mobilization in Soviet Central Asia' in R.A. Lewis, ed., *Geographic Perspectives on Soviet Central Asia.* London and New York: Routledge, 251-78.

Kaiser, R.J. 1994. *The Geography of Nationalism in Russia and the USSR.* Princeton University Press.

—— 1994a. 'Ethnic Demography and Interstate Relations in Central Asia' in Roman Szporluk, ed., *National Identity and Ethnicity in Russia and the New States of Eurasia.* Armonk, NY: M.E. Sharpe, 230-65.

—— 1995. 'Nationalizing the Work Force: Ethnic Restratification in the Newly Independent States', *Post-Soviet Geography* 36(2): February, 87-111.

—— 1997. 'Nationalism and Identity' in M.J. Bradshaw, ed., *Geography and Transition in the Post-Soviet Republics.* Chichester: John Wiley, 9-30.

Kan, G.V. a.o. 1997. *Koreitsy Kazakhstana: illyustrirovannaya istoriya.* N.p.: no publisher mentioned.

Kangas, R.D. 1995. 'State Building and Civil Society in Central Asia' in Vladimir Tismaneanu, ed., *Political Culture and Civil Society in Russia and the New States of Eurasia.* Armonk, NY: M.E. Sharpe, 271-91.

Kappeler, Andreas 1993. *Russland als Vielvölkerreich. Entstehung – Geschichte – Zerfall.* 2nd edn, Munich: C.H. Beck.

Kappert, Petra 1994. 'Azerbajdžan zwischen Nationalismus und religiöser Reaktion' in Peter Nitsche, ed., *Die Nachfolgestaaten der Sowjetunion.* Frankfurt am Main: Peter Lang, 119-30.

Karaörs, Metin 1994. 'Türk Cumhuriyetlerinde ortak bir yazı diline doğru', *Türk Dünyası Araştırmaları* 88:February, 139-51.

Karasik, Th.W., ed. 1992. *USSR: Facts and Figures Annual*, vol. 17. Gulf Breeze, FLA: Academic International Press.

——, ed. 1993. *Russia and Eurasia: Facts and Figures Annual*, vol. 18. Gulf Breeze, FLA: Academic International Press.

Karimi-Hakkak, Ahmed 1989. 'Language Reform Movement and Its

228 *References*

Language: The Case of Persian' in B.H. Jernudd and M.J. Shapiro, eds, *The Politics of Language Purism*. Berlin and New York: Mouton de Gruyter, 81-103.

Karimov, Islam 1998. *Harmoniously Developed Generation Is the Basis of Progress of Uzbekistan*. Tashkent: Sharq.

Karklins, Rasma 1986. *Ethnic Relations in the USSR: The Perspective from Below*. Boston: Geo. Allen and Unwin.

Karsakov, Il'yas 1998. 'Osobennosti transformatsii politicheskoi sistemy Kazakhstana v kontse 80-kh – seredine 90-kh godov', *Tsentral'naya Aziya* 14:75-85.

Kaser, Michael, and Santosh Mehrotra 1996. 'The Central Asian Economies after Independence' in Roy Allison, ed., *Challenges for the Former Soviet South*. Washington, DC: Brookings Institution Press, and London: Royal Institute of International Affairs, 217-306.

Katagoshchina, I.T. 1996. 'Intellektual'nyi potentsial i migratsionnye protsessy v Tsentral'noaziatskom regione', *Vostok. Oriens*, no. 6:70-88.

Kellner-Heinkele, Barbara 2000. 'Biz kimik? – Das Problem mit der Bezeichnung der Staatssprache in der Republik Aserbaidschan', *Folia Orientalia* 36:159-70.

Khalmukhamedov, Aleksandr 1998. 'Islamskii faktor v Uzbekistane', *Svobodnaya Mysl'*, no. 4:50-60.

Khanazarov, Kuchkar 1982. 'Developed Socialism and the Language Situation in the USSR' in *Socialism: Nations and National Relations*. Moscow: USSR Academy of Sciences, 160-76.

Khanazarov, K. Kh. 1982a. *Reshenie natsional'no-yazykovoi problemy v SSSR*. 2nd edn, Moscow: Izdatel'stvo Politicheskoi Literatury.

—— 1990. 'Bilingualism: A Characteristic Feature of Nations and Nationalities under Developed Socialism' in M.B. Olcott a.o., eds, *The Soviet Multinational State. Readings and Documents*. Armonk, NY: M.E. Sharpe, 240-5.

Khasanov, B. Kh. 1987. *Kazakhsko-russkoe dvuyazychie: sotsial'no-lingvisticheskii aspekt*. Alma-Ata: Akademiya Nauk.

—— 1989. *Natsional'nye yazyki, dvuyazychie i mnogoyazychie: poiski i perspektivy*. Alma-Ata: Izdatel'stvo Kazakhstan.

—— 1990. *Kazakhsko-russkoe khudozhestvenno-literaturnoe dvuyazychie*. Alma-Ata: Rauan.

—— 1992. 'Gosudarstvennyi yazyk – osnovnoi priznak lingvisticheskogo suvereniteta nezavisimogo gosudarstva', *Vestnik Akademii Nauk Respubliki Kazakhstan* September: 59-68.

Khazanov, A.M. 1991. *Soviet Nationality Policy During Perestroika*. Falls Church, VA: Delphic Associates.

—— 1995. *After the USSR: Ethnicity, Nationalism, and Politics in the Commonwealth of Independent States*. Madison: University of Wisconsin Press.

—— 1995a. 'The Ethnic Problems of Contemporary Kazakhstan', *CAS* 14(2):243-64.

Kinzer, Stephen 1997. 'Nukus Journal: In Plain English, These Uzbeks Are Going Places', *New York Times* 24 October: A4.

Kirchner, Mark 1999. 'Eine dritte Lateinschrift fur das Kasachische?', MS. To be published in *Festschrift für Erika Taube*, 15 pp.

—— and Wolf Zöller 1996. 'Auf der Suche nach der Staatssprache: Kasachstan spricht mit vielen verschiedenen Zungen', *Das Parlament* 36:30 August, 11.

Kirkwood, J.M. 1991. 'Russian Language Teaching Policy in Soviet Central Asia 1958-86' in Shirin Akiner, ed., *Cultural Change and Continuity in Central Asia*. London and New York: Kegan Paul International, 124-59.

Kloss, Heinz 1971. 'Language Rights of Immigrant Groups', *International Migration Review* 5:250-68.

Kocaoğlu, Timur 1993. 'Türkiye ile Türk cumhuriyetleri arasındaki münasebetlerde ortak alfabe ve imla birliğinin önemi', *Türk Dünyası Tarih Dergisi* 76: April, 17-9.

Koichuev, Turar 1998. 'Kyrgyzskaya Respublika na puti peremen', *Tsentral'naya Aziya* 14:106-15.

Kolstoe, Paul 1995. *Russians in the Former Soviet Republics*. London: Hurst.

—— 1996. 'The New Russian Diaspora: An Identity of Its Own? Possible Identity Trajectories for Russians in the Former Soviet Republic', *Ethnic and Racial Studies* 19(3): July, 609-39.

Kolstø, Pål 1998. 'Anticipating Demographic Superiority: Kazakh Thinking on Integration and Nation Building', *Europe-Asia Studies* 50(1): January, 51-69.

Konarovsky, Mikhail 1994. 'Russia and the Emerging Geopolitical Order in Central Asia' in Ali Banuazizi and Myron Weiner, eds, *The New Geopolitics of Central Asia and its Borderlands*. London: I.B. Tauris, 235-60.

Kopylenko, M.M. 1997. 'Gosudarstvennyi yazyk i ofitsial'nyi yazyk: razgranichenie ponyatii', *Sayasat* May:37-9.

Kopylenko, M.M. and S.T. Saina 1982. *Funktsionirovanie russkogo yazyka v razlichnykh sloyakh kazakhskogo naseleniya*. Alma-Ata: Nauka.

Kosmarskaya, Natal'ya 1998. 'Otstavshie ot potoka: Lyudi ishchut al'-ternativu repatriatsii', *Novoe Vremya* 21: 31 May, 26-7.

—— 1998a. ' "Ya nikuda ne khochu uezzhat" '. Zhizn' v postsovetskoi Kirgizii glazami russkikh', *Vestnik Evrazii* 1998, no. 1-2(4-5):76-100.

Kozlov, Viktor 1988. *The Peoples of the Soviet Union*. London: Hutchinson, and Bloomington: Indiana University Press.

Krag, H.L. 1984. 'The Language Situation in Central Asia – Between National Integrity and Soviet Integration' in E.A. Chylinski, ed.,

Soviet Central Asia: Continuity and Change. Papers from the Conference at Oksbøl, Denmark, February 16-17, 1984. Esbjerg: South Jutland University Press, 57-88.

Kreindler, Isabelle 1991. 'Forging a Soviet People: Ethnolinguistics in Central Asia' in William Fierman, ed., *Soviet Central Asia: The Failed Transformation.* Boulder, CO: Westview Press, 219-31.

—— 1993. 'A Second Missed Opportunity: Russian in Retreat as a Global Language', *International Political Science Review* 14(3): July, 257-74.

—— 1997. 'Multilingualism in the Successor States of the Soviet Union', *Annual Review of Applied Linguistics* 17:91-112.

—— ed., 1982. *The Changing Status of Russian in the Soviet Union* (= *International Journal of the Sociology of Language*, 33). The Hague: Mouton.

—— ed., 1985. *Sociolinguistic Perspectives on Soviet National Languages: Their Past, Present and Future.* Berlin: Mouton de Gruyter.

Kreindler, I.T. 1995. 'Soviet Muslims: Gains and Losses as a Result of Soviet Language Planning' in Yaacov Ro'i, ed., *Muslim Eurasia: Conflicting Legacies.* London: Frank Cass, 187-203.

Kubicek, Paul 1997. 'Regionalism and Nationalism in Central Asia', *Europe-Asia Studies* 49(4):637-55.

Kuchkartayev, Iristay 1993. 'Latin harflı alfabenin Özbekçeye uygulanması üzerine', *Anayurttan Atayurda Türk Dünyası* 1(3): June, 37-8.

Kulchik, Yuriy, Andrey Fadin, Victor Sergeev 1996. *Central Asia After the Empire.* London: Pluto Press.

Kuleshov, S.V. a.o. 1997. *Natsional'naya politika Rossii: istoriya i sovremennost'.* Moscow: Russkii Mir.

Kusherbaev, K.E. 1996. *Ètnopolitika Kazakhstana: sostoyanie i perspektivy.* Almaty: Institut Razvitiya Kazakhstana.

Kustov, I. 1997. 'Problema yazyka. Reaktsiya – migratsiya', *Respublika* 18-24 February.

Kuz'min, A.I. 1998. 'Prichiny i uroki grazhdanskoi voiny', in *Postsovetskaya Tsentral'naya Aziya,* Moscow: Russian Academy of Sciences – Vostochnaya Literatura, 215-71.

Kuznetsova, Sofia 1999. 'The Position of Russians in Kyrghyzstan', *Russia and the Muslim World* 80:23-6.

Kültür Bakanlığı 1992. *Sürekli Türk dili kurultayı.* Ankara: Yayımlar dairesi Başkanlığı.

Laitin, D.D. 1996. 'Language and Nationalism in the Post-Soviet Republics', *Post-Soviet Affairs* 12(1):4-24.

—— 1998. *Identity in Formation: The Russian-Speaking Populations in the Near Abroad.* Ithaca, NY: Cornell University Press.

Landau, J.M. 1993. 'The First Turkish Language Congress' in J.A. Fishman, ed., *The Earliest Stage of Language Planning: The 'First Congress' Phenomenon*. Berlin: Mouton de Gruyter, 271-92.

—— 1994. *The Politics of Pan-Islam: Ideology and Organization*. Oxford: Clarendon Press.

—— 1995. *Pan-Turkism: From Irredentism to Cooperation*. Rev. edn, London: C. Hurst, and Bloomington: Indiana University Press.

—— 1996. 'Language and Ethnopolitics in the Ex-Soviet Muslim Republics' in Yasir Suleiman, ed., *Language and Identity in the Middle East and North Africa*. Richmond (UK): Curzon Press, 133-52.

Lapierre, J.-W. 1988. *Le Pouvoir politique et les langues*. Paris: Presses Universitaires de France.

Lester, Toby 1997. 'New Alphabet Disease?', *Atlantic Monthly* 280(1): July, 20-7. Online posting: BITIG: vol. 8: 13/03 Latin Alphabet in Azerbaijan. Available e-mail: Turkestan-Newsletter@vm.ege.edu.tr. 28 Jan. 1998.

Lewis, Bernard 1961. *The Emergence of Modern Turkey*. London: Oxford University Press.

Lewis, E.G. 1972. *Multilingualism in the Soviet Union: Aspects of Language Policy and its Implementation*. The Hague: Mouton.

—— 1980. *Bilingualism and Bilingual Education: A Comparative Study*. Albuquerque: University of New Mexico Press.

Lewis, G.L. 1984. 'Atatürk's Language Reform as an Aspect of Modernization in the Republic of Turkey' in J.M. Landau, ed., *Atatürk and the Modernization of Turkey*. Boulder, CO: Westview Press, and Leiden: E.J. Brill, 195-213.

Lewis, R.A. 1992. 'The Migration of Russians Outside Their Homeland', *Nationalities Papers* 20(2): 35-40.

Lorenz, Manfred 1994. 'Das Tadschikische – eine Variante des Persischen' in Bert Fragner and Birgit Hoffmann, eds, *Bamberger Mittelasienstudien. Konferenzakten, Bamberg 15.-16. Juni 1990*. Berlin: Klaus Schwarz, 169-78.

Mackey, W.F. 1979. 'Language Policy and Language Planning', *Journal of Communication* 29(2): spring, 48-53.

Mahmudov, Nizamiddin 1997. 'Millî alfabe intiyacı', *Türk Lehçeleri ve Edebiyatı Dergisi* 12: April, 30-4.

Makarova, L.V., G.F. Morozova, T.I. Barzunova 1998. 'Regional'nye aspekty rossiiskoi immigratsii', *SI*, no. 6:48-55.

Malek, Martin 1994. 'Sprachenpolitik in der Gemeinschaft Unabhängiger Staaten (GUS)', *Osteuropa* 44(8): August, 743-59.

Mangott, Gerhard 1996. 'Einführung: Unwillkommene Neue?' in Gerhard Mangott, ed., *Bürden auferlegter Unabhängigkeit. Neue Staaten im post-sowjetischen Zentralasien*. Vienna: Braumüller, 1-4.

Marchenko, Tatiana 1994. 'The New Social and Cultural Situation and the Ouster of the Russian-Speaking Population from the Former Soviet Republics' in Vladimir Shlapentokh a.o., eds, *The New Russian Diaspora*. Armonk, NY: M.E. Sharpe, 141-54.

Marshall, D.F. 1996. 'A Politics of Language: Language as a Symbol in the Dissolution of the Soviet Union and Its Aftermath', *International Journal of the Sociology of Language* 118:7-41.

Maurais, Jacques 1991. 'Les lois linguistiques soviétiques de 1989 et 1990', *Revista de Llengua i Dret* 15: June, 75-90.

―― 1992. 'Redéfinition du statut des langues en Union Soviétique', *Language Problems and Language Planning* 16(1): spring, 1-20.

Mechkovskaya, N.B. 1992. 'Status i funktsii russkogo yazyka v poslednikh sovetskikh zakonakh o yazyke', *Russian Linguistics* 16:79-95.

Medlin, W.K., W.M. Cave, Finley Carpenter 1971. *Education and Development in Central Asia: A Case Study of Social Change in Uzbekistan*. Leiden: E.J. Brill.

Megoran, Nicholas 1997. 'Problems and Possibilities for Higher Education in Uzbekistan: The English Department of Ferghana State University', *CAS* 16(3):353-62.

Mehmedov, Hüsamettin 1992. 'Azerbaycan'da alfabe tartışmalarında ideolojik eğilimleri', in *Türkiye modeli ve Türk kökenli cumhuriyetlerle eski Sovyet halkları*. Ankara: Yeni Forum, 167-74.

Meissner, Boris and Alfred Eisfeld, eds. 1995. *Die GUS-Staaten in Europa und Asien*. Baden-Baden: Nomos.

Melikli, Tofik 1999. 'Azeri mi, Türk mü?', *Türk Dili* 569:May, 403-5.

Melvin, Neil 1995. *Russians Beyond Russia: The Politics of National Identity*. London: Royal Institute of International Affairs.

Mendikulova, G.M. 1998. 'Kazakhskaya diaspora: respublika Kazakhstan: problemy i perspektivy', *Kazakhstan-Spektr: Analiticheskie Issledovaniya* 1(3):73-7.

Mesamed, Vladimir 1996. 'Interethnic Relations in the Republic of Uzbekistan', *CAM* 6:20-6.

―― 1997. 'Linguistic Situation and Language Policy in the Republic of Uzbekistan', *Orient* 38(1): March, 143-56.

―― 1999. 'Tsentral'naya Aziya: yazykovye zakony, titul'nye i prochie natsii', *Novosti Nedeli* 30 September: supplement, 10-11.

Mesbahi, Mohiaddin 1997. 'Tajikistan, Iran, and the International Politics of the "Islamic Factor"', *CAS* 16(2): 141-58.

Mikhailovskaya, E., ed. 1994. *Russkie v blizhnem zarubezh'e*. Moscow.

Mikhal'chenko, V.Yu. 1994. 'Natsional'no-yazykovye konflikty na yazykovom prostranstve byvshego SSSR' in V.M. Solntsev and V.Yu. Mikhal'chenko, eds, *Yazyk v kontekste obshchestvennogo razvitiya. Language in the Context of Social Development*. Moscow: Russian Academy of Sciences, 221-35.

―― 1994a. 'Yazykovye problemy sodruzhestva nezavisimykh gosudarstv' in V.M. Solntsev and V.YU. Mikhal'chenko, eds, *Yazyk v kontekste obshchestvennogo razvitiya. Language in the Context of Social Development*, Moscow: Russian Academy of Sciences, 9-28.

Ministry of National Education, Uzbekistan 1997. *Mustaqil Ŭzbekiston ta"limi*. Tashkent: Sharq.

Moiseev, E.G. 1997. *Mezhdunarodno-pravovye osnovy sotrudnichestva stran SNG*. Moscow: Yurist.

Moldokasımtegin, Kıyas 1995-6. 'Kırgızstan 'da yer isimlerinin değiştirilmesi', *Avrasya Etüdleri* 2(4): winter, 105-18.

Motyl, Alexander 1987. *Will the Non-Russians Rebel? State, Ethnicity and Stability in the USSR*. Ithaca, NY: Cornell University Press.

—— 1990. 'The Demise of the Soviet Language', *Nationalities Papers* 18(1): spring, 14-17.

Musaev, K.M. 1994. 'Demograficheskie protsessy: funktsionirovanie yazykov v Kazakhstane' in Ingeborg Baldauf and Michael Friedrich, eds, *Bamberger Zentralasienstudien. ESCAS IV. Bamberg 8.-12. Oktober 1991*. Berlin: Klaus Schwarz, 153-63.

Mütercimler, Erol 1993. *21. yüzyılın eşiğinde uluslararası sistem ve Türkiye-Türk cumhuriyetleri ilişkiler modeli*. Istanbul: Anahtar.

Naby, Eden 1993. 'Publishing in Central Asia', *CAM* 1:27-30.

—— 1994. 'The Emerging Central Asia. Ethnic and Religious Factions', in Mohiaddin Mesbahi, ed., *Central Asia and the Caucasus after the Soviet Union. Domestic and International Dynamics*. Gainesville, FLA: University of Florida Press, 34-55.

Närimanoğlu, Kâmil Väli 1995. 'Bir daha dilimizin adı haqqında', *Bir* 4:131-42.

Nasyrova, O.D. 1994. 'Yazykovoe stroitel'stvo v Karakalpakstane na sovremennom étape' in V.M. Solntsev and V. Yu. Mikhal'chenko, eds, *Yazyk v kontekste obshchestvennogo razvitiya. Language in the Context of Social Development*. Moscow: Russian Academy of Sciences, 236-48.

Naumova, O.B. 1991. 'Evolution of Nomadic Culture Under Modern Conditions: Traditions and Innovations in Kazakh Culture' in Gary Seaman and Daniel Marks, eds, *Rulers from the Steppe: State Formation on the Eurasian Periphery*. Los Angeles, CA: University of Southern California, 291-307.

—— 1992. 'Nekotorye aspekty formirovaniya sovremennoi bytovoi kultury kazakhov v mnogonatsional'nykh raionakh Kazakhstana' in A.N. Zhilina and S.V. Cheshko, eds, *Sovremennoe razvitie étnicheskikh grupp Srednei Azii i Kazakhstana*. Moscow: Russian Academy of Sciences, vol. I, 5-50.

Nauryzbaev, Zh. 1993. 'Pust' protsvetaet rodnoi yazyk i ryadom s nim – drugie', *Mysl'* no. 8:47-50.

Nazarbaev, Nursultan [1998]. 'Kazakhstan – 2030'. [...] Message of the President of the Country to the People of Kazakhstan. Available: http:// www.kz/articles/state/state_container.asp?Ing=en&art=strategy. 2 July 1998.

Nazarov, B. 1996. 'Mustaqillik davrida til va adabiët ilmi', *Ŭzbekistonda Izhtimoiĭ Fanlar. Obshchestvennye Nauki v Uzbekistane*, no. 6:104-111.

Nelde, P.H. 1989. 'Le contact de langues en tant que conflit linguistique' in F.H. Riedl and Theodor Veiter, eds, *Fédéralisme, régionalisme et droit des groupes ethniques en Europe*. Vienna: Braumüller, 277-87.

Neroznak, V.P., ed., 1995. *Gosudarstvennye yazyki v Rossiiskoi Federatsii: Ėntsiklopedicheskii slovar'-spravochnik*. Moscow: Academia.

Nettleton, Susanna 1992. 'Uzbek Independence and Educational Change', *CAM* 3:19-20.

Nijasow, Saparmurat 1994. *Unabhängigkeit, Demokratie, Wohlstand*. Alma-Ata: Noy.

Nikolaev, Sergei 1994. 'Russians in Uzbekistan' in Vladimir Shlapentokh a.o., eds, *The New Russian Diaspora: Russian Minorities in the Former Soviet Republics*. Armonk, NY: 107-21.

Nissman, David 1993. 'Turkmenistan: Searching for a National Identity' in Ian Bremmer and Ray Taras, eds, *Nation and Politics in the Soviet Successor States*. Cambridge University Press, 384-97.

Niyazi, Aziz 1993. 'The Year of Tumult: Tajikistan After February 1990' in Vitaly Naumkin, ed., *State, Religion and Society in Central Asia: A Post-Soviet Critique*. Reading (England): Ithaca Press, 262-89.

Nizamov, Asliddin 1995. 'Das kulturelle Leben Tadžikistans in der zweiten Jahreshälfte 1994', *Berliner Osteuropa Info* 5: June, 15-16.

Norr, Henry 1985. 'National Languages and Soviet Television: A Statistical Report', *Nationalities Papers* 13(1): spring, 84-105.

Nourzhanov, Kirill 1998. 'Seeking Peace in Tajikistan: Who Is the Odd Man Out?', *CAM* 6:15-24.

—— 1998a. 'Traditional Kinship Structures in Contemporary Tajik Politics' in David Christian and Benjamin Craig, eds, *Worlds of the Silk Roads: Ancient and Modern* (=Silk Road Studies, 2). Turnhout: Brepols, 147-64.

Novak, Yu. 1994. 'Mezhëtnicheskie otnosheniya v Uzbekistane', *SI* 4: 41-52.

Nysanbaev, A., E. Arynov, B. Yesekeyev 1996. *Republic of Kazakstan: Five Years of Independent Development*. Almaty: Academy of Sciences – Institute of Philosophy.

O'Barr, W.M. 1984. 'Asking the Right Questions about Language and Power' in Cheris Kremarae a.o., eds, *Language and Power*. Beverly Hills, CA: Sage 260-80.

Ochs, Michael 1997. 'Turkmenistan: The Quest for Stability and Control' in Karen Dawisha and Bruce Parrott, eds, *Conflict, Cleavage, and Change in Central Asia and the Caucasus*. Cambridge University Press, 312-57.

Olcott, M.B. 1992. 'Kazakhstan's Global Impact', *The Iranian Journal of International Affairs* 4(2): summer, 369-82.

—— 1996. 'How New the New Russia? Demographic Upheavals in Central Asia', *Orbis* 40(4): fall, 537-55.

—— 1997. 'Democratization and the Growth of Political Participation in Kazakstan' in Karen Dawisha and Bruce Parrott, eds, *Conflict, Cleavage, and Change in Central Asia and the Caucasus*. Cambridge: Cambridge University Press, 201-41.

Olimova, Saodat 1998. 'Tadzhikistan – pervaya ostanovka na puti afganskoi migratsii', *Tsentral'naya Aziya i Kavkaz* 1:105-113.

—— 1999. 'Politicheskii Islam i konflikt v Tadzhikistane', *Tsentral'naya Aziya i Kavkaz* 4(5):133-41.

Olson, J.S. 1994. *An Ethnohistorical Dictionary of the Russian and Soviet Empires*. Westport, CT: Greenwood Press.

Omirbekova, M. Sh. a.o., eds, 1997. *Yazykovaya politika v Kazakhstane (1921-1990 gody): Sbornik dokumentov*. Almaty: Qazaq Universiteti.

Orazalinov, S. 1995. 'Delo blagorodnoe i vseobshchee: o glavnykh napra-vleniyakh edinoi gosudarstvennoi yazykovoi politiki', *Mysl'* no. 5:49-53.

Ordoubadian, Reza 1977. 'Azarbayjani: Bilingualism and Politics' in Michel Paradis, ed., *The Fourth LACUS Forum 1977*. Columbia, SC: Kornbeam Press, 303-7.

Ornstein, Jacob 1968. 'Soviet Language Policy: Continuity and Change' in Erich Goldhagen, ed., *Ethnic Minorities in the Soviet Union*. New York: Praeger, 121-46.

Oruzbaeva, B.O. 1994. 'Die kirgizische Sprache als Staatssprache unter neuen Voraussetzungen' in Ingeborg Baldauf and Michael Friedrich, eds, *Bamberger Zentralasienstudien. Konferenzakten ESCAS IV. Bamberg 8.-12. Oktober 1991*. Berlin: Klaus Schwarz, 165-70.

Osipov, A.G. and M.D. Savurov 1992. 'Turki v Uzbekistane: rasselenie, zanyatiya, kul'tura', in A.N. Zhilina and S.V. Cheshko, eds, *Sovremennoe razvitie étnicheskikh grupp Srednei Azii i Kazakhstana*, vol. I, 103-31.

Önder, S.W. 1993. 'Cultural Memory and the Language Artist: A Kazakh Lineage', *Turkish Studies Association Bulletin* 17(2):102-11.

Öner, Mustafa 1997. 'Ortak Türk alfabesi hakkında bazı notlar', *Yeni Türkiye* 3(15): May-June, 207-11.

Öztopçu, Kurtuluş a.o. 1996. *Dictionary of the Turkic Languages. English: Azerbaijani, Kazakh, Kyrgyz, Tatar, Turkish, Turkmen, Uighur, Uzbek*. London and New York: Routledge.

Panarin, S.A. 1994. 'The Ethnohistorical Dynamics of Muslim Societies within Russia and the CIS' in Mohiaddin Mesbahi, ed., *Central Asia and the Caucasus After the Soviet Union: Domestic and International Dynamics*. Gainesville, FLA: University Press of Florida, 17-33.

Paniko, Chris 1994. 'Dual Citizenship in Central Asia', *CAM* 3:18-22.

Pannier, Bruce 1996. 'A Linguistic Dilemma in Kyrgyzstan', *Transition* 24:28-9.

Payne, John 1996. 'Tajikistan and the Tajiks' in Graham Smith, ed., *The Nationalities Question in the Post-Soviet States*. London and New York: Longman, 367-84.

Perks, Dora 1984. 'Overcoming Illiteracy in the USSR' in Marilyn Bechtel and Daniel Rosenberg, eds, *Nations and Peoples: The Soviet Experience*. New York: New World Review Collection, 89-99.

Perry, J.R. 1992. 'Tajikistan's Language Law: Two Years on', *AACAR Bulletin of the Association for the Advancement of Central Asian Research* 5(2):fall, 3-4.

—— 1996. 'Tajik Literature: Seventy Years is Longer Than the Millenium', *World Literature Today* 70(3): summer, 571-3.

—— 1996. 'From Persian to Tajik to Persian: Culture, politics, and law reshape a Central Asian language' in H.I. Aronson, ed., *NSL.8. Linguistic Studies in the Non-Slavic Languages of the Commonwealth of Independent States and the Baltic Republics*. University of Chicago, 279-305.

Perry, John 1997. 'Script and Scripture: The Three Alphabets of Tajik Persian, 1927-1997', *Journal of Central Asian Studies (formerly AACAR Bulletin)* 2 (1), fall/winter: 2-18.

Petrov, N.I. 1998. 'Politicheskaya stabil'nost' v usloviyakh komandno-administrativnogo rezhima' in *Postsovetskaya Tsentral'naya Aziya*. Moscow: Russian Academy of Sciences – Vostochnaya Literatura, 94-121.

—— and M.S. Gafarly 1998. 'Kurs na politicheskuyu stabil'nost' i sotrudnichestvo s sosedyami', in *Postsovetskaya Tsentral'naya Aziya*. Moscow: Russian Academy of Sciences – Vostochnaya Literatura, 36-66.

Pigolkin, A.S. and M.S. Studenikina 1991. 'Republican Language Laws in the USSR: A Comparative Analysis', *Journal of Soviet Nationalities* 2(1): spring, 38-76.

Pilkington, Hilary 1998. *Migration, Displacement and Identity in Post-Soviet Russia*. London and New York: Routledge.

Poliakov, S.P. 1992. *Everyday Islam: Religion and Tradition in Rural Central Asia*. Armonk, NY: M.E. Sharpe.

Pollard, A.P., ed. 1991. *USSR: Facts and Figures Annual*, vol. 15. Gulf Breeze, FLA: Academic International Press.

Pomfret, Richard 1995. *The Economics of Central Asia*. Princeton University Press.

Ponomarev, V. 1991. *Samodeyatel'nye obshchestvennye organizatsii Kazakhstana i Kirgizii (opyt spravochnika)*. Moscow: Institut Issledovaniya Ėkstremal'nykh Protsessov v SSSR.

Pool, Jonathan 1976. 'Developing the Soviet Turkic Tongues: The Language of the Politics of Language', *Slavic Review* 35(3): September, 425-42.

Rakhimov, R.R. 1991. 'K voprosu o sovremennykh tadzhiksko-uzbekskikh mezhnatsional'nykh otnosheniyakh', *Sovetskaya Ėtnografiya* 1:13-20.

Rakowska-Harmstone, Teresa 1970. *Russia and Nationalism in Central Asia: The Case of Tadzhikistan*. Baltimore, MD: Johns Hopkins University Press.

—— 1994. 'Soviet Legacies', *CAM* 3:23-34.

Rashid, Ahmed 1994. *The Resurgence of Central Asia*. Karachi: Oxford University Press.

Robertson, L. R. 1996. 'The Ethnic Composition of Migration in the Former Soviet Union', *Post-Soviet Geography and Economics* 37(2):113-28.

—— ed. 1997. *Russia and Eurasia: Facts and Figures Annual*, vol. 22. Gulf Breeze, FLA: Academic International Press.

—— ed. 1998. *Russia and Eurasia: Facts and Figures Annual*, vol. 24. Gulf Breeze, FLA: Academic International Press.

Robins, Philip 1993. 'Between Sentiment and Self-Interest: Turkey's Policy Toward Azerbaijan and the Central Asian States', *Middle East Journal* 47(4): autumn, 593-610.

Rogers, K.H. 1981. 'Selected Recent Studies in Linguistic Nationalism in the Romance Languages', *Canadian Review of Studies in Nationalism* 8(2): Autumn, 267-83.

Rogers, Rosemarie 1987. 'Language Policy and Language Power: The Case of Soviet Publishing', *Language Problems and Language Planning* 11(1):82-103.

Roig, M.G. 1985. 'El pluralismo lingüístico', *Revista de Estudios Políticos* 48: November-December, 221-32.

Roy, Olivier 1991. 'Ethnies et politique en Asie Centrale', *Revue du Monde Musulman et de la Méditerranée* 59-60(1-2):17-36.

—— 1993. 'Asie Centrale et Kazakhstan: Evolutions dans un environnement complexe' in Roberte Berton-Hogge and M.-A. Crosnier, eds, *Ex-URSS. Les Etats du divorce*. Paris: Etudes de la Documentation Française, 141-53.

Rudensky, Nikolai 1994. 'Russian Minorities in the Newly Independent States: An International Problem in the Domestic Context of Russia Today' in Roman Szporluk, ed., *National Identity and Ethnicity in Russia and the New States of Eurasia*. Armonk, NY: M.E. Sharpe, 58-77.

Rüstämova, T.Z. 1996. *Äski Älifba*. Baku: *Azärbaÿjan Ensiklopediÿasy*.

Rywkin, Michael 1992. 'Post-USSR Political Developments in Former Soviet Central Asia', *Nationalities Papers* 20(2):97-106.
—— 1993. *Moscow's Lost Empire*. Armonk, NY: M.E. Sharpe.
Rzayev, N.M. 1992. 'Türk dünyasının ortak ilmi terim problemleri üzerine', *Türk Dünyası Araştırmaları* 81: December, 189-92.
Rzehak, Lutz 1995. 'Wissenschaft, Hochschulwesen und Unabhängigkeit. Reisebeobachtungen in Usbekistan und Tadshikistan', *Osteuropa* 45(4):329-37.
—— 1999. *Tadschikische Studiengrammatik*. Wiesbaden: Reichert.

Safran, William 1991. 'Diasporas in Modern Societies: Myths of Homeland and Return', *Diaspora* 1(1): spring, 83-99.
Sağlam, Mehmet 1997. 'Türk Cumhuriyetleri ile eğitim ilişkilerimiz', *Yeni Türkiye* 3(15): May-June, 683-4.
Sansone, Vito 1983. *Chez les voisins de l'Afghanistan. L'Asie Centrale Soviétique*. Moscow: Editions du Progrès.
Saray, Mehmet 1996. *Yeni Türk Cumhuriyetleri tarihi*. Ankara: Türk Tarih Kurumu.
Savelieva, Tatiana 1997. 'The Role of Education in the Formation and Development of Language Competence of Women in Uzbekistan Under Conditions of Polyethnicity', *Contemporary Central Asia* (New Delhi) 1(1):44-62.
Savoskul, Sergei 1995. 'Rossiya i russkie na Blizhnem Vostoke', *Ėtnopolis* 3(9):129-40.
Schlyter, B.N. 1997. *Language Policy in Independent Uzbekistan*. Stockholm: Forum for Central Asian Studies.
—— [1998]. 'Language Policies and Language Movements in Central Asia', *IIAS Newsletter Online* 17: 3 pp. Available: http://www.iias.leidenuniv.nl/iiasn/17/regions/17 CAXAO1.html. 22 February 1999.
Schmidt, Gerlind 1995. *Die Bildungsentwicklung in Kasachstan und Usbekistan: Umbruch und Neubeginn im Bildungswesen Mittelasiens*. Frankfurt am Main: Deutsches Institut für Internationale Pädagogische Forschung.
Seckinger, Beverly 1988. 'Implementing Morocco's Arabization Policy: Two Problems of Classification' in Florian Coulmas, ed., *With Forked Tongues: What are National Languages Good For?* Singapore: Karoma Publishers, 68-90.
Seegmiller, Steve and Çiğdem Balım 1998. 'Alphabets for the Turkic Languages: Past, Present and Future' in Lars Johanson, ed., *The Mainz Meeting. Proceedings of the Seventh International Conference on Turkish Linguistics, August 3-6, 1994*. Wiesbaden: Harrassowitz, 627-46.
Seidov, I.S. 1982. 'Ob orfografirovanii sostavnykh terminov, vklyuchayushchikh imya sobstvennoe', *Sovetskaya Tyurkologiya* 1:40-7.

Shahrani, M.N. 1992. 'Muslim Central Asia: Soviet Development Legacies and Future Challenges', *Iranian Journal of International Affairs* 4(2): summer, 331-42.

Shami, Seteney 1999. 'Islam in the Post-Soviet Space: Imaginative Geographies of the Caucasus and Central Asia', *Bulletin of the Royal Institute for Inter-Faith Studies*, I(1): spring, 181-95.

Shamshiev, Bektash 1996. 'Post-Socialist Kyrgyz Literature: Crisis or Renaissance?', *World Literature Today* 70(3):summer, 549-51.

Shapiro, M.J. 1989. 'A Political Approach to Language Purism' in B.H. Jernudd and M.J. Shapiro, eds, *The Politics of Language Purism*. Berlin: Mouton de Gruyter, 21-9.

Sharif, Sergei 1999. 'Diaspora Kazakhstana: razgovor s evreiskim Baronom', *Novosti Nedeli* 29 April, 22-3, supplement.

Shashenkov, Maxim 1994. 'Russia and Central Asia: Emerging Security Links' in Anoushiravan Ehteshami, ed., *From the Gulf to Central Asia: Players in the New Great Game*. University of Exeter Press (England), 168-87.

Shenfield, S.D. 1994. 'Almaty Observations', *CAM* 6:7-12.

Shnirelman, Victor and Galina Komarova 1997. 'Majority as a Minority: The Russian Ethno-Nationalism and Its Ideology in the 1970-1990s' in Hans-Rudolf Wicker, ed., *Rethinking Nationalism and Ethnicity: The Struggle for Meaning and Order in Europe*. Oxford and New York: Berg, 211-24.

Shorish, M.M. 1976. 'The Pedagogical, Linguistic, and Logistical Problems of Teaching Russian to the Local Soviet Central Asians', *Slavic Review* 35(3): September, 443-62.

—— 1984. 'Planning by Decree: The Soviet Language Policy in Central Asia', *Language Problems and Language Planning* 8(1): 35-49.

Shorish, Mobin 1994. 'The Uzbeks and Tajiks: Conflict Resolution and the Soviet Experience' in P.L. Dash, ed., *Russian Dilemma: The Ethnic Aftermath*. Cuttack (India): Arya Prakashan, 53-73.

Shûkurî, Muhammadjân 1994. 'La situation de la langue persane tadjike et les perspectives de son renouveau', *CEMOTI, Cahiers d'Etudes sur la Méditerranée Orientale et le Monde Turco-Iranien* 18: 171-8.

Silver, Brian 1976. 'Bilingualism and Maintenance of the Mother Tongue in Soviet Central Asia', *Slavic Review* 35(3):406-24.

Simon, Gerhard 1986. *Nationalismus und Nationalitätenpolitik in der Sowjetunion*. Baden-Baden: Nomos.

Singer, M.S. 1998. 'Language Follows Power: The Linguistic Free Market in the Old Soviet Bloc', *Foreign Affairs* 77(1): January-February, 19-24.

Sitnyanskii, Georgii 1996. 'Problema reintegratsii byvshego SSSR s tochki zreniya istoricheskogo naslediya narodov Evrazii', *Vestnik Evrazii* 2(3):160-71.

Sjoberg, A.F. 1993. 'Language Structure and Cultural Identity: A Historical Perspective on the Turkic Peoples of Central Asia', *CAS* 12(4): 557-64.

Smith, A.D. 1979. 'Towards a Theory of Ethnic Separatism', *Ethnic and Racial Studies* 2(1): January, 21-37.

Smith, Graham a.o., 1998. *Nation-Building in the Post-Soviet Borderlands. The Politics of National Identities.* Cambridge University Press.

Söegov, Myratgeldi and Rejebov, Nyyazberdi 1993. *Täze Türkmen elipbïü.* Ashgabat: Ruch.

Sokolova, Lyudmila 1998. 'Demograficheskoe razvitie Respubliki Tadzhikistan v perekhodnyi period', *Tsentral'naya Aziya* 14:34-44.

Solchanyk, Roman 1982. 'Language and Education in Soviet Schools', *International Journal of the Sociology of Language* 33:113-18.

Solzhenitsyn, Aleksandr 1998. *Rossiya v obvale.* Moscow: Russkii Put'.

Söylemez, Orhan 1996. '1980 sonrasında Kazak kültürel kimliğinin muhafazası', *Bir* 6:145-65.

Spolsky, Bernard and R.L. Cooper, eds 1977. *Frontiers of Bilingual Education.* Rowley, MA: Newbury.

Stadelbauer, Jörg 1996. *Die Nachfolgestaaten der Sowjetunion. Grossraum zwischen Dauer und Wandel.* Darmstadt: Wissenschaftliche Buchgesellschaft.

State Committee on Statistics of Turkmenistan 1997. *Brief Results of the 1995 National Population Census of Turkmenistan.* Ashgabat.

Steblin-Kamensky, I. 1998. 'Tādjikī', part 1, *Encyclopaedia of Islam*, new edn, vol. X. Leiden: E.J. Brill.

Stölting, Erhard 1991. *Eine Weltmacht zerbricht. Nationalitäten und Religionen in der UdSSR.* 3rd updated and enlarged edition, Frankfurt am Main: Eichborn.

Subtelny, M.E. 1994. 'The Symbiosis of Turk and Tajik' in B. F. Manz, ed., *Central Asia in Historical Perspective.* Boulder, CO: Westview Press, 45-61.

Sultan, Garip 1968. 'Demographic and Cultural Trends among Turkic Peoples of the Soviet Union' in Erich Goldhagen, ed., *Ethnic Minorities in the Soviet Union.* New York: Praeger, 251-73.

Suny, R.G. 1996. 'On the Road to Independence: Cultural Cohesion and Ethnic Revival in a Multinational Society' in R.G. Suny, ed., *Transcaucasia, Nationalism and Social Change.* Rev. edn, Ann Arbor: University of Michigan Press, 377-400.

Svanberg, Ingvar 1996. 'Kazakhstan and the Kazakhs', in Graham Smith, ed., *The Nationalities Question in Post-Soviet States.* London and New York: Longman, 318-33.

Svoik, Petr 1998. 'Natsional'nyi vopros v Kazakhstane: vzglyad "russkoyazychnogo"', *Tsentral'naya Aziya* 15:28-46.

Şahnazarov, Bahtiyar 1996-7. 'Özbekistan'da kültürel çoğulculuk', *Avrasya Etüdleri* 3(4): winter, 95-111.

Şimşir, B.N. 1991. *Azerbaycan'da Türk alfabesi tarihçe*. Ankara: Türk Dil Kurumu.

—— 1995 'Türkmenistan'da Latin alfabesine geçiş hazırlıkları', *Türk Dili* 518:115-38.

T.C. Dışişleri Bakanlığı 1993. *Türkçe konuşan Kafkasya ve İç Asya ülkeleriyle Türkiye arasında iletişimde işbirliği konferansı*. Ankara: TIKA.

Tadjbakhsh, Shahrbanou 1996. 'National Reconciliation: The Imperfect Whim', *CAS* 15(3-4):325-48.

Tarasova, L.V., ed. 1997. *Sotsial'no-ėkonomicheskie problemy migratsii naseleniya Kyrgyzskoi Respubliki (1991-1996 gg.)*. Bishkek: Kyrgyzsko-Rossiskii Slavyanskii Universitet.

Taukina, Rozalana 1999. 'Osveshchenie khroniki sobytii v period prezidentskikh vyborov v Respublike Kazakhstan v SMI', *Tsentral'naya Aziya i Kavkaz* 1(2):173-80.

Tazhutov, A. 1991. 'Gosudarstvennyi yazyk: fakty i realii', *Tochka Zreniya* 2: 1, 3, 31.

Tenishev, E.R. a.o., eds, 1997. *Yazyki mira. Tyurkskie yazyki*. Bishkek: Kyrgyzstan.

Têtu, M. 1988. *La francophonie. Histoire, problématique et perspectives*. Paris: Hachette.

Thom, Françoise 1989. *Newspeak: The Language of Soviet Communism*. London and Lexington: Claridge Press.

Thubron, Colin 1994. *The Lost Heart of Asia*. New York: HarperCollins.

Timirbajew, Wjatscheslaw 1998. 'Multinationales Kyrgysstan', *Wostok* 1: January-February, 17-21.

Tishkov, V.A. 1995. 'The Russians in Central Asia and Kazakhstan' in Yaacov Ro'i, ed., *Muslim Eurasia: Conflicting Legacies*. London: Frank Cass, 289-310.

Tishkov, Valery 1997. *Ethnicity, Nationalism and Conflict in and after the Soviet Union: The Mind Aflame*. London: Sage.

Titov, A.K. 1996. 'The Role of Russian in the Post-Cold-War Era' in K.E. Müller, ed., *Language Status in the Post-Cold-War Era*. Lanham MD: University Press of America, 43-8.

Toker, Yalçın 1992. *Büyük uyanış*. Ankara: Toker Yayınları.

Toktomyshev, Sovetbek 1997. *Universitet budushchego: Kyrgyzskii Gosudarstvennyi Natsional'nyi Universitet: proshloe i nastoyashchee shagi v xxi vek*. Bishkek: KGNU.

Tollefson, J.W. 1991. *Planning Language, Planning Inequality: Language Policy in the Community*. London and New York: Longman.

Tortosa, J.M. 1982. *Política lingüística y lenguas minoritarias*. Madrid: Tecnos.

Tryjarski, Edward 1998. 'Towards Better Mutual Comprehension among Turkic-Speakers' in Touraj Atabaki and John O'Kane, eds, *Post-Soviet Central Asia*. London: I.B. Tauris, 109-17.

Tsagolov, Kim 1998. 'A Russian Official's Analysis of Forced Migration: A Personal Reflection', *The Forced Migration Monitor* 21: January, 1-4.

Tumanyan, E.G. 1994. 'Zakony o yazykakh i vozmozhnost' ikh realizatsii' in V.M. Solntsev and V.Yu. Mikhal'chenko, eds, *Yazyk v kontekste obshchestvennogo razvitiya*. *Language in the Context of Social Development*. Moscow: Russian Academy of Sciences, 72-83.

Tursunov, D.T., ed. 1984. *Russkii yazyk – moguchee sredstvo mezhnatsional'nogo obshcheniya*. Alma-Ata: Mektep.

Türkmen, Fikret 1994. 'The Issue of a Common Turkish Script', *Eurasian Studies* 1: spring, 85-90.

TÜRKSAM (Türkiye Stratejik Araştırmalar ve Eğitim Merkezi) 1999. 'Kırgızstan toplumlararası etnik ilişkiler', *Belgelerle Türk Tarihi Dergisi Dün Bugün Yarın* 24:January, 89-96.

Tütüncü, Mehmet 1998. 'Latin Alphabet in Azerbaijan', *Turkistan Newsletter* 98-13:3 March.

Twining, D.T. 1993. *Guide to the Republics of the Former Soviet Union*. Westport, CT: Greenwood Press.

Uhres, Johann 1996. 'Introduction de l'alphabet ouzbek à graphie latine', *Observatoire de l'Asie Centrale et du Caucase* 1: February, 8, 10.

Um, Haye-kyung 1996. 'The Korean Diaspora in Uzbekistan and Kazakhstan: Social Change, Identity and Music-Making' in K.E. Schulze, Martin Stokes and Colm Campbell, eds., *Nationalism, Minorities and Rights in the Middle East*. London: I.B. Tauris, 217-32.

Urjewicz, Charles 1991. 'L'identité azérie à l'épreuve de l'indépendance', *Revue du Monde Musulman et de la Méditerranée* 59-60(1-2):117-22.

US Department of State 1998. Uzbekistan Country Report on Human Rights Practices for 1997. Released by the Bureau of Democracy, Human Rights and Labor, Jan. 30, 1998.

―――― 1999. Uzbekistan Country Report on Human Rights Practices for 1998. Released by the Bureau of Democracy, Human Rights, and Labor, Feb. 26, 1999.

Usta, Halil Ibrahim 1999. 'Ortak Türk dili ve Mağcan Cumabayev', *Türk Dili* 571:July, 528-32.

Uzel, Nezih 1993. *Adriatik'ten Çin'e Türk dünyası*. Istanbul: İrfan.

Vasil'ev, A.M. 1998. 'Rossiya i Tsentral'naya Aziya' in *Postsovetskaya Tsentral'naya Aziya: Poteri i obreteniya*. Moscow: Russian Academy of Sciences – Vostochnaya Literatura, 5-35.

Vatanabadi, Shouleh 1996. 'Past, Present, Future, and Postcolonial Discourse in Modern Azerbaijani Literature', *World Literature Today* 70(3): summer, 493-7.

Vechkanov, G.S. 1998. *Migratsiya i zanyatost' naseleniya v Rossii.* St. Petersburg: Petropolis.

Veiter, Theodor 1990. 'Die sprachrechtliche Situation in den Staaten in der Mitte Europas', *Archiv des Völkerrechts* 28(1-2):17-75.

Vitkovskaya, Galina, ed. 1996. *Migratsiya russkoyazychnogo naseleniya iz Tsentral'noi Azii : prichiny, posledstviya, perspektivy.* Moscow: Carnegie Endowment for International Peace.

Waxman, Ronald 1973. 'Recent Assimilation Trends in Soviet Central Asia' in Edward Allworth, ed., *The Nationality Question in Soviet Central Asia.* New York: Praeger, 73-85.

Wehrschütz, C. F. 1997. 'Von der Welle zur Springflut? Wanderungs- bewegungen in der ehemaligen Sowjetunion', *Österreichische Militärische Zeitschrift* 35(1):27-36.

Weiner, R.E. 1987. 'Languages Equal and Free?: The Legal Status of Minority Languages in the Soviet Union', *Arizona Journal of International and Comparative Law* 6:73-87.

Weinstein, Brian 1989. 'Francophonie: Purism at the International Level', in B.K. Jernudd and M.J. Shapiro, eds, *The Politics of Language Purism.* Berlin and New York: Mouton de Gruyter, 53-79.

Wheeler, Geoffrey 1977. 'The Turkic Languages of Soviet Muslim Asia: Russian Linguistic Policy', *Middle Eastern Studies* 13(2): May, 208-17.

Willerton, J.P. 1992. *Patronage and Politics in the USSR.* Cambridge University Press.

Wood, R.E. 1981. 'Selected Recent Studies in Linguistic Nationalism in the Germanic Languages', *Canadian Review of Studies in Nationalism* 8(1): spring, 55-84.

Yamskov, A.N. 1994. 'The "New Minorities" in Post-Soviet States: Lin- guistic Orientations and Political Conflict', *Cultural Survival Quarterly* 18(2-3): summer-fall, 58-61.

Yazdani, A.O. 1993. *Geteiltes Aserbaidschan. Blick auf ein bedrohtes Volk.* Berlin: Das Arabische Buch.

Yetkin, Murat 1992. *Ateş hattında aktif politika.* Istanbul: Alan.

Yuldashev, D. 1994. 'Education in Uzbekistan: Reality and Prospects', *CAM* 3:15-17.

Yunusov, Arif 1997. 'Demographic Disaster', *Index on Censorship* 26(4): July-August, 69-73.

—— 1998. 'Postkommunisticheskii Azerbaidzhan: problemy i vozmo- zhnye puti razvitiya', *Mirovaya Ėkonomika i Mezhdunarodnye Otnosheniya*, no. 11:100-11.

Zakaeva, Zinaida and Zaure Sarsenbaeva 1998. 'Mezhėtnicheskie otnosheniya v sovremennom Kazakhstane (opyt kompleksnogo sotsiologicheskogo analiza)', *Tsentral'naya Aziya* 15:46-59.

Zaslavsky, Victor 1997. 'The Soviet Union' in Karen Barkey and Mark von Hagen, eds, *After Empire: Multiethnic Societies and Nation-Building. The Soviet Union and the Russian, Ottoman, and Habsburg Empires.* Boulder, CO: Westview Press, 73-96.

Zdravomyslov, A.G. 1997. *Mezhnatsional'nye konflikty v postsovetskom prostranstve.* Moscow: Aspekt Press.

Zemtsov, Ilya 1985. *The Lexicon of the Soviet Political Language.* Epping (London): Bowker.

Zhilina, A.N and S.V. Cheshko, eds, 1992. *Sovremennoe razvitie etnicheskikh grupp Srednei Azii i Kazakhstana,* vols I-II, Moscow: Russian Academy of Sciences.

Zülfikar, Hamza 1992. 'Özbekistan'da latin harflerine geçiş süreci', *Türk Dili* 489:September, 233-40.

—— 1999. 'Türk cumhuriyetleriyle kurulması beklenen ortak dil üzerine', *Türk Dili* 566: February, 83-9; 567: March, 179-83.

Zviagelskaya, Irina 1995. *The Russian Policy Debate on Central Asia.* London: Royal Institute of International Affairs.

INDEX

Note on abbreviations
Central Asian states are listed in the order followed in our chapters: AZ = Azerbayjan; UZ = Uzbekistan; KA = Kazakhstan; KY = Kyrgyzstan; TU = Turkmenistan; TA = Tajikistan.

See also Note on Transliteration, pp.xiff.

245